M. Elango
11/21/'97

RAHUL DESHMUKH

Teach Yourself
ACTIVE SERVER PAGES®
in 14 days

Teach Yourself
ACTIVE SERVER
PAGES®
in 14 days

Sanjaya Hettihewa
Kelly Held

201 West 103rd Street
Indianapolis, Indiana 46290

President, Sams Publishing Richard K. Swadley

Publishing Manager Dean Miller

Managing Editor Kitty Wilson Jarrett

Director of Marketing Kelli S. Spencer

Product Marketing Managers Wendy Gilbride
Kim Margolius

Associate Product Marketing Manager Jennifer Pock

Marketing Coordinator Linda Beckwith

Acquisitions Editor
Kim Spilker

Development Editor
Sunthar Visuvalingam

Production Editor
Kate Shoup

Indexer
Christine Nelsen

Technical Reviewer
Christopher Haddad

Editorial Coordinators
Mandie Rowell
Katie Wise

Technical Edit Coordinator
Lynette Quinn

Editorial Assistants
Carol Ackerman
Andi Richter
Rhonda Tinch-Mize
Karen Williams

Cover Designer
Tim Amrhein

Book Designer
Gary Adair

Copy Writer
David Reichwein

Production Team Supervisors
Brad Chinn
Charlotte Clapp

Production
Jeanne Clark
Svetlana Dominguez
Sonja Hart
Deirdre Smith

Overview

Contents

Appendixes

Dedication

This book is dedicated to the Microsoft Windows development team for making Windows the best operating system for Web development.

—Sanjaya Hettihewa

I would like to dedicate my work on this book to my family: my aunt, my grandmother, and especially my mother, Dolores, and brothers Bradley and Ethan. They are my biggest fans and supporters. I would just like to return some of their faith and trust.

—Kelly Held

Acknowledgments

Sanjaya Hettihewa

I'm very much indebted to everyone who helped me complete this project. I'd first like to thank Kim Spilker for working with me on this project, and helping me bring it to fruition. Kim's patience, understanding, and confidence helped me complete this project on time. I am also very grateful to Sunthar Visuvalingam, who is the development editor of this book, for all his valuable comments and suggestions. He did an exceptional job refining my work and making this a better book. I do not personally know everyone at Sams.net Publishing who makes books like this possible. All the same, I'd like to thank them for helping me write this book and refine its contents.

Kelly Held

I would like to start by thanking Lynette Quinn, who gave me my first job working with Sams Publishing. Thanks go to Kim Spilker for having the patience to work with me through this first publication. I would like to credit Sunthar Visuvalingam with helping me adapt my technical understanding into meaningful and enlightening tasks for the reader. Kate Shoup also deserves my appreciation. She was very informative and understanding while helping me put this work into a final publishable form.

I would like to acknowledge and thank Jesus Christ my savior for giving me wonderful opportunities and helping me through every day. I would also like to acknowledge Sharon Maloney for believing in me and helping me get where I am today. I cannot find the words to express my indebtedness, so it's lucky that she already knows what I think and feel.

About the Authors

Sanjaya Hettihewa is an accomplished Webmaster and a consultant specializing in integrating Windows NT–based information systems on the Internet. He has been living in the Washington, D.C., area for the past seven years and has done extensive research in deploying Internet information systems utilizing various powerful and unique features of Windows NT. Sanjaya is the author of *Windows NT 4 Web Development* and *Windows NT Internet and Intranet Development*, and the co-author of *Designing and Implementing Internet Information Server*, *Windows NT 3.51 Unleashed*, *FrontPage Unleashed*, *Internet Explorer Unleashed*, and *Internet Information Server Unleashed*, all by Sams and Sams.net Publishing. You can reach Sanjaya at `http://www.NetInnovation.com/` (or, if you prefer the old-fashioned way, `sanjaya@NetInovation.com`).

Kelly Held is a consultant who owns and operates Quantum Consulting Services (QCS), a company providing full-service solutions from hardware to software and networking to Web development. Kelly has spent the past five years helping customers develop a presence in the online community. He has developed and deployed BBSs, intranets, and Internet Web sites. He is currently a Web developer working with the new and powerful Windows NT products. You can see examples of his current work by visiting the QCS Web site at `http://www.qcs-solutions.com`. You can contact Kelly via e-mail at `kelly@qcs-solutions.com` or by phone at 1-800-650-0421.

Tell Us What You Think!

As a reader, you are the most important critic and commentator of our books. We value your opinion and want to know what we're doing right, what we could do better, what areas you'd like to see us publish in, and any other words of wisdom you're willing to pass our way. You can help us make strong books that meet your needs and give you the computer guidance you require.

Do you have access to the World Wide Web? Then check out our site at `http://www.mcp.com`.

> **NOTE**
>
> If you have a technical question about this book, call the technical support line at 317-581-4669.

As the team leader of the group that created this book, I welcome your comments. You can fax, e-mail, or write me directly to let me know what you did or didn't like about this book—as well as what we can do to make our books stronger. Here's the information:

Fax: 317-581-4669

E-mail: `opsys_mgr@sams.mcp.com`

Mail: Dean Miller
          Comments Department
          Sams.net Publishing
          201 W. 103rd Street
          Indianapolis, IN 46290

Introduction

Active Server Pages is revolutionizing the way Web applications are developed almost the same way Windows NT 4 revolutionized client/server computing. Thanks to Active Server Pages, Web developers can now easily make a Web site interactive and provide dynamic and compelling information to users browsing the Web site. Prior to Active Server Pages, the development of a typical interactive Web application meant compiling an executable application using a traditional application development environment such as Visual C++. After the application was compiled, it was copied to a CGI directory of the Web server. Even the slightest change to the application meant recompiling the entire application and replacing the previous version of the executable file. This is unnecessarily resource intensive in a production environment. Active Server Pages solves this problem by providing a more direct and easier way to create Web applications.

All that's required to take advantage of Active Server Pages is familiarity with Visual Basic or a Web scripting language such as JScript/JavaScript or VBScript. Active Server Pages simplifies the lives of Web application developers by providing a mechanism to create sophisticated Web applications via a familiar scripting language such as VBScript, JScript/JavaScript, or Perl. For those readers who are unfamiliar with VBScript, a comprehensive VBScript primer is provided in Appendix A.

Teach Yourself Active Server Pages In 14 Days comprehensively covers all aspects of Active Server Pages in an easy-to-understand format.

How This Book Is Organized

This book is organized into days and weeks. The first week introduces you to Active Server Pages and covers the basics of ASP application development. The second week delves into more advanced topics such as database application development and using other scripting languages, such as Perl. Please refer to the Week in Review and Week at a Glance sections for more information about topics covered in each day. A bonus chapter is included at the end of the book with various practical applications of Active Server Pages. Examples of this book use VBScript. If you are not familiar with VBScript, refer to the comprehensive VBScript primer provided in Appendix A. After reading this book, you will be able to use various capabilities of Active Server Pages to create a richly interactive and dynamic Web site.

Why This Book Is Special

The World Wide Web has experienced phenomenal growth during the last few years. More and more Web sites are relying on Microsoft Windows NT for setting up Internet and intranet Web servers. Active Server Pages, an integral part of IIS, makes it easier to develop powerful Web applications utilizing industry standard technologies such as DAO, ODBC, OLE, COM, and ActiveX. This book covers all aspects of developing ASP applications in a straightforward and easy-to-understand manner.

Who Should Read This Book

This book will teach you everything that's needed to begin developing sophisticated ASP applications. Even if you have little prior knowledge about Web application development, you will be able to easily follow this book. The topics covered in this book are all explained in easy-to-understand terms. Screenshots and diagrams are used extensively to explain various topics. This book should be read by anyone who wishes to utilize the power of Active Server Pages to create a dynamic Web site. The WWW is made up of a very diverse group of people. Likewise, this book has been written for an equally diverse group of people. Specifically, this book is for the following people.

Web Application Developers

Although the WWW was originally used primarily for distributing information, it is increasingly being used for more sophisticated tasks. The WWW is no longer about simply distributing static HTML files. It is about providing dynamic content to millions of users when they want it. If you are a Web application developer, it is crucial that you stay on top of new Web publishing tools and know how and when to utilize them. Active Server Pages is Microsoft's preferred application development environment for developing Web applications. Tips and techniques presented in this book can be used by Web application developers to make the best use of this powerful new Web technology.

Web Site Administrators

The role of Web site administrators is becoming more and more complicated as new Web development applications and technologies are invented. Web site administrators can learn various issues related to developing and deploying ASP applications by reading this book.

Information Systems Architects

This book is of particular value to information systems architects who have been delegated the task of establishing a Web presence and exploring various options available for developing Web applications. With the aid of this book, information systems architects will learn the benefits of using Active Server Pages to develop Web applications.

Windows NT System Administrators

Active Server Pages is an integral part of IIS 3.0. Although system administrators might not be directly responsible for publishing information on the Internet, they need to have a working knowledge of integral Web publishing technologies such as Active Server Pages. They also need to be familiar with various issues, such as security, that arise when Web applications are published on the Internet. With the help of this book, Windows NT system administrators can quickly become familiar with Active Server Pages and learn how to effectively deploy ASP applications on the Web.

WEEK

1

At A Glance

Active Server Pages revolutionizes the way Web applications are built. Traditional server-side application development environments are not optimized for developing interactive Web applications and outputting information formatted in HTML. Active Server Pages is specially designed to make it easier to develop such interactive Web applications and work together with industry-standard Windows technologies such as OLE, ActiveX, ADO, and ODBC. On Day 1, "Introduction to Active Server Pages and IIS," you will be introduced to Active Server Pages and shown how Internet Information Server (IIS) can be used to deploy ASP applications on the Internet.

The fundamentals of ASP application development (such as the uses of loops and control structures) are covered in Day 2, "The Fundamentals of ASP Application Development." At the end of Day 2, you will be able to develop simple ASP applications and understand material presented in days that follow.

The ASP environment allows Web applications to easily interact with users browsing your Web site. Virtually all Web applications interact with users to obtain and display information. On Day 3, "Interacting with Users," you learn how to use HTML, message boxes, input boxes, ActiveX controls, and HTML form elements to interact with users browsing your Web site.

The ASP environment has five intrinsic objects that are used to perform most tasks. The `Request` object is used to retrieve client information and the `Response` object is used to send information to the client. The `Server` object is your utility object that performs miscellaneous tasks and allows you to extend the server. Finally, the `Application` and `Session` objects are used to maintain state. The uses of the five intrinsic ASP objects are covered in Day 4, "Web Application Development with ASP Objects."

The components included with Active Server Pages make it easier to develop complex Web applications. The Advertisement Rotator component can be used to rotate a series of graphic images on a Web page. The Browser Capabilities component can be used to determine the capabilities of the Web browser and make your Web site easier to navigate for those who use less-powerful Web browsers. Various text streams can be manipulated in ASP applications using the Text Stream component. Day 5, "Using ActiveX Components," demonstrates by example how to use the built-in ASP components.

The HTTP protocol retains no information about previous HTTP transactions for future reference. Cookies are used to address this limitation of the HTTP protocol. Active Server Pages simplifies the manipulation of cookies greatly. Day 6, "Tracking HTTP Sessions Using Cookies," demonstrates how to develop Web applications that retain information between HTTP sessions. When a cookie is created, certain information is stored in the user's computer for future reference. When the Web client contacts the Web server responsible for creating the cookie, the information stored in the user's computer (in the form of a cookie) is sent to the Web server. This information can be used either by a client-side or server-side Web application to implement sophisticated Web applications such as shopping carts and personalized Web pages.

On Day 7, "Developing Dynamic and Personalized Content with ASP," you will learn how Active Server Pages can be used to develop highly interactive Web applications that can be customized by users. Feel free to adopt applications presented on Day 7 to provide dynamic and personalized content to users browsing your Web site.

Day 1

Chapter 1

Introduction to Active Server Pages and IIS

Active Server Pages (ASP) is Microsoft's most recent Web server technology, and is designed to make it easier for Web application developers to develop sophisticated Web applications. You are probably familiar with (or have at least heard of) JavaScript and VBScript. ASP is a similar technology, except that ASP applications are executed on the server side. Because ASP supports VBScript, JScript, Perl, and other scripting languages, Web developers need not learn an entirely new language. ASP has been designed to leverage existing knowledge of Web application developers.

NOTE

By default, Active Server Pages only supports VBScript and JScript/JavaScript. Support for additional scripting languages such as Perl can be added as demonstrated in Day 13, "Advanced Topics."

Today you will be introduced to ASP, and shown how you can benefit from some of its unique features and capabilities. ASP makes it easy to develop interactive Web applications. After you read this book, you will find ASP to be one of the most powerful weapons in your arsenal of Web development tools. Although CGI and ISAPI applications were once exclusively used to develop interactive applications, as described in the section "Benefits of Using ASP," there are several distinct advantages in using ASP.

What Is ASP?

ASP is an integral part of the Active Platform, Microsoft's core Internet strategy. The Active Platform is a common set of languages, standards, and services that can be used to develop either Active Desktop (client-side) or Active Server (server-side) applications. The Active Platform paradigm makes it easier and more cost-effective for developers to leverage their skills to develop a broad spectrum of applications that run on the server and on the client. It also makes it very easy to transform a desktop application into a full blown client/server application.

ASP is actually a component that you install on top of your Web server. This component processes files that end with the extension .asp and transmits the result to the client that requested the ASP file. This does not mean that ASP applications render technologies such as Internet Server Application Programming Interface (ISAPI) and Internet Database Connector (IDC) obsolete. Rather, ASP applications complement Web application technologies such as ISAPI and IDC. For example, if you want to create a simple data-entry Web application that does not need to query a database multiple times, you can easily do so using IDC. On the other hand, ASP is more suitable for an application that performs multiple database queries and carries out complex calculations on the data returned. As you can see, ASP technology complements other technologies, integrating with them so that you, the developer, can select which technology to use for each project.

NOTE The relationship between the file extension and the ASP interpreter is initialized by the Registry key HKEY_LOCAL_MACHINE\SYSTEM\ CurrentControlSet\Services\W3SVC\Parameters\Script Map. Notice how the extensions .asa and .asp are linked to …\System32\inetsrv\ ASP\ASP.dll.

Benefits of Using ASP

There are many benefits in using ASP. These benefits make ASP one of the most powerful tools available for developing sophisticated Web applications:

- ☐ ASP development is easy to learn.
- ☐ The ASP development environment makes it easy to leverage existing investments.
- ☐ The ASP development environment makes it easy to leverage existing skills.
- ☐ ASP development is compile free.
- ☐ The ASP environment is extensible.
- ☐ ASP protects proprietary business algorithms and information.

ASP Development Is Easy to Learn

ASP can be used to easily add a new level of interactivity to a Web site. All that's required to take advantage of ASP is familiarity with Visual Basic or a Web scripting language such as JScript/JavaScript or VBScript. Because VBScript resembles BASIC in many ways, it is easy to learn—even if you are new to programming. If you are familiar with C/C++, you will be happy to know that the syntax of JScript/JavaScript is similar to that of C/C++.

The ASP Development Environment Makes It Easy to Leverage Existing Investments

Chances are you have already made significant investments on various productivity and database applications such as Microsoft Office. ASP helps you leverage your investments to the Internet. For example, as demonstrated in Days 8, "Introduction to Web Database Programming Using ActiveX Data Objects," and 9, "Advanced Web Database Programming," database features of ASP can be used to create a Web interface to any ODBC-compliant database.

The ASP Development Environment Makes It Easy to Leverage Existing Skills

ASP simplifies the lives of Web application developers by providing a mechanism for creating sophisticated Web applications using a familiar scripting language such as VBScript, JScript/JavaScript, or Perl. This helps developers who have already invested resources in learning a scripting language such as VBScript, JScript/JavaScript, or Perl. Comprehensive VBScript coverage is provided in Appendix A, "VBScript Primer."

ASP Development Is Compile Free

Prior to ASP, the development of a typical interactive Web application required the compilation of an executable application using a traditional application development environment such as Visual C++. After the application was compiled, it was copied to the CGI directory of the Web server. Even the slightest change to the application required a recompilation of the entire application (or a code module) and the replacement of the previous version of the executable file. This is unnecessarily resource intensive in a production environment. ASP solves this problem by providing a more direct and easier way to create Web applications. After you develop an ASP application, you do not have to compile it. Simply save the file with the .asp extension, and the ASP DLL will process the file when it is requested by a user. Caching is used to enhance the performance of ASP.

The ASP Environment Is Extensible

ASP is fully extensible, and is shipped with several built-in components that can be used for tasks such as allowing database access and creating rotating advertisement banners. In addition to the built-in ASP components, you can develop your custom components as shown in Day 10, "Developing Custom ActiveX Components." You can build your own components using Visual Basic.

ASP Protects Proprietary Business Algorithms and Information

One disadvantage of using client-side scripting languages is that doing so exposes proprietary business algorithms and information. For example, on certain days of the year, a retailer might choose to increase the price of certain items. An example of such a price increase would be a retailer increasing the price of gift wrapping by 20% from December 20th through January 1st. It's certainly not in the best interest of the retailer to make this information public to its customers. If the price increase is implemented using a client-side scripting language such as VBScript, anyone looking at the source code of the Web page will be able to observe various proprietary business algorithms used by the retailer. On the other hand, when ASP is used, users no longer have access to proprietary business algorithms and information because ASP code is executed on the server and only the output is sent to the user.

Do I Need Microsoft Visual InterDev to Develop ASP Applications?

Microsoft Visual InterDev is a rapid application development (RAD) tool for developing ASP applications, but it is not required. ASP technology is included in IIS 3.0. However, you can easily develop complicated Web applications with Microsoft Visual InterDev because it simplifies the process of developing and debugging ASP applications. I highly recommend that you acquire a copy of Microsoft Visual InterDev for developing ASP applications. The capability to easily create ASP database applications is one of the best and most productive features of Visual InterDev.

Requirements for Developing ASP Applications

The requirements for developing ASP applications are basic and can be broken down into two categories: software/hardware requirements, and technical requirements.

The minimum software and hardware requirements for developing ASP applications are

- ☐ A Pentium-based computer.
- ☐ 32MB of RAM.
- ☐ About 100MB of free hard drive space.
- ☐ Windows NT Server 4.0 with TCP/IP networking support properly installed and configured.

NOTE

Although Windows NT Workstation as well as Windows 95 can be used to develop ASP applications, I recommend that you use Windows NT Server due to NT's significant security, performance, and application-integration capabilities. For additional information, see the section in this chapter titled "Do I Really Need Windows NT Server 4?"

- ☐ Internet Information Server 3.0 or better is required if you are using Windows NT Server. Microsoft Personal Web Server (PWS) is required if you are using Windows 95, and Microsoft Peer Web Services is required if you are using Windows NT Workstation. Because the ASP component is actually an ISAPI application, you should be able to develop ASP applications with any ISAPI-compliant Web server by simply downloading the ASP component of IIS 3.0 and installing it. However, you are likely to have better ASP integration with IIS and PWS/Peer Web Services.
- ☐ A database that supports ODBC (such as Microsoft Access or Microsoft SQL Server).
- ☐ Microsoft Visual InterDev is highly recommended but not required.

The technical requirements for developing ASPs are

- ☐ Familiarity with Windows NT 4.
- ☐ A basic understanding of Windows NT security and NTFS (Windows NT File System) permissions, if you are using Windows NT.
- ☐ Familiarity with Visual Basic or a scripting language such as VBScript or JScript/JavaScript, though certainly a plus, is not a requirement.

Why Choose Windows NT and IIS/ASP?

Before you develop ASP applications, it is important to understand the benefits of choosing Windows NT and IIS/ASP to develop Web applications. If you are using Windows NT and UNIX servers to publish Web content, it is especially important that you are aware of various unique features of Windows NT and how you can benefit from them.

There are many advantages to choosing Windows NT and IIS to publish content on the Internet. Windows NT has been developed from the ground up to be the operating system of choice for mission-critical applications. The chief architect of Windows NT is Dave Cutler, designer of the VMS operating system. Along with the NT development team, he combined various aspects of the Mach microkernel (a variant of UNIX developed at Carnegie-Mellon University) and VMS to develop Windows NT. Unlike UNIX, Windows NT lowers the cost of entry, is quickly installed on PC systems, and can be easily maintained.

Why Choose Windows NT?

Windows NT in conjunction with IIS and ASP provide a very powerful platform for developing and deploying Web applications.

Do I Really Need Windows NT Server 4?

ASP applications can also be developed using Windows NT 4.0 Workstation and Windows 95. However, I highly recommend that you use Windows NT Server to deploy your ASP applications for to the following reasons:

- ☐ Windows NT Server yields better performance.
- ☐ Windows NT Server is more secure.
- ☐ Windows NT Server allows for easy integration with enterprise-quality applications such as Microsoft SQL Server.

 NOTE

> If you are using Windows NT Workstation or Windows 95, you will be able to follow exercises in this book with no problems. However, various discussions about Windows NT security and Internet Information Server will not apply to you. After the second day, the focus is on ASP and, for virtually all applications, it does not matter whether you use Windows NT Server/Workstation or Windows 95.

1

Windows NT Server Yields Better Performance

Windows NT Server has been optimized to provide the best performance for network-intensive server applications. On the other hand, Windows 95 and Windows NT Workstation have been optimized to provide the best performance for productivity applications. Therefore, Windows NT Server yields better performance when hosting ASP applications.

Windows NT Server Is More Secure

Because Internet Information Server 3.0 uses NTFS security when run under Windows NT Server 4.0, Windows NT Server is a more secure platform to host ASP applications. Because Windows 95 uses Microsoft Personal Web Server, a watered-down version of Internet Information Server, you will be unable to implement security using NTFS security permissions unless you use Windows NT.

Easy Integration with Enterprise-Quality Applications

Enterprise-quality applications, such as applications in the Microsoft BackOffice Suite (Microsoft SQL Server, Microsoft Exchange Server, and so on), require Windows NT Server. Therefore, choosing to develop your ASP applications using Windows NT Server will make it easier for you to integrate your ASP applications with various components of BackOffice to develop sophisticated Web applications.

How ASP Complements Client-Side Scripting

ASP applications do not replace client-side scripting languages. Rather, they complement client-side scripting languages by providing yet another powerful tool that can be used by Web site developers to develop richly interactive and compelling Web sites. On Day 2, "The Fundamentals of ASP Application Development," you will learn how client-side scripting complements server-side scripting by providing a more richly interactive experience to users.

As shown in Appendix A, you can add a new level of interactivity to your Web pages using client-side scripting. For example, before data in an HTML form is submitted to a Web server for processing, a VBScript subroutine can go over the data and point out errors to the user. However, some Web browsers do not support client-side scripting. When it is not possible to use client-side scripting, server-side scripting can be used to provide users with a rich and interactive experience—even if they use technologically challenged Web browsers. In Day 5, "Using ActiveX Components," you will learn how to use the browser capabilities component to determine whether a Web browser supports client-side scripting.

Using IIS for Publishing ASP Applications

This section covers how to install, configure, and administer Internet Information Server (IIS) for publishing ASP applications. IIS is the foundation of ASP. Therefore, it is crucial that you understand how to install, configure, and administer IIS for publishing ASP applications on the Internet. If you have already installed IIS 3.0, you might want to skim the remainder of this chapter and proceed to Day 2.

Downloading IIS 3.0

Because IIS 3.0 is installed by upgrading your IIS 2.0 installation, make sure IIS 2.0 is already installed on your computer before you proceed. IIS 3.0 can be freely downloaded from the IIS Web site. Information about ordering the IIS 3.0 CD-ROM from Microsoft can also be found at the IIS Web site. For the most up-to-date information about IIS, visit the Internet Information Server Web site at `http://www.microsoft.com/iis`.

When you reach the IIS Web site, select the link to download IIS. You are then presented with a registration Web page, where you enter information such as your name and e-mail address.

IIS 3.0 is actually a collection of components that you add to IIS 2.0. After you submit the registration information, the Web page shown in Figure 1.1 is displayed, allowing you to select components of IIS 3.0 to download. Make sure the Active Server Pages feature is selected.

Figure 1.1.

Select features of IIS to download.

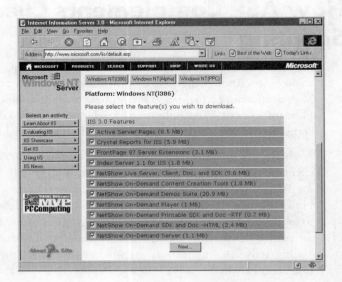

After you enter a download location, you can download the selected features of IIS 3.0 using the Web page shown in Figure 1.2. As you can see, Active Server Pages is a downloadable feature of IIS 3.0. After you download Active Server Pages, proceed to the next section.

Figure 1.2.
Download features of IIS.

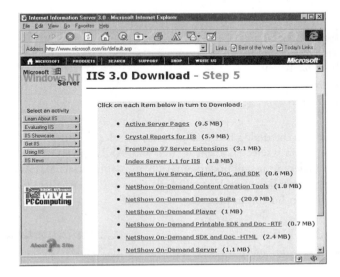

Upgrading IIS 2.0 for Publishing ASP Applications

Execute the Active Server Pages file you downloaded using the Web page shown in Figure 1.2. You will be presented with the ASP license agreement. Read and acknowledge it to proceed to the Active Server Pages Setup program shown in Figure 1.3. Click the Next button to continue.

Figure 1.3.
The Active Server Pages Setup program.

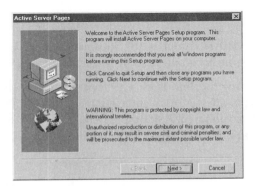

The Active Server Pages Setup program requires the FTP and WWW publishing services to be temporarily stopped while ASP is installed. If the FTP or Web publishing service is running, you will be presented with the dialog box shown in Figure 1.4. Click the Yes button to continue installing ASP.

Figure 1.4.

Temporarily stop the FTP and WWW publishing services to install ASP.

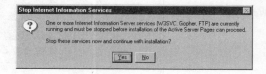

Use the dialog box in Figure 1.5 to select to install options of ASP. Make sure the ODBC driver is selected to ensure that your ASP applications can interact with ODBC data sources. Select to install documentation and samples so you can experiment with them. Also, select to install the Java Virtual Machine so you can perform Java development with ASP. Click the Next button to proceed.

Figure 1.5.

Select to install options of ASP.

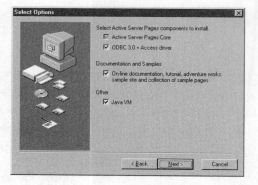

Specify the location of ASP documentation and samples using the dialog box in Figure 1.6. Click the Next button to install Active Server Pages on your computer.

After Internet Information Server is upgraded to support ASP, the dialog box shown in Figure 1.7 provides an installation summary that displays locations of various ASP components. When you install ASP support, you are given the option of selecting where ASP documentation is installed. Browse the sample and tutorial pages to learn more about ASP.

You might need to reboot after ASP is installed on your computer.

Figure 1.6.

Choose the location for documentation and samples.

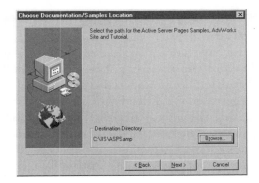

Figure 1.7.

ASP installation summary.

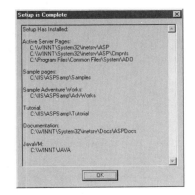

Configuring the WWW Publishing Service

The WWW publishing service of IIS is used to publish Web pages on the Internet. Configure the WWW publishing service by selecting it in Microsoft Internet Service Manager, as shown in Figure 1.8. After you select the WWW publishing service, either double-click or right-click it to select Service Properties.

Figure 1.8.

Microsoft Internet Service Manager.

Configuring the Properties of the WWW Publishing Service

As shown in Figure 1.9, the Service tab of the WWW Service Properties dialog box can be used to configure key aspects of the WWW publishing service. It's recommended that you use default settings for Connection Timeout and Maximum Connections at first. However, after you monitor the number of connections at any given time by using Windows NT Performance Monitor, you might want to increase the Maximum Connections value if you have sufficient network bandwidth to accommodate additional connections. Performance Monitor is a system-administration utility shipped with Windows NT that can be used to monitor various performance statistics of Windows NT resources and applications.

Figure 1.9.

The Service tab of the WWW Service Properties dialog box.

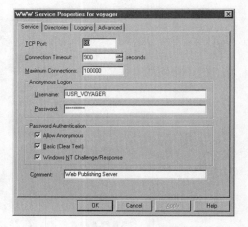

IIS uses Windows NT user accounts and NTFS security to enforce file access permissions. The username and password specified for anonymous logon is used to determine whether an anonymous user requesting an object from IIS is permitted to have that object. It's recommended that IIS be allowed to use the Internet Guest Account (IUSR_VOYAGER) shown in Figure 1.9. Using File Manager, you can control which objects anonymous users can access by assigning file permissions to the Internet Guest Account. The Internet Guest account name is followed by the string IUSR_ and the name of your Windows NT Server.

If your Web site is public, make sure the Allow Anonymous checkbox shown in Figure 1.9 is checked. If you want to protect parts of your Web site with a username and password, make sure the Basic (Clear Text) checkbox is checked.

SECURITY

A third party can monitor HTTP requests made using basic clear-text usernames and passwords because the username and password

information is not encrypted. Unless you have installed a digital security certificate on your Internet server, do not depend on the integrity of clear-text usernames and passwords to protect extremely sensitive information. You can increase security by unchecking the Basic (Clear Text) checkbox and selecting Windows NT Challenge/Response. Although Windows NT Challenge/Response provides you with additional security, your users must use Internet Explorer because it is the only Web browser compatible with Windows NT Challenge/Response authentication.

If you decide to use basic clear-text usernames and passwords, you are warned about the consequences of doing so (as shown in Figure 1.10). As a rule of thumb, never use clear-text passwords to safeguard sensitive data from unauthorized users unless an encryption algorithm such as SSL is used.

Figure 1.10.

You should not use clear-text passwords to restrict access to sensitive data.

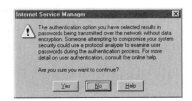

The Windows NT Challenge/Response authentication method is much safer than clear-text user authentication because user authorization information is encrypted before it's transmitted over the Internet. However, because only Internet Explorer is capable of handling Windows NT Challenge/Response authentication, it's recommended that you not use Windows NT Challenge/Response authentication unless you're certain most users visiting your Web site use Internet Explorer.

Finally, you can specify a comment for the WWW publishing service by typing it in the space provided. This comment will show up in Internet Service Manager under Comments. You might want to use the comment field to specify the physical location of the WWW publishing service (as in Building A, Room 421).

Configuring WWW Publishing Service Directories

You can use the Directories tab shown in Figure 1.11 to configure how IIS handles directories. The IIS installation program creates several directory mappings. If FrontPage is installed in the same computer, you will see additional directory mappings.

It's very easy to add directory mappings to your WWW publishing service. For example, you can use the Add button to add a CGI directory mapping to the WWW publishing service. Users using a Web browser can then execute applications in this directory. After you click the

Add button, the Directory Properties dialog box shown in Figure 1.12 appears. In this dialog box, you can select a directory and an *alias* for it. The alias specified in Figure 1.12 for the CGI directory is `cgi-bin`. You can use this alias to execute applications in the `E:\Publish\WWW\CGI-BIN` directory by using a URL such as `http://server.name.com/cgi-bin/application.asp`. Because the `cgi-bin` directory contains applications, the Execute checkbox is selected in Figure 1.12; this enables the WWW publishing service to execute applications requested by users and return the output. To have ASP applications executed on the server, you need to grant execute permission to the directory containing your ASP files.

Figure 1.11.

The Directories tab of the WWW Service Properties dialog box can be used to configure directory mappings.

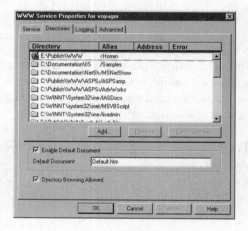

NOTE

If the virtual directory points to a network resource using a universal naming convention (UNC) share name, a username and a password that has access to the share can be specified in the space provided for account information. This option is visible only if a UNC share name is typed in.

NOTE

For ASP to be executed on the Web server, you must grant execute permissions to the directory containing your ASP scripts.

IIS supports virtual servers. You can enable the Virtual Server checkbox if a server has more than one IP address. The virtual server feature is handy for setting up Web servers for several organizations on one server. For example, you can use the Virtual Server feature to host Web servers for www.microsoft.com and www.netscape.com on the same computer (assuming you own both domain names, of course!). Note that properties must be set separately for each virtual server.

Figure 1.12.

The Directory Properties dialog box.

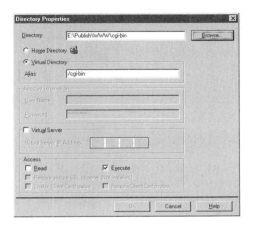

Finally, you can select the Require secure SSL channel checkbox if SSL (Secure Sockets Layer) is installed on your server. SSL encrypts data before it's transmitted to users browsing a Web site.

Use the Enable Default Document checkbox to specify the name of the file that is sent by default if a URL is given without a filename. For example, when a user accesses a Web site with the URL `http://www.company.com/`, the filename specified under Enable Default Document is sent to the user. If the file is not found or if a filename is not specified under Enable Default Document, the user is presented with a list of files and directories, as shown in Figure 1.13 (if directory browsing is allowed). Otherwise, the user is presented with a message similar to the one shown in Figure 1.14.

Figure 1.13.

A list of files and directories appears if a URL without a filename is used and directory browsing is allowed.

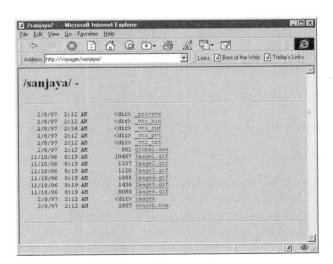

Figure 1.14.

An Access Forbidden message appears if a URL without a filename is used and directory browsing is not allowed.

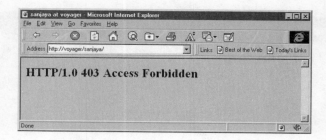

Use the Directory Browsing Allowed checkbox (refer to Figure 1.11) to specify whether IIS should return a list of files and directories if a URL is given with a filename. For example, `http://voyager/sanjaya` refers to a subdirectory. If directory browsing is allowed, the user sees a list of directories (refer to Figure 1.13). On the other hand, if directory browsing is not allowed, the user sees a message similar to the one shown in Figure 1.14.

Logging Web Publishing Service Accesses

Web server accesses can be logged either to a SQL/ODBC database or to a plain-text file. Configure WWW publishing service access logging by using the Logging tab shown in Figure 1.15. Unless you have special software to analyze data logged to a SQL/ODBC database, it's recommended that you allow IIS to log Web server accesses to a plain-text file.

Figure 1.15.

The Logging tab of the WWW Service Properties dialog box.

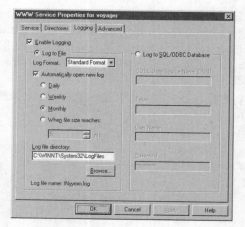

Web Publishing Service Access Control

The Advanced tab of the WWW Service Properties dialog box, shown in Figure 1.16, is used to grant and deny access to various computers on the Internet. You might want to use this dialog box to deny access to one or more Internet computers.

Figure 1.16.

The Advanced tab of the WWW Service Properties dialog box.

For example, it's possible to deny access to a computer named www.hacker.com by selecting the Denied Access radio button and clicking the Add button. You can use the dialog box shown in Figure 1.17 to specify which IP addresses should be denied access. If you don't know the IP address of a computer but do know its domain name (in this case, www.hacker.com), simply click the ellipsis button shown in Figure 1.17, and enter the domain name, as shown in Figure 1.18.

Figure 1.17.

The Deny Access On dialog box.

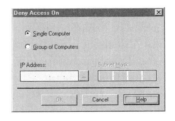

Figure 1.18.

You can use the DNS Lookup dialog box to look up an Internet computer by its domain name.

The Limit Network Use checkbox (refer to Figure 1.16) is handy for limiting network bandwidth that will be used by all Internet services (managed by IIS) running on the computer being administered. Use Performance Monitor to determine network bandwidth used by IIS before changing the default value. If it's necessary to use this option to severely limit network bandwidth, it's a good indication that you need to upgrade your Internet link.

Summary

ASP can be used to easily add a new level of interactivity to your Web site. Traditional server-side application development environments are not optimized for developing interactive Web applications and outputting information formatted in HTML. ASP is specially designed to make it easier to develop interactive Web applications and to work together with industry-standard Windows technologies such as OLE, ActiveX, ADO, and ODBC.

You are now aware of various unique features and capabilities of ASP and how you can use these capabilities to develop interactive Web applications. Today you were introduced to ASP and the benefits of using Windows NT and IIS to develop Web applications. The pace of this book will increase considerably, so get some rest to be ready for the next two weeks! By this time next week, you will be wondering how you ever got along without ASP!

Internet Information Server is used to publish Web pages on the Internet. Various options of the Web publishing server can be configured by invoking Microsoft Internet Service Manager and selecting to configure the WWW publishing service.

What's Next

You are now ready to begin developing ASP applications. Tomorrow's lesson covers the fundamentals of ASP application development, including the structure and syntax of ASP applications. You'll also learn about mixing scripting language in ASP applications, as well as about using conditional structures. By the end of the day, you will have learned how to include useful ASP subroutines in server-side include (SSI) files.

In the meantime, I recommend that you go over the ASP documentation whenever you have some free time. A link to ASP documentation is placed in the Microsoft Internet Server documentation folder in the Windows NT Start menu if you selected to install ASP documentation.

Q&A

Q Is Microsoft Visual InterDev required to develop ASP applications?

A No. Microsoft Visual InterDev is a RAD (rapid application development) tool for creating ASP applications.

Q Which version of Internet Information Server do you need to develop ASP applications?

A Internet Information Server version 3.0 or better if you are using Windows NT Server. Personal Web Server if you are using Windows 95, and Peer Web Services if you are using Windows NT Workstation.

Q Can ASP applications be developed with scripting languages other than VBScript?

A Yes. ASP supports JScript right out of the box. Scripting engines for additional languages can be installed to work with ASP.

Q Do you have to install Microsoft Internet Information Server 2.0 before upgrading to Internet Information Server 3.0?

A Yes. IIS 3.0 is installed by upgrading IIS 2.0.

Q How do you configure IIS to execute ASP applications on the server?

A By selecting to configure the WWW publishing service of Internet Service Manager and granting execute permissions to the directory containing your ASP scripts.

Q How do you implement security on ASP applications?

A IIS respects Windows NT NTFS security. Therefore, you can use File Manager to specify NTFS security settings for ASP files.

Chapter 2

The Fundamentals of ASP Application Development

Today you will learn the fundamentals of ASP application development. Read this chapter carefully because information presented in upcoming days builds on information presented today. The fundamentals of ASP application development are very easy to understand. If you are familiar with basic HTML markup tags, you will have no difficulty learning how to convert a typical Web page to an ASP application. In order to develop ASP applications, you must be familiar with a scripting language such as VBScript, JScript, or Perl. The examples in this book are all in VBScript. If you are not familiar with VBScript, please consult Appendix A, "VBScript Primer."

NOTE Although the sample applications you see in this and upcoming chapters were developed using Microsoft Visual InterDev, you do not need Microsoft Visual InterDev to develop ASP applications. All you need is a text editor (yes, even Notepad will do!), a Web browser, and IIS 3.0 or Microsoft Personal Web server with ASP extensions installed. See Day 11, "Introduction to Microsoft Visual InterDev," and Day 12, "Developing Active Server Pages with Visual InterDev," to learn how to develop ASP applications using Microsoft Visual InterDev.

The Syntax of ASP Applications

Before you develop ASP applications, it is important that you understand their syntax. An ASP application is simply a Web page with additional scripting commands that are executed on the server. An ASP application is composed primarily of the following elements:

- ☐ HTML code
- ☐ Script delimiters
- ☐ Script code
- ☐ ActiveX components
- ☐ ASP objects

The only difference between a typical Web page and an ASP application is the presence of ASP script delimiters. Listing 2.1 illustrates a typical ASP application with various ASP script delimiters. The output of the ASP application in Listing 2.1 is shown in Figure 2.1.

NOTE An ASP application is a text file that contains script commands that are executed by the Web server. The ASP application is parsed and executed by the Web server's ASP interpreter, allowing the generation of dynamic HTML content. The standard ASP parser understands the scripting languages VBScript and JScript. ASP statements are embedded between ASP delimiters. Additionally, server-side ActiveX components may be instantiated and natively accessed.

2

Listing 2.1. Components of a typical ASP application.

```
 1: <%@ LANGUAGE="VBSCRIPT" %>
 2:
 3: <SCRIPT RUNAT=SERVER LANGUAGE=VBSCRIPT>
 4:
 5: Sub SayHello ()
 6:
 7:   Response.Write("<H1>Hello! Today's date is " & Date & " </H1>")
 8:
 9: End Sub
10:
11: </SCRIPT>
12:
13: <HTML>
14: <HEAD>
15: <META NAME="GENERATOR" Content="Microsoft Visual InterDev 1.0">
16: <META HTTP-EQUIV="Content-Type" content="text/html; charset=iso-8859-1">
17: <TITLE>Syntax of ASP Applications</TITLE>
18: </HEAD>
19: <BODY bgcolor="#DBFFBF" link="#0000FF" vlink="#800080">
20:
21: <!-- Insert HTML here -->
22:
23: <%= "<H2>This line of text is displayed as output </H2>" %>
24:
25: <%
26:
27:   Call SayHello ()
28:   Response.Write ("<HR>")
29:
30: %>
31:
32: </BODY>
33: </HTML>
```

Figure 2.1.

*The output of the
ASP application in
Listing 2.1.*

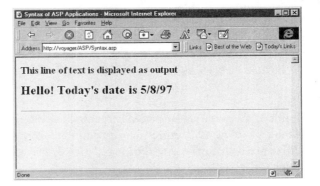

ANALYSIS   The scripting language used by the ASP application is specified using the statement `<%@ LANGUAGE="VBSCRIPT" %>`. This statement is placed at the beginning of the ASP application, as shown in line 1. ASP subroutines are enclosed between the delimiters `<SCRIPT RUNAT=SERVER LANGUAGE=VBSCRIPT>` and `</SCRIPT>`. The scripting language of the subroutine(s) is specified using the LANGUAGE argument. Refer to lines 3–11 for an example of using the `<SCRIPT>` delimiter to define an ASP subroutine.

 NOTE

> The LANGUAGE keyword may equal any supported scripting language such as JScript.

NOTE

> The RUNAT=SERVER statement is required to denote that the script commands should be executed by the server. Otherwise, the commands will be embedded in the HTML file sent to the client.

You can easily output any expression by enclosing it between the delimiters `<%=` and `%>`. For example, in order to display the string of text `This line of text is displayed as output` on the Web page, the statement `<%= "<H2>This line of text is displayed as output </H2>" %>` is used in line 23. You can also use the statement `Response.Write` to output the value of an expression. Use `Response.Write` when you need to output a value in the middle of a subroutine. Use the delimiters `<%=` and `%>` to output the value of an expression when you need to quickly display the value of an expression in the middle of HTML code.

Do	Don't

DO use `Response.Write` to output the value of an expression within an ASP script block (ASP script blocks are enclosed between the delimiters `<%` and `%>`). Only include ASP expressions (not statements) between the script delimiters `<%=` and `%>`.

Inline ASP statements are placed between the delimiters `<%` and `%>`, as shown in lines 25–30. Think of inline ASP expressions as inline images you include in Web pages. The only difference is that instead of the image being displayed, the output of the ASP statements is displayed.

Hello World! Active Server Pages

It is very easy to write the classic Hello World! application using ASP. At first, the Hello World! application in Listing 2.2 will seem like a typical Web page. However, the Web page in Listing 2.2. contains ASP scripting statements. Unlike a typical Web page, the ASP application in Listing 2.2 contains ASP scripting delimiters. These scripting delimiters cause various statements to be executed on the server before the requested Web page is sent to the user. The statement in line 13 of Listing 2.2, `<%= "Hello World!<BR> The time now is " & time & " on " & date %>`, displays the string `Hello World!` with the current date and time. Notice how the VBScript string concatenation operator (&) is used to combine the two string expressions with the result of the `time` and `date` functions. The output of the application in Listing 2.2 is shown in Figure 2.2.

Listing 2.2. ASP version of the classic Hello World! application.

```
 1: <%@ LANGUAGE="VBSCRIPT" %>
 2:
 3: <HTML>
 4: <HEAD>
 5: <META NAME="GENERATOR" Content="Microsoft Visual InterDev 1.0">
 6: <META HTTP-EQUIV="Content-Type" content="text/html; charset=iso-8859-1">
 7: <TITLE>Hello World, Active Server Pages!</TITLE>
 8: </HEAD>
 9: <BODY bgcolor="#DBFFBF" link="#0000FF" vlink="#800080">
10:
11: <FONT SIZE=6 FACE="Comic Sans MS">
12:
13: <%= "Hello World!<BR> The time now is " & time & " on " & date %>
14:
15: </FONT>
16:
17: </BODY>
18: </HTML>
```

Figure 2.2.

The output of the Hello World! application in Listing 2.2.

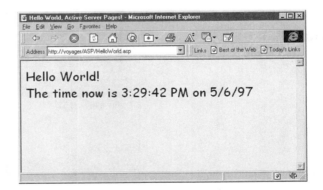

Hello World! VBScript

ASP applications can use VBScript to script various commands. The application in Listing 2.3 illustrates the use of VBScript to declare a subroutine within an ASP application. Lines 3–12 of Listing 2.3 declare a VBScript subroutine that displays the current date. The VBScript subroutine is then executed with the statement in line 22. The output of the ASP application in Listing 2.3 can be found in Figure 2.3. As shown in Listing 2.3, you can easily leverage your VBScript skills to the Internet when developing ASP applications.

Listing 2.3. VBScript version of the classic Hello World! application.

```
 1: <%@ LANGUAGE="VBSCRIPT" %>
 2:
 3: <SCRIPT RUNAT=SERVER LANGUAGE=VBSCRIPT>
 4:
 5: Sub UserDefinedVBScriptFunction ()
 6:
 7:   Response.Write("<H2>UserDefinedVBScriptFunction has been called.<BR>")
 8:   Response.Write("Today's date is " & Date )
 9:
10: End Sub
11:
12: </SCRIPT>
13:
14: <HTML>
15: <HEAD>
16: <META NAME="GENERATOR" Content="Microsoft Visual InterDev 1.0">
17: <META HTTP-EQUIV="Content-Type" content="text/html; charset=iso-8859-1">
18: <TITLE>Hello World, VBScript!</TITLE>
19: </HEAD>
20: <BODY bgcolor="#DBFFBF" link="#0000FF" vlink="#800080">
21:
22: <% Call UserDefinedVBScriptFunction %>
23:
24: </BODY>
25: </HTML>
```

Figure 2.3.

The output of the ASP application in Listing 2.3.

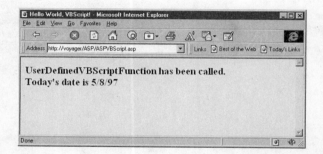

Hello World! JScript

ASP applications can also use JScript to script various commands. The application in Listing 2.4 illustrates the use of JScript to declare a subroutine within an ASP application. Lines 3–13 of Listing 2.4 declare a JScript subroutine that displays the current time. The JScript subroutine is then executed with the statement in line 23. The output of the ASP application in Listing 2.4 can be found in Figure 2.4. As shown in Listing 2.4, you can easily leverage your JScript skills to the Internet when developing ASP applications.

Listing 2.4. JScript version of the classic Hello World! application.

```
 1: <%@ LANGUAGE="VBSCRIPT" %>
 2:
 3: <SCRIPT RUNAT=SERVER LANGUAGE=JSCRIPT>
 4:
 5: function  UserDefinedJScriptFunction ()
 6: {
 7:   var DateObject = new Date()
 8:   Response.Write("<H2>UserDefinedJScriptFunction has been called.<BR>")
 9:   Response.Write("The current time is " + DateObject.getHours() + " : " +
10:                  DateObject.getMinutes() + " : " + DateObject.getSeconds())
11: }
12:
13: </SCRIPT>
14:
15: <HTML>
16: <HEAD>
17: <META NAME="GENERATOR" Content="Microsoft Visual InterDev 1.0">
18: <META HTTP-EQUIV="Content-Type" content="text/html; charset=iso-8859-1">
19: <TITLE>Document Title</TITLE>
20: </HEAD>
21: <BODY bgcolor="#DBFFBF" link="#0000FF" vlink="#800080">
22:
23: <% Call UserDefinedJScriptFunction %>
24:
25: </BODY>
26: </HTML>
```

Figure 2.4.

The output of the ASP application in Listing 2.4.

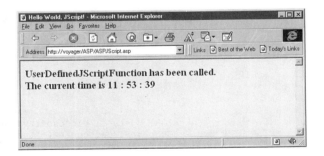

Mixing Scripting Languages

It is possible to mix scripting languages in an ASP application. The application in Listing 2.5 demonstrates this. If you mix scripting languages, develop subroutines that use only one scripting language with clearly defined input and output. Lines 3–12 declare a VBScript subroutine, and lines 15–25 declare a JScript subroutine. The two subroutines are called in lines 36 and 39. The output of the application in Listing 2.5 is shown in Figure 2.5.

Do	Don't

DO stick to one scripting language to avoid possible confusion.

DON'T mix scripting languages unless you have a very good reason for doing so (such as the need to use a powerful and useful feature of each scripting language).

Listing 2.5. Mixing scripting languages.

```
 1: <%@ LANGUAGE="VBSCRIPT" %>
 2:
 3: <SCRIPT RUNAT=SERVER LANGUAGE=VBSCRIPT>
 4:
 5: Sub UserDefinedVBScriptFunction ()
 6:
 7:   Response.Write("<H2>UserDefinedVBScriptFunction has been called.<BR>")
 8:   Response.Write("Today's date is " & Date )
 9:
10: End Sub
11:
12: </SCRIPT>
13:
14:
15: <SCRIPT RUNAT=SERVER LANGUAGE=JSCRIPT>
16:
17: function  UserDefinedJScriptFunction ()
18: {
19:   var DateObject = new Date()
20:   Response.Write("<H2>UserDefinedJScriptFunction has been called.<BR>")
21:   Response.Write("Today's time is " + DateObject.getHours() + " : " +
22:                   DateObject.getMinutes() + " : " + DateObject.getSeconds())
23: }
24:
25: </SCRIPT>
26:
27: <HTML>
28: <HEAD>
29: <META NAME="GENERATOR" Content="Microsoft Visual InterDev 1.0">
30: <META HTTP-EQUIV="Content-Type" content="text/html; charset=iso-8859-1">
31: <TITLE>Mixing Scripting Languages</TITLE>
```

2

```
32: </HEAD>
33: <BODY bgcolor="#DBFFBF" link="#0000FF" vlink="#800080">
34:
35: <H1>About to call VBScript subroutine</H1>
36: <% Call UserDefinedVBScriptFunction %>
37:
38: <H1>About to call JScript subroutine</H1>
39: <% Call UserDefinedJScriptFunction %>
40:
41: </BODY>
42: </HTML>
```

Figure 2.5.

*The output of the
ASP application in
Listing 2.5.*

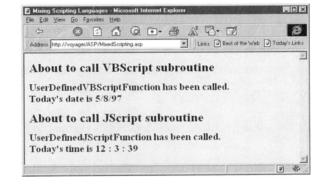

Using Loops for Repetitive Tasks

Loops can be used to perform iterative statements. The application in Listing 2.6 demonstrates the use of a loop within an ASP application to add some flair to the classic Hello World! application. The loop in lines 15–26 displays the string `Hello World!` one character at a time, followed by a table with increasing width (the background color of the table is set to black). For additional information about VBScript loops, see Appendix A. The output of the application in Listing 2.6 is shown in Figure 2.6.

 NOTE

> You can nest one loop inside another loop to perform various iterative actions.

Listing 2.6. Using loops for repetitive tasks.

```
1: <%@ LANGUAGE="VBSCRIPT" %>
2:
3: <HTML>
```

continues

Listing 2.6. continued

```
 4: <HEAD>
 5: <META NAME="GENERATOR" Content="Microsoft Visual InterDev 1.0">
 6: <META HTTP-EQUIV="Content-Type" content="text/html; charset=iso-8859-1">
 7: <TITLE>Hello World!</TITLE>
 8: </HEAD>
 9: <BODY bgcolor="#DBFFBF" link="#0000FF" vlink="#800080">
10:
11: <FONT SIZE=3 FACE="ARIAL">
12:
13: <%
14: Greeting = "HELLO WORLD!"
15: For RowCount = 1 to Len(Greeting)
16: %>
17:
18: <TABLE>
19: <TR>
20: <TD BGCOLOR=000000 WIDTH=<%= (RowCount^2)+(RowCount*15)%>>+</TD>
21: <TD><%= Left(Greeting,1) %></TD></TR>
22: </TABLE>
23:
24: <%
25: Greeting = Right(Greeting, Len(Greeting)-1)
26: Next
27: %>
28:
29: </FONT>
30:
31: <HR>
32:
33: <B>The time now is <%= Time %> on <%= Date %>.</B>
34:
35: </BODY>
36: </HTML>
```

Figure 2.6.

A loop is used to add flair to the classic Hello World! application.

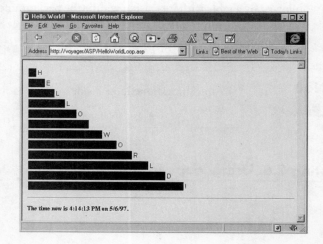

Using Conditional Statements for Flow Control

Conditional statements can be used to control the flow of an ASP application. The application in Listing 2.7 uses an If…Then…Else control structure to display a greeting based on the time of day the Web page is invoked (see Figure 2.7 for the output). See Appendix A for additional information about VBScript flow control structures.

Listing 2.7. Using conditional statements for flow control.

```
 1: <%@ LANGUAGE="VBSCRIPT" %>
 2: <HTML>
 3: <HEAD>
 4: <META NAME="GENERATOR" Content="Microsoft Visual InterDev 1.0">
 5: <META HTTP-EQUIV="Content-Type" content="text/html; charset=iso-8859-1">
 6: <TITLE>Conditional Statements</TITLE>
 7: </HEAD>
 8: <body bgcolor="#DBFFBF" link="#0000FF" vlink="#800080">
 9: <H1> Hi! </H1>
10: <FONT Face="Comic Sans MS" Size=6>
11: <%
12: If (Hour(Time) < 12) Then
13:    Response.Write "Good morning!"
14: ElseIf (Hour(Time) < 3)  Then
15:    Response.Write "Good afternoon!"
16: Else
17:    Response.Write "Good evening!"
18: End If
19: %>
20: </FONT>
21: <HR>
22: The current time is <%= Time %>.
23: </BODY>
24: </HTML>
```

Figure 2.7.

Conditional statements are used to display a custom message based on the time of day.

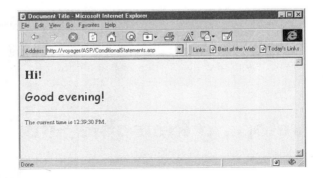

Using Server-Side Includes

Server-side includes (SSI) can be used with Active Server Pages. If you are familiar with C/C++, think of SSI as preprocessor directives. Server-side includes can be used to include ASP subroutines contained in other files. You might want to create a separate file containing your favorite ASP subroutines and include that file in other ASP applications using SSI. SSI can also be used to implement certain company policies. For example, a subroutine in an SSI file can calculate a sale price using a certain formula. At a later time, if the formula used to calculate the sale price is changed, only one file needs to be updated. Other ASP applications that use the SSI file will automatically use the new formula to calculate sale prices after the SSI file is updated with the new formula. There are two ways in which you can include SSI files in ASP applications: virtual pathnames and relative pathnames.

WARNING

> You cannot use an ASP statement to generate the name of a file to include because ASP statements are processed after all external files are included.

Using Virtual Pathnames

You can include files relative to the path of the virtual root directory of the Web server using the `<!--#INCLUDE VIRTUAL="/VIRTUAL/Path/Of/File.inc"-->` statement. Use virtual pathnames to implement global policies and subroutines that are common to many applications.

Using Relative File Pathnames

Files relative to the path of the current file can be included using the `<!--#INCLUDE FILE="Relative/Path/Of/File.inc"-->` statement. Use relative pathnames to implement policies and subroutines that are unique to the application being developed.

Do	Don't

DO give a file an `.inc` extension when you create one with useful subroutines that you plan to include in other ASP applications.

Developing Reusable Subroutines

When you develop ASP subroutines, always try to reuse code you have already written. That way, you can use subroutines you have already perfected when developing future applications. Not only will this cut back in development time, it will make your applications more efficient because you will be using subroutines that have undergone several cycles of reuse and optimization.

Developing ASP Pages with Client-Side Scripts

It is possible to develop ASP applications with client-side scripting. By doing so, you can take advantage of scripting features of the Active Desktop (which is composed of the Active Server and the Active Client). In order to include client-side scripting in an ASP application, simply include the client-side scripting code in the ASP application. The ASP interpreter ignores client-side scripting code and does not attempt to execute it on the server.

Hello World! Active Server Pages (the Personalized Version)

It is very easy to develop an interactive version of the classic Hello World! application. When the Hello World! application in Listing 2.8 is invoked, the Web page in Figure 2.8 is displayed. This Web page allows the user to enter his name.

Listing 2.8. Hello World! Active Server Pages (the personalized version).

```
 1: <!DOCTYPE HTML PUBLIC "-//IETF//DTD HTML//EN">
 2: <html>
 3:
 4: <head>
 5: <meta http-equiv="Content-Type"
 6: content="text/html; charset=iso-8859-1">
 7: <meta name="Template"
 8: content="C:\PROGRA~1\MICROS~2\Office\html.dot">
 9: <meta name="GENERATOR" content="Microsoft FrontPage 2.0">
10: <title>Hello World, Active Server Pages! (Interactive Version)</title>
11: </head>
12:
13: <body bgcolor="#DBFFBF" link="#0000FF" vlink="#800080">
14:
15: <% IF (Request.QueryString("NameOfUser") = "") THEN %>
16:
17: <p>
18: <img src="/Graphics/Lines/Colorful_SquiggleD8.gif" width="424"
19: height="18">
20: </p>
21:
```

continues

Listing 2.8. continued

```
22: <table border="0" cellpadding="7" cellspacing="0" width="492">
23:     <tr>
24:         <td valign="top" bgcolor="#FFFFFF">Welcome to the
25:         exciting and dynamic world of Web application development
26:         with Active Server Pages! Please enter your name and
27:         press the button!</td>
28:     </tr>
29: </table>
30:
31: <p> </p>
32:
33: <form action="/ASP/HelloWorldInteractive.asp">
34:     <p>Please enter your name here and press the button <input
35:     type="text" size="20" maxlength="30" name="NameOfUser"
36:     width="24"> <input type="submit"
37:     value="Please press this button after typing your name."> </p>
38: </form>
39:
40: <% ELSE %>
41:
42: <p><font color="#000000" size="5">
43: <strong>Hello World!</strong>
44: </font></p>
45:
46: <p><font color="#FF0000" size="5" face="Arial">
47: <em><%= Request.QueryString("NameOfUser") %>,</em></font>
48: <font color="#0000FF" size="4" face="Comic Sans MS">
49: welcome to the fun and exciting world of ASP application development!
50: </font></p>
51:
52: <form action="/ASP/HelloWorldInteractive.asp">
53:     <p><input type="submit"
54:     value="Please click here to start over again."> </p>
55: </form>
56:
57: <% END IF %>
58:
59: </body>
60: </html>
```

Figure 2.8.

*The Hello World!
application requests the
user's name.*

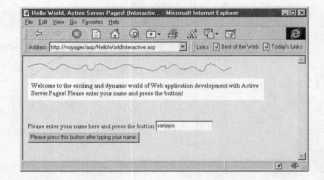

After the user's name is entered, the ASP application greets the user with his name, as shown in Figure 2.9. Notice how line 33 of Listing 2.8 submits the user's name to the same file the user invoked. In line 15, the variable `NameOfUser` is examined to determine whether the user has specified a name in the HTML form. If a name is specified, the ASP application greets the user with that name. Otherwise, the application requests that the user provide a name. ASP applications can obtain the value of a form variable using the `Request.QueryString` method.

Figure 2.9.

The Hello World! application greets the user with his name.

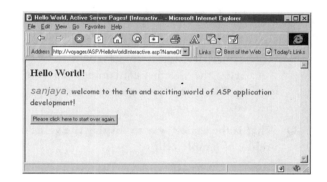

Summary

Active Server Pages can be used to easily develop Web applications and publish them on the Internet. The fundamentals of ASP application development are easy to learn. ASP applications differ from typical Web pages in that special scripting delimiters are used to separate ASP code from the rest of the Web page. Useful ASP subroutines can be included in an SSI file. Subroutines contained in an SSI file can be easily called by other ASP applications.

What's Next?

The application in Listing 2.8 showed you a glimpse of the power of interactive ASP applications. Tomorrow, you will learn more about interacting with users browsing your Web site and developing compelling, interactive Web applications.

Q&A

Q Is it possible to mix scripting languages in an ASP application?

A Yes, it is possible. However, this is discouraged because it can lead to confusion when developing complex Web applications.

Q **How does IIS determine whether a certain Web page is an ASP application?**

A IIS does this by examining the file extension of the Web page. If the file extension is `.asp`, the Web page is executed on the server as an ASP application.

Q **So in order to publish an ASP application on the Internet, all that's needed to do is save the file with the extension `.asp`?**

A Not quite. You also need to make sure the directory in which the file is saved is given execute permissions. This is done by performing the following steps:

  1. Invoke Microsoft Internet Service Manager.

  2. Select to modify the properties of the WWW publishing service.

  3. Choose the directories tab.

  4. Select the directory containing the ASP file and click the Edit Properties button. When the Directory Properties dialog box appears, make sure the Execute checkbox is checked.

Q **What is the easiest way to display the value of the variable `InterestRate` in the middle of a table cell?**

A `<TD> <%= InterestRate %> </TD>`

Q **I need to implement a subroutine that calculates the insurance premium of a car when certain pieces of information are passed into the function as arguments. I anticipate that this subroutine will be called by several other ASP applications. Should I include this subroutine in a virtual or a relative SSI file?**

A You should use a virtual SSI so that other applications can easily refer to the subroutine without being concerned about the directory structure of your application.

Exercises

  1. Modify the application in Listing 2.7 to greet the user with one of 10 messages based on the number of seconds past the minute of the current system time.

  2. Convert the ASP code you created in Exercise 1 to an ASP subroutine and include it in a SSI file.

  3. Develop a new ASP application that calls the subroutine in the SSI file created in Exercise 2.

2

Chapter 3

Interacting with Users

Nearly all Web applications interact with users browsing a Web site. Sometimes this interaction is indirect. For example, depending on the time of day, the Web application might greet the user with "Good morning!" or "Good evening!" Although the greeting is displayed on the user's Web browser, the interactive and dynamic nature of the Web page is not always obvious because the user did nothing special to execute the Web application. At other times, the interaction between the Web application and the user is very visible and direct—as in the case of an online mortgage payment calculator application.

Today you will learn how ASP applications can interact with users via ActiveX controls, message boxes, input boxes, HTML form elements, and of course, HTML text. By the end of the day, you will be able to create compelling, interactive ASP applications that fully exploit capabilities of the Active Desktop to obtain user input.

NOTE

Before you proceed, it is important that you understand that nearly all user input occurs on the client side. Therefore, you should be aware of the limitations of certain Web browsers. For example, if a Web browser does not support VBScript, you will not be able to use the `InputBox` and `MsgBox` functions.

Even if most of your users do not use a Web browser that supports ActiveX or VBScript, your ASP applications can interact with users using HTML forms as shown later in this chapter in the section titled "Using HTML Forms."

There are several ways an ASP application can obtain user input. Depending on the application and circumstances, you will have to select one or more of the following methods to obtain user input:

☐ The `InputBox` function—This function is used to display a window on the user's screen for the purpose of obtaining text input from the user. A Web browser that supports VBScript is required in order for this function to work.

☐ The `MsgBox` function—This function displays a message on the user's screen with one or more buttons the user can click to respond. A Web browser that supports VBScript is required in order for this function to work.

☐ Data-entry objects of HTML forms—Such objects include textboxes, selection lists, and checkboxes. This method will work with all Web browsers that support HTML forms.

☐ ActiveX controls—These can be used to obtain input from users when the application requires more control over various attributes of the data-entry fields. A Web browser that supports ActiveX is required in order for this method to work.

The `InputBox` Function

The `InputBox` function is displayed by a client-side VBScript subroutine. Because the `InputBox` function is a feature of VBScript, you should make sure your users' Web browsers support VBScript before you use this function. The `InputBox` function obtains input from the user by presenting a dialog box with a data entry field. The syntax of the `InputBox` command is as follows:

```
InputBox(<Prompt>,<Title>,<Default>,<X>,<Y>)
```

Arguments enclosed in pointed brackets can be replaced with the following values:

☐ `<Prompt>`—Dialog box prompt.

☐ <Title>—Title of dialog box.

☐ <Default>—Default input value.

☐ <X>—Horizontal position, in number of twips, from the left side of the screen. (A *twip* is $\frac{1}{20}$ of a printer's point, which is $\frac{1}{1,440}$ of an inch.)

☐ <Y>—Vertical position, in number of twips, from the top of the screen.

Using the InputBox Function

Listing 3.1 demonstrates how an ASP application can obtain input from a user via the InputBox function. The InputBox function is used by the ASP application to obtain the user's name and the height of the tree that will be drawn by the ASP application.

Listing 3.1. The InputBox function is used to obtain input by an ASP application.

```
1: <%@ LANGUAGE="VBSCRIPT" %>
2: <SCRIPT LANGUAGE="VBSCRIPT" RUNAT=SERVER>
3: Sub DrawTree ()
4:
5:    TreeHeight = Request.QueryString("TreeHeight")
6:    UserInput = Request.QueryString("Name")
7:
8:    Response.Write "<PRE>"
9:    For LoopCountVariable = 0 To (TreeHeight - 1)
10:      Response.Write "Hello " & UserInput & "!"
11:      For AsterisksCountVariable = 0 To (TreeHeight-LoopCountVariable)
12:        Response.Write " "
13:      Next
14:      For AsterisksCountVariable = 0 To (LoopCountVariable*2)
15:        Response.Write "*"
16:      Next
17:      Response.Write "<BR>"
18:    Next
19:    For LineCountVariable = 0 To ((TreeHeight / 3) - 1)
20:      For SpaceCountVariable = 0 To ( 7 + Len(UserInput) + (TreeHeight))
21:        Response.Write " "
22:      Next
23:      Response.Write "***<BR>"
24:    Next
25:    Response.Write "</PRE><HR>"
26:    Response.Write "<A HREF=InputBox.asp>Click here to start over.</A>"
27:
28: End Sub
29: </SCRIPT>
30: <HTML>
31: <HEAD>
32: <META NAME="GENERATOR" Content="Microsoft Visual InterDev 1.0">
33: <META HTTP-EQUIV="Content-Type" content="text/html; charset=iso-8859-1">
34: <TITLE>Using The InputBox Function For User Input</TITLE>
35: </HEAD>
```

continues

Listing 3.1. continued

```
36: <BODY BGCOLOR="FFFFFF">
37: <B>
38:
39: <%
40:   If NOT (IsEmpty(Request.QueryString("TreeHeight"))) Then
41:     Call DrawTree
42:   Else %>
43:     <FORM ACTION="InputBox.asp" METHOD="GET" NAME="DataForm">
44:         <INPUT TYPE=HIDDEN NAME="Name">
45:         <INPUT TYPE=HIDDEN NAME="TreeHeight">
46:     </FORM>
47:     <SCRIPT LANGUAGE="VBScript">
48: <!--
49:
50: Sub window_onLoad()
51:
52:   Name = InputBox ("Please enter your name and press enter", _
53:               "The InputBox function is used to obtain your name", _
54:               "Please type your name here", 300, 200)
55:   Do
56:     TreeHeight = InputBox ("Please enter the height of your tree", _
57:               "Please enter the height of your tree (1-20)", _
58:               "Please type the height of your tree here",200,200)
59:     If NOT((TreeHeight>=1) AND (TreeHeight<=20)) Then
60:       MsgBox "Please enter a height between 1 and 20."
61:     End If
62:   Loop Until ((TreeHeight>=1) AND (TreeHeight<=20))
63:
64:   DataForm.Name.value=Name
65:   DataForm.TreeHeight.value=TreeHeight
66:   DataForm.Submit
67:
68: end sub
69: -->
70:     </SCRIPT>
71: <%
72:   End If
73: %>
74:
75:   </B>
76: </BODY>
77: </HTML>
```

NOTE

The VBScript subroutine window_onLoad is always executed before the user can manipulate elements of the Web page. Therefore, InputBox statements should be placed inside the window_onLoad subroutine, as shown in line 50 of Listing 3.1, to ensure that the input boxes are displayed as soon as the Web page is loaded.

When the Web page in Listing 3.1 is invoked, it displays the input box shown in Figure 3.1 to obtain the user's name. This input box is created by lines 52–54 in Listing 3.1.

Figure 3.1.

The ASP application uses the InputBox *function to obtain the user's name.*

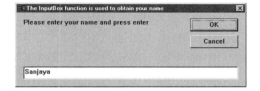

After the user types his name and presses Enter, the input box shown in Figure 3.2 is displayed. This input box is used to obtain the height of the tree that will be drawn by the ASP application. This input box is generated by lines 56–58.

Figure 3.2.

An input box is used to obtain the height of the tree.

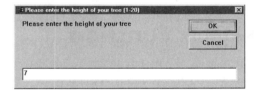

The Do...Loop Until iterative structure, defined in lines 55–62, ensures that a number between 1 and 20 is entered as the height of the tree. If an invalid number is entered, the message box shown in Figure 3.3 is displayed, and the user is returned to the input box shown in Figure 3.2.

Figure 3.3.

Invalid tree heights are rejected by the Do...Loop Until *iterative structure.*

After the user's name and the height of the tree is obtained, the ASP application generates the Web page shown in Figure 3.4.

The ASP application in Listing 3.1 demonstrates how the InputBox function is used to obtain user input. Notice how lines 64–66 of Listing 3.1 populate the HTML form variables with values and then submit the HTML form to the ASP application. The two HTML form variables that are used to transfer the user's name and the tree height are declared in lines 44 and 45 as hidden HTML form variables. This is a trick that can be used to send information to an ASP application if the information was not directly obtained from an HTML form. You can simply declare a hidden HTML form variable and use it to send information to ASP applications.

Figure 3.4.

The Web page generated by the ASP application.

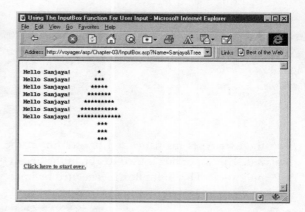

The MsgBox Function

Although using the MsgBox function might seem a bit complicated at first, it can add a professional touch to your ASP application. The MsgBox function displays a message box. The syntax of the MsgBox command is as follows:

```
MsgBox <MessageBoxPrompt>,<ButtonStyle>,<Title>
```

Replace <MessageBoxPrompt> with the prompt of the message box and <Title> with the title of the message box. By replacing <ButtonStyle> with values shown in Table 3.1, a message box can be customized. For example, an OK dialog box with a warning-message icon can be created by replacing <ButtonStyle> with 48. Note that <ButtonStyle> and <Title> are optional arguments.

NOTE

The MsgBox function is a feature of VBScript. Your ASP applications can use the MsgBox function only if your users' Web browsers support VBScript.

Table 3.1. Message box codes.

Button type	Button description
0	OK
1	OK and Cancel
2	Abort, Retry, and Ignore

Button type	Button description
3	Yes, No, and Cancel
4	Yes and No
5	Retry and Cancel
16	Critical Message icon (see Figure 3.5)
32	Warning Query icon (see Figure 3.6)
48	Warning Message icon (see Figure 3.7)
64	Information Message icon (see Figure 3.8)
256	Second button is default
512	Third button is default
4096	Message box always appears on top of all other windows until the user responds to the message box

NOTE

The VBScript subroutine `window_onLoad` is always executed before the user can manipulate elements of the Web page. Therefore, `MsgBox` statements should be placed inside the `window_onLoad` subroutine to ensure that the message boxes are displayed as soon as the Web page is loaded.

For your reference, Figures 3.5–3.8 show the types of message boxes that can be created through the use of the `MsgBox` function.

Figure 3.5.
The Critical Message box.

Figure 3.6.
The Warning Query box.

Figure 3.7.
The Warning Message box.

Figure 3.8.

The Information Message box.

The application in Listing 3.2 demonstrates how an ASP application can display a message box on the user's desktop using the MsgBox function. ASP applications can use the MsgBox function to display critical information to users. For example, the application in Listing 3.2 demonstrates how the MsgBox function can be used to remind the user that the information he is about to see is confidential (see Figure 3.9).

Listing 3.2. The MsgBox function is used by an ASP application.

```
 1: <%@ LANGUAGE="VBSCRIPT" %>
 2:
 3:      <SCRIPT LANGUAGE="VBScript">
 4: <!--
 5:
 6: Sub window_onLoad()
 7:
 8:   MsgBox "The information you are about to see is confidential!", _
 9:          16 ,"Confidential information - keep it private!"
10:
11: end sub
12: -->
13:      </SCRIPT>
14:
15: <HTML>
16: <HEAD>
17: <META NAME="GENERATOR" Content="Microsoft Visual InterDev 1.0">
18: <META HTTP-EQUIV="Content-Type" content="text/html; charset=iso-8859-1">
19: <TITLE>Using The MsgBox Function</TITLE>
20: </HEAD>
21: <BODY BGCOLOR="FFFFFF">
22:
23: <H1>Confidential information goes here!</H1>
24:
25: </BODY>
26: </HTML>
```

There are many practical applications of the MsgBox function. For example, you can use the famous Abort, Retry, or Ignore message box in an ASP application if a certain action cannot be immediately performed. The user can then decide whether he wants to retry the action, ignore the action, or abort the task.

Figure 3.9.

The message box displayed by the ASP application in Listing 3.2.

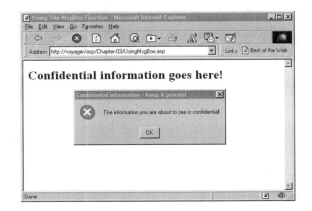

Using HTML Forms

Virtually all Web browsers support HTML forms, so ASP applications can use HTML forms to communicate with virtually anyone browsing your Web site. The application in Listing 3.3 demonstrates how an ASP application can communicate with users through the use of HTML forms. An ASP application can easily determine the value of an HTML form variable using the `Request.QueryString` method. For example, `Request.QueryString("name")` returns the value of the `"name"` variable.

Listing 3.3. An ASP application that uses an HTML form for data input.

```
 1: <%@ LANGUAGE="VBSCRIPT" %>
 2:
 3: <HTML>
 4: <HEAD>
 5: <META NAME="GENERATOR" Content="Microsoft Visual InterDev 1.0">
 6: <META HTTP-EQUIV="Content-Type" content="text/html; charset=iso-8859-1">
 7: <TITLE>Using An HTML Form For Data Entry</TITLE>
 8: </HEAD>
 9: <BODY>
10:
11: <H1>
12: <%
13:   If NOT (IsEmpty(Request.QueryString("Name"))) Then
14:     Response.Write ("Hi " & Request.QueryString("Name") )
15:   Else %>
16:     Please enter your name <BR>
17:     <FORM ACTION="HTMLFormInput.asp" METHOD="GET" NAME="DataForm">
18:         <INPUT TYPE=Text NAME="Name" Size="35"
19:          VALUE="Please enter your name here">
20:         <INPUT TYPE="SUBMIT" VALUE="Submit name to ASP application">
21:     </FORM>
22: <%
```

continues

Listing 3.3. continued

```
23:   End If
24: %>
25: </H1>
26:
27: </BODY>
28: </HTML>
```

TIP

It is a good programming practice to include default data values to guide the user into entering valid data.

When the ASP application in Listing 3.3 is invoked, the Web page shown in Figure 3.10 is displayed. The form in this Web page is linked to the ASP application that generated the HTML form. After the Submit name to ASP application button is clicked, the name entered in the text box is sent to the ASP application.

When the HTML form in Figure 3.10 is submitted, the ASP application in Listing 3.3 generates the Web page shown in Figure 3.11.

Figure 3.10.

An HTML form data-entry field is used to type in a value.

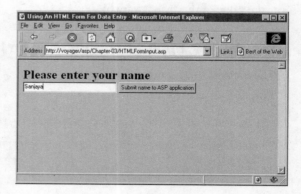

Figure 3.11.

The value of the HTML form field is sent to the ASP application.

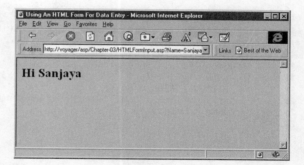

Using ActiveX Controls

As long as the Web browser supports ActiveX, ActiveX controls can be used by ASP applications to obtain input from users. The application in Listing 3.4 demonstrates how ASP applications can communicate with users through the use of ActiveX controls. Because ActiveX controls are not directly supported by HTML forms, a small trick is employed to transfer the values of ActiveX controls to an ASP application. When the information is submitted for processing, a VBScript subroutine copies the values of the ActiveX controls to hidden HTML form variables. The HTML form is then submitted to the ASP application.

Listing 3.4. An ASP application that uses ActiveX controls for data input.

```
 1: <%@ LANGUAGE="VBSCRIPT" %>
 2:
 3: <SCRIPT LANGUAGE="VBScript">
 4: <!--
 5: Sub SubmitButton_onClick()
 6:
 7:   DataForm.Name.value=UserName.Value
 8:   DataForm.Submit
 9:
10: end sub
11: -->
12: </SCRIPT>
13:
14: <HTML>
15: <HEAD>
16: <META NAME="GENERATOR" Content="Microsoft Visual InterDev 1.0">
17: <META HTTP-EQUIV="Content-Type" content="text/html; charset=iso-8859-1">
18: <TITLE>Using ActiveX Controls For Data Entry</TITLE>
19: </HEAD>
20: <BODY BGCOLOR=FFFFFF>
21:
22: <H1>
23: <%
24:   If NOT (IsEmpty(Request.QueryString("Name"))) Then
25:     Response.Write ("Hi " & Request.QueryString("Name") )
26:   Else %>
27:     Please enter your name <BR>
28:     <OBJECT ID="UserName" WIDTH=300 HEIGHT=37
29:      CLASSID="CLSID:8BD21D10-EC42-11CE-9E0D-00AA006002F3">
30:        <PARAM NAME="VariousPropertyBits" VALUE="746604571">
31:        <PARAM NAME="BackColor" VALUE="8454143">
32:        <PARAM NAME="Size" VALUE="7938;979">
33:        <PARAM NAME="Value" VALUE="Please type your name here">
34:        <PARAM NAME="BorderColor" VALUE="0">
35:        <PARAM NAME="FontName" VALUE="Comic Sans MS">
36:        <PARAM NAME="FontHeight" VALUE="315">
37:        <PARAM NAME="FontCharSet" VALUE="0">
38:        <PARAM NAME="FontPitchAndFamily" VALUE="2">
```

continues

Listing 3.4. continued

```
39:        </OBJECT>
40:        <FORM ACTION="ActiveXInput.asp" METHOD="GET"
41:             NAME="DataForm">
42:           <INPUT TYPE=HIDDEN NAME="Name">
43:           <INPUT TYPE=Button Name=SubmitButton
44:                  VALUE="Submit name to ASP application">
45:        </FORM>
46: <%
47:    End If
48: %>
49: </H1>
50:
51: </BODY>
52: </HTML>
```

When the ASP application in Listing 3.4 is invoked, the Web page shown in Figure 3.12 is displayed. The user employs the textbox ActiveX control shown in Figure 3.12 to interact with the ASP application by providing his name.

 NOTE

The TextBox control is an ActiveX control that is included with Internet Explorer.

Figure 3.12.

An ActiveX control is used to obtain input from the user.

After the Submit name to ASP application button is clicked, the name entered by the user is sent to the ASP application through the use of a hidden form field. Line 7 of Listing 3.4 copies the value entered by the user to the hidden HTML form field. The ASP application then generates the Web page shown in Figure 3.13.

3

Figure 3.13.

The value of the ActiveX control is sent to the ASP application.

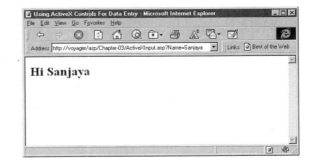

Summary

Nearly all Web applications interact with users to obtain and display information. Today you learned how to use HTML, message boxes, input boxes, ActiveX controls, and HTML form elements to interact with users browsing your Web site. Use ActiveX controls to interact with users when you are certain they use a Web browser that supports ActiveX; ActiveX controls provide additional control over various attributes of data-entry objects.

What's Next?

The built-in objects shipped with Active Server Pages are very useful when developing ASP applications. Tomorrow you will learn how the Application, Request, Response, Server, and Session objects can be used to develop ASP applications.

Q&A

Q How can an ASP application obtain input from users?

A ASP applications can obtain input from users through the use of message boxes, input boxes, ActiveX controls, and HTML form fields.

Q If I'm not sure whether a Web browser supports ActiveX or VBScript, how can my ASP application obtain input?

A Virtually all Web browsers can handle HTML forms. Your ASP application can use an HTML form to obtain data.

Q How can I transfer a value obtained via an input box to an ASP application?

A A VBScript subroutine can transfer the value to a hidden HTML form variable and submit the HTML form to the ASP application.

Exercises

1. Create an ASP application that uses two message boxes to obtain two numbers and use the MsgBox function to display the sum of the two numbers.

2. Add an ActiveX control to the ASP application in Exercise 1 to obtain the user's name and greet the user.

Chapter **4**

Web Application Development with ASP Objects

by Kelly Held

In order to effectively use ASP, you must understand something about Object Oriented Programming (OOP). There are many excellent books on this subject; this chapter does not attempt to cover it in depth because only a basic understanding is required. This chapter touches on the collections, methods, and properties of those objects.

TIP   Sams and Sams.net have many good books on OOP. *Teach Yourself Java in 21 Days* (Sams.net) and *Teach Yourself Visual Basic 5 in 21 Days* (Sams) are good choices because both relate closely to IIS and the Web.

OOP Basics

The basic building block of object-oriented programming is the object itself. The object is an abstract and generic concept that is very powerful in programming. You need to learn only enough about objects to become comfortable with their naming conventions.

An object is a self-contained component, an abstract representation of a concrete thing. Objects can fit together with other objects in a predefined way and can even contain other objects. Think of an object as being like a computer; the computer itself might contain other objects such as drives, which might also contain objects such as files.

Each object has properties that define its attributes. An object's properties tell you something specific about the object or its contents. Properties differentiate one object from another and determine its state and qualities. For example, a computer might be a PC, a Macintosh, or a mainframe, and it might be on or off.

Each object also has methods that define how that object behaves as well as how an object interacts with other objects. Sticking with the computer example, a method might define how to turn it on or how it is controlled (how you interact with it). If you are used to programming, you might feel more comfortable thinking of methods as functions; but in the OOP paradigm, they are called methods.

Finally, there are collections. Collections are groups of objects of the same type. An object and a collection are both containers, but of a different type. An object will contain zero or more collections that are all different in nature, while a collection will contain zero or more objects that are all alike in nature. For example, ASP uses only five basic objects to accomplish its tasks. In turn, each object has its own properties, methods, and collections. Each collection might then have its own properties.

For example, in ASP you have a Request object that contains many properties and different collections that relate to how client browsers make requests. One of those collections is called the Form collection. This collection contains only information that was entered by the user and the properties of that information. Notice the fine line between objects and connections. Objects can always contain another level of varied information but collections cannot. Collections are made up of the most basic information.

4

The task for today is to fit everything together, and to get the overall view of how everything works to make your ASP applications. The five objects that comprise ASP are

- [ ] The Request object
- [ ] The Response object
- [ ] The Server object
- [ ] The Application object
- [ ] The Session object

If you understand these five objects, you understand ASP. There is, of course, a lot more to cover. This chapter is not meant to be an in-depth reference for ASP objects, but rather contains descriptions of the most powerful and most frequently used objects and methods. By the end of the day you should have a basic understanding of how to use each object listed.

The HTTP Protocol

Before you can use the ASP objects to start programming, you need to understand a bit about how the World Wide Web functions and how the exchange of information occurs. To get information from the browser and to have the server send content to the client browser, the server and browser must have a set way to communicate. The methodology that defines how the communication process occurs is defined by HTTP.

HTTP is based on the client/server or request/response paradigm. There are three important things about HTTP of which you should be aware:

- [ ] HTTP is connectionless. After a request as been made, the client disconnects from the server and waits for a response. The server must re-establish the connection after it processes the request. Each request must receive a response from the server telling the client the status of the request.

- [ ] HTTP is media independent. Any type of data can be sent by HTTP as long as both the client and browser know how to handle the data content. How content is handled is determined by a standard labeling schema. This labeling, or content-typing, schema is defined by the MIME specification discussed later in this section.

- [ ] HTTP is stateless. This is a direct result of HTTP's being connectionless. The server and client are aware of each other only during a request. Afterward, each forgets the other. For this reason, neither the client nor the browser can retain information between different requests or across Web pages. However, ASP enables the server to store information, or maintain state, between client requests.

4

A client browser that wants to view content must request that content from the server. The client browser sends a client request that contains the location, or Uniform Resource Locator (URL), of the desired content as well as extra information regarding the request and the client. There are really two parts to a client request. The request itself is contained in the HTTP command. The extra information (such as time, browser version, form information from the user, and so on) is contained in what is called an *HTTP header*.

After the server receives a request for a page, several things happen:

1. The server determines whether the page exists. (Technically, this is the third step and happens only after the server translates the URL to a physical path and then ensures that the client has rights to access the document.)

2. The server processes the HTTP headers.

3. The server determines the page's content type based on the page's extension and supported MIME types.

4. The server processes the page executing any ASP script if necessary. Normally, output is sent as the page is processed, but you can use ASP and the Response object to change this behavior in order to trap errors or for other reasons.

5. The server attaches HTTP headers and sends the content. At the very least, headers must inform the client browser of two things:

   ☐ The Status header tells the client browser the status of its request. The Status header is represented by a status code and a status message. The most common standard server status codes are listed in Table 4.1.

   ☐ If the server is sending content, the headers also must specify the type of content being sent so that the client will know how to handle it. ContentType is one of the MIME types as defined by RFC 1521. A listing of the most common types appears in Table 4.2.

NOTE

This is a simple breakdown of what happens during an HTTP request, and does not include all possibilities. Although this book focuses on ASP, there are subjects other than ASP that must be considered, such as MIME type and HTTP. Microsoft designed ASP to do most of the work for you, so you can write applications without delving too deeply into either subject.

Nonetheless, there are some applications that require knowledge of MIME types and further understanding of HTTP. You can find the MIME types supported by IIS in the IIS documentation. More

4

information on MIME types can be found in RFC 1521. You can find more HTTP response codes in the HTTP 1.0 specification as defined by RFC 1945. You can find more information about HTTP and MIME on the Internet at `http://ds.internic.net`. Try `http://ds.internic.net/rfc/rfc2068.txt` if you need more specifics on HTTP.

Table 4.1. Common HTTP status codes.

Code	Description
200	The request was successful and the data is being sent. You will never see this code on your browser, but every page you load successfully has this code attached.
301	The requested content has moved permanently to a new location. If the new location is given, your browser will probably send you automatically to the new location. However, some browsers might not, so you might see this code in your browser and even use it as a programmer to redirect users to the new location.
302	The requested content has temporarily moved to a new location. This code is handled by the browser in the same way as 301, and is used the same way in your programming.
404	The requested content could not be located on the server. No file is sent, and this ugly message is displayed on the user's browser.
500	The server encountered an internal error and the request cannot be processed. This status almost always indicates that you have done some bad bit of coding and need to fix it. Usually an error message is attached.

Table 4.2. Common MIME types and subtypes.

Type/subtype	Description
text/html	HTML file. Specifies that the client browser should look for and interpret HTML code for display.
text/plain	Indicates plain ASCII text. Specifies that the browser should only display text and not try to parse code.

continues

Table 4.2. continued

Type/subtype	Description
image/gif	Indicates a GIF-type graphics file. Indicates that the browser should handle this code internally and display the image inline or (according to user configuration) start a third-party application to view the image.
image/jpeg	Indicates a JPEG-encoded graphics file. Handled by the client browser in the same way as the GIF file.

So headers are used by the client to send information and by the server to inform the client about the information it will be sending. They can also be used to send extra information back to the client browser.

This exchange of headers and commands seems like too much to handle when you just want to process a form! Luckily there is ASP. For the most part, ASP hides all the ugly details of the HTTP protocol. You just need to understand the basics.

Using the Response Object to Send the Information to the Browser

Now that you have the basics down, you can start doing something with ASP. You will start today by learning how to write information and control its flow to the client browser. Later you will learn how to get information from the client browser; then you will learn how to store that information for further use.

Controlling HTTP Output

There are several ways you can directly control and manipulate the HTTP output. The following ASP properties and methods can be used separately or in tandem to produce the desired results:

- [ ] The Status property
- [ ] The ContentType property
- [ ] The AddHeader method
- [ ] The Redirect method
- [ ] The BinaryWrite method

The most common reasons for manipulating HTTP are for generating on-the-fly graphics applications such as graphical page counters, requesting authentication, and redirecting users. There are other reasons, but try to keep the ones listed here foremost in your mind as you learn to manipulate the HTTP data stream using ASP.

As discussed previously, the minimum headers required by the client browser to process your information are `ContentType` and `Status`. Normally, IIS handles header generation for you, but for those of you who need a little more control, there are the `ContentType` and `Status` properties. These properties replace server-generated headers. The syntax of the `ContentType` property is as follows:

```
Response.ContentType = type/subtype
```

The `ContentType` must be in the MIME type/subtype schema. `ContentType` can be any supported type that is in the MIME specification. You might use this code to introduce an unknown MIME type or to change the MIME type and send a different file than originally requested. This is especially useful when you are generating graphics on the fly, such as in a graphical counter application.

The syntax of the `Status` property is as follows:

```
Response.Status = status
```

`Status` should include both the three-digit status code and the brief description. This header is used in conjunction with the `ContentType` property to create on-the fly graphics. You might also use it to require authentication (`Status 401`).

WARNING

All `Response` properties must be set before any HTML or other screen output (such as Java applets) is sent to the browser; otherwise, an error is generated. These statements (if used) should be among the first in your ASP scripts and must appear before the <HTML> tag.

A method that relates closely to the `Status` property is the `Redirect` method. Using the `Status` property to set the HTTP `Status` header to a value of `302` or `301` tells the client browser only that the page has moved; it does not divulge the page's new location. The `Redirect` method tells the browser where the page has moved and allows capable browsers to automatically redirect.

The `Redirect` method does two things to ensure that the client browser can obtain to the new page location. First, it sends the HTTP `Status` header with the code `302 Object Moved` like so:

```
HTTP/1.0 302 Object Moved
Location URL
```

Then, the method automatically generates a link to the new URL in HTML form. All other output is ignored. In this way, clients that do not support automatic redirection are not left out in the cold. The syntax of the Redirect method is as follows:

```
Response.Redirect(URL)
```

The AddHeader method allows you to define custom headers and header values in the HTTP stream. You should avoid the use of the underscore character (_) in your header; instead, use a dash (-). The correct syntax for the AddHeader method is as follows:

```
Response.AddHeader headername, headervalue
```

You cannot use the AddHeader method to replace the value of an existing header. Any attempt to do so will generate an error. The AddHeader method is primarily for advanced use. In most cases, the browser will not know what to do with your header anyway, so you will probably never use this method.

The BinaryWrite method is used to write data directly to the HTTP stream without translation. Note that this method will not send the contents of a file, but only a data stream. This method is useful when sending small graphics, multimedia, or other nontext files. The syntax of the BinaryWrite method is as follows:

```
Response.BinaryWrite data
```

Binary data is usually too long to send in a typed-in data string. It is either generated by an object or loaded from a file.

To see how these methods might be used, take the example of a graphical page counter that generates graphics on the fly using ASP. You might place the following tag in your HTML code where you want the image to appear:

```
<IMG SRC="count.asp">
```

The count.asp file is not an image, but it might produce one. Normally, the server assumes the output to be text/html, so you want to change that. You do not need to worry about how to generate binary code; just pretend you have magically done it and stored the results in the variable numpic. Given this, Listing 4.1 shows the necessary steps to send the picture to the client browser.

Listing 4.1. count.asp: Using BinaryWrite to send a generated image.

```
<% Response.Status("200")
Response.ContentType("image/gif")
' numpic is magically generated here.
BinaryWrite numpic
%>
```

Controlling How the Server Processes ASP Scripts

One thing you must have control over is how the server processes your scripts and sends the output to the client browser. Normally, output is sent to the browser while the page is being processed. However, you can also buffer content. Buffered content is not sent to the client browser until the script is completely processed or until the `Flush` or `End` method (discussed later in this section) is called.

Use buffering to test information or to look for errors before sending output to the user. If you detect an error in processing or receive invalid information, you can stop processing or redirect the user. When buffering is enabled, the server will honor keep-alive requests from the client. Keep-alive requests ask the server not to close the connection after the request, but to leave the connection open until the request is complete. This might save some time because the server does not have to re-establish the connection. However, keep-alive requests could be bad news when you are processing a long script in a high-traffic environment. This is because there is a limited amount of network bandwidth and a limited number of connections that can be serviced at one time. In a high-traffic environment, the network and server resources should not be used by an idle connection waiting on script output.

Buffering is controlled by the `Buffer` property. It is either `TRUE (1)` or `FALSE (0)`. To set the `Buffer` property, use the following syntax:

```
Response.Buffer = [TRUE¦FALSE]
```

By default, buffering is off. The default value for all scripts can be altered in the Registry. Use the `BufferingOn` flag to set the default behavior. The `Buffer` property must be set in the very beginning of the script, before any headers are written.

The `Flush` method works with the page-buffering property. To flush the contents of the buffer out to the user before the end of the script, use the following call:

```
Response.Flush
```

If the `Response.Buffer` property is not set to `TRUE`, the call to `Flush` will return an error.

The `End` method stops processing of the ASP script and returns the results. All commands after the `End` method are ignored.

The `Clear` method erases the contents of a buffered page, but not the headers. Use the `Clear` method to keep the user from seeing the output of the page up to the point of the `Clear` call.

To see how you might use all these properties together, consider a form called `fill-out-form.htm`, where you require the user to input his birthday. You do not need to consider a whole form, just the following line:

```
Birthday (mandatory): <input name="birthday">
```

4

If you use the POST method to return the data to the server, you could use the following script to make sure the user's birthday is filled in. If not, you could send the user back to the form after clearing the buffer. The following code shows how to do just that:

```
<%Response.Buffer%>
<HTML><HEAD>
<TITLE>Your Birthday </TITLE></HEAD>
if Request.Form("birthday") = "" then
Response.Clear
Response.Redirect("fill-out-form.htm")
Response.End
Else%>
<BODY>
Your birthday is <%=Request.Form("birthday")%>
<%end if%>
</BODY>
</HTML>
```

The Expires and ExpiresAbsolute Properties

To save downloading time, many client browsers cache content on the local hard disk. When a user requests content, the client browser looks in the cache and loads from there. If the content cannot be found in cache, the server is contacted. If you change your content often, it is possible that the user might not see the most recent content displayed. The Expires and ExpiresAbsolute properties tell the client browser how long it should cache the page on the local hard disk or local memory. If neither property is specified, that page will expire immediately and will not be placed in the client browser's cache. The syntax of the Expires properties is as follows:

```
Response.Expires = number
```

number is the time in minutes before a page expires. Setting this to 0 causes the document to not be cached.

ExpiresAbsolute lets you specify the date and time that the page will expire. If no time is specified, the page expires on midnight of that day. The date and time must be provided in a GMT format that conforms to RFC 1123. The ExpiresAbsolute property has the following syntax:

```
Response.ExpiresAbsolute = [date time]
```

If you are using VBScript, your dates and times should be enclosed in pound (#) signs. For example, a page that expires on my birthday in 1998 would use

```
Response.ExpiresAbsolute = #July 10, 1998 16:00:00#
```

The AppendToLog Method

IIS can be configured to log requests. Each page request is a separate line or record in a database. See the IIS documentation or *Internet Information Server 3.0 Unleashed* for more information about logging. The `AppendToLog` method appends the specified string to the server log when the file is processed. This can be any string and might be useful for tracking if you use Crystal Reports that come with IIS 3.0. To append a string to the server logs, use the following syntax:

```
Response.AppendToLog String
```

The `Write` and `ImplicitWrite` **Methods**

Use the `Response.Write` method to write text to the data stream. Method calls and variables inside the `Write` method will be evaluated and only the result will be written to the client browser. For example, you could use the `Write` method to display the value in the variable count as follows:

```
Response.Write("The Counter says" & count)
```

If you are in the middle of an HTML code and need to evaluate an expression or retrieve the contents of a variable, you can use a shortcut to the `Write` method. The following line produces the same output as the previous one:

```
The Counter Says <%=count%>
```

The equal sign must immediately follow the <% delimiter. Although only one expression at a time can be evaluated in this manner, it is quicker than using the full syntax of the `Write` method.

Write a Cookie with the `Cookies` Collection

Cookies are wonderful things that help the client browser and server retain information, or maintain state, across different pages. Basically, cookies contain information that the client stores for the server. The client sends cookies back to the server as part of the HTTP request. Cookies can contain any type of information and have a great number of uses, but are usually used only to maintain state information. Cookies will be covered in much greater detail on Day 6, "Tracking HTTP Sessions Using Cookies."

A cookie crumbles in four ways. First, all cookies must have a name/value pair. Second, cookies can have *keys* (extra name/value pairs that are stored in the cookie). When a cookie has keys, it is called a *dictionary*. Finally, a cookie has properties and attributes. Each cookie has the attribute `HasKeys`, which is either `TRUE` or `FALSE` (Boolean 1 or 0 if you did not declare a language) depending on whether the cookie is a dictionary. Look for Microsoft to add more attributes to cookies in the next version of ASP.

Cookies have four optional properties that can be set, and one property that is intrinsic and therefore read-only (see Table 4.3).

Table 4.3. Cookie properties.

Property name	Description
Domain	Specifies the domain that must be requested (in the HTTP page request) for the cookie to be returned to the server. In other words, it specifies which domain this cookie belongs to. If no domain is set, the domain of the current page is used.
Expires	This sets the date/time the cookie expires. If no date is set, the cookie is lost when the user exits the client browser.
Path	Specifies the path that must be requested for the client to return the cookie. In other words, it specifies which page the cookie belongs to. If one is not specified, the path of the current page is used.
Secure	This property is either TRUE or FALSE. There must be a secure connection for the client to return the cookie.

To set a property, use the following:

```
Response.Cookies(cookiename).Property = PropertyValue
```

To set a cookie's name and value, use the following:

```
Response.Cookies(cookiename) = cookievalue
```

To set the key values, use the following:

```
Response.Cookies(cookiename)(keyname) = keyvalue
```

Keys are discussed in more detail later in this chapter in the section titled "The Cookies Collection." If you are familiar with Perl, you will notice that cookie dictionaries closely resemble associative arrays.

WARNING

If a cookie already exists and you want to assign new keys or properties, you must specify the old keys and properties with the new ones. This is because each new cookie overwrites the existing one.

Because cookies are stored in headers, they must be written before the first <HTML> tag appears unless you have enabled page buffering. In that case, headers are not written until the end of the script or until the Flush method is called.

Imagine you run a huge search engine. You want to save information about the last items a visitor to your search engine used (this really happens at the Microsoft site—you should try it). To do so, use a cookie with a really big expiration date. Listing 4.2 shows how you would write a cookie to the browser to preserve this information for the next visit.

Listing 4.2. Writing a sample cookie.

```
<%
Response.Cookies("searchstring") = "MSDN AND Interdev"
Response.Cookies("searchstring").Expires = "July 31, 2000"
Response.Cookies("searchstring").Domain = "www.microsoft.com"
Response.Cookies("searchstring").Path = "/search"
Response.Cookies("Type").Secure = FALSE
%>
```

If you write the same cookie again, the information previously stored in the cookie and all its properties are destroyed.

Using the Request Object to Obtain Client Information

When a client browser communicates with the server using HTTP, that browser sends many things besides the name of the requested page. Here I will provide a brief list of what is sent and how it is extracted without covering all the ways in which the information might be used:

- ☐ Environment variables
- ☐ Certificate information
- ☐ Cookies
- ☐ User-supplied information from forms

All this information is encoded and passed in HTTP headers, and it is not always easy to extract. ASP does the job of extracting, decoding and organizing all the information for you. The only thing ASP does not do is determine how this information is used; that is *your* job. With this information, you might do any of the following tasks and more:

- ☐ Validate a user.
- ☐ Get information about the user and client browser.
- ☐ Store information for later use (maintain state).

ASP stores the information in collections within the Request object. By making calls to Request.*collection*, you can easily extract the information you want.

4

The `ServerVariables` **Collection**

The first collection with which you want to become familiar is the `ServerVariables` collection. This collection stores information about the client browser, server, and user. The available information and some of its uses are shown in Table 4.4. The syntax of this collection is as follows:

```
Request.ServerVariables("variablename")
```

If you are familiar with CGI, you will recognize some the variables in Table 4.4. There are other variables that Microsoft has added for functionality. Note that the variable names listed in the table must be contained in quotation marks when referencing the `ServerVariables` collection.

Table 4.4. The most common `ServerVariables` and their uses.

Variable	Description
`"CONTENT_TYPE"`	The data type of the content. Used when the client is sending attached content to the server. For example, form uploads would qualify, as would HTTP `POST` and `PUT` requests.
`"PATH_INFO"`	The path to the current script. Could be used for self-referencing URLs.
`"PATH_TRANSLATED"`	A translated version of `PATH_INFO` that takes the path and performs any necessary virtual-to-physical mapping. This is useful if you need to know the physical location of your script on a remote server where you have no browsing access.
`"QUERY_STRING"`	The URL-encoded information that is sent via either the `GET` or `POST` method (see the section "The `Form` and `QueryString` Collections" for more information).
`"REMOTE_ADDR"`	The IP address of the remote host making the request. This can be useful for logging or as an extra way of authenticating clients.
`"REMOTE_HOST"`	The fully qualified domain name of the host making the request. If this information is not available, `"REMOTE_ADDR"` will be set and this variable left empty.
`"REQUEST_METHOD"`	The method used to make the request. The most common methods are `GET` and `POST`. You will use this later today to determine which `Request` collection is appropriate for gathering user information.

4

Variable	Description
"SCRIPT_NAME"	Returns the virtual path to the script being executed. This is used for self-referencing URLs. For example, a form that calls itself in the ACTION attribute of the <FORM> tag is a self-referencing form.
"SERVER_NAME"	The server's hostname or IP address.
"SERVER_SOFTWARE"	The name and version of the software the server is running. Version information is also given. The format is *name*/*version*.

TIP

ALL_HTTP (not listed in Table 4.4) returns all the headers sent by the client in the order they were sent. They are simply listed, not delimited.

The Form **and** QueryString **Collections**

These important collections in the Request object are for extracting information from forms or queries sent by the browser to the server. There are two ways the client can send information to the server: the GET and POST methods. Before you look at each collection, you should become somewhat familiar with the different methods of sending information to the server.

Before the browser sends the information, it encodes it using a scheme called URL encoding. In this schema, name/value pairs are joined with equal signs and different pairs are separated by the ampersand.

```
name1=value1&name2=value2&name3=value3
```

Spaces are removed and replaced with the + character, and any other nonalphanumeric characters are replaced with a hexadecimal value according to RFC 1738. After the information is encoded, it is sent to the server.

NOTE

RFC stands for *request for comments*. RFCs are the traditional way that Internet standards come about. A group submits a suggested standard or procedure as an RFC, an open discussion ensues, and changes are made. Finally, the original group submits a final RFC that defines a standard. Adherence to these standards is voluntary; people can propose and use other standards. The point of the RFC process is to define a standard way of doing things. You'll find an RFC for most tasks you want to accomplish.

The GET method sends the encoded user information appended to the page request. The page and the encoded information are separated by the ? character.

```
http://www.test.com/form.asp?name1=value1&name2=value2&name3=value3
```

The GET method produces a long, ugly string that appears in your server logs, in the browser's Location: box, and for most browsers, at the top of sheets printed off the Web. Not only is this ugly, it's a potential security hazard: The information in the string is visible to everyone. Never use the GET method if you have passwords or other sensitive information in a form. Finally, the GET method has a size limitation: Only 1,024 characters can be in a request string. This method should be avoided when possible, but you will see that it is useful for passing information in ASP from page to page without using the <FORM> tag.

NOTE

This book discusses forms only briefly, so if you don't have a good HTML book, you should get one (consider *Teach Yourself HTML in 21 Days*). Nonetheless, the HTML standard is everchanging, so keep up to date by visiting http://www.w3.org for information on the latest standards.

The POST method transfers information via HTTP headers. The information is encoded as it was previously and put into a header called QUERY_STRING. Note that you can post information only to files that are executable and that can read the query string; otherwise, you will receive an error. Listing 4.3 contains code that has a simple form that we will use as an example throughout the rest of the chapter. The completed form appears as shown in Figure 4.1.

Listing 4.3. The sample HTML login form.

```
1:   <HTML>
2:   <HEAD>
3:   <TITLE>Sample Form</TITLE>
4:   </HEAD>
5:   <BODY>
```

```
 6:  <P Align=center> This is a Sample Form </P>
 7:  <FORM action="test.asp" method=POST>
 8:  <TABLE><TR>
 9:  <TD>Name:</TD>
10:  <TD><INPUT name="name"></TD></TR>
11:  <TR><TD>Nick Name:</TD>
12:  <TD><INPUT name="name"></TD></TR>
13:  <TR><TD>Password:</TD>
14:  <TD><INPUT type=password name="pass"></TD></TR>
15:  <INPUT type=hidden name="hide" value="a hidden value">
16:  </TABLE>
17:  <INPUT type=submit> <INPUT type=reset>
18:  </FORM>
19:  </BODY>
20:  </HTML>
```

Figure 4.1.

The completed sample HTML form.

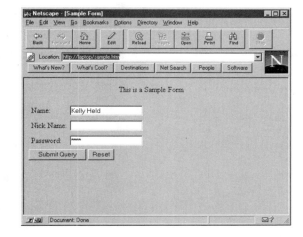

If you replace line 7 of Listing 4.3 with the following line, you receive the error shown in Figure 4.2 because `test.html` is not executable:

```
<form action=test.html method=POST>
```

In these examples, `test.html` is simply a blank file that produces a blank screen on your browser.

However, if you replace line 7 in Listing 4.3 with the following line, there is no error:

```
<form action test.html method=GET>
```

Look at Figure 4.3; notice how even the hidden and password information is shown in the `Location:` box.

Figure 4.2.

Trying to POST *to a nonexecutable file.*

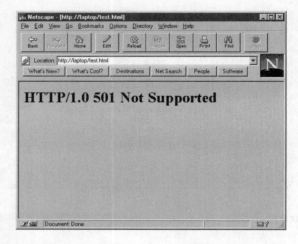

Figure 4.3.

Using the GET *method to transfer information.*

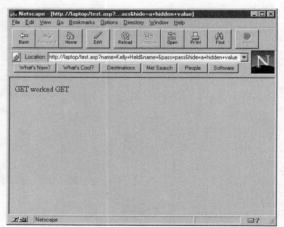

After the information successfully reaches the server, it must be decoded into a useful format. This used to be a problem for Web developers, but luckily, it is not a problem for you. ASP accomplishes this task automatically and, as mentioned, puts the information into collections. Two collections in the Request object let you get at user-submitted form information: the Form collection for the POST method and the QueryString collection for the GET method.

The Form **Collection**

The Form collection is used to extract information sent via the POST method.

```
Request.Form(variablename)[(index)¦.Count]
```

The `Request.Form(variablename)` method automatically decodes the encoded string if you call it using a valid *variablename*. If you need access to the raw encoded data, call `Request.Form` without any variables.

The `Count` method is there to expose a common stumbling block for many when dealing with HTML forms. One form variable can hold many values (that is, it can be an array). `Count` returns the number of values in the array. `Count` returns 1 if the variable is not an array, and 0 if the variable does not exist in the collection.

The *index* argument is used to extract a certain value from a form variable that is actually an array. Index numbers start at 1 (not 0). If you call a variable that has multiple values without the *index* argument, the result is a comma-delimited string containing all the values.

The `QueryString` Collection

The `QueryString` collection helps you extract and decode information sent through the use of the `GET` method.

```
Request.QueryString(variablename)[(index)¦.Count]
```

The behavior of the `Request.QueryString(variablename)` method is exactly like the `Request.Form` method. If you need access to the raw data, then call `Request.QueryString` without parameters.

A Simple Example

You can use the HTML code in Listing 4.3 to produce a form. Listing 4.4 is an ASP script that decodes the information and prints it to the browser.

Listing 4.4. `Test.asp` **is used to decode the login form in Listing 4.3.**

```
1:  <HTML>
2:  <% Select Case Request.ServerVariables("Request_Method")
3:  Case "GET"
4:  If Request.QueryString("name").Count > 1 then %>
5:  Name = <%=Request.QueryString("name")(1)%> <BR>
6:  Nick Name = <%=Request.QueryString("name")(2)%> <BR>
7:  <%else%>
8:  Name = <%=Request.QueryString("name")%> <BR>
9:  <%end if%>
10: Password = <%=Request.QueryString("pass")%> <BR>
11: Hidden Field = <%=Request.QueryString("hide")%> <BR>
12: Raw Data: = <%=Request.QueryString%>
13: <%Case "POST"
14: If Request.Form("name").Count > 1 then %>
15: Name = <%=Request.Form("name")(1)%> <BR>
16: Nick Name = <%=Request.Form("name")(2)%> <BR>
```

continues

Listing 4.4. continued

```
17: <%else%>
18: Name = <%=Request.Form("name")%> <BR>
19: <%end if%>
20: Password = <%=Request.Form("pass")%> <BR>
21: Hidden Field = <%=Request.Form("hide")%> <BR>
22: Raw Data: = <%=Request.Form%>
23: <%end select%>
24: </HTML>
```

ANALYSIS   Line 2 determines which method was used to transfer the information. In most cases you will already know this information and automatically use the appropriate collection; however, using the wrong collection will produce an error. The output (see Figure 4.4) is the same using either collection.

Figure 4.4.

Output of Listing 4.4.

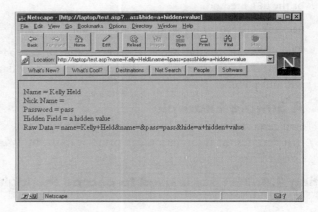

Line 4 tests whether name is an array (of course, you know that it is and that the else condition will never be executed, but this is just an example). Note that even if the user did not enter a nickname, name is still an array with the second element blank.

Notice that the code requires knowledge of the form. There is a quicker and easier way to write this code, which you will learn about in the section "Using Iterators to Loop Through Data."

The Cookies Collection

Cookies must be written before they can be retrieved. You learned how to write a cookie earlier today. Now you are concerned only with reading the information from an existing cookie. The client browser sends cookies to the server in HTTP headers (which means they are encoded).

Just to show an example of what a cookie might look like, consider a cookie with the name name and value Bradley & Ethan. The HTTP request the browser sends might look like the following:

```
GET /index.html HTTP/1.0
HTTP_COOKIE: name=Bradley+%26+Ethan
```

Luckily, you do not have to sort through headers or decode strings. ASP decodes the cookie and places it into the cookie collection for you. You just need to call the collection using the name of the cookie as illustrated here:

```
variable = Request.Cookies(cookiename)
```

For example, Request.Cookies("name") produces the text Bradley & Ethan. Pretty simple isn't it? You don't even need to know anything about HTTP headers.

As mentioned, when a cookie contains more than one name/value pair, it is called a dictionary and the HASKEYS attribute is TRUE. Now consider a cookie called name that has two name/value pairs. The key, or name, for the first pair is names with the value Bradley & Ethan; the key for the second is ages with values 20 & 17. To read a cookie with keys, use the following syntax:

```
variable = Request.Cookies(cookiename)(keyname)
```

For example, to see the key ages for the cookie name, use

```
Request.Cookies("name")("ages")
```

Be careful when using cookies because the Cookies collection behaves differently depending on its attributes. If a cookie has keys and you do not include a key value in a call to Request.Cookies, you will receive all the key's name/value pairs in query-string (undecoded) form. Using the previous sample cookie with keys ages and names and making this call:

```
Request.Cookies(cookiename)
```

would give the following result:

```
AGES=20+%26+17&NAMES=Bradley+%26+Ethan
```

If you are not sure whether a cookie is a dictionary, check whether a call to Request.Cookies.HasKeys returns TRUE (1) or FALSE (0). Listing 4.5 determines whether the cookie has keys and then prints the value of each key that exists. The output for a cookie with keys is shown in Figure 4.5.

Listing 4.5. Checking for keys and printing values.

```
1:  <HTML>
2:  <%if Request.Cookies("name").Haskeys = 1 then %>
3:  Cookie has keys! <BR>
4:  <%for each key in Request.Cookies("name")%>
5:  Key <%=key%> = <%=Request.Cookies("name")(key)%> <BR>
6:  <%next
7:  else%>
8:  No Keys for cookie! <BR>
9:  Name = <%=Request.Cookies("name")%> <BR>
10: <%end if%>
11: </HTML>
```

ANALYSIS Line 2 checks for keys. Notice that because Listing 4.5 did not declare a language, you must use numerical evaluators. Line 4 loops through each key. We will talk more about using iterators and loops in the section "Using Iterators to Loop Through Data."

Figure 4.5.
*Output of Listing 4.5 for
a cookie with keys.*

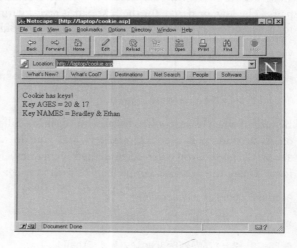

WARNING If a browser sends two cookies with the same name, only the cookie with the deeper path structure is stored in the Cookies collection. You'll learn more about the path properties of cookies on Day 6.

The ClientCertificate Collection

This collection contains the client certificate information (as defined by the X.509 standard) for SSL3/PCT1 requests. SSL3 and PCT1 are secure protocols that encode your information and keep it safe from prying eyes on the Web. Certificates are encrypted codes that uniquely and positively identify a client or server. When certificates exist on both the client and server, public-key encryption can be used to encrypt content transferred between them. Certificates should be obtained from an issuing authority so they are guaranteed to be unique and authentic.

IIS (or Peer Web Server) must be configured to request certificate information. By default, it is not configured to request this information. Unless you are dealing with very sensitive information, client certificates are not really necessary. Understanding the X.509 standard is really an advanced topic, but it might be something you want to look into after you become proficient in ASP.

Using Iterators to Loop Through Data

One good thing to know is how to use iterators and for each loops. You can save a lot of time coding if the NAME attribute of the <FORM> tag matches the variable you use in your scripting. Using iterator loops becomes even more useful and efficient when you move on to storing values in the Session or Application objects (discussed in the section "Using the Session and Application Objects to Maintain State"), and in database applications (see Day 8, "Introduction to Web Database Programming Using ActiveX Data Objects").

Listing 4.6 is a sample HTML form. This form gathers typical user information that will later be processed in an ASP file using loops.

Listing 4.6. HTML code for a sample form.

```
<HTML>
<Body>
<TITLE>A Simple Form</TITLE>
<P ALIGN=CENTER> A SIMPLE FORM
<BR>
Please fill out all information for fields that
not apply answer N/A.
<FORM ACTION=/SCRIPTS/SIMPLE.ASP METHOD=POST>
<TABLE><TR>
<TD>FIRST NAME:</TD>
<TD><INPUT NAME="FNAME"></TD></TR>
<TR><TD>LAST NAME:</TD>
<TD><INPUT NAME="LNAME"></TD></TR>
<TR><TD>PHONE: </TD>
<TD><INPUT NAME="PHONE"></TD></TR>
<TR><TD>EMAIL:</TD>
<TD><INPUT NAME="EMAIL"></TD><TR>
</TABLE>
CHILDREN'S FIRST NAME:<BR>
<INPUT NAME="CHILDREN"><BR>
<INPUT NAME="CHILDREN"><BR>
```

continues

Listing 4.6. continued

```
<INPUT NAME="CHILDREN"><BR>
<INPUT NAME="CHILDREN"><BR>
<INPUT TYPE=SUBMIT><INPUT TYPE=RESET>
</FORM>
</BODY>
</HTML>
```

Figure 4.6 shows the sample form as my mother might fill it out.

Figure 4.6.

The completed sample form.

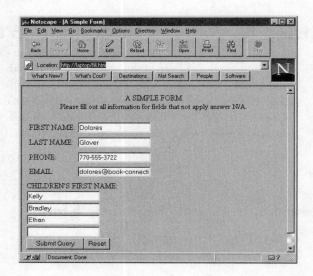

You can get each *variablename* by making a call to the Request.Form(*variablename*). However, when you are writing ASP code you do not want to constantly refer back to the HTML code to find the NAME attribute that matches *variablename*. If you are processing a whole form this way, it is also easy to skip a *variablename* in your code if you are not careful. An efficient way around these problems is to use iterator loops.

An iterator is the dummy variable used in a for or foreach loop. For example, the following code snippet prints each name/value pair from the HTML form in Listing 4.6.

```
<%foreach iterator in Request.Form%>
The variable <%=iterator%> is <%Request.Form(iterator)<BR>
<%next%>
```

This code would produce the following result if the form contained the data in Figure 4.6:

```
Fname = Dolores

Lname = Glover

Phone = 770-555-3722

CHILDREN = Kelly, Bradley, Ethan
```

Remember that a name in an HTML form can be an array (that is, it can hold more than one variable). To extract and print the values that this form places in the Form collection, use the following code:

```
<% for each key in Request.Form
for index 1 to Request.Form(key).Count%>
<%=key%>  = <%=Request.Form(key)(index)%> <BR>
<%next
next%>
```

The output this time is slightly different:

```
Fname = Dolores

Lname = Glover

Phone = 770-555-3722

CHILDREN = Kelly

CHILDREN = Bradley

CHILDREN = Ethan
```

You could also use another for each loop, but the important thing to remember when nesting loops is that each loop must have unique iterators. In the following code, you get the same output using the unique iterators key and item in a for each loop instead of a for/next loop.

```
<% for each key in Request.Form
for each item in Request.Form(key)%>
<%=key%> = <%=Request.Form(item)%> <BR>
<%next
next%>
```

You also can use iterator loops to test the content of the information as well extract information. A small bit of code that tests for blanks in the form follows:

```
<%for each key in Request.Form
if Request.Form(key)= "" then%>
You left the field <%=key%> blank! Please go back and fill out the form
➥correctly
<%exit loop
end if
next%>
```

The important thing to remember is that if you have done a little conceptual planning, you will save a lot of coding and processor time later.

The Server Object

The Server object is probably the least-used object. This object contains one property and four methods. Microsoft calls it a *utility object*, which is about right, since the methods and properties here are needed to extend ASP with custom objects (see Day 5, "Using ActiveX Components") and for special tasks that fit nowhere else. These methods are

- ☐ The ScriptTimeOut property
- ☐ The HTMLEncode method
- ☐ The URLEncode method
- ☐ The MapPath method
- ☐ The CreateObject method

The ScriptTimeOut Property

The behavior of your Web server is controlled primarily through the Server Manager. The only control you should expect to have through the Server object is over how the server processes your ASP scripts. Script buffering is handled through the Response object, but you can control a script's TimeOut through the Server object like so:

```
Server.ScriptTimeOut(seconds)
```

Any script that runs longer than the specified value is assumed to have misbehaved and will be terminated to free system resources. The default value is 90 seconds. The default can be changed only through the Registry; the ScriptTimeOut property applies to the current page only.

WARNING

> You should change the value of the ScriptTimeOut property only if you want it to be greater than the default value. If you set the value for less than the default value, nothing is accomplished because IIS continues to process the script until the default value is reached.

The HTMLEncode and URLEncode Methods

There might be times when you'll need to parse or encode your data strings so they can be used by other programs or methods. You might think these methods belong in the Response object, but you might not always want to encode data just to send it back to the client browser. You might encode it before saving it to a file or database, so these methods really belong more to the Server object.

URL encoding replaces whitespace with the + character, and then all nonalphanumeric characters are replaced by hexadecimal values according to RFC 1783.

```
variablename = Server.URLEncode("<h1>Quantum Consulting Services</H1>")
```

stores the string

```
%3CH1%3EQuantum+Consulting+Services%3C%2fH1%3E
```

in *variablename*.

There are many special and nonalphanumeric characters in HTML. In order to display these characters correctly on the client browser's screen, you must map them to their respective hexadecimal codes or an entity code as defined in RFC 1738. Then use the ampersand (&) followed by entity code and a semicolon (;), or use the ampersand followed by the pound sign (#) followed by a hexadecimal code followed by the semicolon.

For example, to display the string

```
<H1>Kelly & Sharon's Page</H1>
```

on the client browser, the HTML code would be

```
&lt;H1&gt; Kelly &amp; Sharon's Page &lt;/H1&gt;
```

Luckily, you do not have to keep up with a table of entity codes, and you will not find one in this book. All you need is the HTMLEncode method. To correctly display the preceding code on the browser, all you need to use is

```
<%=Server.HTMLEncode("<h1> Kelly & Sharon's Page </h1>")%>
```

The MapPath Method

The Server object has information about the virtual, relative, and physical paths of your server machine, and it knows how to map one to the other. You might need to map paths in order to create directories or to manipulate files on the server using the physical path. Use the MapPath method to map a virtual or relative path to the corresponding physical path like so:

```
variablename = Server.MapPath(pathname)
```

If *pathname* begins with a forward slash or a backslash, the method maps the path as a full virtual path (that is, from the drive's root directory to the virtual directory specified and then down to the directory tree specified). Otherwise, *pathname* is mapped relative to the directory where the ASP file that called the method resides. If you have your Web server and ASP set up using the defaults, you would obtain the following results from an ASP file run in the c:\inetpub\scripts directory:

```
<%=Server.MapPath("/scripts")%>
<%=Server.MapPath("scripts")%>
```

The browser would display

```
c:\inetpub\scripts
c:\inetpub\scripts\scripts
```

WARNING

The MapPath method does not check to see whether the path actually exists. Knowing this could be useful if you are going to create directories.

The CreateObject **Method**

You will use the Server object primarily to create instances of server components. You will learn more about server components on Day 5. To create an instance of a server component, use the CreateObject method like so:

```
Set objectname = Server.CreateObject(ProgID)
```

You must use Set with the Server.CreateObject method. ProgID is the registered name of your object. You will learn more about registering your objects tomorrow. It is important to note that objectname cannot be the same as one of the four built-in objects in ASP. You can destroy a previously created object with the following:

```
Set objectname = Nothing
```

Object instances are by default destroyed when the page finishes being processed.

Using the Session **and** Application **Objects to Maintain State**

One of the problems facing Web developers since the inception of HTTP is that HTTP is a stateless protocol. It connects, sends information, and then disconnects to free resources. This is not a problem if you simply want to display content, but in order for the Web to grow and be successful, it must be a truly interactive medium.

For the client and server to interact, there must be some preservation of information, or state, from one request to the next. CGI programmers have found many inventive ways to maintain state using the HTML and CGI environment variables available to them, but in this case, the server is doing all the work of maintaining state. The best solution was proposed and implemented by Netscape, and many others soon followed. The solution was called a *cookie*. A cookie is simply a container for information, and behaves much like an associative array with name/value pairs. But although cookies offer a better solution, there remains much work

4

to be done to ensure that the state of all the variables needed is maintained across different client requests on the server.

In steps Microsoft with ASP. ASP makes it simple to maintain state without worrying about cookie logic, HTTP headers, and the like. Microsoft has given you two object containers in which to store information. The best part is that they work just as you would expect (of course, they still have their little quirks and pitfalls). All and all, ASP maintains state in a manner much more simple and intuitive than CGI or HTML tricks.

WARNING

> ASP actually uses cookies to maintain state, but they hide the logic from you in the Session and Application objects. Some client browsers do not support cookies. In these browsers, ASP cannot maintain state across pages.

The Session and Application objects magically solve your problems of maintaining state. They differ only in their scopes. *Scope* defines what information is available to which users.

Information stored in the Session object is available only to the client that created the information in that object. This information has *session scope*. An ASP-based application is made up of all the ASP files in a virtual directory plus all ASP files that are in subdirectories of the virtual directory. Information stored in the Application object is available to all users who access this ASP-based application. This information is said to have *application scope*. Variables and object instances created in a script but not stored the in the Application or Session object expire after the script is processed. These variables and objects are said to have *page scope*.

Common Pitfalls of the Session and Application Objects

The Application and Session objects can contain variables, arrays, or other objects. There are only three big pitfalls you need to worry about:

☐ You cannot directly manipulate arrays stored in either object. If you try the following code, it will fail.

```
Session(Array)(arrayindex) = value
```

This code does not put *value* into the *arrayindex* position of *Array*, which is stored in the Session object. The code would also fail for an Application object because both objects are implemented as collections. In the previous code, *value* is indexed into the collection at *arrayindex* and overwrites any existing objects in the collection. If you need to change information in an array that is stored in the `Application` or `Session` object, you should first retrieve a working copy. Make your changes to the copy and then store the updated copy in the `Session` or `Application` object.

☐ You must use the `Set` keyword to store objects in the `Application` or `Session` objects when you are using VBScript as your primary language.

```
Set Session("objname") = Server.CreateObject("componentobject")
```

☐ You cannot store any of the five built-in ASP objects in the `Session` or `Application` object.

WARNING

When storing objects, you must also consider the type of threading model the object uses. Threading models are discussed in greater detail on Day 6. Only objects that are *both* free *and* apartment threaded can be stored in `Application` or `Session` objects.

The `Session` Object

A new `Session` object is created each time a user who does not already have a session ID requests an ASP script. The server knows if a browser already has a session because the `SessionID` cookie is sent with the request for the ASP script. Session information persists until the `Session.Abandon` method is called or until the `Session.TimeOut` property is reached. The default `TimeOut` property is 20 minutes. The `TimeOut` clock is reset each time a user makes a new request or refreshes the last request, so a session can last for much longer than 20 minutes if the user is active.

Each session has a unique ID that is assigned by the server at creation. You can glean this value by checking the property `Session.SessionID`. This property is read-only.

WARNING

The `SessionID` is always unique among other `SessionID`s during any specific server service runtime. You should not use the `SessionID` property to generate primary keys in a database because the server might generate the same `SessionID` during different runtimes (stops and starts).

4

..cion **Object**

..on object is created just before the first `Session` object. An `Application` object
..estroyed until the server is shut down, or until the `global.asa` file (discussed in the
next section) is modified and all users are disconnected.

Because many users have access to the `Application` object, you must worry about concurrency.
Concurrency refers to the problem of two users' trying to change the same data at the same
time. There is no problem with many users' simultaneously reading the same information,
but any time you need to change information in the `Application` object, you must have
exclusive access. To gain exclusive access, use the `Lock` method like so:

```
Application.Lock
```

After you make the necessary changes, you should release your exclusive rights so that others
may make changes. Release your rights by using the `UnLock` method like so:

```
Application.UnLock
```

To illustrate uses of both the `Application` and `Session` objects, consider an application where
you have received information (via `POST`) from a user form and you need to store it for later
processing on another page. This information is needed only by this user, so the information
can safely be stored in the `Session` object. The following code stores all the information from
the form into the `Session` object using the iteration loops that you learned about earlier.

```
<% For each key in Request.Form
Session(key)=Request.Form(key)
next %>
```

As you see, a little planning goes a long way. No matter how long the form is or what
information is requested, you have successfully stored it for later processing in just three lines
of code!

You want everyone to know how many people have filled out your form, so keep a counter
running. This counter information must be available to everyone, so you should store it in
the `Application` object. You can modify the code to increment the number of visitors like so:

```
<%Application.Lock
Application("numfilled-out")=Application("numfilled-out") +1
Application.Unlock
For each key in Request.Form
Session(key)=Request.Form(key)
next %>
```

`Session` and `Application` objects can be modified from a page (as you have done) or based
on an event (as you will see in the next section).

The `global.asa` File

The `global.asa` file is an optional file that relates directly to the `Application` and `Session` objects. It has two purposes:

- [ ] To define how object events are handled
- [ ] To allow you to create component object instances with application or session scope

The `global.asa` file must be named `global.asa` and must appear in the root directory of your ASP-based application. Inside the `global.asa` file are two containers: the object container `<OBJECT>` and the script container `<SCRIPT>`. Code is contained within `<SCRIPT></SCRIPT>` tags, and object declarations are made between `<OBJECT>` tags.

The `<OBJECT>` tag has the following attributes:

```
<OBJECT RUNAT=Server SCOPE=Scope ID=Identifier
➥{PROGID="progID"¦CLASSID="ClassID"}>
```

Currently, the only choice for the `RUNAT` attribute for both tags is `SERVER`. `SCOPE` is either `Application` or `Session`. The `Identifier` is the name you assign to the object you create.

Objects are not created until they are referenced by a script. This saves system resources and time at session and application start-up.

The `<SCRIPT>` tag has the following attributes:

```
<SCRIPT LANGUAGE=ScriptLanguage RUNAT=SERVER>
```

`ScriptLanguage` might be any supported scripting language, but it will most often have the value `VBScript`.

WARNING

> Object tags are self contained. You should not place an `<OBJECT>` tag inside a `<SCRIPT>` tag. No declarations or code should appear outside either the `<SCRIPT>` or the `<OBJECT>` tag.

The `Application` and `Session` objects each have two events: `OnStart` and `OnEnd`. If you are using VBScript, each event is treated as a `SUB` and has the form where `Object_Event` is `Application_OnStart`, `Application_OnEnd`, `Session_OnStart`, or `Session_OnEnd`:

```
<SCRIPT LANGUAGE=ScriptLanguage RUNAT=SERVER>
SUB Object_Event
'Your event code here
END SUB
'Other Event SUBs written in VBScript
</SCRIPT>
```

Not all objects and/or methods are available in all events. This will become apparent as you understand how the application uses events to fire the global.asa file. Any procedures you write are available only locally within the global.asa file and cannot be called directly from an ASP file.

At this point, it would be a good idea to look at a sample global.asa file just to get a feel for the general format. Listing 4.7 is an example about which you will receive more detailed information in the next section.

Listing 4.7. A sample global.asa file.

```
1: <SCRIPT LANGUAGE=VBScript RUNAT=SERVER>
2: SUB Application_OnStart
3: 'load count from file if it exists
4: END SUB
5:
6: SUB Session_OnStart
7: Application.Lock
8: Application("count") = Application("count") + 1
9: Application.Unlock
10: END SUB
11:
12: SUB Application_OnEnd
13: 'code to write to the count file
14: END SUB
15: </SCRIPT>
```

Firing Sequence of the global.asa File

Application objects are created when the first user connects to an ASP-based application and requests a session. When the Application object is created, the server looks for the global.asa file. If this file exists, the script for the Application_OnStart event is processed. Next, the Session object is created. The creation of the Session object signals the Session_OnStart event. Script in the global.asa file executed before the page request that triggers the object creation is processed. When the Session object times out or the Session.Abandon method is called, the Session_OnEnd event is triggered. Code for the Session_OnEnd event in global.asa is processed before the Session object is destroyed. When the server shuts down, the Application_OnEnd event is triggered. All sessions are destroyed and all Session_OnEnd code is processed. Code for the Application_OnEnd event in the global.asa file is then processed before the Application object is destroyed.

If the global.asa file is changed, the server will recompile it. To recompile the file, the server must destroy the current Application and Session objects and restart. First, the server processes all active requests. The server will not process more requests until the

Application_OnEnd event has been processed. Users who try to connect during this time will receive the message The request cannot be processed while the application is restarted. After the active requests are processed, the following occurs:

1. The active sessions are abandoned. This triggers the Session_OnEnd event for each session.
2. The application is abandoned. This triggers the Application_OnEnd event.
3. Further requests restart the Application object and create new Session objects. This will trigger the Application_OnStart and Session_OnStart events.

Special Event Consideration

Each event has its own quirks and considerations. Table 4.5 can help you find these quirks and avoid pitfalls.

Table 4.5. Event considerations.

Event	Considerations
Application_OnStart	The only intrinsic ASP objects available to this event are the Server and Application objects. Calls to any of the other three will generate an error.
Session_OnStart	All intrinsic ASP objects are available to this event. If the event calls the Redirect or End method, the following script and the requested page are not processed. For this reason, you should call these methods last in your scripts. You might use the Redirect method in this event to ensure that a user starts at the correct page and does not jump into the middle of an ASP-based application.
Application_OnEnd	Only the Application and Server objects are available to this event.
Session_OnEnd	Only the Application, Server, and Session objects are available to this event. You cannot call the Server.MapPath method in this event

Understanding the Sample global.asa File

Now that you know more, you will want to re-examine Listing 4.7. The whole file is really concerned with keeping track of how many sessions have been started on the server. The more complex parts, such as loading information from files and saving information to files, have been glossed over for now.

When the application starts, line 3 contains code that loads the previous count from a file. Each new session increments the count by one. Notice that this is not a page counter, but rather a session counter. Line 7 locks the Application object, line 8 increments it, and line 9 releases it. This happens only at the start of each new session.

When the application is terminated, line 13 writes the number of counts to disk for safekeeping until the application is restarted.

Summary

ASP has five intrinsic objects that are used to do all the work. You can add other component objects to extend the server, but the built-in objects handle the most common tasks. The Request object is used to retrieve client information; the Response object is used to send information to the client. The Server object is your utility object that performs miscellaneous tasks and allows you to extend the server. Finally, the Application and Session objects are used to maintain state. That's all there is to ASP. But to be a successful Web developer, you should familiarize yourself with subjects such as the fundamentals of the HTTP protocol and MIME types.

What's Next

Tomorrow you will look at how to create your own custom objects. You can use these objects to extend ASP and the server to do tasks that are much more advanced.

Q&A

Q How many intrinsic objects are in ASP?

A Five.

Q What are the three important properties of HTTP?

A It is connectionless, it is media independent, and it is stateless.

Q It the global.asa file mandatory?

A No. It is an optional way to execute code based on events.

Exercises

1. Using the Expires property, configure code to terminate information in the user's cache after 24 hours.
2. Visit http://ds.internic.net/rfc/rfc2068.txt and read up on HTTP and MIME.

Chapter 5

Using ActiveX Components

Active Server Pages is shipped with several useful built-in components. These components can be used in ASP applications to handle common Web development tasks. Today you will learn how to use the following components to develop ASP applications:

- [ ] The Advertisement Rotator component
- [ ] The Browser Capabilities component
- [ ] The File Access/Text Stream component

The ASP environment also includes a Database Access component. See Day 8, "Introduction to Web Database Programming Using ActiveX Data Objects," and Day 9, "Advanced Web Database Programming," to learn how to use the ASP Database Access component to develop Web database applications. In addition to the Database Access component, the ASP environment also includes a Content Linking component for creating a table of contents for Web pages.

The Advertisement Rotator Component

The Advertisement Rotator component is ideal for displaying a series of graphic images each time a user visits your Web page. You might use this control to display useful messages or to generate a new source of revenue by advertising other Web sites or products. You can also use the Advertisement Rotator component to entice users to visit various parts of your Web site. It is very easy to rotate a series of images using this component.

 NOTE

The user has to reload the Web page to see a different graphic as opposed to a series of images being displayed one by one by an animated GIF file.

First, develop a Rotator Schedule file for the images. A Rotator Schedule file is simply a text file containing information about the images to be rotated, and consists of two sections separated by an asterisk (*). The first section contains a list of keyword value pairs that may be omitted (in which case, default values are assumed). The following keywords can be used in the first section of the Rotator Schedule file:

- ☐ REDIRECT—URL of file that implements redirection
- ☐ WIDTH—Width of advertisements in pixels
- ☐ HEIGHT—Height of advertisements in pixels
- ☐ BORDER—Size of border

Table 5.1 lists default values of the keywords contained in the first section of the Rotator Schedule file.

Table 5.1. Default values of keywords.

Keyword	Default value
REDIRECT	N/A
WIDTH	440
HEIGHT	60
BORDER	1

 TIP

Set BORDER to 0 to delete the border around advertisements.

The second section of the Rotator Schedule file contains information about each image to be rotated. Each image requires four lines of information:

☐ The first line contains the URL of the advertisement image (as in /images/graphic.jpg).

☐ The second line contains the URL of the Web page to which the graphic is linked. If an advertisement graphic does not have a URL, simply include a hyphen (-).

☐ The third line contains a text description of the graphic. This description is displayed by Web browsers that do not display graphics. Other Web browsers, such as Internet Explorer, display the description of the graphic in a balloon if the user rests the mouse pointer on the graphic.

☐ The last line contains a number (between 0 and 4,294,967,295) that represents how frequently the advertisement image is displayed. Say one graphic has a frequency of 1 and another graphic has a frequency of 9. The graphic with a frequency of 1 will be displayed 10% of the time, and the graphic with a frequency of 9 will be displayed 90% of the time.

The ASP application in Listing 5.1 demonstrates how to rotate the three advertisement images shown in Figure 5.1.

Listing 5.1. The ASP application that rotates the three images shown in Figure 5.1.

```
 1: <%@ LANGUAGE="VBSCRIPT" %>
 2:
 3: <HTML>
 4: <HEAD>
 5: <META NAME="GENERATOR" Content="Microsoft Visual InterDev 1.0">
 6: <META HTTP-EQUIV="Content-Type" content="text/html; charset=iso-8859-1">
 7: <TITLE>Advertisement Rotator Web Page</TITLE>
 8: </HEAD>
 9: <BODY BGCOLOR=FFFFFF>
10:
11: <%
12: ' The Advertisement Rotator object is instantiated.
13:     Set AdRotator = Server.CreateObject("MSWC.AdRotator")
14: %>
15:
16: <H2>
17: The following image is rotated using the Advertisement Rotator object
18: </H2>
19:
```

continues

Listing 5.1. continued

```
20: <!--
21: The GetAdvertisement method of the Advertisement Rotator object
22: is used to display an advertisement image.
23: -->
24:
25: <%= AdRotator.GetAdvertisement ("Advertisements.txt") %>
26:
27: </BODY>
28: </HTML>
```

Figure 5.1.

The images to be rotated by the Advertisement Rotator component.

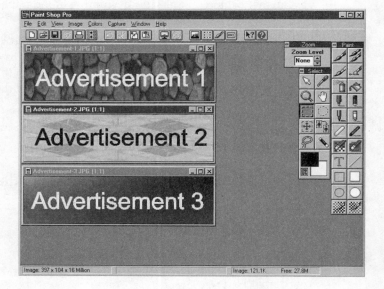

All that's needed to develop an ASP application that rotates images is to create a Rotator Schedule file and include two ASP statements in your ASP application. The first line instantiates the Advertisement Rotator component, as shown in line 13 of Listing 5.1. Afterwards, images can be displayed using the GetAdvertisement method of the Advertisement Rotator component and specifying the Rotator Schedule file as shown in line 25 of Listing 5.1. Images will then be rotated each time a user visits the Web page, as shown in Figures 5.2 and 5.3.

Figure 5.2.

The ASP application displays advertisement 2.

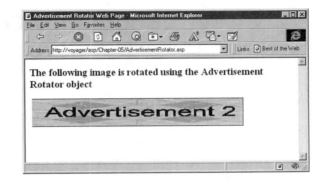

Figure 5.3.

The ASP application displays advertisement 1.

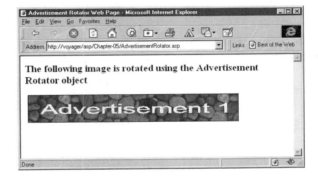

The Rotator Schedule file of the ASP application is shown in Listing 5.2. Notice how the asterisk in line 2 separates the two sections of the file.

Listing 5.2. The Rotator Schedule file used by the ASP application in Listing 5.1.

```
 1: BORDER     4
 2: *
 3: Advertisement-1.jpg
 4: -
 5: Description of advertisement 1
 6: 10
 7: Advertisement-2.jpg
 8: -
 9: Description of advertisement 2
10: 20
11: Advertisement-3.jpg
12: -
13: Description of advertisement 3
14: 30
```

The Browser Capabilities Component

The Browser Capabilities component is very useful for developing cross-browser Web applications. When developing Web applications, you cannot assume that all your users employ the latest version of Internet Explorer. Use the Browser Capabilities component to determine which browser is employed by your users and what features that browser supports. To use the Browser Capabilities component, you must first instantiate it using the ASP statement `<% Set BrowserCapabilities = Server.CreateObject("MSWC.BrowserType") %>`. After the Browser Capabilities component is instantiated, you can determine capabilities of the Web browser using the syntax `BrowserCapabilities.<Keyword>`. `<Keyword>` can be replaced with any value in the Keyword column of Table 5.2. For example, `BrowserCapabilities.tables` returns `TRUE` if the Web browser supports tables.

Table 5.2. Information that can be obtained using the Browser Capabilities component.

Keyword	Description
browser	Name of the Web browser.
platform	Operating system being used.
version	Version of the Web browser.
majorver	Major version number.
minorver	Minor version number.
frames	Does the Web browser support frames?
tables	Does the Web browser support tables?
cookies	Does the Web browser support cookies?
backgroundsounds	Does the Web browser support background sounds?
vbscript	Does the Web browser support VBScript?
javascript	Does the Web browser support JavaScript?

The ASP application in Listing 5.3 reports the capabilities of the Web browser, as shown in Figures 5.4 and 5.5. Notice how the Browser Capabilities component correctly reports capabilities of Internet Explorer 3.01 and Netscape Navigator 3.0.

Listing 5.3. Determining capabilities of the browser.

```
 1: <%@ LANGUAGE="VBSCRIPT" %>
 2:
 3: <HTML>
 4: <HEAD>
 5: <META NAME="GENERATOR" Content="Microsoft Visual InterDev 1.0">
 6: <META HTTP-EQUIV="Content-Type" content="text/html; charset=iso-8859-1">
 7: <TITLE>Determining Capabilities Of The Browser</TITLE>
 8: </HEAD>
 9:
10: <BODY BGCOLOR=FFFFFF>
11:
12: <H2>
13: The Browser Capabilities Component can be used
14: to determine the capabilities of the browser.
15: </H2>
16:
17:
18: <%  Set BrowserCapabilities = Server.CreateObject("MSWC.BrowserType") %>
19:
20: <TABLE>
21: <TR>
22: <TD>
23: Name of the Web browser
24: </TD>
25: <TD>
26: <%= BrowserCapabilities.browser     %>
27: </TD></TR>
28: <TR><TD>
29: Operating system being used
30: </TD>
31: <TD>
32: <%= BrowserCapabilities.platform    %>
33: </TD></TR>
34: <TR><TD>
35: Version of the Web browser
36: </TD>
37: <TD>
38: <%= BrowserCapabilities.version %>
39: </TD></TR>
40: <TR><TD>
41: Major version number
42: </TD>
43: <TD>
44: <%= BrowserCapabilities.majorver %>
45: </TD></TR>
46: <TR><TD>
47: Minor version number
48: </TD>
49: <TD>
```

continues

Listing 5.3. continued

```
 50: <%= BrowserCapabilities.minorver %>
 51: </TD></TR>
 52: <TR><TD>
 53: Does the Web browser support frames?
 54: </TD>
 55: <TD>
 56: <%If BrowserCapabilities.frames Then %>
 57: True
 58: <%Else %>
 59: False
 60: <%End If%>
 61: </TD></TR>
 62: <TR><TD>
 63: Does the Web browser support tables?
 64: </TD>
 65: <TD>
 66: <%If BrowserCapabilities.tables  Then%>
 67: True
 68: <%Else %>
 69: False
 70: <%End If%>
 71: </TD></TR>
 72: <TR><TD>
 73: Does the Web browser support cookies?
 74: </TD>
 75: <TD>
 76: <%If BrowserCapabilities.cookies Then%>
 77: True
 78: <%Else %>
 79: False
 80: <%End If%>
 81: </TD></TR>
 82: <TR><TD>
 83: Does the Web browser support background sounds?
 84: </TD>
 85: <TD>
 86: <%If BrowserCapabilities.backgroundsounds Then%>
 87: True
 88: <%Else %>
 89: False
 90: <%End If%>
 91: </TD></TR>
 92: <TR><TD>
 93: Does the Web browser support VBScript?
 94: </TD>
 95: <TD>
 96: <%If BrowserCapabilities.vbscript Then%>
 97: True
 98: <%Else %>
 99: False
100: <%End If%>
101: </TD></TR>
102: <TR><TD>
```

5

```
103: Does the Web browser support JavaScript?
104: </TD>
105: <TD>
106: <%If BrowserCapabilities.javascript Then%>
107: True
108: <%Else %>
109: False
110: <%End If%>
111: </TD>
112: </TR>
113: </TABLE>
114:
115: </BODY>
116: </HTML>
```

Figure 5.4.

Capabilities of Internet Explorer 3.01 as reported by the Browser Capabilities component.

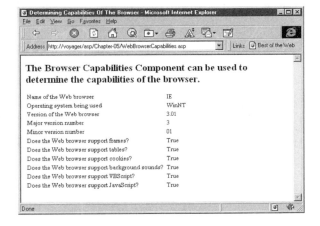

Figure 5.5.

Capabilities of Netscape Navigator 3.0 as reported by the Browser Capabilities component.

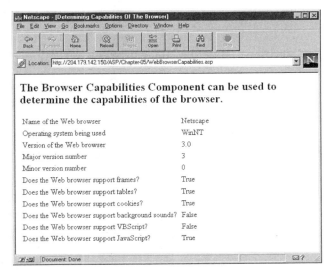

You now know how to use the Browser Capabilities component to determine the capabilities of the browser. Use this component to make it easier for users who employ technologically challenged Web browsers to navigate your Web site.

The Text Stream Component

The Text Stream component enables ASP applications to access the server file system. This component was designed to make it easy to manage text streams within ASP applications. The Text Stream component uses the FileSystem object to read and write text streams to files. The FileSystem object has two methods that can be used to manipulate text streams:

- [ ] CreateTextFile—Creates a text file and returns a TextStream object that can be used to read or write text.
- [ ] OpenTextFile—Can be used to read from a text file or append text to it.

NOTE   It is possible to have two or more instances of the same application running at the same time. In cases such as this, use file locking to ensure that multiple instances of the same application do not attempt to modify the same file.

Before methods of the FileSystem object can be used, the object must be instantiated with the following ASP statement:

```
Set FileStreamObject = CreateObject("Scripting.FileSystemObject")
```

After the FileSystem object is instantiated, you can use either the CreateTextFile method or the OpenTextFile method to manipulate text streams.

Properties of the TextStream Object

When reading a text stream, properties of the TextStream object (listed in Table 5.3) can be used to monitor your current position in the file.

Table 5.3. Properties of the TextStream object.

Property	Description
AtEndOfLine	Used to determine whether you are at the end of the line when reading characters from a text stream. This property is very useful when you read a file one character at a time using the Read method.

Property	Description
AtEndOfStream	Used to determine whether you are at the end of the text stream. This property is useful when you read a file an entire line at a time using the ReadLine method.
Column	Used to determine how many characters you have currently read from the beginning of the line.
Line	Used to determine how many lines you have read so far.

Methods of the TextStream Object

In addition to the Close method, the TextStream object has methods that can be used to read, write, and skip text. The Close method simply closes the TextStream object. Tables 5.4–5.6 list various methods of the TextStream object.

Table 5.4. Methods of the TextStream object used to read information (used only with input streams).

Method	Description
Read	Used to read text one character at a time.
ReadAll	This method should not be used for very large files. The ReadAll method causes the contents of the entire TextStream to be loaded into memory.
ReadLine	Used to read an entire line of text.

Table 5.5. Methods of the TextStream object used to write information (used only with output streams).

Method	Description
Write	Writes a string of characters to the output stream. (A carriage return is not included at the end of the line.)
WriteLine	Writes a string of characters to the output stream and follows it with a carriage return.
WriteBlankLines	Used to insert blank lines. The number of blank lines can be specified as a parameter.

5

Table 5.6. Methods of the `TextStream` object used to skip lines (used only with input streams).

Method	Description
Skip	Skips the specified number of characters.
SkipLine	Skips the current line and proceeds to the next line.

Using the `CreateTextFile` Method

The `CreateTextFile` method is used to create a text file. After the text file is created, the `CreateTextFile` method returns a `TextStream` object that can be used to read or write text. The syntax of the `CreateTextFile` method is as follows:

```
Set FileStreamObject = CreateObject("Scripting.FileSystemObject")
FileStreamObject.CreateTextFile (<NameOfFile>,<Overwrite>, <Unicode>)
```

<NameOfFile> is the name of the file to be created. *<Overwrite>* contains a Boolean value. If the value is TRUE, existing files are overwritten. If the value is FALSE, existing files are not overwritten. Likewise, *<Unicode>* contains a Boolean value. If the value is TRUE, the file is created as a unicode file. If the value is FALSE, the file is created as an ASCII file. If you omit this argument, a file type of ASCII is assumed. For most purposes, ASCII file type will work fine. Use unicode only if the range of the ASCII character set is not sufficient to store your text.

The ASP application in Listing 5.4 creates a text file named `TextFile.txt` and writes the string `Hello World!`.

Listing 5.4. Using the `CreateTextFile` method.

```
1: Set FileStreamObject = CreateObject("Scripting.FileSystemObject")
2: Set WriteStream = FileStreamObject.CreateTextFile("TextFile.txt", True)
3: WriteStream.WriteLine("Hello World!")
4: WriteStream.Close
```

Using the `OpenTextFile` Method

The `OpenTextFile` method can be used to read from a text file or to append text to it. The syntax of the `OpenTextFile` method is as follows:

```
Set FileStreamObject = CreateObject("Scripting.FileSystemObject")
Set TextStream = FileStreamObject.OpenTextFile (<FileName>, <Mode>,<Create>)
```

5

The parameters *<Mode>* and *<Create>* are optional.

<FileName> is the name of the file to be opened. *<Mode>* is used to specify the input/output mode of the text stream. Files can be opened either in input or output mode. Replace *<Mode>* with ForReading to open the file for reading (input) and ForAppending to open the file for appending (output). *<Create>* is an optional Boolean argument that determines whether a new file should be created if the specified *<FileName>* does not exist. Replace *<Create>* with TRUE to create a new file if *<FileName>* does not exist. Replace *<Create>* with FALSE otherwise.

The ASP application in Listing 5.4 creates a text file named TextFile.txt and writes the string Hello World!. Afterwards, it reads and displays the contents of TextFile.txt. See Figure 5.6 for the output of the ASP application in Listing 5.5.

Listing 5.5. Using the OpenTextFile method.

```
 1: <%@ LANGUAGE="VBSCRIPT" %>
 2:
 3: <HTML>
 4: <HEAD>
 5: <META NAME="GENERATOR" Content="Microsoft Visual InterDev 1.0">
 6: <META HTTP-EQUIV="Content-Type" content="text/html; charset=iso-8859-1">
 7: <TITLE>Manipulating Text Streams</TITLE>
 8: </HEAD>
 9: <BODY BGCOLOR=FFFFFF>
10:
11: <H2>
12: The FileSystemObject can be used to manipulate
13: text streams.
14: </H2>
15:
16: <H3>
17: Now creating "TextFile.txt" ...
18: </H3>
19:
20: <%
21:   Set FileStreamObject = CreateObject("Scripting.FileSystemObject")
22:   Set WriteStream = _
23:     FileStreamObject.CreateTextFile(Server.MapPath ("/ASP/Chapter-05") _
24:     & "\TextFile.txt", True)
25:   WriteStream.WriteLine("Hello World!")
26:   WriteStream.Close
27:
28: %>
29:
```

continues

5

Listing 5.5. continued

```
30: <H3>
31: Now reading and displaying the contents of "TextFile.txt" ...
32: </H3>
33:
34: <%
35:   Set FileStreamObject = CreateObject("Scripting.FileSystemObject")
36:   Set ReadStream = FileStreamObject.OpenTextFile ( _
37:     Server.MapPath ("/ASP/Chapter-05") _
38:     & "\TextFile.txt", 1)
39:
40:   While not ReadStream.AtEndOfStream
41:     Response.Write ReadStream.Readline
42:     ReadStream.SkipLine()
43:   Wend
44:   Set ReadStream=Nothing
45: %>
46:
47: </BODY>
48: </HTML>
```

TIP

FileSystemObject creates new files in the current directory. Chances are you do not know the current directory of your computer at any given time (try guessing your computer's current directory!). To avoid looking all over your hard drive(s) for files you create, use the Server.MapPath method to specify a pathname relative to the document root directory of your Web server. Refer to lines 23–24 of Listing 5.5 for an example of how the Server.MapPath method is used to specify the path of the text file TextFile.txt.

Figure 5.6.

Output of the ASP application in Listing 5.5.

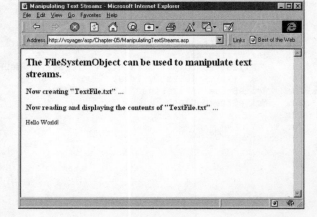

Summary

The components included with Active Server Pages make it easier to create complex Web applications. The Advertisement Rotator component can be used to rotate a series of images on a Web page. The Browser Capabilities component can be used to determine the capabilities of your user's Web browser; using this component, you can make your Web site easier to navigate for those who use less powerful browsers. Various text streams can be manipulated in ASP applications through the use of the Text Stream component.

What's Next?

The HTTP protocol retains no information about previous HTTP transactions for future reference. Cookies are used to address this limitation of the HTTP protocol. Active Server Pages simplifies the manipulation of cookies greatly. Tomorrow, you will learn how to develop Web applications that retain information between HTTP sessions. Cookies can be used to implement sophisticated Web applications such as shopping carts and personalized Web pages.

Q&A

Q **Which method of the `FileSystem` object can be used to append text?**

A The `OpenTextFile` method.

Q **Should you use ASCII mode or unicode mode to create a regular text file?**

A The ASCII mode is recommended for regular text files.

Q **Which ASP statement should you use to create a text file called `NumVisits.txt` if the file does not already exist?**

A The following ASP code creates a text file called `NumVisits.txt` if the file does not already exist:

```
1: Set FileStreamObject = CreateObject("Scripting.FileSystemObject")
2: Set WriteStream = FileStreamObject.CreateTextFile("NumVisits.txt",
   ➥False)
```

Exercises

1. Create an ASP application that implements a guest book using a text file.

2. Create an ASP application that adds the name of the Web browser being used to a text file each time the application is invoked. The application creates a new text file if a file does not already exist. The text filename has the format *MMDDYYYY*. For example, if today's date is July 15, 1997, the text file created will be named `07151997.txt`.

Chapter 6

Tracking HTTP Sessions Using Cookies

HTTP is a stateless protocol. Although this makes HTTP efficient for distributing information, it makes it harder for Web applications to track HTTP sessions and retain certain information between each one. Cookies have been implemented to address this limitation of HTTP. When a Web server receives an HTTP request, it fulfills it and terminates the connection between the Web server and the Web client. No information about the HTTP transaction is retained for future reference. This is a major obstacle for Web applications, such as online shopping-cart applications, that need to remember certain information between connections. Figure 6.1 shows an example of a typical HTTP transaction. Notice how no information about the HTTP transaction is retained after the HTTP connection between the Web server and the Web client is broken.

Figure 6.1.

A typical HTTP transaction that does not use cookies.

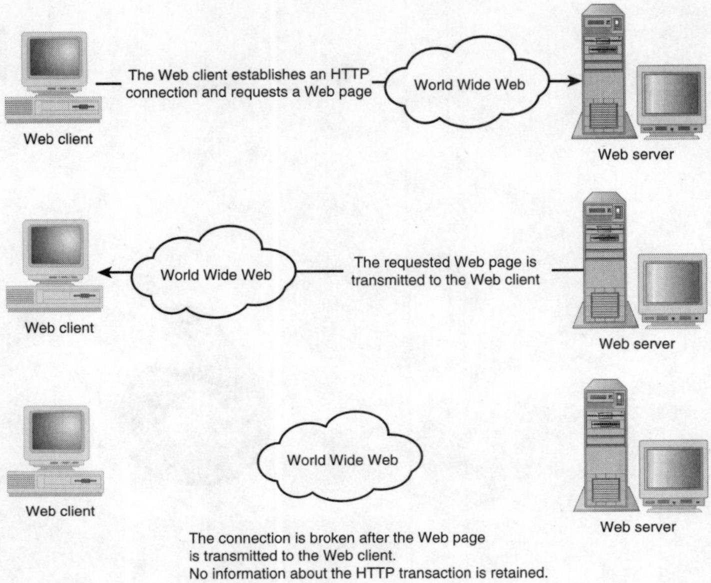

The Web client establishes an HTTP connection and requests a Web page

Web client
World Wide Web
Web server

The requested Web page is transmitted to the Web client

Web client
World Wide Web
Web server

World Wide Web

Web client
Web server

The connection is broken after the Web page is transmitted to the Web client.
No information about the HTTP transaction is retained.

Figure 6.2 demonstrates how a cookie is used to retain information about an HTTP transaction. The cookie, `"Repeat=Yes"`, can be created by an ASP application. A server- or client-side application can examine the cookie to determine whether the Web client is a repeat visitor.

Cookies can be used to develop sophisticated Web applications that retain certain pieces of information between HTTP sessions. See Figure 6.3 for an example of how cookies can be used to make it easier for users to get information they need. Users visit the MovieLink Web page, shown in Figure 6.3, to find out about movies playing in various areas of the U.S.; to learn about movies playing in their area, users simply provide their zip code. Because it is a hassle for users to type their zip code each time they want to find out which movies are playing in their area, a cookie containing the user's zip code can be created and stored in the user's computer. Notice how the MovieLink Web page remembers my zip code (20910) and city (Silver Spring).

6

Figure 6.2.

An HTTP transaction that uses cookies to remember certain information between sessions.

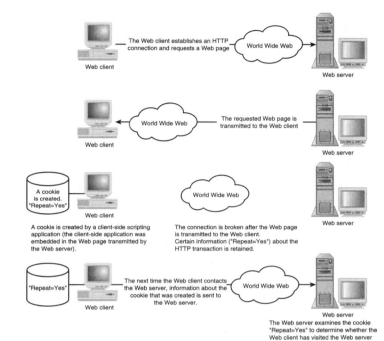

Figure 6.3.

Cookies can be used to avoid asking the same question ("What's your zip code?") each time a user visits your Web page.

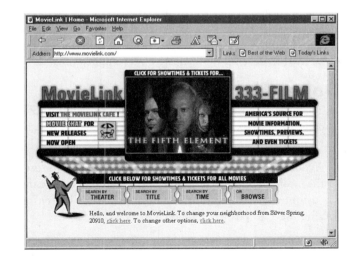

> **URL**
>
> Visit the following Web page for additional information about client-side persistent cookies and how they are used to retain information between HTTP sessions:
>
> `http://home.netscape.com/newsref/std/cookie_spec.html`

Applications of Cookies

There are numerous practical applications of cookies. Examples of information that can be retained between HTTP sessions with the aid of cookies include

- [ ] Personal information—User's name, geographic location (country, state/province, zip code), time zone, and account number (if applicable)
- [ ] Personal preferences—Preferred background color/bitmap, background music (be sure to include the option of no background music if you implement a cookie for this purpose), preferred typeface for the text of Web pages (font name, point size, color)
- [ ] Information about an online transaction—Items in shopping cart, time spent shopping, shopping cart expiration time/date

The section later in this chapter titled "Using Cookies in ASP Applications" demonstrates how cookies are used in an actual ASP application to retain information between HTTP transactions. Let's explore some of the applications of cookies and outline how cookies can be used to develop sophisticated Web applications.

Online Shopping Carts

The Internet is being used more and more to conduct business transactions. Online shopping carts use cookies to keep track of items selected by the customer from a product catalog (see Figure 6.4).

A cookie is updated each time an item is selected by the user. When the user finishes shopping, the online shopping cart application examines cookie information created as a result of the customer selecting various items for purchase. The customer can pay for the selected items after they are verified, as shown in Figure 6.5.

6

Figure 6.4.

An online product catalog linked to an online shopping cart.

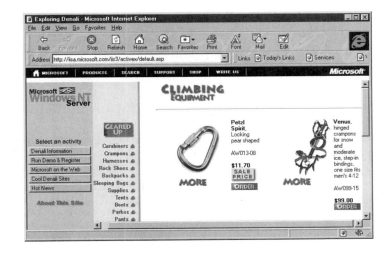

Figure 6.5.

An online shopping-cart application keeps track of items selected for purchase by the customer.

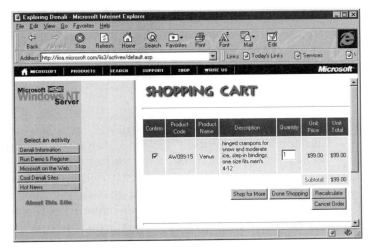

Customized Web Pages

Customized Web pages can be dynamically created to provide personalized content to users browsing a Web site. Customized Web pages enhance the experience of browsing by presenting information in which the user is most likely interested.

The Microsoft Network default home page is shown in Figure 6.6. Notice how it provides the option of creating a personalized Start page.

URL

Visit the Microsoft Network home page to explore how personalized Web pages are dynamically created by the Web server with the aid of cookies.

`http://www.msn.com/`

Figure 6.6.

The default home page of the Microsoft Network.

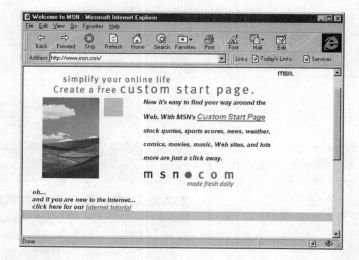

Customization categories of the Microsoft Network home page are shown in Figure 6.7. Before you create your own custom Start page on the Microsoft Network, enable the Warn before accepting cookies checkbox by selecting View | Options from the Internet Explorer menu bar and selecting the Advanced tab (see Figure 6.8). You will then be able to observe how cookies are created to store certain information. More and more Web pages are using cookies to store information. You might want to turn off the warning message if you find it annoying.

After the Warn before accepting cookies checkbox is enabled, you can monitor the creation of cookies as shown in Figure 6.9. The cookie in Figure 6.9 is created the first time a user visits the Microsoft Network home page.

Figure 6.7.

Customization categories of the Microsoft Network home page.

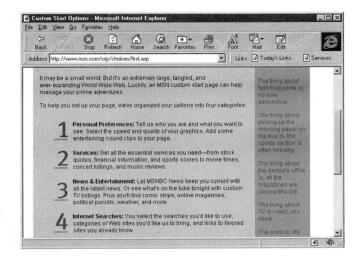

Figure 6.8.

Enable the Warn before accepting cookies checkbox.

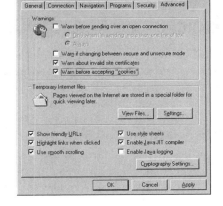

Figure 6.9.

If the checkbox in Figure 6.8 is enabled, a warning message is displayed when a cookie is created.

See Figure 6.10 for the personalized Start page of the Microsoft Network. Notice how the personalized page is significantly different from the default page shown in Figure 6.6.

Figure 6.10.

The customized Start page of the Microsoft Network.

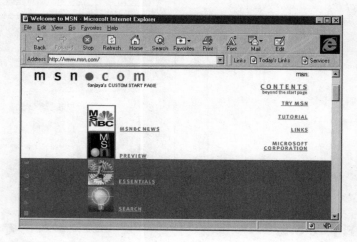

Drawbacks of Using Cookies

Although client-side cookies are powerful tools for developing sophisticated Web applications, there are a number of drawbacks associated with using cookies. It is important that you consider these drawbacks before you deploy Web applications that rely on cookies to accurately identify and authenticate users.

Cookies Can Be Lost

Cookies can be lost. Never depend on cookies to store valuable and irreplaceable information. Such information should always be stored in a server-side database. Cookie information is stored in the user's hard drive. Cookies created by Internet Explorer can be found in the `Cookies` subdirectory of your Windows NT directory (for example `C:\WINNT\Cookies`), as shown in Figure 6.11. (Netscape Communicator stores cookies in the text file `bookmark.htm` in the Netscape Communicator application settings directory.)

Cookie files can be corrupted, deleted, or overwritten when you install a new version of a Web browser (this could be due to a badly written setup application). When using cookies, be prepared for a user to lose the file used to store cookies. A practical contingency plan to address the case of lost cookies is proposed later in this chapter in the section titled "Addressing the Drawbacks of Using Cookies."

6

Figure 6.11.

Cookies created by Internet Explorer can be found in the `Cookies` *subdirectory of your Windows NT directory.*

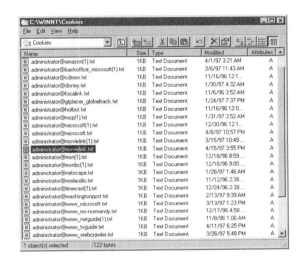

Cookies Can Be Changed by Users

Technically inclined users may be able to figure out how to change the value of a cookie. Never assume cookie information is authentic. If you are using a cookie to determine the last time a user visited a Web page, it is okay to rely on the value of a cookie. However, it is not a good idea to rely on the value of a cookie to determine a user's account balance. (Have you ever wished you could reset the balance of your credit card by editing a file on your computer? If credit-card companies used client-side cookies to store account balances, you would be able to make that wish a reality!)

As a rule of thumb, use cookies to store nonconfidential information. If you need to store confidential information for future reference, store it in a server-side database, and assign an identification code and password to the user. Store the identification code in a client-side cookie and ask the user for his password before allowing him to perform a transaction (say, buy a laptop computer) using the information (credit-card number) stored in your database.

Cookies Can Be Copied

Cookies are not universally unique even if you create a universally unique cookie for each HTTP transaction. It is possible for two computers to have the exact same cookie information. Never use cookies to store information that's unique to the user's computer (screen resolution, color depth, operating system, and so on).

Cookies Can Be Stolen

As discussed in the previous section, cookie information can be copied with or without the consent or knowledge of the owner of the cookie file.

6

WARNING

> You should never authenticate a user based only on the value of a cookie. Use a password to verify the user's identity.

Web Browser Compatibility Issues

Both Internet Explorer and Netscape Navigator support client-side persistent cookies. Although Internet Explorer and Netscape Navigator account for over 95% of all Web browsers used to navigate the Internet, some users may still be using other Web browsers that do not support cookies. When designing Web pages, be sure to take this into consideration. Always provide a URL that can be used by a technologically challenged Web browser to access the information.

Addressing the Drawbacks of Using Cookies

As discussed earlier, cookie information can be lost or altered. A solution to this problem is to store all cookie information (username, e-mail address, preferences) in a server-side database. Only a reference to the data stored in the server-side database (such as the record number) is contained in the client-side cookie. When this is implemented, the user can simply provide his e-mail address and password to restore the client-side cookie containing the reference to the server-side database. This ensures that a user does not have to re-enter all information in the event a cookie is lost.

Consider assigning a password to each user for validation purposes. This prevents the misuse of stolen cookies because only those who know the password can use the cookie. You might want to employ the user's e-mail address as the user ID to make it easy to remember.

Using Cookies in ASP Applications

It is very easy to use cookies in ASP applications. These applications manipulate cookies using the Response and Request objects of Active Server Pages.

Creating Cookies

The Response object is used to create a cookie and set its attributes. Cookies are created using the following syntax:

```
Response.Cookies (NameOfCookie) = ValueOfCookie
```

NOTE

> Always place ASP statements used to generate cookies at the beginning of the HTML file. Cookies should be generated before any HTML text is sent to the browser.

NameOfCookie is the name of the cookie to be created. If *NameOfCookie* already exists, its value will be replaced with the new value. *ValueOfCookie* is the value of the cookie to be created. The following ASP statement creates a cookie named "TimeZone" with the value "Eastern".

```
Response.Cookies("TimeZone") = "Eastern"
```

Setting Attributes of Cookies

Cookies can contain various attributes, such as when the cookie expires and to which domains the cookie is sent. The attributes of a cookie can be changed using the following syntax:

```
Response.Cookies(NameOfCookie).CookieAttribute = ValueOfCookieAttribute
```

NameOfCookie is the name of the cookie whose attribute is about to be changed. *CookieAttribute* is the attribute of the cookie to be changed, and can be replaced with one of the values described in Table 6.1. *ValueOfCookieAttribute* is the value of the cookie attribute.

Table 6.1. Cookie attributes.

Name	Description of the cookie
Expires	Used to specify when the cookie expires. This is a write-only attribute.
Domain	Used to specify to which domains the cookie is sent. This is a write-only attribute.
Path	Used to specify requests originating from the path to which the cookie is sent. The default path is the path of the ASP application. This is a write-only attribute.
Secure	Used to specify whether the cookie is secure. This is a write-only attribute.
HasKeys	Used to specify whether the cookie has keys. This is a read-only attribute.

The following ASP statements create a cookie named "TimeZone", assign it the value "Eastern", and set it to expire on February 29, 2000.

```
Response.Cookies("TimeZone") = "Eastern"
Response.Cookies("TimeZone").Expires = "February 29, 2000"
```

Finding the Values of Cookies

The Request object is used to retrieve the value of a cookie. The following ASP statement retrieves the value of the cookie named *NameOfCookie*:

```
Request.Cookies(NameOfCookie)
```

Before attempting to access the value of a cookie subkey, use the HasKeys attribute to ensure that the cookie has a subkey. You can obtain the value of a cookie subkey using the following syntax:

```
Request.Cookies(NameOfCookie)(NameOfSubKey)
```

You can easily determine whether a cookie has subkeys using the following ASP statement. If the result is TRUE, the cookie has subkeys; if the result is FALSE, the cookie does not have subkeys.

```
Request.Cookies(NameOfCookie).HasKeys
```

So the value of the cookie named "NameOfCookie" can be retrieved using the following ASP statement:

```
Request.Cookies("NameOfCookie")
```

An ASP Application That Uses Cookies

The ASP application in Listing 6.1 demonstrates how an ASP application uses the Response and Request objects to retain information between HTTP sessions using cookies. Client-side persistent cookies are used to keep track of when and how many times the user has invoked the ASP application. The Web page in Figure 6.12 is displayed the first time a user invokes the ASP application in Listing 6.1.

Listing 6.1. Using cookies to retain information between HTTP sessions.

```
 1: <%@ LANGUAGE="VBSCRIPT" %>
 2:
 3: <% LastAccessTime = Request.Cookies ("LastTime") %>
 4: <% LastAccessDate = Request.Cookies ("LastDate") %>
 5:
 6: <%
 7: If (Request.Cookies ("NumVisits")="") Then
 8:    Response.Cookies ("NumVisits") = 0
 9: Else
10:    Response.Cookies ("NumVisits") = Request.Cookies ("NumVisits") + 1
11: End If
12: %>
13:
14: <% Response.Cookies ("LastDate") = Date %>
15: <% Response.Cookies ("LastTime") = Time %>
16:
17: <!DOCTYPE HTML PUBLIC "-//IETF//DTD HTML//EN">
18: <html>
19:
20: <head>
21: <meta http-equiv="Content-Type"
22: content="text/html; charset=iso-8859-1">
23: <meta name="GENERATOR" content="Microsoft FrontPage 2.0">
24: <title>Using Cookies In ASP Applications</title>
25: </head>
26:
27: <body bgcolor="#FDFFA4">
28:
29: <p><font size="4" face="Arial"><STRONG>
30: Welcome to the dynamic and personalized world of ASP
31: application development with client-side persistent cookies!
32: </STRONG></font></p>
```

```
33:
34: <p>When you access this Web page, three cookies are created. The
35: first cookie counts the number of times you have visited this Web
36: page. The other two cookies are used to determine the date and
37: time you last visited this Web page.</p>
38: <div align="center"><center>
39:
40: <table border="4" width="300">
41:     <tr>
42:         <td>
43:         <CENTER>
44:         <% IF (Request.Cookies ("NumVisits")=0) THEN %>
45:
46:         <font color="#0000FF" face="Comic Sans MS">
47:         Welcome!<br>
48:         This is the first time you are visiting this Web page!
49:         </font><br>
50:
51:         <% ELSE %>
52:
53:         <p><font color="#400000" size="4"><strong>
54:         Thanks for visiting this Web page again! You have
55:         visited this Web page a total of
56:         <%= Request.Cookies ("NumVisits") %> time(s).
57:         </strong></font></p>
58:
59:         <% END IF %>
60:         </CENTER>
61:         </td>
62:     </tr>
63: </table>
64: </center></div>
65:
66: <hr>
67:
68: <p>
69: <font color="#FF0000" size="4" face="Comic Sans MS"><strong>
70:
71: The Current time is <%= Time %> on <%= Date %> <BR>
72:
73: <% IF (Request.Cookies ("NumVisits")>0) THEN %>
74:
75:    You last accessed this Web page
76:    at <%= LastAccessTime %>
77:    on <%= LastAccessDate %>
78:
79: <% END IF %>
80: </strong></font>
81:
82: <HR>
83:
84: <A HREF="/ASP/Chapter-06/DeleteCookies.asp">
85: Select this link to delete all cookies created for this page</A>
86:
87: </p>
88: </body>
89: </html>
```

Figure 6.12.

This page appears the first time the ASP application in Listing 6.1 is invoked.

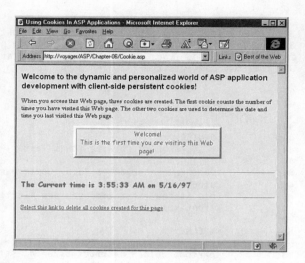

When the ASP application in Listing 6.1 is invoked a second time by the same user, the Web page shown in Figure 6.13 is displayed.

The hyperlink defined in lines 84–85 of Listing 6.1 points to the ASP application in Listing 6.2. Lines 3–5 of the ASP application in Listing 6.2 delete cookies created by the ASP application in Listing 6.1. Notice how the cookies are deleted through the use of the Expire attribute of the Response object to specify an expiration date that has already passed. After the cookies are deleted, the Web page shown in Figure 6.14 appears.

Figure 6.13.

This page appears after the ASP application in Listing 6.1 is loaded a second time by the same user.

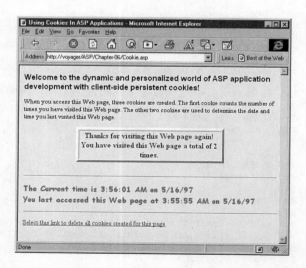

Listing 6.2. The ASP application that deletes cookies created by the ASP application in Listing 6.1.

```
 1: <%@ LANGUAGE="VBSCRIPT" %>
 2:
 3: <% Response.Cookies ("NumVisits").Expires = "January 1, 1997" %>
 4: <% Response.Cookies ("LastDate").Expires = "January 1, 1997" %>
 5: <% Response.Cookies ("LastTime").Expires = "January 1, 1997" %>
 6:
 7: <HTML>
 8: <HEAD>
 9: <META NAME="GENERATOR" Content="Microsoft Visual InterDev 1.0">
10: <META HTTP-EQUIV="Content-Type" content="text/html; charset=iso-8859-1">
11: <TITLE>Cookies Are Deleted</TITLE>
12: </HEAD>
13: <BODY BGCOLOR="FFFFFF">
14:
15: <H1>Cookies Are Deleted</H1>
16:
17: <A HREF="/ASP/Chapter-06/Cookie.asp">
18: Click here to start over</A>
19:
20: </BODY>
21: </HTML>
```

Figure 6.14.

The Web page generated by the ASP application in Listing 6.2.

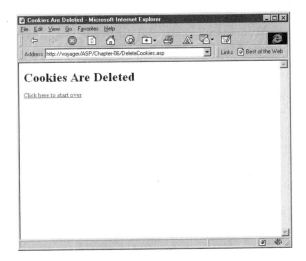

Summary

Cookies can be used to develop sophisticated Web applications that retain information between HTTP sessions. When a cookie is created, certain information is stored in the user's computer for future reference. When the Web client contacts the Web server responsible for creating the cookie, the information stored in the user's computer (in the form of a cookie) is sent to the Web server. This information can be used either by a client- or server-side Web application to implement sophisticated Web applications such as shopping carts and personalized Web pages. For additional information about developing ASP applications that use cookies, see Day 7, "Developing Dynamic and Personalized Content with ASP."

What's Next

Today you learned how cookies can be used to address a limitation of the HTTP protocol. Cookies can be used to add a new level of interactivity and personalization to a Web page. Tomorrow you will learn more about developing dynamic and personalized Web applications using client-side persistent cookies.

Q&A

Q Which ASP object is used to create a cookie?

A The Response ASP object is used to create a cookie.

Q Which ASP object is used to retrieve the value of a cookie?

A The Request ASP object is used to retrieve the value of a cookie.

Q What is the ASP statement used to delete a cookie named "EMailAddress"?

A Delete a cookie by setting an expiration date that has already passed. The following statement deletes the cookie named "EMailAddress":

```
Response.Cookie("EmailAddress").Expires = "January 1, 1997"
```

Exercises

1. Modify the application in Listing 6.1 to use custom text and background colors.
2. Modify the application in Listing 6.1 to use a custom font for text.
3. Modify the application in Listing 6.1 to obtain the user's name, store it in a cookie, and use it to personally greet the user the next time the ASP application is invoked.

Chapter 7

Developing Dynamic and Personalized Content with ASP

Yesterday you learned how cookies can be used to retain information between HTTP sessions. Today you will learn how to develop ASP applications that output dynamic and personalized content with the aid of cookies. Various ASP applications that produce dynamic and personalized output will be presented throughout the day to demonstrate how ASP applications can be used to add a new level of interactivity and personalization to your Web site.

When developing dynamic and personalized Web applications, it is very important that you consider those users who might not employ the latest version of Internet Explorer. Although Web browsers such as Internet Explorer support the latest innovations and technologies in the Web industry, not all Web browsers are created equal. When you develop Web applications that use technologies such as client-side scripting, do not disregard users who use technologically challenged browsers. Design your Web applications so that someone using a less powerful Web browser can access the information without having to change operating systems or upgrade Web browsers!

You should also avoid intruding on your Web users. User interaction can sometimes provide a more rich and compelling Web browsing experience (for example, by displaying custom greetings and prompts that include the user's name). Nonetheless, the user should have the option of refraining from answering questions, of simply accessing the information he needs. Notice how the ASP application in Listing 7.1 attempts to enhance the user's Web browsing experience (by displaying personalized greetings) while not getting in his way. For example, if a user refuses to provide his name, the ASP application in Listing 7.1 refrains from displaying more message boxes that ask for it.

 TIP

> When developing ASP applications that use cookies to retain information between HTTP sessions, ensure that users can change the values of or delete cookies through the selection a hyperlink. For example, if a user moves to another zip code, he should be able to update the cookie containing this information by selecting a hyperlink.

Developing Web Pages with Personalized User Greetings

The ASP application outlined in Figure 7.1 greets users with their names. (Figure 7.1 represents an outline of the ASP application in Listing 7.1.) After the user's name is obtained, client-side cookies are used to store the name. Study the program outline in Figure 7.1, and you will realize that the ASP application has been designed to handle a variety of situations. For example, although obtaining the user's name via a dialog box adds a professional touch to your Web application, not all Web browsers support the VBScript function InputBox. To address this issue, the Browser Capabilities component you learned about in Day 5, "Using ActiveX Components," is used to determine whether the user's Web browser supports VBScript. If it does, a dialog box is displayed. If it does not, an HTML form is used to obtain the user's name. The ASP application in Figure 7.1 does not fail, and does not display a message asking the user to upgrade her Web browser. I encourage you to model your ASP applications after the one outlined in Figure 7.1. Always anticipate the situations your Web application is likely to encounter and use the flexibility of Active Server Pages to address them.

Figure 7.1.

Outline of the ASP application in Listing 7.1.

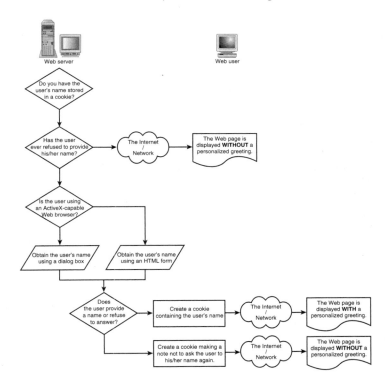

NOTE

The capability to easily develop cross-browser applications using the Browser Capabilities component is a very powerful feature of Active Server Pages.

Browsing the Personalized User Greeting Application with Internet Explorer

The dialog box shown in Figure 7.2 is displayed when the personalized user greeting application is accessed via Internet Explorer. This dialog box is generated by the VBScript subroutine defined in lines 53–74 of Listing 7.1.

Figure 7.2.

A dialog box is used to obtain the user's name.

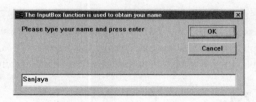

After the user's name is provided through the dialog box shown in Figure 7.2, the ASP application generates the Web page shown in Figure 7.3. Notice how the name provided in Figure 7.2 is sent to the ASP application by appending it to the URL of the ASP application. The ASP application examines the query string and creates a cookie containing the user's name in lines 7–8 of Listing 7.1. Select the Reload Personalized Greeting application hyperlink to proceed to the Web page shown in Figure 7.4.

Figure 7.3.

The ASP application generates a cookie and greets the user.

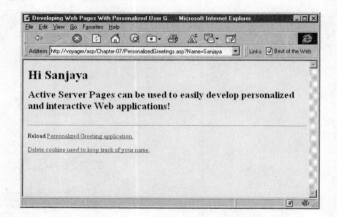

Compare the URL of the Web page in Figure 7.3 to the URL of the Web page in Figure 7.4. Notice how the URL in Figure 7.4 does not have the user's name appended to it. Nonetheless, the ASP application still greets the user with his name. This is because in Figure 7.3, the ASP application obtained the user's name by examining the query string, while the application in Figure 7.4 obtained the user's name by examining the cookie created in Figure 7.3. If the user reboots his computer and reloads the Web page, he will again be greeted with his name because it is stored in a client-side cookie. The user selects the Delete cookies used to keep track of your name hyperlink to delete the cookie containing his name.

When the Delete cookies used to keep track of your name hyperlink is selected, the ASP application in Listing 7.2 deletes the cookie containing the user's name and displays the Web page shown in Figure 7.5.

Figure 7.4.

The ASP application greets the user through by using the cookie created in Figure 7.3.

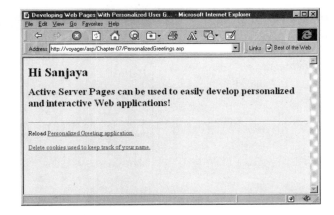

Figure 7.5.

The ASP application deletes the cookie containing the user's name.

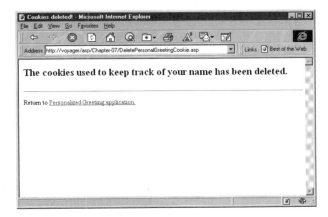

If the ASP application is invoked after the cookie containing the user's name is deleted, the user will be asked for his name via the dialog box shown in Figure 7.2. If at this point the user clicks the Cancel button, the ASP application displays the Web page shown in Figure 7.6. The ASP application then creates a cookie to note that the user refused to provide his name (see lines 13–14 of Listing 7.1). This cookie reminds the ASP application to refrain from asking the user for his name in the future.

7

Figure 7.6.

A generic greeting is displayed if the user refuses to provide a name.

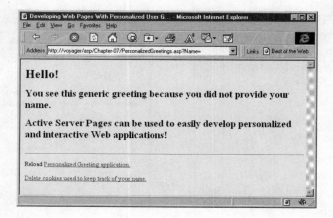

Listing 7.1. The personalized user greeting application.

```
 1: <%@ LANGUAGE="VBSCRIPT" %>
 2:
 3: <%
 4:
 5: ' If the user provides us a name, a cookie is created
 6:
 7: If Not (Request.QueryString("Name")="") Then
 8:   Response.Cookies ("Name") = Request.QueryString("Name")
 9:
10: ' If the user does not provide us his/her name, a cookie
11: ' is created to make sure we do not keep on asking for it.
12:
13: ElseIf (InStr(Request.QueryString,"Name")=1) Then
14:   Response.Cookies ("UserRefusedInput") = "TRUE"
15: End If
16: %>
17:
18: <HTML>
19: <HEAD>
20: <META NAME="GENERATOR" Content="Microsoft Visual InterDev 1.0">
21: <META HTTP-EQUIV="Content-Type" content="text/html; charset=iso-8859-1">
22: <TITLE>Developing Web Pages With Personalized User Greetings</TITLE>
23: </HEAD>
24: <BODY bgcolor="#FDFFA4">
25:
26: <%
27:
28: ' The user is asked for his/her name.
29:
30:   If ((Request.Cookies ("Name")="") AND _
31:     ((Request.QueryString("Name"))="") ) AND _
32:     (Not(Request.Cookies ("UserRefusedInput")="TRUE")) Then
33: %>
34:
```

```
35: <%
36: ' The BrowserCapabilities object is created to determine if
37: ' the Web browser supports VBScript
38: Set BrowserCapabilities = Server.CreateObject("MSWC.BrowserType")
39: %>
40:
41: <%
42: ' If the Web browser supports VBScript, use the
43: ' InputBox function to obtain input.
44:
45: If (BrowserCapabilities.vbscript = TRUE) Then
46: %>
47:
48: <FORM ACTION="PersonalizedGreetings.asp"
49:         METHOD="GET" NAME="DataForm">
50:     <INPUT TYPE=HIDDEN NAME="Name">
51: </FORM>
52:
53: <SCRIPT LANGUAGE="VBScript">
54: <!--
55:
56: Sub window_onLoad()
57:
58: ' The InputBox function is used to obtain the user's name.
59: ' This is an example of taking maximum use of the
60: ' interactive capabilities of the browser.
61:
62:     Name = InputBox ("Please type your name and press enter", _
63:                 "The InputBox function is used to obtain your name", _
64:                 "Please type your name here", 300, 200)
65:
66: ' The user's name is submitted to the ASP application for
67: ' processing.
68:
69:     DataForm.Name.value=Name
70:     DataForm.Submit
71:
72: end sub
73: -->
74: </SCRIPT>
75:
76: <!--
77: If the Web browser does not support VBScript, an HTML form
78: is used to obtain user input.
79: -->
80:
81: <% Else %>
82:
83: Please type your name and press the button
84: <FORM ACTION="PersonalizedGreetings.asp"
85:         METHOD="GET" NAME="DataForm">
86:     <INPUT TYPE=TEXTBOX NAME="Name">
87:     <INPUT TYPE=Submit VALUE="Please type your name and press this button">
```

continues

7

Listing 7.1. continued

```
88: </FORM>
89: <P>
90: <% End If %>
91:
92: <!--
93: If the user did not refuse input, the user is greeted with
94: his/her name.
95: -->
96:
97: <% ElseIf Not (Request.Cookies ("UserRefusedInput")="TRUE") Then %>
98:
99: <H1>
100: Hi <%= Request.Cookies ("Name") %>
101: </H1>
102:
103: <!--
104: If the user refused input, the user is not greeted with
105: his/her name.
106: -->
107:
108: <% Else %>
109:
110: <H1>
111: Hello!
112: </H1>
113: <H2>
114: You see this generic greeting because you did not
115: provide your name.
116: </H2>
117:
118: <% End If %>
119:
120: <H2>
121: Active Server Pages can be used to easily develop personalized
122: and interactive Web applications!
123: </H2>
124:
125: <HR>
126:
127: Reload <a href="PersonalizedGreetings.asp">
128: Personalized Greeting application.</a>
129:
130: <P>
131:
132: <A HREF="DeletePersonalGreetingCookie.asp">
133: Delete cookies used to keep track of your name.</A>
134:
135: </BODY>
136: </HTML>
```

The ASP application in Listing 7.2 deletes cookies created by the ASP application in Listing 7.1 by setting the expiration date of both cookies to a previous date.

Listing 7.2. Deletes cookies created by the ASP application in Listing 7.1.

```
<%@ LANGUAGE="VBSCRIPT" %>
<%
Response.Cookies ("Name").Expires = "January 1, 1997"
Response.Cookies ("UserRefusedInput").Expires = "January 1, 1997"
%>
<html>
<head>
<meta name="GENERATOR" content="Microsoft Visual InterDev 1.0">
<meta http-equiv="Content-Type"
content="text/html; charset=iso-8859-1">
<title>Cookies deleted!</title>
</head>
<body bgcolor="FFFFFF">
<h2>
The cookies used to keep track of your name has been
deleted.
</h2>
<hr>
<p>Return to <a href="PersonalizedGreetings.asp">
Personalized Greeting application.</a> </p>
</body>
</html>
```

Browsing the Personalized User Greeting Application with Netscape Navigator

The personalized user greeting application has been designed to work with Web browsers that do not yet support VBScript. This section explores how the ASP application handles a Web browser (Netscape Navigator 3.0) that does not support VBScript. Figure 7.7 illustrates the application in Listing 7.1 being browsed with Netscape Navigator. Notice how an HTML form is used to obtain the user's name because Netscape Navigator 3.0 does not support VBScript.

After the HTML form in Figure 7.7 is submitted, the user is greeted with the Web page shown in Figure 7.8. If the user submits the HTML form in Figure 7.7 without providing his name, the Web page in Figure 7.9 is displayed, and the user is not asked for his name again.

7

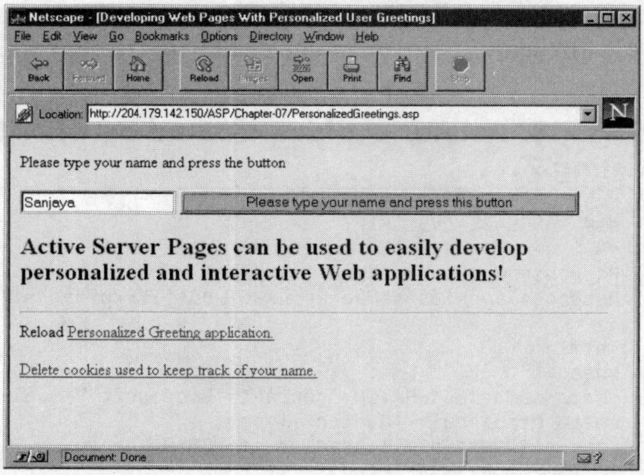

Figure 7.7.

*An HTML form is used
to obtain the user's name
because Netscape
Navigator 3.0 does not
support VBScript.*

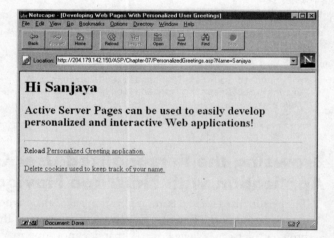

Figure 7.8.

*The user is greeted with
his name.*

The ASP application in Listing 7.1 demonstrates how to develop a cross-browser application
that adds a new level of interactivity to a Web site. Feel free to use and modify the ASP
application in Listing 7.1 to add a new level of interactivity to your Web site.

Figure 7.9.

The user is greeted with a generic greeting if no name is provided.

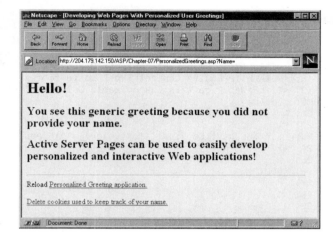

Allowing Users to Select Custom Web Page Colors

Colors and background images can be used to create attractive Web pages. The ASP application in Listing 7.3 demonstrates how to develop an ASP application with customizable colors, allowing users to set the page's colors to their liking. The colors selected by the user are stored in client-side cookies for future reference.

Listing 7.3. The Select Colors ASP application.

```
 1: <%@ LANGUAGE="VBSCRIPT" %>
 2:
 3: <%
 4:
 5: ' If the user has selected text and background colors,
 6: ' cookies are used to remember the values between
 7: ' HTTP sessions.
 8:
 9: If Not (Request.QueryString("Text")="") Then
10:   Response.Cookies ("TextColor") = Request.QueryString("Text")
11:   Response.Cookies ("BackgroundColor") = Request.QueryString("Background")
12: End If
13: %>
14:
```

continues

7

Listing 7.3. continued

```
15: <HTML>
16: <HEAD>
17: <META NAME="GENERATOR" Content="Microsoft Visual InterDev 1.0">
18: <META HTTP-EQUIV="Content-Type" content="text/html; charset=iso-8859-1">
19: <TITLE>Web Page With Customizable Colors</TITLE>
20: </HEAD>
21:
22: <%
23:    If (Request.Cookies ("TextColor")="") Then
24: %>
25:
26: <BODY>
27:
28: <%
29:    Else
30: %>
31:
32: <BODY
33:    BGCOLOR=<%= Request.Cookies ("BackgroundColor") %>
34:    TEXT=<%= Request.Cookies ("TextColor") %>
35: >
36:
37: <%
38:    End If
39: %>
40:
41: <font face="Comic Sans MS">
42: <STRONG>
43: The Web page colors of this ASP application can be
44: modified. by selecting the hyperlink you see below!
45: </STRONG>
46: </font>
47:
48: <P>
49:
50: <A HREF="SelectWebPageColors.html">
51: Select this hyperlink to modify Web page colors.</A>
52:
53: <HR>
54:
55: <A HREF="DeleteColorCookies.asp">
56: Select this hyperlink to delete cookies used to
57: store Web page colors.</A>
58:
59: </BODY>
60: </HTML>
```

The Web page in Figure 7.10 is displayed the first time the ASP application in Listing 7.3 is invoked. Click the Select this hyperlink to modify Web page colors hyperlink to choose custom Web page colors.

Figure 7.10.

The Web page displayed before custom colors are selected.

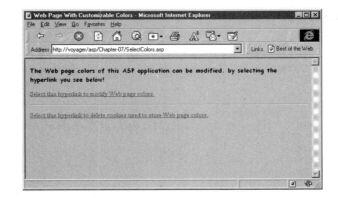

The Web page in Figure 7.11, which is generated by Listing 7.4, can be used to select various colors. After the user selects his custom Web page colors and clicks the Submit selected colors button, the selected colors are transmitted to the ASP application in Listing 7.3.

Listing 7.4. The Web page used to select colors.

```
<!DOCTYPE HTML PUBLIC "-//IETF//DTD HTML//EN">
<html>
<head>
<meta http-equiv="Content-Type"
content="text/html; charset=iso-8859-1">
<meta name="GENERATOR"
content="Microsoft FrontPage (Visual InterDev Edition) 2.0">
<title>Please Use This Web Page To Select Colors of Web Page
Elements</title>
</head>
<body bgcolor="#FFFFFF">
<p align="center"><font face="Verdana"><strong>Please select the
colors of Web page elements</strong></font></p>
<div align="center"><center>
<FORM ACTION="SelectColors.asp"
      METHOD="GET" NAME="DataForm">
<table border="4" width="450">
    <tr>
        <td>
<TABLE>
<TR>
<TD BGCOLOR=99FF99>
<font face="Comic Sans MS">
<strong>Please select the background color</strong>
</font>
</TD>
</TR>
<TR>
```

continues

Listing 7.4. continued

```
<TD BGCOLOR=CCCCCC>
<INPUT TYPE="RADIO" NAME="Background" VALUE="CCCCCC" CHECKED>
CCCCCC
</TD>
</TR>
<TR>
<TD BGCOLOR=FFFF99>
<INPUT TYPE="RADIO" NAME="Background" VALUE="FFFF99">
FFFF99
</TD>
</TR>
<TR>
<TD BGCOLOR=CCFF99>
<INPUT TYPE="RADIO" NAME="Background" VALUE="CCFF99">
CCFF99
</TD>
</TR>
<TR>
<TD BGCOLOR=999933>
<INPUT TYPE="RADIO" NAME="Background" VALUE="999933">
999933
</TD>
</TR>
<TR>
<TD BGCOLOR=004400>
<INPUT TYPE="RADIO" NAME="Background" VALUE="004400">
<FONT COLOR=FFFFFF>004400</FONT>
</TD>
</TR>
<TR>
<TD BGCOLOR=000000>
<INPUT TYPE="RADIO" NAME="Background" VALUE="000000">
<FONT COLOR=FFFFFF>000000</FONT>
</TD>
</TR>
</TABLE>
        </td>
        <td>
<TABLE>
<TR>
<TD BGCOLOR=99FF99>
<font face="Comic Sans MS">
<strong>Please select the text color</strong>
</font>
</TD>
</TR>
<TR>
<TD BGCOLOR=CCCCCC>
<INPUT TYPE="RADIO" NAME="Text" VALUE="CCCCCC" CHECKED>
CCCCCC
</TD>
</TR>
<TR>
```

```
<TD BGCOLOR=FFFF99>
<INPUT TYPE="RADIO" NAME="Text" VALUE="FFFF99">
FFFF99
</TD>
</TR>
<TR>
<TD BGCOLOR=CCFF99>
<INPUT TYPE="RADIO" NAME="Text" VALUE="CCFF99">
CCFF99
</TD>
</TR>
<TR>
<TD BGCOLOR=999933>
<INPUT TYPE="RADIO" NAME="Text" VALUE="999933">
999933
</TD>
</TR>
<TR>
<TD BGCOLOR=004400>
<INPUT TYPE="RADIO" NAME="Text" VALUE="004400">
<FONT COLOR=FFFFFF>004400</FONT>
</TD>
</TR>
<TR>
<TD BGCOLOR=000000>
<INPUT TYPE="RADIO" NAME="Text" VALUE="000000" CHECKED>
<FONT COLOR=FFFFFF>000000</FONT>
</TD>
</TR>
</TABLE>
        </td>
    </tr>
</table>
</center></div>
  <INPUT TYPE=Submit VALUE="Submit selected colors">
</FORM>
</body>
</html>
```

Figure 7.11.

*Custom colors are selected
via this page.*

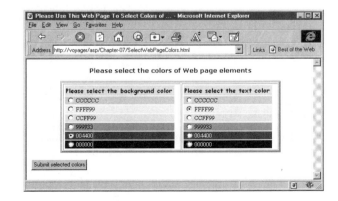

The ASP application examines the query string appended to the URL to determine what colors were selected in the Web page shown in Figure 7.11. Lines 9–12 of Listing 7.3 create two cookies to retain the background and text color selected by the user. Lines 32–35 change the default background and text colors of the Web page.

Figure 7.12.

The Web page in Figure 7.10 with custom colors.

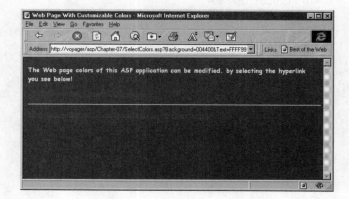

Click the Select this hyperlink to delete cookies used to store Web page colors hyperlink to delete cookies storing colors selected in Figure 7.11 and reset the Web page. The ASP application in Listing 7.5 deletes the cookies by specifying an expiration date that has already passed. The Web page in Figure 7.13, which is generated by the ASP application in Listing 7.5, confirms that the cookies have been deleted.

Listing 7.5. The ASP application that deletes cookies used to store colors.

```
<%@ LANGUAGE="VBSCRIPT" %>
<%
Response.Cookies ("TextColor").Expires = "January 1, 1997"
Response.Cookies ("BackgroundColor").Expires = "January 1, 1997"
%>
<HTML>
<HEAD>
<META NAME="GENERATOR" Content="Microsoft Visual InterDev 1.0">
<META HTTP-EQUIV="Content-Type" content="text/html; charset=iso-8859-1">
<TITLE>Cookies Deleted!</TITLE>
</HEAD>
<BODY BGCOLOR=FFFFFF>
<H2>
The cookies used to store color codes have been
deleted.
</H2>
```

```
<HR>
<A HREF=SelectColors.asp>
Return to ASP application
</A>
</BODY>
</HTML>
```

Figure 7.13.

*This page confirms that
the cookies used to store
custom colors have been
deleted.*

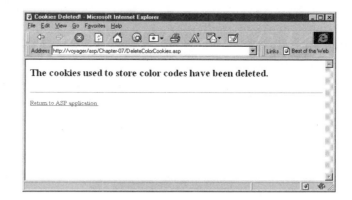

Allowing Users to Select Specific Information They Need

The ASP application in Listing 7.6 can be used when certain information should be displayed on the Web page only if that information is useful to the user. For example, the home page of a corporate intranet might display the day's cafeteria menu. This information is not useful for those who eat elsewhere or bring their own food. The ASP application in Listing 7.6 can be used to display specific information only if users choose to view it.

Listing 7.6. This ASP application displays the weather in selected cities.

```
1: <%@ LANGUAGE="VBSCRIPT" %>
2:
3: <%
4: If Not (Request.QueryString("City")="") Then
5:   Response.Cookies ("Cities") = Request.QueryString("City")
6: End If
7: %>
8:
```

continues

7

Listing 7.6. continued

```
 9: <HTML>
10: <HEAD>
11: <META NAME="GENERATOR" Content="Microsoft Visual InterDev 1.0">
12: <META HTTP-EQUIV="Content-Type" content="text/html; charset=iso-8859-1">
13: <TITLE>Find Out The Weather In Selected Cities</TITLE>
14: </HEAD>
15:
16: <BODY BGCOLOR=FFFFCC>
17:
18: <font face="Comic Sans MS">
19: <STRONG>
20: This Web page displays the weather in selected cities.
21: Cities can be selected using the hyperlink below.
22: </STRONG>
23: </font>
24:
25: <P>
26:
27: <TABLE>
28: <%
29: If (InStr (Request.Cookies("Cities"),"WashingtonDC")>0) Then
30: %>
31: <TR>
32: <TD WIDTH=400>
33: The weather in Washington DC is...
34: <IMG ALIGN=RIGHT SRC=DC.jpg><P>
35: </TD>
36: </TR>
37: <%
38: End If
39: If (InStr (Request.Cookies("Cities"),"NewYork")>0) Then
40: %>
41: <TR>
42: <TD WIDTH=400>
43: The weather in New York is...
44: <IMG ALIGN=RIGHT SRC=NY.jpg><P>
45: </TD>
46: </TR>
47: <%
48: End If
49: If (InStr (Request.Cookies("Cities"),"Redmond")>0) Then
50: %>
51: <TR>
52: <TD WIDTH=400>
53: The weather in Redmond is...
54: <IMG ALIGN=RIGHT SRC=Redmond.jpg><P>
55: </TD>
56: </TR>
57: <%
58: End If
59: If (InStr (Request.Cookies("Cities"),"Chicago")>0) Then
60: %>
61: <TR>
62: <TD WIDTH=400>
63: The weather in Chicago is...
64: <IMG ALIGN=RIGHT SRC=Chicago.jpg><P>
```

```
65: </TD>
66: </TR>
67: <%
68: End If
69: %>
70: </TABLE>
71:
72: <P>
73:
74: <A HREF="SelectCities.html">
75: Select this hyperlink to select cities.</A>
76:
77: <HR>
78:
79: <A HREF="DeleteCities.asp">
80: Select this hyperlink to delete cookies used to
81: store city names.</A>
82:
83: </BODY>
84: </HTML>
```

The Web page in Figure 7.14 is displayed when the ASP application in Listing 7.6 is invoked. The user clicks the Select this hyperlink to select cities hyperlink to view the weather of the city that interests him.

Figure 7.14.

The Web page generated by the ASP application in Listing 7.6.

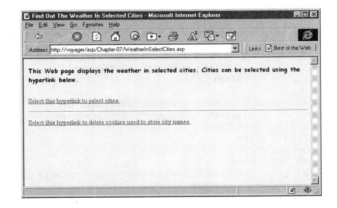

Various cities can be selected using the Web page shown in Figure 7.15, which is generated by the HTML page in Listing 7.7.

7

Listing 7.7. The Web page used to select cities.

```
 1: <HTML>
 2: <HEAD>
 3: <META NAME="GENERATOR" Content="Microsoft Visual InterDev 1.0">
 4: <META HTTP-EQUIV="Content-Type" content="text/html; charset=iso-8859-1">
 5: <TITLE>Please select cities you are interested in</TITLE>
 6: </HEAD>
 7:
 8: <BODY BGCOLOR=FFFFFF>
 9:
10: <H2>
11: Please select cities you are interested in
12: </H2>
13:
14: <FORM ACTION="WeatherInSelectCities.asp"
15:       METHOD="GET">
16:
17: <table border="4" width="450">
18:     <tr>
19:         <td>
20:             <INPUT TYPE=CHECKBOX NAME=City
21:             VALUE="WashingtonDC"><B>Washington DC</B>
22:         </td>
23:         <td>
24:             <INPUT TYPE=CHECKBOX NAME=City
25:             VALUE="NewYork"><B>New York</B>
26:         </td>
27:     </tr>
28:     <tr>
29:         <td>
30:             <INPUT TYPE=CHECKBOX NAME=City
31:             VALUE="Redmond"><B>Redmond</B>
32:         </td>
33:         <td>
34:             <INPUT TYPE=CHECKBOX NAME=City
35:             VALUE="Chicago"><B>Chicago</B>
36:         </td>
37:     </tr>
38:     <tr>
39:         <td>
40:             <INPUT TYPE=Submit VALUE="Submit selected cities">
41:             </FORM>
42:         </td>
43:     </tr>
44: </table>
45:
46:
47: </BODY>
48: </HTML>
```

Figure 7.15.

Selecting cities.

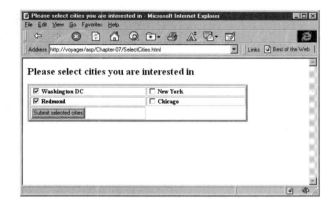

After submitting the cities selected in the Web page shown in Figure 7.15, the ASP application generates the Web page shown in Figure 7.16. Notice how the weather of the cities selected in Figure 7.15 is displayed by the ASP application in Listing 7.6. Lines 3–7 of Listing 7.6 generate a cookie to save the selected cities for future reference.

Figure 7.16.

The weather of the cities selected in the Web page shown in Figure 7.15.

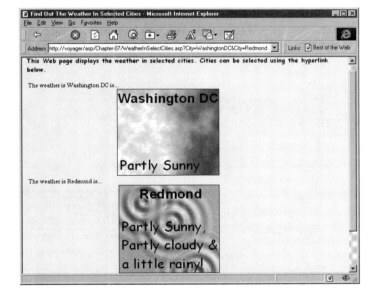

Users can delete the cookie created to store the names of the cities by clicking the Select this hyperlink to delete cookies used to store city names hyperlink. The ASP application in Listing 7.8 deletes the cookie by setting an expiration date that has already passed (see line 4) and generates the Web page shown in Figure 7.17.

Listing 7.8. The ASP application that deletes cookies used to retain city names.

```
 1: <%@ LANGUAGE="VBSCRIPT" %>
 2:
 3: <%
 4: Response.Cookies ("Cities").Expires = "January 1, 1997"
 5: %>
 6:
 7: <HTML>
 8: <HEAD>
 9: <META NAME="GENERATOR" Content="Microsoft Visual InterDev 1.0">
10: <META HTTP-EQUIV="Content-Type" content="text/html; charset=iso-8859-1">
11: <TITLE>Cities Deleted</TITLE>
12: </HEAD>
13: <BODY BGCOLOR=FFFFFF>
14:
15: <H2>
16: The cookies used to store city names have been
17: deleted.
18: </H2>
19:
20: <HR>
21:
22: <A HREF=WeatherInSelectCities.asp>
23: Return to ASP application
24: </A>
25:
26: </BODY>
27: </HTML>
```

Figure 7.17.

The cookie used to store names of cities is deleted.

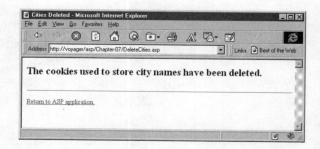

Summary

Active Server Pages can be used to develop highly interactive Web applications that can be customized by users. When you develop Web applications that use cookies to keep track of information between HTTP sessions, always include a hyperlink that can be used to modify or reset values stored in cookies. The ASP applications presented today can be modified to add a new level of interactivity to your Web site.

What's Next?

ASP applications can interface with any ODBC database. Active Server Pages includes a database component that can be used to easily manipulate any ODBC data source. Tomorrow you will learn the fundamentals of ASP Web database development and how to publish databases on the Web using ASP applications.

Q&A

Q How can an ASP application determine whether a Web browser supports VBScript?

A The Browser Capabilities component can be used to determine the capabilities of the Web browser (including whether it supports VBScript).

Q In addition to support of HTML, what is the minimum Web browser requirement for applications presented today?

A The Web browser should support client-side cookies in order for ASP applications to store information obtained from the user for future reference.

Q If a Web browser does not support cookies, what can I do?

A The cookies' values can be stored in a server-side database. In this case, the user needs to provide a unique key to access the information stored in the database.

Q If a server-side database is used to store information obtained from the user because the user's Web browser does not support cookies, can I use his IP address to store and retrieve the data?

A This is not a very effective method because very few Web users have static IP addresses.

Q Roughly what percentage of Web users use Web browsers that support cookies?

A More than 95% of users use either Internet Explorer or Netscape Navigator, and both of these browsers support cookies.

7

Exercises

1. Modify the ASP application that displays the weather in selected cities so that the user can specify when the cookie expires.
2. Modify the ASP application that displays the weather in selected cities so that the user can specify the font as well as text and background colors.

WEEK

1

In Review

As demonstrated in the past seven days, Active Server Pages can be used to easily add a new level of interactivity to a Web site. Traditional server-side application development environments are not optimized for developing interactive Web applications and outputting information formatted in HTML. Active Server Pages is designed to make it easier to develop interactive Web applications and work together with industry standard Windows technologies such as OLE, ActiveX, ADO, and ODBC. Internet Information Server is used to publish Web pages on the Internet. Various options of the Web Publishing Service can be configured by invoking Microsoft Internet Service Manager and selecting to configure the WWW publishing service.

1
2
3
4
5
6
7

Active Server Pages enables you to easily develop Web applications and publish them on the Internet. The fundamentals of ASP application development are easy to learn. ASP applications differ little from typical Web pages, except for the special scripting delimiters used to separate ASP code from the rest of the Web page. Useful ASP subroutines can be included in a server-side include (SSI) file. Subroutines contained in an SSI file can be easily called by other ASP applications.

Virtually all Web applications interact with users to obtain and display information. You learned how to use HTML, message boxes, input boxes, ActiveX controls, and HTML form elements to interact with users browsing your Web site. Use ActiveX controls to interact with users when you are certain your users use a Web browser that supports ActiveX (in an intranet environment, for example).

ASP has five intrinsic objects that are used to perform most tasks. The `Request` object is used to retrieve client information, and the `Response` object is used to send information to the client. The `Server` object is your utility object that performs miscellaneous tasks and allows you to extend the server. Finally, the `Application` and `Session` objects are used to maintain state. You can create your own custom ASP components as shown in Day 10, "Developing Custom ActiveX Components."

The components included with Active Server Pages make it easier to develop complex Web applications. The Advertisement Rotator component can be used to rotate a series of images on a Web page. The Browser Capabilities component can be used to determine the capabilities of the Web browser and make your Web site easier to navigate for those who use less powerful Web browsers. Various text streams can be manipulated in ASP applications through the use of the Text Stream component.

Cookies are used to develop sophisticated Web applications that retain information between HTTP sessions. When a cookie is created, certain information is stored in the user's computer for future reference. When the Web client contacts the Web server responsible for creating the cookie, the information stored in the cookie in the user's computer is sent to the Web server. This information can be used to implement sophisticated Web applications such as shopping carts and personalized Web pages.

Active Server Pages can be used to create dynamic and personalized content for users browsing your Web site. On Day 7, "Developing Dynamic and Personalized Content with ASP," you will learn how Active Server Pages can be used to develop highly interactive Web applications that can be customized by users.

WEEK 2

8

9

10

11

12

13

14

At A Glance

During the first week, you learned the basics of ASP application development. Material presented in the second week builds on tips and techniques you learned during the first week. Various advanced topics such as building database applications, developing custom ASP components, and using other scripting languages such as Perl are covered in Week 2. At the end of the second week, you are shown how to create a CD cataloging database using Active Server Pages to reinforce what you have learned during the last two weeks.

On Days 8, "Introduction to Web Database Programming Using ActiveX Data Objects," and 9, "Advanced Web Database Programming," you will learn how to use the Data Access Component and ActiveX Data Objects (ADOs) to easily interface with databases. ADO's advantages include speed, small disk footprint, low memory usage, and the capability to function in a connectionless and stateless environment like the Internet. ADO (and OLE DB) exposes data from a data provider in a tabular form. As you will learn on Day 9, various components and utilities that can be freely downloaded from Microsoft's Web site can be used to aid in the development of ASP database applications (or even port Internet Database Connector applications to ASP). Both Microsoft Visual InterDev and Microsoft Access support Active Server Pages and can be used to easily develop Web interfaces to databases using Active Server Pages. Because there is usually more than one way to carry out a database transaction when using Active Server Pages, your challenge is to understand ADO and use the best method.

You can develop your own custom ASP components to extend the capabilities of the ASP environment. Custom ASP components can be developed using a variety of application development environments (Visual C++, Visual J++, and so on) that allow the creation of ActiveX controls. As shown in Day 10, "Developing Custom ActiveX Components," Visual Basic 5.0 can be easily used to develop custom ASP components. If you are familiar with VBScript, your VBScript skills can be easily leveraged to develop custom ASP components because the syntax of Visual Basic is very similar to VBScript. Custom ASP components promote data encapsulation, ease of code distribution, security, and centralized code management. At the end of Day 10, you will be shown how Visual Basic and Active Server Pages can be used to develop a Web e-mail gateway.

Microsoft Visual InterDev is the newest member of Microsoft's Visual Studio family. Visual InterDev is designed to make you more productive as a Web developer by making your life easier through the use of visual tools and an Integrated Development Environment (IDE). Day 11, "Introduction to Microsoft Visual InterDev," introduces you to Microsoft Visual InterDev and demonstrates how the Visual InterDev IDE can be used to develop ASP applications. Day 12, "Developing Active Server Pages with Visual InterDev," covers more advanced Visual InterDev topics, such as database application development.

Various advanced topics, such as security and ASP Registry entries, are covered in Day 13, "Advanced Topics." Day 13 also demonstrates how to extend the capabilities of Active Server Pages by using additional scripting language engines, such as Perl.

Active Server Pages is ideal for developing Web database applications, as shown in Day 14, "Developing a CD Cataloging System with ASP." The Active Database component that is included with Active Server Pages can be used to easily create Web interfaces to ODBC databases. Step-by-step instructions are provided in Day 14 to guide you through all the stages of developing a CD cataloging database.

Chapter **8**

Introduction to Web Database Programming Using ActiveX Data Objects

By Kelly Held

The Data Access component is the feature in ASP that makes it possible to interface your database directly with your server. This component is prepackaged with ASP, but you have not seen it yet because it deserves a day of its own. The Data Access component uses ActiveX Data Objects (ADO) to expose database functionality. Let's take a look at Microsoft's ADO object model, shown in Figure 8.1.

Figure 8.1.
Microsoft's ADO object model.

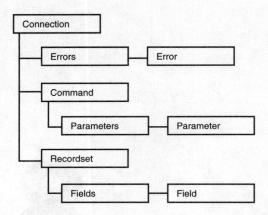

We will concentrate our efforts on the three exposed objects, which are the Connection, Command, and Recordset objects. *Exposed objects* are those that you can access directly without interfacing with another object first. In ADO, the Recordset object is the most important, and the others exist to facilitate the creation of the Recordset object. The important thing to remember about ADO is that its main purpose is data access and manipulation. Design and reporting are for the most part left to HTML.

ADO is just a data-access programming model. If you are familiar with Microsoft's other models (such as DAO or RDO), you will be able to quickly pick up on ADO (in fact, if you know and like DAO or RDO, you will probably find that you like ADO better because it is easier to use). If you are not familiar with them, do not worry; ADO is a high-level language that is easy to use.

Do	**Don't**

DON'T bring your Web site to its knees by choosing the wrong data provider. Although ADO and ODBC can connect you to any data provider, some have limitations. The DOA engine of Microsoft Access is insufficient for enterprise solutions. SQL Server or another third-party product with ODBC drivers is a better choice for applications on the Internet and large intranets. However, because it is the simplest solution, this book will be using Microsoft Access.

Setting Up ODBC and a System DSN

Today you will develop the skills you need to work with databases and write many sample applications. You will need one of the files on the MCP Web site called guestbook.mdb. You can place the file anywhere you like, but a good suggestion is to create a new directory called C:Inetpub\databases and place the file there.

Do	Don't

DON'T place databases or files with sensitive information in a directory on the system where your server has read permissions. Anything in a directory that has read permissions can be downloaded or viewed by a client browser.

ODBC (Open DataBase Connectivity) drivers allow you to access ODBC-compliant data stores. In the language of ADO, ODBC is your data provider. ODBC is controlled from the Windows Control Panel. To access a database, you must create a DSN.

There are various types of DSNs you can create. The User DSN is specific to a certain computer and user. It is easy to access because it has a simple name. However, you cannot use a User DSN in a Web applicaton because many users need access to the file.

Instead, you must create a System DSN or a File DSN. A System DSN is available to all users and system services on the server. A System DSN is easy to access because it can be assigned a simple name. File DSNs are not machine or user specific, so they are more portable than System DSNs but not as easy to access. Today you will create a System DSN; on Day 11, "Introduction to Microsoft Visual InterDev," you will learn how to create a File DSN.

 TIP

ODBC 3.0 adds a new feature called *connection pooling*, but it is disabled by default. You must have Service Pack 2 for NT Server 4 (free from the Microsoft Web site) installed to use connection pooling. It is a great way to increase your performance if you use ODBC a lot. You can find out more information on connection pooling in the Microsoft Active Server Pages Roadmap documentation (http://your_server_name/iasdocs/aspdocs/ref/comp/compref_13.htm, by default).

To create a System DSN, you must be a member of the Administrators group. Open the Windows Control Panel and double-click the ODBC32 icon to bring up the ODBC32 applet. Click the System DSN tab. If you installed the samples that came with ASP, you should already have two System DSN entries so that ADO can use the Microsoft Access data stores that came with ASP. Your screen should resemble Figure 8.2.

To use a data store, you must have the ODBC driver for that product. ODBC32 ships with drivers for Microsoft Access and SQL Server. If you need other drivers, you should contact your product vendor to see whether they are available. You can also visit the Microsoft Web site and look at Knowledge Base Article Q159674.

Figure 8.2.

Creating a system DSN in the ODBC32 applet.

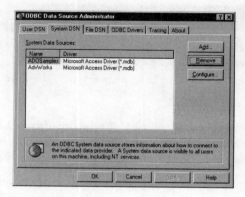

To add a new DSN, do the following:

1. Click the Add button shown in Figure 8.2.
2. Choose Microsoft Access Driver (*.mdb) from the list of installed drivers.
3. Click Finish.
4. Enter the DSN name guestbook. This is the name you will use with the Connection object. It is totally arbitrary, but should be descriptive.
5. Type the optional description.
6. In the Database box, choose Select.
7. Choose the guestbook.mdb file.
8. Click OK.

Figure 8.3 shows how the entered information should look after you are finished. The location of your guestbook.mdb might be slightly different from the figure according to what you did when you installed the file.

Figure 8.3.

Creating the Guestbook DSN.

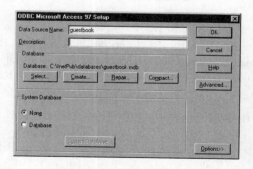

Do	Don't

DO notice that you can perform database maintenance from the screen shown in Figure 8.3. If you are adding and deleting a lot of records, you will want to compact your database often to keep its size down.

Click the Advanced button. From here, you can specify a username and password for accessing the file. This file requires no special username or password to access. You might want to password-protect your sensitive database files in case they fall off the Web into the wrong hands. There are some more advanced options that allow you to have more control over how a connection to your database is made. However, you should not need to change any of these for most applications. Click OK to get back to the screen in Figure 8.3.

Click the Options>> button. You can manually set the driver properties from here. Page Timeout defines the maximum time (in tenths of a second) a page will remain in the buffer if unused. Buffer Size sets the size of the buffer used to transfer information to and from the disk. Buffer Size should be set to 512 and the Page Timeout set to 5. 512 is a balanced buffer size and sufficient for most applications. However, if you are transferring large amounts of data and have plenty of memory, you can increase the buffer size to help performance. Just remember that you are putting a greater load on your server if you change these options. Click OK to finish setting up your system DSN.

On Day 11, you will learn how to set up a File DSN. Later today you will learn how to set up the equivalent of a File DSN without using ODBC32 Administrator. Close the ODBC32 Administrator applet.

The Connection Object

In the ADO object model shown in Figure 8.1, you can see that the Connection object is directly related to the Command and Recordset objects. Although the other objects can be created independently, they cannot communicate with the data source without going through the Connection object.

The primary function of the Connection object is to specify a data provider. You can also use the Connection object to execute simple commands and return reporting record sets. More complex commands such as deleting and modifying records can be realized with the Command and Recordset objects.

Getting Connected

Now that you have specified a System DSN, you can connect to it. You can create a connection to the Guestbook DSN using the code in Listing 8.1.

Listing 8.1. Connecting to the Guestbook DSN.

```
1: set ConnObj = Server.CreateObject("ADODB.Connection")
2: ConnObj.ConnectionTimeout = timeinseconds
3: ConnObj.Open "guestbook"
4: ConnObj.CommandTimeOut = timeinseconds
```

ANALYSIS It is that simple. Now that you have opened a connection you can send commands to and create record sets from. Line 1 creates an instance of the ADO connection object. ADO will try to create objects for you if you forget, but by creating them yourself, you save processor time and avoid possible errors.

Line 2 sets the `ConnectionTimeOut` property. The `ConnectionTimeOut` property sets the maximum time that ADO will wait for a connection to be established with the data provider. This value defaults to 15 seconds, so you do not have to explicitly state this property unless network latency or load begins to cause timeouts. Notice that this property is set before the connection is opened in the next line.

Line 3 opens the `Connection` object. After the connection is open, you can start doing work such as creating record sets and sending commands.

Line 4 sets the `CommandTimeOut` property. This property sets the maximum time in seconds that ADO will wait for a data provider to finish executing a command. This command defaults to 30 seconds, so you do not have to set it unless you have intensive commands or a high server load. Setting this property to 0 will cause ADO to wait indefinitely for a command to process.

Considering Performance and Data Protection

You are probably itching to start sending commands and creating record sets, but you should not dive in just yet (especially if you are at all concerned about your application's performance or your data integrity). Examine the following lines of code:

```
1: <!--#include virtual="/ASPSAMP/SAMPLES/ADOVBS.INC"-->
2: set ConnObj = Server.CreateObject("ADODB.Connection")
3: ConnObj.Mode = adModeRead
4: ConnObj.Open "guestbook"
```

ANALYSIS The type of access you have to your data is set via the `Mode` property in line 3. This connection is now set for read-only; any attempt to alter data at the data provider will create an error. All record sets created from this connection are also read-only. Commands that try to add records or edit a record will produce an error.

The question in your mind is probably "Why set this at all?" There are two answers:

- ☐ Explicitly setting the mode saves ADO the time of trying to figure it out. This is true with a lot of properties in ADO. ADO or your data provider will figure it out, but you can save a lot of processor time with a little extra code that explicitly tells ADO what you want to do.

- ☐ A high-performance database application must be well planned, and you must consider and understand several points that are not discussed until later today (see the section "Understanding Record Sets"). What you do today can be done blindly (for the most part), but if you plan to do much more than the simple guestbook or if you expect many people to be accessing your guestbook at once, you should consider things more carefully.

The Mode in line 3 must be set before the Connection object is opened (line 4). The available Mode values are listed in Table 8.1.

Table 8.1. Mode values.

Constant	Description
adModeUnknown	The permissions have not yet been set or cannot be determined (default).
adModeRead	Read-only permissions. AddNew or attempted edits will fail.
adModeWrite	Write-only permissions. Used mostly to affect tables with SQL statements such as INSERT INTO.
adModeReadWrite	Read/write permissions.
adModeShareDenyRead	Prevents others from opening connection with read permissions. This way others cannot see your changes until you have finished and closed the connection.
AdModeShareDenyWrite	Prevents others from opening connection with write permissions. This is one way to ensure that no one else is changing information that you are accessing.
adModeShareExclusive	Prevents others from opening connection with read/ write permissions. Use this to ensure that no one interferes with or sees your reads or edits until you have closed the connection.
adModeShareDenyNone	Prevents others from opening connection with any permissions.

NOTE

> ADO refers to some of its properties as numbers. IsolationLevel, LockType, CursorType, and Mode are all integer arguments. However, keeping up with which numbers represent which properties is no fun and indeed not required. Instead of numbers, you can use ADO constants as defined in Microsoft's ADO Verbs include file.
>
> To use the ADO constant values listed in Table 8.1, you must include a file in the beginning of your .asp code. To include Microsoft's ADO Verb file, use the line `<!--#include virtual="/ASPSAMP/SAMPLES/ADOVBS.INC"-->` (as in line 1 of the previous code). Your path will be different if you installed ASP elsewhere.

One other thing to avoid is redundancy in your code. If you use the Connection object to produce a record set that many users need, you might store it in the Application or Session objects (refer to Day 4, "Web Application Development with ASP Objects"). Fetching a new record set through the Connection object for each user is inefficient. However, resist the temptation to store the Connection object because the connection is inactive most of the time. To increase performance without carrying around the Connection object, use connection pooling as discussed earlier.

Using the Execute Method to Return and Modify Data

All things considered, what can you actually do with the connection you have created and with the Connection object? You can, at this point, do only two things: You can send commands to the data provider and you can retrieve data for reporting. You do both of these by using the Execute method. In this section, you will see how to pass commands through the connection and later you will see how to retrieve a record set.

Listing 8.2 shows how you can use the Execute method along with what you already know to add your name to the guestbook. Fill in your information in the code.

Listing 8.2. Add your name to the database with Addme.asp.

```
1: <!--#include virtual="/ASPSAMP/SAMPLES/ADOVBS.INC"-->
2: <% set ConnObj = Server.CreateObject("ADODB.Connection")
3: ConnObj.Mode = adModeWrite
4: ConnObj.Open "driver = {Microsoft Access Driver (*.mdb)};dbq
5: ➥= c:\Inetpub\databases\guestbook.mdb"
6: Line1 = "INSERT INTO tblguestbook (fname,lname,phone,"
7: Line2 = "email,homepage, dateadded) VALUES ('your first name',"
```

```
8: Line3 = "'your last name', 'your phone', 'your email',"
9: Line4 = "'your homepage','" & now() & "')"
10: CommandText = Line1 & Line2 & Line3 & Line4
11: ConnObj.Execute CommandText, RecordsAffected, adCmdText %>
12: <HTML>
13: <%=RecordsAffected%> record(s) were added sucessfully!
14: </HTML>
15: <%ConnObj.Close%>
```

ANALYSIS   The first thing to notice about addme.asp is that you made the connection a little differently in line 4. When making a connection, you need to specify at the very least a driver and a database. Earlier today you associated guestbook.mdb and Microsoft Access Driver with the Guestbook DSN. You used this DSN to open your first Connection object. This is all the information you need; this way you can make the connection without having the administrative access.

Lines 6–9 are used to build the SQL statement, and line 10 combines everything.

Do	Don't

DO pick up a book about SQL. SQL is quite an extensive topic and often offers better and more efficient ways to do things than ADO alone. *Teach Yourself SQL in 21 Days, Second Edition,* by Sams Publishing, is highly recommended.

Line 11 uses the Execute method to tell the data provider to process the command. The Execute method takes three arguments:

☐ The purpose of the first argument is obvious: This is the command itself. This command can be a textual command or it can be the name of a stored procedure at the data provider.

☐ The second argument of the Execute method is RecordsAffected. This argument tells you how many records you affected. In this example, you knew you were only affecting one record, but in some cases you might not be so sure. You can use this read-only argument to find out. Notice that you used this argument later in line 13 to make sure the command had the expected result.

☐ The third argument of the Execute method is the Options argument, which is there to save processor time. It tells the data provider what type of operation the CommandText specifies. If the Options argument is omitted, the data provider will figure out what type of operation was requested. As with Mode, you save time by explicitly specifying the Option argument. Table 8.2 describes the valid Options arguments.

Table 8.2. Valid options.

Constant	CommandText type
adCmdText	Textual SQL command to be processed by the provider.
adCmdTable	CommandText refers to a stored table.
adCmdStoredProc	CommandText refers to a stored procedure.
adCmdUnknown	Unknown, the data provider resolves. This is the default.

You should not have any questions about the remaining code except maybe the last line. In line 15, you are finished with the Connection object, so you close it. You also need to close the Connection object if you want to change its properties.

Be careful not to close the connection too early in your code because closing the connection affects other things. Closing the connection sets the ActiveConnection property of other objects to null. Any record sets associated with the connection are also closed, so be sure you are finished with everything before calling the Close method.

NOTE

Imagine that there was a way to do things 10 times faster! There is in some cases: It is called a *transaction*. Transactions are faster because they use RAM instead of the hard disk to process your commands and store the results. Nevertheless, this can be a double-edged sword because an error in the middle of a transaction means all the work from the beginning is lost.

Using transactions is easy. They are really wrappers. Anything you do can be done more quickly inside a transaction. To use transactions, you need only three simple methods. BeginTrans signals the start of your data-processing that you want to do in RAM. After your data-processing code, you need to check for errors. If there are no errors, you commit changes using the CommitTrans method. If errors are present, you will want to abandon any changes by using the RollbackTrans method. Following is an example of the structure of a transaction:

```
ConnObj.BeginTrans
Your data processing code here
If ConnObj.Errors.Count = 0 then
ConnObj.CommitTrans
else
ConnObj.RollbackTrans
```

8

TIP

If you are typing code from this book instead of using the files on the MCP Web site, it is easy to make mistakes. If you make a mistake, an error message might not always appear—the expected output just isn't there. In fact, there are error codes, but if your application generates an error after some HTML code has been sent, your browser might not display the error correctly. To see the error message and where the code stopped, use the View Source feature of your browser, which allows you to see the raw HTML code.

There is almost no room for error handling in ADO because, unlike VBScript, 90% of the errors produced will halt your application with no `ResumeNext` possible. See Microsoft's documentation for more information about ADO's `Error` collection.

The `Recordset` **Object**

This object is the workhorse of ADO. Almost everything you do in ADO in done with a record set. You have not used one yet, but you are about to create your first one. *Record sets* are tabular objects that contain your data. The values are on the row axis and the fields are on the column axis. For a more in-depth discussion of record sets, see the section "Understanding Record Sets" later today.

If you have a copy of Microsoft Access, you might want to open the database and become familiar with its design at this point. There are only two objects in the database: a table named `tblguestbook` and a query named `findme`. Table 8.3 shows the design of `tblguestbook`.

Table 8.3. Fields in `tblguestbook`.

Field	Description	Type	Size (characters)
no	Visitor number	Auto	(long integer)
fname	First name	Text	50
lname	Last name	Text	50
phone	Phone number	Text	50
email	E-mail	Text	50
homepage	Home page URL	Text	50
dateadded	Date visited	Date/time	N/A

Listing 8.3 for `findme.asp` is an extension of Listing 8.2. Instead of inserting your name as a record, you are going to find your record. For this application, you input your first name (see Figure 8.4) and it returns your visitor number (see Figure 8.5).

Listing 8.3. Find your Record `findme.asp`.

```
1: <!--#include virtual="/ASPSAMP/SAMPLES/ADOVBS.INC"-->
2: <% set ConnObj = Server.CreateObject("ADODB.Connection")
3: Set RstObj = Server.CreateObject("ADODB.Recordset")
4: RstObj.CursorType = adOpenForwardOnly
5: RstObj.LockType = adLockReadOnly
6: ConnObj.Mode = adModeRead
7: If Request.Form = "" then %>
8: <HTML>
9: Input your first name.
10: <FORM Method=POST>
11: <INPUT name="fname">
12: <BR><INPUT type=submit>
13: </FORM>
14: </HTML>
15: <%else
16: name=Request.Form("fname")
17: ConnObj.Open "Driver={Microsoft Access Driver (*.mdb)};DBQ
18: ➥=C:\Inetpub\databases\guestbook.mdb"
19: Line1 ="SELECT DISTINCTROW tblguestbook.* FROM tblguestbook"
20: Line2=" WHERE (((tblguestbook.fname)='" & name & "'))"
21: CommandText = Line1 & Line2
22: set RstObj = ConnObj.Execute (CommandText, RecordsAffected, adCmdText) %>
23: <HTML>
24: Your Vistor Number is <%=RstObj("no")%>
25: </HTML>
26: <%end if%>
```

ANALYSIS This program might return the wrong number if there is more than one person in the database with your first name. One of the exercises at the end of today is to fix this problem. In line 2, you define the Recordset object. If you don't define the record set, ADO will automatically create one for you, but you do not have any control over the properties of an automatically created record set.

In lines 4 and 5, you set the properties for this record set. You must set most of the record set's properties before you open it. Only set those properties that are sufficient for your needs. In this example, your needs are simple, so the record set is simple. For more information about CursorTypes and LockTypes, see the section "Understanding Record Sets" later today.

Figure 8.4.

Entering your name in findme.asp.

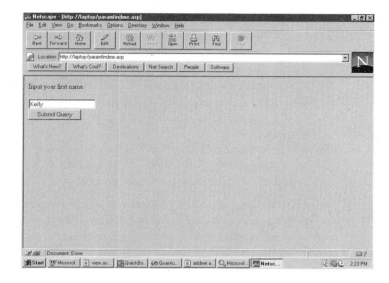

Figure 8.5.

Results of findme.asp.

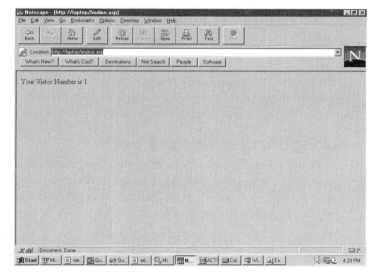

NOTE
> If you are not very concerned about performance and your task is reporting, you can set ADO create all your objects for you with the default properties. The default properties for a record set are adForwardOnly and adLockReadOnly. You cannot do much more than reporting with these record sets, but sometimes that's all you need.

The code from lines 7–15 handles the form. You have enough knowledge of VBScript to easily follow processing of the form. If the `Request.Form` collection is empty, the form is displayed; if not, the database is accessed and the result is output.

The next interesting line is line 22. Here you use the `Execute` method again, but this time you are returning records so there are two things different between this line and line 11 of `addme.asp`. First, because your command returns results, you need to use parentheses around your arguments. Second, you must have some place to put the results of the command. That place is the `Recordset` object. Notice that you must use the `Set` keyword.

Finally, you printed the value of one of the fields. To access the value of a field, you simply use the same form as in line 24. Be sure that you put the field name in quotations. Later today you will learn how to step through and print field names and field values using the `Field` object.

So far you have created both connections and record sets, but you have not done anything really exciting yet because you do not quite have all the tools. In the next section you will learn how to move around in record sets; after that, you will learn how to manipulate record sets.

Navigating a Record Set

A record set might contain one or many records. It is important to know where you are in a record set because all changes or reads occur record by record. So changes or reads affect only the *current record*. There are three ways to change the current record in a record set. They are incrementally forward, incrementally backward, or with bookmarks.

Listing 8.4, `view.asp`, is an application that lists all the records in the guestbook in an HTML table. You learn how to move around, as well as how to use the `Fields` collection.

Listing 8.4. List all the record sets in the guestbook with `view.asp`.

```
1: <!--#include virtual="/ASPSAMP/SAMPLES/ADOVBS.INC"-->
2: <%Set ConnObj = Server.CreateObject("ADODB.Connection")
3: Set RstObj = Server.CreateObject("ADODB.Recordset")
4: ConnObj.Open "guestbook"
```

```
5: RstObj.Open "tblguestbook",ConnObj,adOpenKeySet,,adCmdTable
6: RstObj.MoveLast
7: vistors = RstObj("no")
8: RstObj.MoveFirst %>
9: <HTML> <HEAD> <TITLE>Guest Book</TITLE> </HEAD> <BODY>
10: <%=vistors%> people have signed the guestbook.<P>
11: <TABLE border=1><TR>
12: <TH>NO.</TH><TH colspan=2>Name</TH><TH>Phone</TH><TH>Email</TH>
13: <TH>HomePage</TH><TH>Date Added</TH></TR>
14: <%do until RstObj.EOF%>
15: <TR>
16: <%for each x in RstObj.Fields
17: if x.Value <> "" then%>
18: <TD><%=Server.HTMLEncode(x.Value)%></TD>
19: <%else%>
20: <TD>NULL</TD>
21: <%end if
22: next
23: RstObj.MoveNext%>
24: </TR>
25: <%Loop%>
26: </TABLE> </BODY> </HTML>
```

The output of the code in Listing 8.4 is shown in Figure 8.6.

Figure 8.6.

Viewing the guestbook as an HTML table.

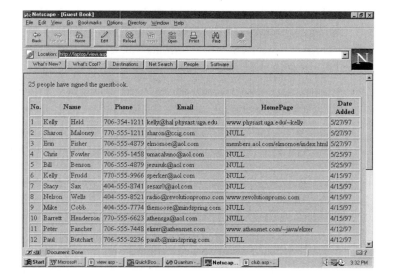

ANALYSIS In view.asp, you go back to opening the connection using the DSN you set up earlier. The Recordset object was opened directly using the Open method. When using the Open method with the Recordset object, the syntax is as follows:

```
RstObj.Open Source, ActiveConnection, CursorType, LockType, Options
```

In this case, the source was a table in the ConnObj connection, so you specified adCmdTable for the Options argument. Notice that you have to change the cursor from an adForwardOnly cursor to an adKeySet cursor so that you could move freely in the record set.

To display your data, you used the Value property of the Fields collection. The Fields collection contains all the Field objects in your database. That means you can loop through each field in the Fields collection (line 16) and obtain the value using the Value property (line 18) without having to call each field individually as you have done before. Notice that the code uses the HTMLEncode method on line 12 to correctly display the field's value on the client browser.

When working with databases, it is important to correctly deal with NULL values (line 17). NULL values caused by optional fields can cause endless problems in your data. Your database must be designed so that NULL fields do not cause a problem when data is added. When extracting data, you should remember that ASP methods such as HTMLEncode do not handle NULL strings and will generate an error if you try to process one.

When you open a record set, the current record is the first record. To move around in the record set, you can use the traditional single-step methods or the sized-steps discussed later. Today you will only use the single-step methods.

MoveNext and MovePrevious are single-step methods and do exactly what you would expect. MoveFirst and MoveLast jump to the first or last record in the record set, respectively.

Besides all records in a record set, there are two other positions you need to know about. There is the BOF position, which occurs before the first record, and the EOF position, which occurs after the last record. If you try to move before the BOF or past the EOF position, you will generate an error. When you are in the BOF or EOF position, the corresponding BOF or EOF property is set to TRUE. To avoid errors in record set navigation, check for the EOF or BOF property using if…then statements or using do while/until loops.

In Listing 8.4, you started out by moving to the last record in the record set to get the total number of visitors (lines 6 and 7). Then you moved back to the start of the record set (line 8) so you could step through it later. You stepped through the record set using the MoveNext method (line 23) that is embedded in a do until loop (line 14), which ensures that you do not go past the EOF position.

8

Do	Don't

DON'T attempt to read or modify the current record when the BOF or EOF property is TRUE; when either of these properties is TRUE, it signifies that there is no current record. Any attempt to read or modify the current record will generate an error. Don't try it.

TIP

ADO has two other features for navigation that are a little more advanced. The first feature is called pages, which are arbitrary groups of records that act as the current record. Pages are not very useful for editing because you must lock the whole page to change a record on a page! Pages are used primarily for reporting and display. You can provide controls, such as ActiveX, for moving from page to page.

The second feature is called a bookmark. Bookmarks allow you jump around arbitrarily in a record set. Your data provider must support pages or bookmarks before you can use them. See the Microsoft ADO documentation for more information.

TIP

When moving forward or backward in a record set in ADO, you can choose your step size by using the Move method like so:

```
RstObj.Move Numrecords , Start
```

If *NumRecords* is greater than zero, the move is forward. If *NumRecords* is less than zero, the move is backward. *Start* is an optional argument that specifies a bookmark. Be careful not to move past BOF or EOF.

Using the Filter Property to Find Information

The Filter property allows you to filter a record set to one that contains only those records that meet a specified criteria. You can filter a record set in one of three ways: by using criteria strings, an array of bookmarks, or criterion constants.

Listing 8.5, filter.asp, is the code for an application that allows you to filter the record set for people with your first name. Almost 100% of the code except the filter is reused from other sections, so the discussion in this section focuses on filtering. The results of filter.asp are shown in Figure 8.7.

Listing 8.5. Filtering a record set with `filter.asp`.

```
 1: <!--#include virtual="/ASPSAMP/SAMPLES/ADOVBS.INC"-->
 2: <%Set ConnObj = Server.CreateObject("ADODB.Connection")
 3: Set RstObj = Server.CreateObject("ADODB.Recordset")
 4: ConnObj.Open "guestbook"
 5: if Request.Form = "" then %>
 6: <HTML>
 7: Filter on First Name.
 8: <FORM method=POST> <TABLE>
 9: <TR><TD>First Name:</TD><TD><input name ="fname"></TD></TR>
10: </TABLE> <P> <INPUT type=submit> <INPUT type=reset>
11: </FORM></HTML>
12: <%else
13: RstObj.Open "tblguestbook",ConnObj,adOpenKeySet,adCmdTable
14: RstObj.Filter = "[fname] = '" & Request.Form("fname") & "'"%>
15: <HTML> <HEAD> <TITLE>Guest Book</TITLE> </HEAD> <BODY>
16: Filter = &quot;[fname] = '<%=Request.Form("fname")%>'&quot;
17: <P><TABLE border=1><TR>
18: <TH>No.<TH colspan=2>Name</TH><TH>Phone</TH><TH>Email</TH>
19: <TH>HomePage</TH><TH>Date Added</TH></TR>
20: <%do until RstObj.EOF%>
21: <TR>
22: <%for each field in RstObj.Fields
23: if field.Value <> "" then%>
24: <TD><%=Server.HTMLEncode(field.Value)%></TD>
25: <%else%>
26: <TD>NULL</TD>
27: <%end if
28: next
29: RstObj.MoveNext%>
30: </TR>
31: <%Loop%>
32: </TABLE> </BODY> </HTML>
33: <%Rst.Filter adFilterNone
34: end if%>
```

ANALYSIS   Criteria strings allow you to filter the record set using operator logic on field/value pairs. Field names should appear in brackets. How the value appears depends on the data type of the field. Strings should appear in single quotes (') and dates should appear between pound signs (#). In Listing 8.5, you use a single clause to filter the record set (line 14).

A criteria string can consist of multiple clauses joined by AND statements. There are seven valid operators: =, <, >, <=, >=, <>, and LIKE. If the operator is LIKE, the value can have the wildcards * or % as the last character in the string. You can build more complicated filters—for example, a filter for both name and phone number would look like the following line:

```
RstObj.Filter = "[name] = 'Kelly' AND [phone] LIKE '706*'"
```

8

Figure 8.7.

Results of `filter.asp`.

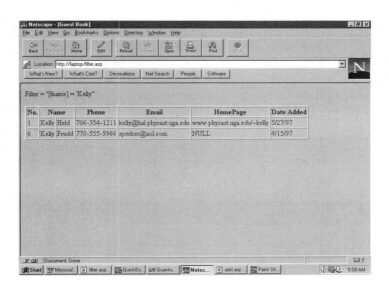

TIP The use of brackets with field names is only required when the field name contains spaces. However, you can always use brackets to delimit your field names, and it is suggested that you do so for readability purposes.

There is a second type of filter used in Listing 8.5 called a criterion constant (line 33). Criterion constants filter the record set by an intrinsic attribute. These filterable attributes are listed in Table 8.4. Criterion constants are also called `FilterGroupEnum` values by ADO.

Table 8.4. Valid `FilterGroupEnum` values for the `Filter` property.

Constant	Filtering action
`adFilterNone`	Removes all filters and restores all records to the current cursor. Setting the filter to a null string (`RstObj.Filter = ""`) has the same effect.
`adFilterPendingRecords`	The filter shows all records edited in batch mode but not yet committed. See the section "Understanding Record Sets" later today for more information on batch mode.
`adFilterAffectedRecords`	The filter shows all records affected by the last `CancelBatch`, `Delete`, `Resync`, or `UpdateBatch` method.
`adFilterFetchedRecords`	The filter shows the results of the last fetch from the database.

Your Filter in line 33 serves no purpose except to illustrate the use of criterion constants, because the record set is closed at the end of the page anyway. However, you could easily extend this application to filter on more criteria using different operators, or you could filter based on criterion constants (see Exercise 2).

Adding, Deleting, and Modifying Records

When you need to modify or add records to the record set, you have several choices. Blind adding of records does not require a cursor or record set at all, but can be done with the SQL statement INSERT INTO and the Execute method of the Connection or Command objects (refer to Listing 8.1). The same is true for blind deletes.

Do	Don't

DO use SQL statements or stored procedures to add and delete records from a data provider without building a record set. Not having to create a record set saves a lot of time and is much more efficient than the AddNew or Delete methods discussed later. Use SQL statements and stored procedures when you can.

If you must read the data before adding a record, you can use the AddNew method with the appropriate cursor. To delete a record from a record set opened for editing, you can use the Delete method.

In this section, you will develop an application that allows you to view the guestbook listing and choose between adding a new entry, editing an existing entry, or deleting an entry. This application is contained in two files. The file listedit.asp is on the MCP Web site but is not listed here. It is basically a slight modification of view.asp (refer to Listing 8.4). The important modifications from view.asp to listedit.asp will be pointed out in a moment. Figure 8.8 shows the output of listedit.asp.

To select a record to edit or delete, click that record's visitor number. To add a new record, use the button at the top of the page. Listedit.asp posts its output to edit.asp in Listing 8.6.

If you choose to add a record, the output of edit.asp looks like Figure 8.9, which is just a blank form with an Add button. If you choose to modify an existing record, the output of edit.asp looks like Figure 8.10. The record you selected is filtered and displayed so you can make changes or choose to delete the record.

Figure 8.8.
Output of
`listedit.asp.`

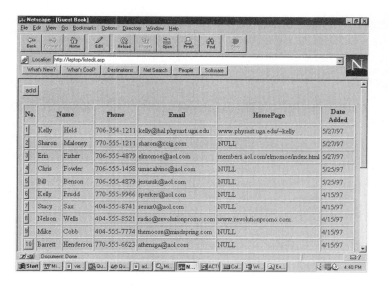

Figure 8.9.
Adding a new record to the guestbook.

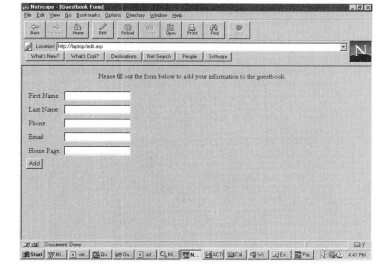

Figure 8.10.

Modifying an existing record in the guestbook.

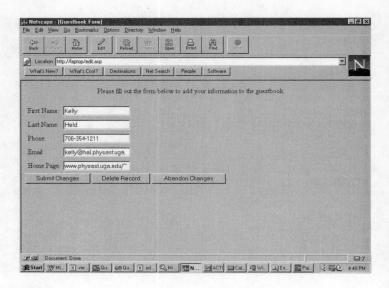

Listing 8.6. ASP code for `edit.asp`.

```
1: <!--#include virtual="/ASPSAMP/SAMPLES/ADOVBS.INC"-->
2: <%if Request.Form("action")="" then
3: ' part one display the forms
4: myarray = ARRAY ("First Name:","Last Name:","Phone:","Email:","Home Page:")
5: set RstObj = Session("RstObj")
6: if Request.Form("button") <> "add" then
7:  RstObj.Filter = "[no] = '" & Request.Form("button") & "'"
8: Session("no") = Request.Form("button")
9: end if%>
10: <HTML> <HEAD> <TITLE>Guestbook Form</TITLE> </HEAD> <BODY>
11: <P align=center> Please fill out the form below to add your
12:➥information to the guestbook.
13: <FORM method = POST> <TABLE>
14: <%for each x in RstObj.Fields
15: if x.Name <> "no" then
16:  if x.Name <> "dateadded" then %>
17:   <TR><TD><%=myarray(count)%></TD>
18:   <%count = count + 1
19:    if Request.Form("button") <> "add" then%>
20:     <TD><input name ="<%=x.Name%>" value="<%=x.Value%>"></TD></TR>
21:    <%else%>
22:     <TD><input name ="<%=x.Name%>"></TD></TR>
23:    <%end if
24:  end if
25: end if
26: next%>
27: </TABLE>
```

8

```
28: <%if Request.Form("button") <> "add" then%>
29:  <INPUT type=submit name="action" value="Submit Changes">
30:  <INPUT type=submit name="action" value="Delete Record">
31:  <INPUT type=submit name="action" value="Abandon Changes">
32: <%else%>
33:  <INPUT type=submit name="action" value="Add">
34: <%end if%>
35: </FORM> </BODY> </HTML>
36: <%'part 2 handle actions
37: else
38: Set ConnObj = Server.CreateObject("ADODB.Connection")
39: Set RstObj = Server.CreateObject("ADODB.Recordset")
40: ConnObj.Open "guestbook"
41: RstObj.Open "tblguestbook",ConnObj,adOpenKeySet,adCmdTable
42: Select Case Request.Form("action")
43: Case "Add"
44: count =1
45:   RstObj.AddNew
46:   for each x in Request.Form
47:   if Request.Form(x) <> "" then
48:    if x <> "ACTION" then%>
49:    <% RstObj(x) = Request.Form(x)
50:    end if
51:   end if
52:   next
53:   RstObj("dateadded")=now()
54:   RstObj.Update %>
55: <HTML>
56: Record Added<BR>
57: Click <a href="listedit.asp">here</a> to see new entry
58: </HTML>
59: <%Case "Delete Record"
60: RstObj.Filter = "[no] = '" & Session("no") & "'"
61: RstObj.Delete%>
62: <HTML>
63: Record Deleted<BR>
64: Click <a href="listedit.asp">here</a> to go back to table.
65: </HTML>
66: <%Case "Submit Changes"
67: RstObj.Filter = "[no] = '" & Session("no") & "'"
68: for each x in Request.Form
69: if Request.Form(x) <> "" then
70: if x <> "ACTION" then
71: RstObj(x)=Request.Form(x)
72: end if
73: end if
74: next%>
75: <HTML>
76: Record Changed<BR>
77: Click <a href="listedit.asp">here</a> to see changes.
78: </HTML>
79: <%Case "Abandon Changes"
80: Response.Redirect("listedit.asp")
81: end select
82: end if%>
```

ANALYSIS There are two parts to edit.asp. At the start of the program, the code checks whether any actions have been requested (line 2). If not, it displays either the add screen (refer to Figure 8.9) or the edit screen (refer to Figure 8.10) based on the value of the button variable (line 6) passed from listedit.asp. The appropriate form is displayed, and you choose one of the form buttons. Each button performs an action that is posted back to the form as the variable action.

If you are modifying a record (button<>"add"), the record's visitor number passed from listedit.asp is used to filter the record set (line 7). The information from the current record is then used to fill in the values of the form fields (line 20) so you can make changes.

Do	Don't

DO use the technique of storing data in the Session object when it is used only for reporting and needs to be accessed across many pages. Listedit.asp stores a copy of the record set in the Session object (refer to Day 4) so that it can be used in line 5 of edit.asp.

You can only use this technique for reporting because you cannot make changes to the data stored in the Session object. You can see that this is true in part two, starting with line 36, where the connection had to be reopened to make changes to the data.

Part two is really the part you are interested in. This part handles the action of adding, deleting, or making changes to a record. The code uses a select case method, which is useful when you have more than two possible states of a variable.

To add a record, use the AddNew method. There are two ways to call the AddNew method. You could pass the fields and values in the following format where Fields and Values are arrays:

```
RstObj.AddNew fields, Values
```

Changes made are immediately committed to the record set if you use this method.

Alternatively, you could add the fields as is done in the code (lines 45–54) between the AddNew and Update methods. Changes to the database are not committed until the Update method is called or until you move off the current record. If you want to abandon your changes, you need to call the CancelUpdate method.

To edit a record, you first need to filter the record set so that the current record is the one you want to edit. Line 67 uses the value of the no field stored in the Session object to accomplish this task. After you are on the correct record, you can start making changes. There is no edit mode in ASP; you just do it. Changes are committed immediately, so be careful

8

when editing. If you are concerned about this, you should use a cursor that allows batch editing (see the section "Understanding Record Sets" later today) and use the `CancelBatch` and `UpdateBatch` methods.

Deleting a record in ADO is easy. Just make sure you are on the correct record (line 60) and then call the `Delete` method (line 61). The current record is deleted, but your position in the record set does not change. After you move off of or a delete a record, you cannot move back to it. If you click the Abandon Changes button in Figure 8.10, you are redirected to `listedit.asp`.

There is one more thing to notice before you move on to the last section: The code was planned to be easy to process. The names of the variables from the form correspond exactly to the names of the fields in the database. This makes it easy to use a loop to process the information quickly.

The Command Object

The `Command` object offers another way to construct and create instances of the `Recordset` object. The `Command` object represents a command to be processed by the data provider. Because not all data providers have the capability to process commands, the `Command` object is actually optional. However, most data providers do support command processing as well as parameters. The two places where this object really shines is for storing procedures and for using parameters.

Putting It Together with the Parameters Collection

Parameters are placeholders in your command or stored procedure. Parameterized queries and procedures can accept parameters at runtime. A parameter is like a variable in that it stores a value, but there is one important difference between variables and parameters in ADO: All variables in ADO are of type Variant. Parameters interact directly with your data provider, so they must have the same characteristics as the fields with which they are associated and must be declared correctly.

Parameterized queries and stored procedures are useful for operations that you perform often but for which you change the criteria. Using parameters is an alternative to creating SQL statements on the fly as you saw in `findme.asp` (refer to Listing 8.2).

The application in Listing 8.7 is called `paramfindme.asp`. It is a reworked version of Listing 8.2 that shows a little more information and uses parameters instead of building a SQL statement. First you input the first name of the person you want to find (see Figure 8.11). The application returns all the records with the matching first names, as shown in Figure 8.12.

Listing 8.7. Code for `paramfindme.asp`.

```
 1: <!--#include virtual="/ASPSAMP/SAMPLES/ADOVBS.INC"-->
 2: <%Set ConnObj = Server.CreateObject("ADODB.Connection")
 3: Set RstObj = Server.CreateObject("ADODB.Recordset")
 4: set CmdObj = Server.CreateObject("ADODB.Command")
 5: if Request.Form = "" then %>
 6:   <HTML>
 7:   Input your first name.
 8:   <FORM Method=POST>
 9:   <INPUT name="fname">
10:   <BR><INPUT type=submit>
11:   </FORM> </HTML>
12: <%else
13:   ConnObj.Open "guestbook"
14:   RstObj.ActiveConnection = ConnObj
15:   CmdObj.ActiveConnection = ConnObj
16:   CmdObj.CommandText = "Findme"
17:   set ParamObj = CmdObj.CreateParameter
18: ➥(,adVarChar,,50,Request.Form("fname"))
19:   CmdObj.Parameters.Append ParamObj
20:   set RstObj = CmdObj.Execute (,,adCmdStoredProc)%>
21:   <HTML> <TABLE border=1> <TR>
22:   <TH>No.<TH colspan=2>Name</TH><TH>Phone</TH><TH>Email</TH>
23:   <TH>HomePage</TH><TH>Date Added</TH></TR>
24:   <%do until RstObj.EOF%>
25:     <TR>
26:     <%for each x in RstObj.Fields
27:       if x.Value <> "" then%>
28:        <TD><%=Server.HTMLEncode(x.Value)%></TD>
29:       <%else%>
30:          <TD>NULL</TD>
31:       <%end if
32:     next
33:     RstObj.MoveNext%>
34:     </TR>
35:   <%Loop%>
36:   </TABLE> </HTML>
37: <%end if%>
```

ANALYSIS Again, most of our code is recycled from the other applications. You could have actually used a filter to get this information, but if you are pulling from a table, it is sometimes best to use stored procedures and/or SQL.

The code works with a stored query in the database called `findme`. The procedure has one parameter: the first name. Because the data provider cannot communicate with the user at runtime to get the value of this parameter, you have to create this parameter yourself and pass it to the data provider. It is even possible to have textual SQL commands that contain parameters. You can incorporate the text command and the parameters as part of a `Command` object and pass them to the data provider for processing.

8

Figure 8.11.

Inputting the parameter.

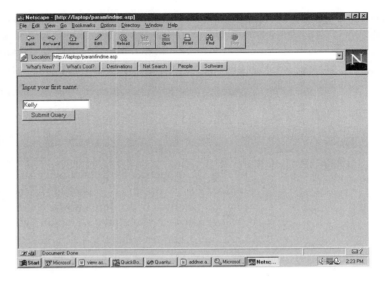

Figure 8.12.

The resulting table for `paramfindme.asp`.

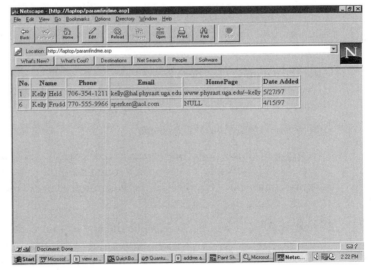

The `Parameters` collection belongs to the `Command` object, so before you can create a parameter, you have to create a `Command` object (line 4). After creating the `Command` object, you have to associate it with a `Connection` object via the `ActiveConnection` property (line 15). The `ActiveConnection` property must be set before the `Execute` method is called or an error is generated.

When creating a parameter, you should know four things. You need to know the name of the parameter, the value you want to assign to the parameter, the data type of the field associated with the parameter, and the size of the field associated with the parameter. Use the CreateParameter method to construct a parameter as follows (be sure to use the Set keyword):

```
Set ParamObj = CmdObj.CreateParameter(Name,Type,Size,Value)
```

NOTE The name of the parameter is really not necessary as long as you know the order in which the parameters are required. You just have to make sure that the properties of the parameter match the field with which you want the parameter to be associated. The size argument might not be necessary either, depending on which data type the field is. Know your database and stored procedures, and you will not have a problem.

If you know your database, providing the correct values for the type and size arguments will not be a problem. AdVarChar type, which is predominant in ASP/ADO, requires a size argument. Some of the other data types might not require a size argument. For more information about data types and their ADO constants, see the Microsoft ADO documentation.

After the parameter has been created, you need to add it to the Parameters collection using the Append method as shown in line 19. You can delete parameters from your collection with the Delete method using the following syntax:

```
CmdObj.Parameters.Delete ParamObj
```

Everything is almost done, but you still need to set the CommandText property of the Command object. Line 16 sets it to the name of a stored procedure (findme), but it could be a table or a textual command. After that is done, you just need to call the Execute method to get things moving at the data provider's end.

If your command returns records like the one in your code, you must store the result in a record set using the Set keyword (line 20). Parentheses are also necessary when your command returns a record set, but should not be used if no records are returned. Notice that you told the data provider what type of command (adStoredProc) it was receiving to save time.

Understanding Record Sets

This section is a little more advanced, but is necessary for your successful use of ADO. After you finish this section, you should have a better understanding of record sets and cursors. However, it's not necessary that you finish this section today; you might want to tackle it later if you do not feel good about working with ADO right away.

Before you jump into record sets, take a quick look at how you interface with the data provider to create a record set. It is quite possible to use ADO without ever knowing anything about OLE or ODBC, but the wise developer wants to *understand* ADO and data access so he can use it more effectively. Object linking and embedding applied to databases (OLE DB) is Microsoft's new object-oriented application interface (API).

APIs have that low-level coding that you as a Web developer probably want to avoid. ActiveX itself is a language-neutral wrapper that exposes OLE functionality through high-level scripting languages. ADO is an ActiveX product, so you can use the advantages of OLE DB without coding in C++.

OLE DB was designed to give the developer access to a wide range of data storage systems. Microsoft's Open Database Connectivity (ODBC) product already gave developers an interface to relational data stores that were based on Structured Query Language (SQL). The idea of OLE DB is not to replace ODBC, but to extend it.

In OLE DB, there are three categories: interfaces data consumers, data providers, and service providers. Consumers take data from OLE DB interfaces, and providers expose data to OLE interfaces. For our purposes then, your ADO application is a consumer and ODBC is the provider. However, service providers are both data consumers and providers. These products are standalone products that can be seamlessly integrated with OLE DB.

OLE DB 1.0 exposes data in a tabular form. This is independent of the original data store. So although you are currently using ODBC to expose SQL data stores, you might soon be using ADO and OLE DB to look at e-mail stores, spreadsheets, or any data store you can imagine.

Understanding Record Sets and Cursors

The whole point of a database is to read, create, and manipulate data. Almost all of these operations require or can be accomplished with the Recordset object. The idea behind ADO is to allow you to get at your data easily, but if you do not understand record sets and the Recordset object in ADO, you are not getting what you want in terms of performance and data protection.

ADO exposes data in tabular form. This is an important consideration because the underlying data store might not be tabular (such as a text file). Each row in tabular form is a complete record. Record sets in ADO are container objects for records in which data is arranged in tabular form. It is important to realize that record sets are representations of your data derived from the data store, but they are not the data store itself. ADO does not work directly with your data store. It can neither read nor write directly to your data provider's store. Reading data, creating data, and manipulating data must be done within record sets. Changes made to your record sets are later made to the data store by the data provider.

When you are inside a record set, there are three things that must be determined: your place, your navigation abilities, and your connection to the data store (or rather, your ability to change and see changes to the underlying data). Cursors determine the behavior of your record set.

Bookmarks

Navigation within a record set is a complex thing. Going back and forth record by record is actually easy, but keeping up with where you are and jumping around is not. Here is why: SQL is used to create record sets. SQL is a set-based language, without physical rows in a set. The cursor transforms the set into columns and rows. There are no record numbers in ODBC data stores because there are no physical rows. A record's place in the record set is determined by the WHERE and ORDER BY statements in SQL. To refer to specific records, you must use the bookmark. Not all cursors support bookmarks (see Table 8.6 later in this chapter).

Don't let this discussion on bookmarks scare you. You just need to understand that if you want to jump directly to certain records inside a record set, the cursor you choose (and the data provider) needs to support bookmarks.

Understanding Concurrency and Interference

The Internet and intranets are multi-user environments. It is possible to allow many users access to your data concurrently. If you are just reading data, this is not really a problem. But if two people are trying to change the same data at the same time, corruption can occur. If data is being edited by one person and used by another, you can run into interference problems. *Interference* is the problem of data interaction caused by data being changed during an operation.

Neither interference nor corruption are desirable results, but they are inherent in a multi-user system. The problem is that you want many people to use the data at one time, but you do not want interference or corruption. The solution is not really a solution at all; it is a trade-off. This is one area where you cannot have the best of both worlds. Depending on your needs, you must choose the cursor properties that produce results acceptable for your situation. (Remember: Cursors determine the behavior of your record set.)

Lock Types and Isolation Levels

To avoid data corruption, you use locks. Locks ensure that only one user at a time is changing the given data. There are three basic types of locks:

- ☐ Read-only—All the data in the cursor is locked from changes or additions.

- ☐ Pessimistic—Locks the current record or current page in the cursor. Other users cannot make changes to the current record or page of records until the user has moved on or closed the record set. Pessimistic locking can cause serious concurrency issues if the edit takes a while (for example, if someone goes home or to lunch without closing the record set, or if a crash occurs while the record is being edited).

- ☐ Optimistic—Locks the record just before it is updated, not when the record becomes current. Records are normally updated as you move from record to record, but you can perform batch updating if you set your lock type to Batch Optimistic. Batch updating works much like a transaction. Changes are committed to memory, but not made to the data store until you call the `BatchUpdate` method.

Table 8.5 examines lock types.

Table 8.5. Lock types.

Type	Descriptions
adLockReadOnly	Read-only. You cannot alter the data or add new records to the data.
adLockPessimistic	Pessimistic locking locks the data record by record or page by page when the record or page becomes current. No one else can edit the current record while it is locked.
adLockOptimistic	Optimistic locking occurs record by record, but records are only locked just before they are updated. This allows concurrency, but means that two people can be editing the same data at the same time.
adLockBatchOptimistic	Optimistic batch updates are required for batch update mode as opposed to immediate update mode.

When a cursor used by one application or user interacts with a cursor from another application or user, problems of interference can arise. There are three types of problems that can occur with interacting cursors:

- ☐ Dirty reads—This is a common problem that results when a cursor is allowed to see changes made by others that have not yet been committed. One cursor uses the noncommitted data from the first cursor. The editing cursor then abandons or rolls back the changes. For example, one user changes a record's price from $50 to $25 dollars. While that user is editing, a second user processes a customer's order based on the $25 price. The first user realizes he is on the wrong record and abandons the update. The customer got a great deal, but the company loses money because of a dirty read.

☐ Nonrepeatable reads—This type of interference occurs when data is changed from one read to the next. Say a customer calls to check on the availability of an item, and two are available. The customer is disconnected and must call back. When the customer tries to process the order a second time, no items remain.

This might seem to be the same as a dirty read, but it is not. With a dirty read, changes are abandoned and the problem could have been solved if the first user could have seen the second user's committed transactions. With nonrepeatable reads, the fix is not so easy because changes were kept.

☐ Phantom reads—This kind of interference occurs when one transaction depends on data that is modified by another transaction during editing. It is similar to a nonrepeatable read, but subtly different. Say the customer is a firm with many buyers. The first buyer calls with a big order that puts the firm at its credit limit. While the first order is being entered, another buyer calls with a smaller order that is committed before the first one. Suddenly there is not enough credit for the first order even though there was when the transaction began. The solution involves locking the records so that changes cannot be made by others while this record is in use.

Interference in transactions is handled with the IsolationLevel property of the Connection object. To deal with interference in other record sets, you use a combination of cursor and lock types. Isolation levels define when and whether you can see and affect changes made by other cursors. By more or less isolating an operation from others, you can either resolve or exacerbate these three problems.

In ADO, isolation levels are defined in the CursorType property. Different cursors afford different levels of isolation. Cursor types also define navigational abilities, so there is a lot more to be considered. Table 8.6 takes a look at each cursor type.

Table 8.6. Cursor types in ADO.

Name	ADO constant	Description
Dynamic	adOpenDynamic	This is the most powerful cursor, and requires the most resources to maintain. This type of cursor can see changes made by other users to the underlying data as they are made. Bookmarks (if the

Name	ADO constant	Description
		data provider supports them) are supported as well as backward and forward navigation.
Keyset	adOpenKeyset	The keyset cursor is almost as powerful as the dynamic cursor. It supports bookmarks and forward and backward navigation. Edits to the underlying data can been seen after they have been committed, but additions and deletions of records cannot be seen without a re-query.
Static	adOpenStatic	This is sometimes called the *snapshot cursor*. Bookmarks and forward and backward navigation are all supported, but changes to the underlying data are not seen without a re-query.
Forward Only	adOpenForwardOnly	This cursor is like the static cursor except that only forward navigation is supported.

Choosing the Right Cursor for the Job

Choosing the right cursor for the job is very important for performance and usability. The most important thing you must know in advance is what you want to do. Time spent planning will save coding time at development and processor time at completion.

Remember that there is work for the data provider and ADO in building and maintaining a cursor. You want to choose a cursor type that will fit your needs, but no more. This saves resources at the data provider and in ADO, so the client browser will see the results more quickly. It might even be more than a matter of speed. On the Internet and large intranets, choosing the wrong cursor can bring the system to its knees because there are so many concurrent users.

> **TIP**
>
> Some data providers, such as SQL 6.5, have a feature called a *server-side cursor*. This type of cursor cuts down on network traffic and uses the SQL server's resources instead of your IIS server's resources. Of course, this is only helpful if these products are installed on separate machines. If they are not, you are probably putting too much load on one server.

There are three different things you might want to do with your data that determine what type of record set you need. You might want to only report, you might need to edit, or you might need to blindly add and delete records. There are cases where you need to do a little of each in your applications, but it is best to break these tasks up and use different cursors where appropriate instead of using the most powerful cursor at all times.

The first and easiest task is simple reading or reporting. Reporting requires only forward motion, and a read-only lock will work fine because you are not going to make changes, additions, or deletions. If you are reporting and want to see changes to the underlying data as they are made (for example a stock reporting program), you might be tempted to use the dynamic or keyset cursors because they are less isolated. However, this is a mistake because of the overhead required to build this more powerful cursor. A better solution is to use one of the more economic cursor types (static or forward only) and periodically requery to your data provider to keep your record set up to date.

The next task you might need to perform on your data is an edit. Your first decision is what type of lock to use. High-traffic sites have a better chance of concurrent edits and need tighter locking to ensure that data corruption does not occur. However, pessimistic locking can curtail concurrency. Low-traffic sites or record sets can safely use optimistic locking. Batch operations can use only optimistic locking. However, some operations require batch processing. Consider using the MODE property to help resolve locking issues in this case.

The second question you should ask is what type of isolation your transaction needs and what navigation capabilities it should have. If data is highly interactive (for example, an ordering system), chances are you want to perform your operations in low isolations and with tight locks. If your operations are not affected by others making changes to data and you do not need bookmarks, you can use the static or forward-only cursor with lock types appropriate for the expected traffic. As you can see, the possibilities are endless; it is just a matter of understanding your situation and your application needs.

Finally, there are some cases where records must be blindly added or deleted (for example, in a guestbook). Although you can build a cursor and use the AddNew or Delete methods, this might be the wrong approach. You can add or delete records directly to the provider without building a cursor at all. You simply use SQL commands; the data provider handles all other issues.

8

Summary

Today you learned about the Data Access component and ActiveX Data Objects. ADO's advantages include speed, small disk footprint, low memory usage, and the capability to function in a connectionless environment such as the Internet. ADOs get data from the data provider in a tabular form. The most important exposed object in ADO is the Recordset object. The other exposed objects and methods enable the creation or manipulation of the Recordset object. Finally, performance should always be a consideration when you are developing. There is usually more than one way to accomplish a task. Your challenge is to understand ADO and find the best method.

What's Next

Tomorrow you will learn more about using ASP and databases. You will be using Microsoft add-ons and third-party applications to connect to databases using ASP.

Q&A

Q **What are the three exposed objects in ADO? Are any of these always supported?**

A The Connection, Command, and Recordset objects. The Command object is optional because not all data providers can process commands.

Q **What is the best method for blindly inserting or deleting records into a base table?**

A Use SQL commands with the Execute method. This saves time because you do not have to create a record set.

Q **Describe the characteristics and uses of the default cursor (record set) that is created by the Command and Connection objects.**

A These objects can create only read-only, forward-only record sets.

Q **What function do the optional Options arguments of the Execute and Open methods serve?**

A Explicitly specifying the command type in the Options argument saves the data provider the trouble (and processor time) of doing it for you.

Exercises

1. Fix the problem of multiple records in `findme.asp` and have it list more than just your visitor number.

   Hint: Use more form fields to narrow your search. You could even use a filter instead of a SQL statement.

2. Expand `filter.asp` to include multiple filters. If you are ambitious, you can combine Exercises 1 and 2!

   Hint: You can only apply one filter, so you need a big long filter string with AND connecting the different criteria.

3. Expand the `paramfindme.asp` application to include searching on more than one parameter. Be careful keeping correlating parameters and fields.

Chapter 9

Advanced Web Database Programming

Yesterday you learned the fundamentals of developing database applications using Active Server Pages and ActiveX data objects. Today you will explore advanced database topics that can be used to easily develop sophisticated Web applications. At the end of the day, you will be able to perform the following tasks:

☐ Use the Internet Database Connector for simple database transactions

☐ Distinguish the differences between the Internet Database Connector and Active Server Pages

☐ Convert IDC scripts to ASP applications

☐ Use the HTML Table Formatter control to format information presented to users

☐ Use Microsoft Access to create ASP applications

The Quotations Database

All database applications discussed today use the quotations database shown in Figure 9.1. This is a Microsoft Access database used to store various quotations. As shown in Figure 9.1, the quotations database consists of four data fields.

Figure 9.1.

The data fields of the quotations database.

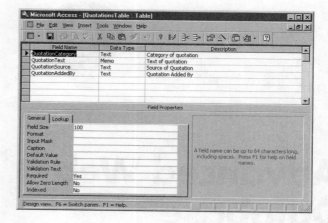

The quotations database contains a list of quotations, as shown in Figure 9.2. Internet Database Connector (IDC) and Active Server Pages (ASP) applications discussed today manipulate the data in the quotations database.

Figure 9.2.

The data in the quotations database.

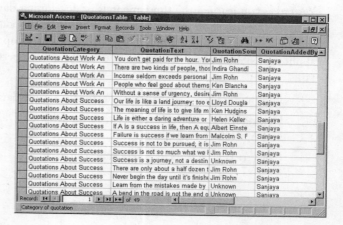

In order for Active Server Pages to be able to interface with the quotations database, a system DSN must be created in the manner shown on Day 8, "Introduction to Web Database Programming Using ActiveX Data Objects." For the purposes of applications presented today, a system DSN by the name of `QuotationsDatabase` has been created.

Using the Internet Database Connector for Simple Database Transactions

In this section, you will learn how to publish a database on the Internet with the Internet Database Connector. Prior to Active Server Pages, databases were primarily published on the Web with IIS using the Internet Database Connector.

NOTE

If you are familiar with developing IDC applications, you might want to skim this section, and then proceed to the next section ("Differences Between IDC and ASP").

TIP

You can easily publish a Microsoft Access 97 database on the Web by selecting Save As HTML from the File menu.

The quotations form shown in Figure 9.3 can be used to browse quotations of the Microsoft Access database shown in Figure 9.2. See Listing 9.1 for the source code of the IDC file that generates the Web page shown in Figure 9.3. The IDC file in Listing 9.1 contains a SQL statement that extracts data from the `QuotationsDatabase` system data source name. The extracted data is displayed by the HTML extensions file (see Listing 9.2) defined in Line 2 of Listing 9.1. The `<%BeginDetail%>` and `<%EndDetail%>` block defined in Lines 32–40 of Listing 9.2 display the information retrieved from the database.

Listing 9.1. The quotations form IDC file.

```
1: Datasource:QuotationsDatabase
2: Template:QuotationsForm_1.htx
3: SQLStatement:SELECT * FROM [QuotationsTable]
4: Password:
5: Username:
```

Figure 9.3.

The quotations form
(IDC/HTX version).

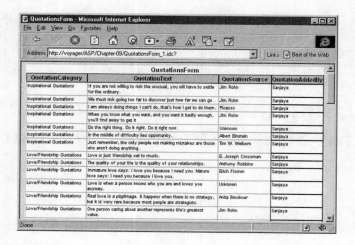

Listing 9.2. The quotations form HTML extensions file.

```
 1: <HTML>
 2:
 3: <TITLE>Quotations Form</TITLE>
 4:
 5: <BODY background = sky.jpg>
 6:
 7: <TABLE BORDER=1 BGCOLOR=#ffffff CELLSPACING=0>
 8: <FONT FACE="Arial" COLOR=#000000>
 9: <CAPTION><B>QuotationsForm</B></CAPTION>
10:
11: <THEAD>
12: <TR>
13: <TH BGCOLOR=#c0c0c0 BORDERCOLOR=#000000 >
14: <FONT SIZE=2 FACE="Arial" COLOR=#000000>
15: QuotationCategory</FONT></TH>
16:
17: <TH BGCOLOR=#c0c0c0 BORDERCOLOR=#000000 >
18: <FONT SIZE=2 FACE="Arial" COLOR=#000000>
19: QuotationText</FONT></TH>
20:
21: <TH BGCOLOR=#c0c0c0 BORDERCOLOR=#000000 >
22: <FONT SIZE=2 FACE="Arial" COLOR=#000000>
23: QuotationSource</FONT></TH>
24:
25: <TH BGCOLOR=#c0c0c0 BORDERCOLOR=#000000 >
26: <FONT SIZE=2 FACE="Arial" COLOR=#000000>
27: QuotationAddedBy</FONT></TH>
28:
29: </TR>
30: </THEAD>
31: <TBODY>
32: <%BeginDetail%>
33: <TR VALIGN=TOP>
```

```
34: <TD BORDERCOLOR=#c0c0c0 ><FONT SIZE=1 FACE="Arial"
    ➥COLOR=#000000><%QuotationCategory%><BR></FONT></TD>
35: <TD BORDERCOLOR=#c0c0c0 ><FONT SIZE=1 FACE="Arial"
    ➥COLOR=#000000><%QuotationText%><BR></FONT></TD>
36: <TD BORDERCOLOR=#c0c0c0 ><FONT SIZE=1 FACE="Arial"
    ➥COLOR=#000000><%QuotationSource%><BR></FONT></TD>
37: <TD BORDERCOLOR=#000000 ><FONT SIZE=1 FACE="Arial"
    ➥COLOR=#000000><%QuotationAddedBy%><BR></FONT></TD>
38:
39: </TR>
40: <%EndDetail%>
41: </TBODY>
42: <TFOOT></TFOOT>
43: </TABLE>
44:
45: </BODY>
46:
47: </HTML>
```

Differences Between IDC and ASP

There are several differences between the Internet Database Connector and Active Server Pages. The biggest difference is ASP's capability to maintain several database connections to manipulate data. IDC applications are limited to a single database connection at a time. This is a major limitation when you develop Web applications that require several database connections.

Unlike the Internet Database Connector, Active Server Pages supports several different scripting languages (JavaScript, VBScript, Perl, and so on); you can use the scripting language with which you are most familiar.

As you will be shown on Day 10, "Developing Custom ActiveX Components," any language that allows the creation of ActiveX controls (such as Visual Basic) can be used to extend Active Server Pages. IDC applications, on the other hand, cannot be extended through the use of other languages.

If an IDC application fails to execute for any reason, a generic error message is displayed to the user. ASP applications can be programmed to display customized, user-friendly error messages that are more helpful to the user.

As you can see, Active Server Pages is far better suited for developing Web database applications. The flexibility and features offered by Active Server Pages can be used to undertake virtually any Web database project.

Converting IDC Scripts to ASP Applications

If you are familiar with Windows NT Web development, chances are you are familiar with the Internet Database Connector. You might already have various IDC scripts set up on your Web server. If you have been postponing porting your IDC scripts to Active Server Pages, there is good news. Microsoft has developed an application that can be used to port IDC applications to Active Server Pages. This section demonstrates how to convert the IDC application in Listings 9.1 and 9.2 to Active Server Pages.

Download the application used to convert IDC scripts to ASP applications by visiting http://www.microsoft.com/iis/usingiis/developing/samples/. After you download the conversion utility, copy it to a temporary directory and execute it. After the conversion utility is installed, invoke the Web page in the IDC2ASP Windows NT Start menu to learn how to convert your IDC files to ASP.

After the IDC/HTX conversion utility is installed, log on to the directory you selected to install the IDC/HTX conversion utility and use the following syntax to convert IDC/HTX files to ASP:

```
IDC2ASP /I<PathToIDCFiles> /O<PathToTheASPDirectory> *.idc
```

For example, the following command was used to convert the IDC/HTX files in Listings 9.1 and 9.2:

```
C:\Program Files\IDC2ASP>IDC2ASP /IE:\Publish\WWW\ASP\Chapter-09
➥/OE:\Publish\WWW\ASP\Chapter-09 *.idc
```

Listing 9.3 shows the ASP file generated by the IDC/HTX utility. The output of the ASP file can be found in Figure 9.4. Compare Figure 9.4 to Figure 9.3 and notice how the output of the ASP file and the IDC file is identical. But unlike the IDC file, the ASP file can be customized using various ASP statements and components.

Listing 9.3. Source code of the quotations form (ASP version of Listings 9.1 and 9.2).

```
 1: <%@ LANGUAGE="VBScript" %>
 2: <!--#include file="ADOVBS.inc"-->
 3: <!--#include file="IASUtil.asp"-->
 4:
 5: <%
 6: Set Connection = Server.CreateObject("ADODB.Connection")
 7:
 8: Connection.Open "DSN=QuotationsDatabase; UID=; PWD="
 9:
10: SQLStmt = "SELECT * FROM [QuotationsTable] "
```

```
11:
12: Set RS = Connection.Execute(SQLStmt)
13: %>
14: <HTML>
15:
16: <TITLE>Quotations Form</TITLE>
17:
18: <BODY background = sky.jpg>
19:
20: <TABLE BORDER=1 BGCOLOR=#ffffff CELLSPACING=0>
21: <FONT FACE="Arial" COLOR=#000000>
22: <CAPTION><B>QuotationsForm</B></CAPTION>
23:
24: <THEAD>
25: <TR>
26: <TH BGCOLOR=#c0c0c0 BORDERCOLOR=#000000 >
27: <FONT SIZE=2 FACE="Arial" COLOR=#000000>
28: QuotationCategory</FONT></TH>
29:
30: <TH BGCOLOR=#c0c0c0 BORDERCOLOR=#000000 >
31: <FONT SIZE=2 FACE="Arial" COLOR=#000000>
32: QuotationText</FONT></TH>
33:
34: <TH BGCOLOR=#c0c0c0 BORDERCOLOR=#000000 >
35: <FONT SIZE=2 FACE="Arial" COLOR=#000000>
36: QuotationSource</FONT></TH>
37:
38: <TH BGCOLOR=#c0c0c0 BORDERCOLOR=#000000 >
39: <FONT SIZE=2 FACE="Arial" COLOR=#000000>
40: QuotationAddedBy</FONT></TH>
41:
42: </TR>
43: </THEAD>
44: <TBODY>
45: <%
46:    CurrentRecord = 0
47:    Do While CheckRS(RS)%>
48: <TR VALIGN=TOP>
49: <TD BORDERCOLOR=#c0c0c0 ><FONT SIZE=1 FACE="Arial"
    ➥COLOR=#000000><%= RS("QuotationCategory") %><BR></FONT></TD>
50: <TD BORDERCOLOR=#c0c0c0 ><FONT SIZE=1 FACE="Arial"
    ➥COLOR=#000000><%= RS("QuotationText") %><BR></FONT></TD>
51: <TD BORDERCOLOR=#c0c0c0 ><FONT SIZE=1 FACE="Arial"
    ➥COLOR=#000000><%= RS("QuotationSource") %><BR></FONT></TD>
52: <TD BORDERCOLOR=#000000 ><FONT SIZE=1 FACE="Arial"
    ➥COLOR=#000000><%= RS("QuotationAddedBy") %><BR></FONT></TD>
53:
54: </TR>
55: <%          RS.MoveNext
56:    CurrentRecord = CurrentRecord + 1
57:    Loop
58: %>
59: </TBODY>
60: <TFOOT></TFOOT>
61: </TABLE>
```

continues

Listing 9.3. continued

```
62:
63: </BODY>
64:
65: </HTML>
66: <% Connection.Close %>
```

Figure 9.4.
*The quotations form
(ASP version).*

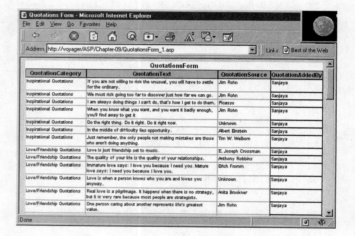

Using the HTML Table Formatter Control to Format Information Presented to Users

The HTML Table Formatter control can be used to easily format and display information retrieved from a database, as shown in Figure 9.5.

Download the HTML Table Formatter control by visiting http://www.microsoft.com/iis/usingiis/developing/samples/. After you download the control, copy the distribution file to a temporary directory and execute it. Use the dialog box shown in Figure 9.6 to specify the target directory of the ASP component. I suggest that you install the ASP component in the C:\WINNT\system32\inetsrv\ASP\Cmpnts directory so that all your ASP components reside at the same place.

After the ASP component is copied to the directory you specified, you will see a text file. Read it for the most up-to-date information about the HTML Table Formatter control. Install the control as specified in the readme.txt file.

Figure 9.5.

The HTML Table Formatter control can be used to format information retrieved from a database.

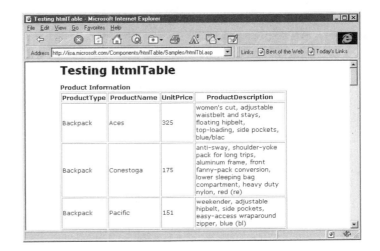

Figure 9.6.

Specify the target directory of the HTML Table Formatter control.

> **NOTE**
>
> The Java Virtual Machine and the Java SDK should be installed on every IIS server on which you will be using the HTML Table Formatter control. The latest version of the Java Virtual machine can be downloaded from http://www.microsoft.com/java.

After the HTML Table Formatter control is installed, it can be used to format and display the contents of a record set, as shown in Listing 9.4. Notice how it is not necessary to manually declare a table to display the values of a record set; instead, the AutoFormat() method of the HTML Table Formatter control can be used to format and display information in a record set (see line 14).

Listing 9.4. The HTML Table Formatter control is used to display the data in a record set.

```
1: <%
2:   Set DatabaseConnection = _
3:     Server.CreateObject ("ADODB.Connection")
4:   DatabaseConnection.Open "DSN=QuotationsDatabase; UID=; PWD="
5:
6:   Set RecordSet = _
7:     DatabaseConnection.Execute ("SELECT * FROM [QuotationsTable]")
8:
9:   Set HTMLTableControl = _
10:     Server.CreateObject("IISSample.HTMLTable")
11:
12:   HTMLTableControl.Borders = True
13:   HTMLTableControl.HeadingRow = True
14:   HTMLTableControl.AutoFormat(RecordSet)
15: %>
```

Using Microsoft Access to Create ASP Applications

This section demonstrates how the Microsoft Access Publish to the Web wizard can be used to create a Web interface to a Microsoft Access database. To use the Microsoft Access Publish to the Web wizard, launch Microsoft Access, load a database, and select File | Save As HTML from the menu bar. The Microsoft Access Publish to the Web wizard, shown in Figure 9.7, appears. Click the Next button.

Figure 9.7.

The Microsoft Access Publish to the Web wizard.

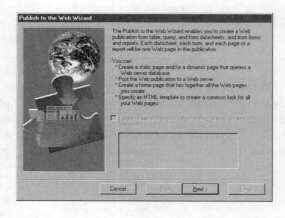

Use the dialog box shown in Figure 9.8 to select objects of the database to convert to HTML. You can select any combination of tables, queries, forms, and reports. After you select the objects, click the Next button.

Figure 9.8.
Select objects of the database to convert to HTML.

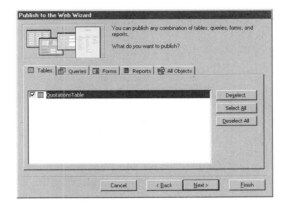

The dialog box shown in Figure 9.9 is used to specify the template used to format the results of the ASP application. You can pick a different template by clicking the Browse button. After you select a template, click the Next button.

Figure 9.9.
Select the template file used to format the output.

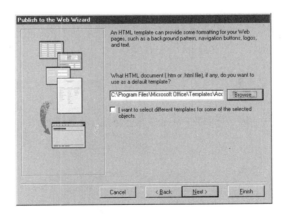

NOTE

The Microsoft Access Publish to the Web wizard might not copy all the supporting graphic files to your target directory. If this happens, you can manually copy the files from C:\Program Files\Microsoft Office\Templates\Access.

The Microsoft Access Publish to the Web wizard can create a static HTML file, a dynamic Internet Database Connector (IDC/HTX) file, or a dynamic Active Server Pages file. For the purpose of this exercise, select to create a dynamic Active Server Pages file, as shown in Figure 9.10.

Figure 9.10.

Select to create a dynamic ASP file.

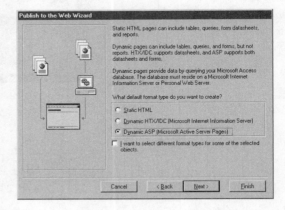

Before the ASP application can be used, a system data source name (DSN) must be created for it. If you have already created one, provide the name of the data source, as shown in Figure 9.11. You must also specify the IIS URL of the location where you want to create the ASP files. For example, if the document root directory of your Web server is E:\Publish\WWW and you want the ASP files to be created in the directory E:\Publish\WWW\ASP, specify the URL http://Your.Server.com/ASP.

Figure 9.11.

Specify the DSN and server URL information.

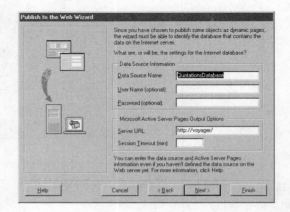

Use the dialog box shown in Figure 9.12 to specify the location of the ASP files. Make sure the directory you specify is an executable physical (or virtual) directory of IIS. Click Next to proceed to the dialog box shown in Figure 9.13.

Figure 9.12.

Specify the location of the ASP files.

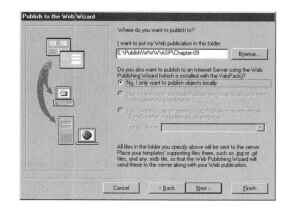

Microsoft Access can automatically create a home page for the database components you selected to convert to HTML in Figure 9.8. Specify the ASP application's home page information, as shown in Figure 9.13, and click the Next button.

Figure 9.13.

Specify the home page information.

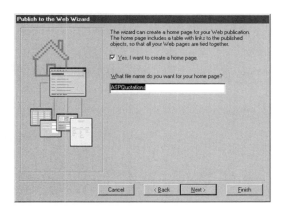

The dialog box shown in Figure 9.14 can be used to save the settings you specified for future use. If you want to save your settings, enable the checkbox and provide a profile name. Click Finish to create the ASP files.

Figure 9.14.

The ASP settings can be saved for future use.

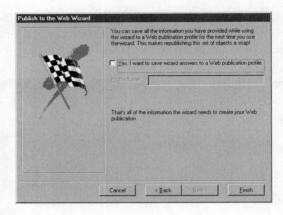

That's all the information Microsoft Access needs to create an ASP interface to your database. After you click Finish, the Microsoft Access Publish to the Web wizard creates an ASP application that can be used to browse your database, as shown in Figure 9.15. For your reference, the source code of the ASP file created by Microsoft Access is provided in Listing 9.5.

Figure 9.15.

The ASP file can be used to browse the Microsoft Access database using a Web browser.

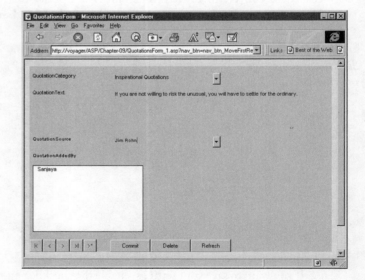

Listing 9.5. The Active Server Pages file generated by Microsoft Access.

```
 1: <%
 2: If IsObject(Session("QuotationsDatabase_conn")) Then
 3:     Set conn = Session("QuotationsDatabase_conn")
 4: Else
 5:     Set conn = Server.CreateObject("ADODB.Connection")
 6:     conn.open "QuotationsDatabase","",""
 7:     Set Session("QuotationsDatabase_conn") = conn
 8: End If
 9: %>
10: <%
11: If IsObject(Session("Form_QuotationsForm_rs")) Then
12:     Set rs = Session("Form_QuotationsForm_rs")
13: Else
14:     sql = "SELECT * FROM [QuotationsTable]"
15:     Set rs = Server.CreateObject("ADODB.Recordset")
16:     rs.Open sql, conn, 3, 3
17:     If rs.eof Then
18:         rs.AddNew
19:     End If
20:     Set Session("Form_QuotationsForm_rs") = rs
21: End If
22: %>
23: <SCRIPT LANGUAGE=VBScript>
24: <!--
25: Dim rgszCtrls(12, 2)
26: Dim cMaxCtrls
27: cMaxCtrls = 12
28: Sub AddCtrlToList(szCtrl, szCtrlSrc)
29:     Dim i
30:     for i = 1 to cMaxCtrls
31:         if rgszCtrls(i, 1) = szCtrl Then Exit Sub
32:         if rgszCtrls(i, 1) = "" Then
33:             rgszCtrls(i, 1) = szCtrl
34:             rgszCtrls(i, 2) = szCtrlSrc
35:             Exit Sub
36:         End If
37:     next
38: End Sub
39:
40: Sub UpdateRefreshBtn()
41:     nav_btn_MoveCancelUpdate.Caption = "Cancel"
42: End Sub
43:
44: Function MakeHTMLValue(szVal)
45:     Dim i
```

continues

Listing 9.5. continued

```
46:        Dim szRet
47:        for i = 1 to Len(szVal)
48:            ch = Mid(szVal, i, 1)
49:            if ch = " " Then
50:                szRet = szRet & "%20"
51:            elseif ch = "&" Then
52:                szRet = szRet & "%26"
53:            elseif ch = "#" Then
54:                szRet = szRet & "%23"
55:            elseif ch = """" Then
56:                szRet = szRet & "%22"
57:            elseif ch = ";" Then
58:                szRet = szRet & "%3B"
59:            elseif ch = ":" Then
60:                szRet = szRet & "%3A"
61:            elseif ch = "'" Then
62:                szRet = szRet & "%27"
63:            else
64:                szRet = szRet & Mid(szVal, i, 1)
65:            end if
66:        next
67:        MakeHTMLValue = szRet
68: End Function
69:
70: Function GetCtrlQueryString()
71:        Dim szRet
72:        Dim i
73:        for i = 1 to cMaxCtrls
74:            if rgszCtrls(i, 1) = "" Then Exit For
75:            szRet = szRet & rgszCtrls(i, 2) & "=" &
76: MakeHTMLValue(QuotationsForm_1alx.Controls(rgszCtrls(i, 1)).Value) &
77: "&"
78:        next
79:        GetCtrlQueryString = szRet
80: End Function
81:
82: <%
83: If IsObject(Session("RS_QuotationsForm_QuotationAddedBy")) Then
84:        Set tempRS = Session("RS_QuotationsForm_QuotationAddedBy")
85: Else
86:        sql = "SELECT DISTINCT QuotationsTable.QuotationAddedBy FROM
87: QuotationsTable ORDER BY QuotationsTable.QuotationAddedBy "
88:        Set tempRS = Server.CreateObject("ADODB.Recordset")
89:        tempRS.Open sql, conn, 3, 3
90:        Set Session("RS_QuotationsForm_QuotationAddedBy") = tempRS
91:        tempRS.MoveFirst
92: End If
93: tempRS.MoveLast
94: %>
95:
96: Dim QuotationAddedBy_tempList(<% =tempRS.RecordCount %>, 1)
```

```
 97:
 98: <%
 99: tempRS.MoveFirst
100: I = 0
101: do while Not tempRS.eof
102:     If tempRS.Fields(0).value = rs.Fields("QuotationAddedBy").Value
103: Then
104:
105:         selectedVarQuotationAddedBy = cstr(tempRS.Fields(0).value)
106:
107:     End If
108:     %>
109:     QuotationAddedBy_tempList( <% =I %> , 0)= "<%
110: =tempRS.Fields(0).value %>"
111:     <%
112:     tempRS.MoveNext
113:     I = I+1
114: loop
115: %>
116:
117: <%
118: If IsObject(Session("RS_QuotationsForm_QuotationSource")) Then
119:     Set tempRS = Session("RS_QuotationsForm_QuotationSource")
120: Else
121:     sql = "SELECT DISTINCT QuotationsTable.QuotationSource FROM
122: QuotationsTable "
123:     Set tempRS = Server.CreateObject("ADODB.Recordset")
124:     tempRS.Open sql, conn, 3, 3
125:     Set Session("RS_QuotationsForm_QuotationSource") = tempRS
126:     tempRS.MoveFirst
127: End If
128: tempRS.MoveLast
129: %>
130:
131: Dim QuotationSource_tempList(<% =tempRS.RecordCount %>, 1)
132:
133: <%
134: tempRS.MoveFirst
135: I = 0
136: do while Not tempRS.eof
137:     If tempRS.Fields(0).value = rs.Fields("QuotationSource").Value Then
138:
139:         selectedVarQuotationSource = cstr(tempRS.Fields(0).value)
140:
141:     End If
142:     %>
143:     QuotationSource_tempList( <% =I %> , 0)= "<%
144: =tempRS.Fields(0).value %>"
145:     <%
146:     tempRS.MoveNext
147:     I = I+1
```

continues

Listing 9.5. continued

```
148: loop
149: %>
150:
151: dim QuotationCategory_tempList(9, 1)
152: QuotationCategory_tempList( <% =0 %> , 0)= "<% ="Inspirational
153: Quotations" %>"
154: QuotationCategory_tempList( <% =1 %> , 0)= "<% ="Love/Friendship
155: Quotations" %>"
156: QuotationCategory_tempList( <% =2 %> , 0)= "<% ="Quotations About
157: Dreams, Aspirations And Goals" %>"
158: QuotationCategory_tempList( <% =3 %> , 0)= "<% ="Quotations About Time"
159: %>"
160: QuotationCategory_tempList( <% =4 %> , 0)= "<% ="Quotations About Work
161: And Education" %>"
162: QuotationCategory_tempList( <% =5 %> , 0)= "<% ="Quotations About
163: Success In Life" %>"
164: QuotationCategory_tempList( <% =6 %> , 0)= "<% ="Quotations About
165: Computers And The Information Systems Industry" %>"
166: QuotationCategory_tempList( <% =7 %> , 0)= "<% ="Quotations About
167: Communication And Human Interaction" %>"
168: QuotationCategory_tempList( <% =8 %> , 0)= "<% ="Humorous Quotations"
169: %>"
170:
171: Sub QuotationsForm_1alx_OnLoad()
172:     QuotationAddedBy.list = QuotationAddedBy_tempList
173:     QuotationSource.list = QuotationSource_tempList
174:     QuotationCategory.list = QuotationCategory_tempList
175: End Sub
176:
177: Sub QuotationAddedBy_AfterUpdate()
178:     call AddCtrlToList("QuotationAddedBy", "QuotationAddedBy")
179:     call UpdateRefreshBtn()
180: End Sub
181:
182: Sub QuotationSource_AfterUpdate()
183:     call AddCtrlToList("QuotationSource", "QuotationSource")
184:     call UpdateRefreshBtn()
185: End Sub
186:
187: Sub QuotationText_AfterUpdate()
188:     call AddCtrlToList("QuotationText", "QuotationText")
189:     call UpdateRefreshBtn()
190: End Sub
191:
192: Sub QuotationCategory_AfterUpdate()
193:     call AddCtrlToList("QuotationCategory", "QuotationCategory")
194:     call UpdateRefreshBtn()
195: End Sub
196:
197: Sub nav_btn_MoveFirstRecord_Click()
198:     Window.Location.Href =
```

9

```
199: "http://voyager/ASP/Chapter-09/QuotationsForm_1.asp?nav_btn=nav_btn_Mov
200: eFirstRecord&" & GetCtrlQueryString()
201: End Sub
202:
203: Sub nav_btn_MovePrevRecord_Click()
204:     Window.Location.Href =
205: "http://voyager/ASP/Chapter-09/QuotationsForm_1.asp?nav_btn=nav_btn_Mov
206: ePrevRecord&" & GetCtrlQueryString()
207: End Sub
208:
209: Sub nav_btn_MoveNextRecord_Click()
210:     Window.Location.Href =
211: "http://voyager/ASP/Chapter-09/QuotationsForm_1.asp?nav_btn=nav_btn_Mov
212: eNextRecord&" & GetCtrlQueryString()
213: End Sub
214:
215: Sub nav_btn_MoveLastRecord_Click()
216:     Window.Location.Href =
217: "http://voyager/ASP/Chapter-09/QuotationsForm_1.asp?nav_btn=nav_btn_Mov
218: eLastRecord&" & GetCtrlQueryString()
219: End Sub
220:
221: Sub nav_btn_MoveAddRecord_Click()
222:     Window.Location.Href =
223: "http://voyager/ASP/Chapter-09/QuotationsForm_1.asp?nav_btn=nav_btn_Mov
224: eAddRecord&" & GetCtrlQueryString()
225: End Sub
226:
227: Sub nav_btn_MoveCommitRecord_Click()
228:     Window.Location.Href =
229: "http://voyager/ASP/Chapter-09/QuotationsForm_1.asp?nav_btn=nav_btn_Mov
230: eCommitRecord&" & GetCtrlQueryString()
231: End Sub
232:
233: Sub nav_btn_MoveCancelUpdate_Click()
234:     Window.Location.Href =
235: "http://voyager/ASP/Chapter-09/QuotationsForm_1.asp?nav_btn=nav_btn_Mov
236: eCancelUpdate&"
237: End Sub
238:
239: Sub nav_btn_MoveDeleteRecord_Click()
240:     If MsgBox("Press OK to delete current record", 1,
241: "QuotationsForm_1") =1 Then
242:         Window.Location.Href =
243: "http://voyager/ASP/Chapter-09/QuotationsForm_1.asp?nav_btn=nav_btn_Mov
244: eDeleteRecord&"
245:     End If
246: End Sub
247:
248: -->
249: </SCRIPT>
250: <DIV ID="QuotationsForm_1alx"
```

9

continues

Listing 9.5. continued

```
251:  STYLE="LAYOUT:FIXED;HEIGHT:402;WIDTH:630;">
252:  <OBJECT ID="QuotationAddedBy"
253:  CLASSID="CLSID:8BD21D20-EC42-11CE-9E0D-00AA006002F3"
254:  STYLE="TOP:214;LEFT:6;WIDTH:231;HEIGHT:147;TABINDEX:3;ZINDEX:0;">
255:  <PARAM NAME="Value" VALUE="<%=selectedVarQuotationAddedBy%>">
256:  <PARAM NAME="BackStyle" VALUE="1">
257:  <PARAM NAME="BackColor" VALUE="16777215">
258:  <PARAM NAME="BorderStyle" VALUE="1">
259:  <PARAM NAME="BorderColor" VALUE="0">
260:  <PARAM NAME="DisplayStyle" VALUE="2">
261:  <PARAM NAME="ForeColor" VALUE="0">
262:  <PARAM NAME="FontHeight" VALUE="160">
263:  <PARAM NAME="FontName" VALUE="Arial">
264:  <PARAM NAME="Size" VALUE="6006;3822">
265:  <PARAM NAME="SpecialEffect" VALUE="1">
266:  <PARAM NAME="BoundColumn" VALUE="1">
267:  <PARAM NAME="VariousPropertyBits" VALUE="746588187">
268:  </OBJECT>
269:  <OBJECT ID="QuotationAddedBy_Label"
270:  CLASSID="CLSID:978C9E23-D4B0-11CE-BF2D-00AA003F40D0"
271:  STYLE="TOP:187;LEFT:6;WIDTH:156;HEIGHT:27;ZINDEX:1;">
272:  <PARAM NAME="BackStyle" VALUE="0">
273:  <PARAM NAME="Caption" VALUE="QuotationAddedBy">
274:  <PARAM NAME="ForeColor" VALUE="0">
275:  <PARAM NAME="FontHeight" VALUE="160">
276:  <PARAM NAME="FontName" VALUE="Arial">
277:  <PARAM NAME="Size" VALUE="4056;702">
278:  <PARAM NAME="SpecialEffect" VALUE="0">
279:  <PARAM NAME="VariousPropertyBits" VALUE="8388627">
280:  </OBJECT>
281:  <OBJECT ID="QuotationSource"
282:  CLASSID="CLSID:8BD21D30-EC42-11CE-9E0D-00AA006002F3"
283:  STYLE="TOP:151;LEFT:168;WIDTH:231;HEIGHT:27;TABINDEX:2;ZINDEX:2;">
284:  <PARAM NAME="Value" VALUE="<%=selectedVarQuotationSource%>">
285:  <PARAM NAME="BackStyle" VALUE="0">
286:  <PARAM NAME="BorderStyle" VALUE="1">
287:  <PARAM NAME="BorderColor" VALUE="12632256">
288:  <PARAM NAME="DisplayStyle" VALUE="3">
289:  <PARAM NAME="ForeColor" VALUE="0">
290:  <PARAM NAME="FontHeight" VALUE="160">
291:  <PARAM NAME="ShowDropButtonWhen" VALUE="2">
292:  <PARAM NAME="FontName" VALUE="Arial">
293:  <PARAM NAME="Size" VALUE="6006;702">
294:  <PARAM NAME="SpecialEffect" VALUE="0">
295:  <PARAM NAME="ListRows" VALUE="8">
296:  <PARAM NAME="BoundColumn" VALUE="1">
297:  <PARAM NAME="VariousPropertyBits" VALUE="746604563">
298:  </OBJECT>
299:  <OBJECT ID="QuotationSource_Label"
300:  CLASSID="CLSID:978C9E23-D4B0-11CE-BF2D-00AA003F40D0"
```

```
301: STYLE="TOP:151;LEFT:6;WIDTH:156;HEIGHT:27;ZINDEX:3;">
302: <PARAM NAME="BackStyle" VALUE="0">
303: <PARAM NAME="Caption" VALUE="QuotationSource">
304: <PARAM NAME="ForeColor" VALUE="0">
305: <PARAM NAME="FontHeight" VALUE="160">
306: <PARAM NAME="FontName" VALUE="Arial">
307: <PARAM NAME="Size" VALUE="4056;702">
308: <PARAM NAME="SpecialEffect" VALUE="0">
309: <PARAM NAME="VariousPropertyBits" VALUE="8388627">
310: </OBJECT>
311: <OBJECT ID="QuotationText"
312: CLASSID="CLSID:8BD21D10-EC42-11CE-9E0D-00AA006002F3"
313: STYLE="TOP:49;LEFT:168;WIDTH:456;HEIGHT:90;TABINDEX:1;ZINDEX:4;">
314: <%If Not IsNull(rs.Fields("QuotationText").Value) Then%>
315: <PARAM NAME="Value"
316: VALUE="<%=Server.HTMLEncode(rs.Fields("QuotationText").Value)%>">
317: <%End If%>
318: <PARAM NAME="BackStyle" VALUE="0">
319: <PARAM NAME="BorderStyle" VALUE="1">
320: <PARAM NAME="BorderColor" VALUE="12632256">
321: <PARAM NAME="ForeColor" VALUE="0">
322: <PARAM NAME="FontHeight" VALUE="160">
323: <PARAM NAME="FontName" VALUE="Arial">
324: <PARAM NAME="Size" VALUE="11856;2340">
325: <PARAM NAME="SpecialEffect" VALUE="0">
326: <PARAM NAME="VariousPropertyBits" VALUE="2894088211">
327: </OBJECT>
328: <OBJECT ID="QuotationText_Label"
329: CLASSID="CLSID:978C9E23-D4B0-11CE-BF2D-00AA003F40D0"
330: STYLE="TOP:49;LEFT:6;WIDTH:156;HEIGHT:27;ZINDEX:5;">
331: <PARAM NAME="BackStyle" VALUE="0">
332: <PARAM NAME="Caption" VALUE="QuotationText">
333: <PARAM NAME="ForeColor" VALUE="0">
334: <PARAM NAME="FontHeight" VALUE="160">
335: <PARAM NAME="FontName" VALUE="Arial">
336: <PARAM NAME="Size" VALUE="4056;702">
337: <PARAM NAME="SpecialEffect" VALUE="0">
338: <PARAM NAME="VariousPropertyBits" VALUE="8388627">
339: </OBJECT>
340: <OBJECT ID="QuotationCategory"
341: CLASSID="CLSID:8BD21D30-EC42-11CE-9E0D-00AA006002F3"
342: STYLE="TOP:13;LEFT:168;WIDTH:231;HEIGHT:27;TABINDEX:0;ZINDEX:6;">
343: <%If Not IsNull(rs.Fields("QuotationCategory").Value) Then%>
344: <PARAM NAME="Value"
345: VALUE="<%=Server.HTMLEncode(rs.Fields("QuotationCategory").Value)%>">
346: <%End If%>
347: <PARAM NAME="BackStyle" VALUE="0">
348: <PARAM NAME="BorderStyle" VALUE="1">
349: <PARAM NAME="BorderColor" VALUE="12632256">
350: <PARAM NAME="DisplayStyle" VALUE="3">
351: <PARAM NAME="ForeColor" VALUE="0">
352: <PARAM NAME="FontHeight" VALUE="160">
```

9

continues

Listing 9.5. continued

```
353: <PARAM NAME="ShowDropButtonWhen" VALUE="2">
354: <PARAM NAME="FontName" VALUE="Arial">
355: <PARAM NAME="Size" VALUE="6006;702">
356: <PARAM NAME="SpecialEffect" VALUE="0">
357: <PARAM NAME="ListRows" VALUE="8">
358: <PARAM NAME="BoundColumn" VALUE="1">
359: <PARAM NAME="VariousPropertyBits" VALUE="746604563">
360: </OBJECT>
361: <OBJECT ID="QuotationCategory_Label"
362: CLASSID="CLSID:978C9E23-D4B0-11CE-BF2D-00AA003F40D0"
363: STYLE="TOP:13;LEFT:6;WIDTH:156;HEIGHT:27;ZINDEX:7;">
364: <PARAM NAME="BackStyle" VALUE="0">
365: <PARAM NAME="Caption" VALUE="QuotationCategory">
366: <PARAM NAME="ForeColor" VALUE="0">
367: <PARAM NAME="FontHeight" VALUE="160">
368: <PARAM NAME="FontName" VALUE="Arial">
369: <PARAM NAME="Size" VALUE="4056;702">
370: <PARAM NAME="SpecialEffect" VALUE="0">
371: <PARAM NAME="VariousPropertyBits" VALUE="8388627">
372: </OBJECT>
373: <OBJECT ID="nav_btn_MoveCancelUpdate"
374: CLASSID="CLSID:D7053240-CE69-11CD-A777-00DD01143C57"
375: STYLE="TOP:374;LEFT:336;WIDTH:84;HEIGHT:28;ZINDEX:0;">
376: <PARAM NAME="BackStyle" VALUE="0">
377: <PARAM NAME="Caption" VALUE="Refresh">
378: <PARAM NAME="ParagraphAlign" VALUE="3">
379: <PARAM NAME="ForeColor" VALUE="0">
380: <PARAM NAME="Size" VALUE="2184;728">
381: <PARAM NAME="SpecialEffect" VALUE="0">
382: <PARAM NAME="VariousPropertyBits" VALUE="2">
383: </OBJECT>
384: <OBJECT ID="nav_btn_MoveDeleteRecord"
385: CLASSID="CLSID:D7053240-CE69-11CD-A777-00DD01143C57"
386: STYLE="TOP:374;LEFT:252;WIDTH:84;HEIGHT:28;ZINDEX:1;">
387: <PARAM NAME="BackStyle" VALUE="0">
388: <PARAM NAME="Caption" VALUE="Delete">
389: <PARAM NAME="ParagraphAlign" VALUE="3">
390: <PARAM NAME="ForeColor" VALUE="0">
391: <PARAM NAME="Size" VALUE="2184;728">
392: <PARAM NAME="SpecialEffect" VALUE="0">
393: <PARAM NAME="VariousPropertyBits" VALUE="2">
394: </OBJECT>
395: <OBJECT ID="nav_btn_MoveCommitRecord"
396: CLASSID="CLSID:D7053240-CE69-11CD-A777-00DD01143C57"
397: STYLE="TOP:374;LEFT:168;WIDTH:84;HEIGHT:28;ZINDEX:2;">
398: <PARAM NAME="BackStyle" VALUE="0">
399: <PARAM NAME="Caption" VALUE="Commit">
400: <PARAM NAME="ParagraphAlign" VALUE="3">
401: <PARAM NAME="ForeColor" VALUE="0">
402: <PARAM NAME="Size" VALUE="2184;728">
403: <PARAM NAME="SpecialEffect" VALUE="0">
```

```
404: <PARAM NAME="VariousPropertyBits" VALUE="2">
405: </OBJECT>
406: <OBJECT ID="nav_btn_MoveAddRecord"
407: CLASSID="CLSID:D7053240-CE69-11CD-A777-00DD01143C57"
408: STYLE="TOP:374;LEFT:112;WIDTH:28;HEIGHT:28;ZINDEX:3;">
409: <PARAM NAME="BackStyle" VALUE="0">
410: <PARAM NAME="Caption" VALUE="&gt;*">
411: <PARAM NAME="ParagraphAlign" VALUE="3">
412: <PARAM NAME="ForeColor" VALUE="0">
413: <PARAM NAME="Size" VALUE="728;728">
414: <PARAM NAME="SpecialEffect" VALUE="0">
415: <PARAM NAME="VariousPropertyBits" VALUE="2">
416: </OBJECT>
417: <OBJECT ID="nav_btn_MoveLastRecord"
418: CLASSID="CLSID:D7053240-CE69-11CD-A777-00DD01143C57"
419: STYLE="TOP:374;LEFT:84;WIDTH:28;HEIGHT:28;ZINDEX:4;">
420: <PARAM NAME="BackStyle" VALUE="0">
421: <PARAM NAME="Caption" VALUE="&gt;¦">
422: <PARAM NAME="ParagraphAlign" VALUE="3">
423: <PARAM NAME="ForeColor" VALUE="0">
424: <PARAM NAME="Size" VALUE="728;728">
425: <PARAM NAME="SpecialEffect" VALUE="0">
426: <PARAM NAME="VariousPropertyBits" VALUE="2">
427: </OBJECT>
428: <OBJECT ID="nav_btn_MoveNextRecord"
429: CLASSID="CLSID:D7053240-CE69-11CD-A777-00DD01143C57"
430: STYLE="TOP:374;LEFT:56;WIDTH:28;HEIGHT:28;ZINDEX:5;">
431: <PARAM NAME="BackStyle" VALUE="0">
432: <PARAM NAME="Caption" VALUE="&gt;">
433: <PARAM NAME="ParagraphAlign" VALUE="3">
434: <PARAM NAME="ForeColor" VALUE="0">
435: <PARAM NAME="Size" VALUE="728;728">
436: <PARAM NAME="SpecialEffect" VALUE="0">
437: <PARAM NAME="VariousPropertyBits" VALUE="2">
438: </OBJECT>
439: <OBJECT ID="nav_btn_MovePrevRecord"
440: CLASSID="CLSID:D7053240-CE69-11CD-A777-00DD01143C57"
441: STYLE="TOP:374;LEFT:28;WIDTH:28;HEIGHT:28;ZINDEX:6;">
442: <PARAM NAME="BackStyle" VALUE="0">
443: <PARAM NAME="Caption" VALUE="&lt;">
444: <PARAM NAME="ParagraphAlign" VALUE="3">
445: <PARAM NAME="ForeColor" VALUE="0">
446: <PARAM NAME="Size" VALUE="728;728">
447: <PARAM NAME="SpecialEffect" VALUE="0">
448: <PARAM NAME="VariousPropertyBits" VALUE="2">
449: </OBJECT>
450: <OBJECT ID="nav_btn_MoveFirstRecord"
451: CLASSID="CLSID:D7053240-CE69-11CD-A777-00DD01143C57"
452: STYLE="TOP:374;LEFT:0;WIDTH:28;HEIGHT:28;ZINDEX:7;">
453: <PARAM NAME="BackStyle" VALUE="0">
454: <PARAM NAME="Caption" VALUE="¦&lt;">
455: <PARAM NAME="ParagraphAlign" VALUE="3">
456: <PARAM NAME="ForeColor" VALUE="0">
```

continues

Listing 9.5. continued

```
457: <PARAM NAME="Size" VALUE="728;728">
458: <PARAM NAME="SpecialEffect" VALUE="0">
459: <PARAM NAME="VariousPropertyBits" VALUE="2">
460: </OBJECT>
461: </DIV>
```

ANALYSIS   The ASP application in Listing 9.5 demonstrates how to use style sheets to develop richly formatted Web applications.

Summary

Although IIS 3.0 supports the Internet Database Connector, Active Server Pages is far more suitable for developing dynamic Web database applications. Various components and utilities that can be freely downloaded from Microsoft's Web site can be used to aid in the development of ASP applications (or even to port IDC applications to ASP). Microsoft Visual InterDev and Microsoft Access support Active Server Pages and can be used to easily develop Web interfaces to databases. Microsoft Access databases can be published on the Web by creating a system DSN for the database and selecting File | Save As HTML from the menu bar.

What's Next?

You can extend the capabilities of Active Server Pages by developing your own custom ASP components. Tomorrow, you will learn how Visual Basic 5.0 can be used to develop custom ASP components. Your VBScript skills can be easily leveraged to develop custom ASP components because the syntax of Visual Basic is very similar to VBScript.

Q&A

Q I need to develop a simple Web database application. Should I use the Internet Database Connector or Active Server Pages?

A You should use Active Server Pages because it is well suited for both simple and complicated Web database projects. Although a Web database application might initially appear to be simple, using Active Server Pages to develop the database application gives you the flexibility to modify the database application at a later time if necessary.

Q After downloading and installing the IDC/HTX conversion utility, which command should I give to convert all the IDC files in the directory `c:\Publish\WWW\Scripts\Database` to Active Server Pages?

A `IDC2ASP /Ic:\Publish\WWW\Scripts\Database`
↪`/Oc:\Publish\WWW\Scripts\Database *.idc`

Exercises

1. Create an address book using Microsoft Access and port it to the Web using the Microsoft Access Publish to the Web wizard.

2. Create a System DSN for the address book database created in Exercise 1.

3. Use the HTML Table Formatter control to display the contents of the address book database created in Exercise 1 using the System DSN created in Exercise 2.

Chapter **10**

Developing Custom ActiveX Components

On Day 5, "Using ActiveX Components," you learned how to use components supplied with Active Server Pages to develop interactive Web applications. Today you will learn how to develop your own custom ASP components using Visual Basic (VB) 5.0. Any language that allows the creation of ActiveX controls (such as Visual C++, Visual J++, Delphi, and so on) can be used to develop custom ASP components. Because the syntax of Visual Basic is very similar to the syntax of VBScript, Visual Basic 5.0 is used in examples presented today. At the end of the day you will be able to leverage your VBScript/Visual Basic skills to develop custom ASP components. For those of you who have already used Visual Basic, you will quickly realize how creating a custom ASP component is as straightforward as developing a typical VB application.

Benefits of Developing Custom ASP Components

You might be wondering why you should go to the trouble of creating custom ASP components when you can simply use VBScript, JScript, or another client-side scripting language to write your ASP applications. Some of the benefits of developing custom ASP components include

- ☐ Centralized code management
- ☐ The black box model
- ☐ Access to API functions
- ☐ Mix-and-match programming languages
- ☐ Security
- ☐ Protection of proprietary algorithms
- ☐ Ease of alteration
- ☐ Ease of distribution

Centralized Code Management

When business logic is implemented as an ASP component, you can centrally manage the business logic code without being concerned about everyone having access to the latest revision of the code.

The Black Box Model

ASP components support the black box model. The term *black box model* refers to an object that operates in a predictable and consistent manner when proper input is provided. For example, consider a radar detector. The user need only know how to turn it on and how to supply the power in order to use it. The logic required to detect laser and radar from police speed-detection equipment is contained within the radar detector unit, and the user need not know how the technology works in order to use the device. Likewise, ASP components hide details of implementation from the user. All the user needs to know to use an ASP component is what the ASP component does and how to provide input. The logic required to process the input is contained within the ASP component.

Access to API Functions

When developing custom ASP components, you can use numerous Windows API functions to obtain and process information. The custom ASP component you will build later today uses a Windows API function to obtain system memory resources of the Web server. Not only do custom ASP components give you access to the Windows API, but access is also provided to additional server resources such as memory, disk, network, and running processes.

10

Mix-and-Match Programming Languages

Because any language capable of creating an ActiveX control can be used to develop custom ASP components, Active Server Pages can be employed to make the best use of features of many languages such as Visual Basic, C++, Java, Delphi, and so on. This is a major benefit of using Active Server Pages; virtually no other Web application development environment gives more freedom in selecting the language you use to develop custom components.

Security

Windows NT security can be used to ensure the security of ASP components that contain sensitive information (for example, a database query that requires a secret password). If the database query is implemented using a simple ASP statement, anyone with access to the ASP page (graphic designers, Web page editors, contractors, consultants, temporary employees, and so on) can find out the password. This might not be desirable in some cases. In such a case, the database query can be carried out by an ASP component, and Windows NT security can be used to ensure the security of the ASP component.

Protection of Proprietary Algorithms

ASP components protect proprietary algorithms in that implementation details are hidden from the user. An example of this would be an application that calculates the cost of a project when certain information is provided. Due to the proprietary nature of the formula used to calculate the cost of the project, the formula can be embedded in an ASP component.

Ease of Alteration

ASP components can be easily modified when business formulas and conditions change. Think of an online storefront (which happens to sell ASP components) that is implemented with Active Server Pages. Every week, the store puts certain ASP components on sale. The percentage to subtract is calculated using a complex business formula. If the formula is included in each ASP page, any slight change to the formula would require several pages to be updated. On the other hand, if the formula is contained in an ASP component that is used by the ASP pages, the formula can be easily altered.

Ease of Distribution

ASP components can be easily distributed after they are created. All that's required to use an ASP component after it is developed is to register it on the server. (If the component was developed on the server, Visual Basic automatically registers it for you.) See the section "Distributing ASP Components" to learn more about registering and distributing ASP components.

Benefits of Using Visual Basic 5.0

Visual Basic 5.0 is a powerful, easy-to-use application development environment. Although previous versions of Visual Basic provided an easy-to-use rapid application development environment, there was a tradeoff in performance. Microsoft has increased the performance of VB 5.0 by including a native code compiler and an enhanced P-code interpreter. VB can also be used to easily develop ActiveX controls that can be hosted on Internet Explorer and IIS 3.0, as well as on Visual C++, Microsoft Office, and other VB applications (to name a few). VB 5.0 includes many useful features that can save you time when developing applications. Visual Basic 5.0's speed and access to a rich library of ActiveX controls and Microsoft sample code make Visual Basic an ideal application development environment for creating custom ASP components. Have you ever had to press F1 or refer to a manual to find out the syntax of a particular function? Thanks to code completion, VB 5.0 makes this a thing of the past. As soon as you type the name of a function, a ToolTip shows you the function's syntax and return type. This feature is also useful for locating a member function of an object. As soon as you type the name of an object and follow it with a period, VB 5.0 displays all the member functions of the object in a ToolTip.

Developing a Custom ASP Component

This section demonstrates how easy it is to develop a custom ASP component using VB 5.0. The component developed in this section can be used to determine the memory resources of the Web server. The VB component uses a Win32 API function to obtain system memory resource information. To begin creating your first custom ASP component, start VB 5.0; the New Project window appears (see Figure 10.1). Select to create an ActiveX DLL project and click the Open button. If you do not see the window in Figure 10.1, select File | New Project from the menu bar or press Ctrl+N.

NOTE

> ActiveX wrapper functions that will provide access to any Windows API function can be created.

Figure 10.1.

*Select to create an
ActiveX DLL project.*

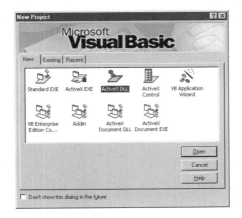

Visual Basic creates a project with default project and class names. Before you add code to the VB application, provide more descriptive project class names. Locate the project settings window and replace the default name of the project (Project1) with something more descriptive, such as VBComponent (see Figure 10.2).

Figure 10.2.

*Give the VB project a
descriptive name.*

Next, replace the default name of the project class (Class1) with something more descriptive (such as SystemInformation), as shown in Figure 10.3.

NOTE

The project class name becomes the name of the ASP component referenced by the ASP application.

Figure 10.3.

Give a descriptive name to the default class of the project.

You are now ready to begin writing VB code. The API function that can be used to determine system memory resources is GlobalMemoryStatus(). In order to call a Win32 API function from Visual Basic, you need the function prototype and the data structure of the API function. Therefore, before you proceed, you need the function prototype and the data structure used by the API function GlobalMemoryStatus(). Fortunately, Visual Basic ships with a utility that can be used to easily locate the function prototype and the data structures of an API function. Locate the file APILOAD.EXE in the \Program Files\DevStudio\VB\Winapi\ directory and execute it (assuming you installed Visual Basic in the directory \Program Files\DevStudio\VB\). You will see the application window shown in Figure 10.4.

NOTE

A MAPI32.txt file is also available for using various MAPI functions.

Figure 10.4.

The API Viewer application can be used to locate API function prototypes and data structures.

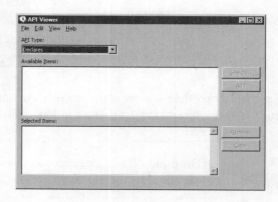

10

Select File | Load Text File from the menu bar and select Win32api.txt, as shown in Figure 10.5. The first time you execute APILOAD.EXE, you will be asked whether the text file should be converted to a database. Answer yes to improve the performance of the API Viewer application.

Figure 10.5.

Select the file Win32api.txt.

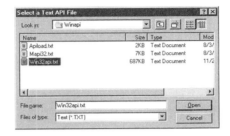

After converting the text file to a database, API Viewer loads information about API functions, types, and constants so you can easily browse items. The Copy button is used to copy the selected items to a clipboard so you can later paste them to your VB application. Because you need the declaration for the GlobalMemoryStatus() function, type the string GlobalMemoryStatus() into the listbox. After you see the GlobalMemoryStatus() function highlighted, double-click it to see its function definition (see Figure 10.6). Pay particular attention to the data type of the argument of the API function (lpBuffer As MEMORYSTATUS).

Figure 10.6.

The function prototype of the GlobalMemory Status() *function.*

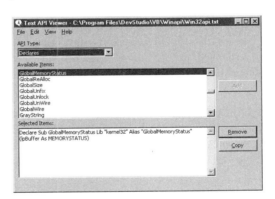

To obtain information from the API function, you must pass it a data structure of MEMORYSTATUS type. Your next task is to locate the data structure definition of MEMORYSTATUS type. Select Types from the API Type listbox, and type the string MEMORYSTATUS into the Available Items listbox. After MEMORYSTATUS is highlighted, double-click it to see its data structure definition, as shown in Figure 10.7.

> **NOTE**
>
> API functions are very useful for interfacing with various Windows resources. In order to use an API function, you must declare it and the data structure(s) it uses. The APILOAD.EXE application can be used to easily obtain the declaration used to call an API function along with the data structure(s) it uses.

Figure 10.7.

The data structure definition of MEMORYSTATUS.

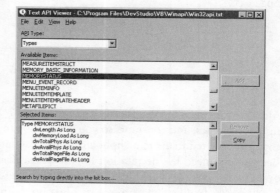

Notice how both the function definition and the data structure definition are in the Selected Items textbox. To transfer this information to the clipboard, click Copy. Next, switch back to Visual Basic and double-click the SystemInformation class module. Locate the Declarations module of the SystemInformation class and paste the information from the clipboard (see Figure 10.8). This is a good time to comment the code you pasted from the clipboard so you can easily identify it at a later time.

Listing 10.1 contains the full source code of the VB ASP component that can be used to obtain memory resource values of the Web server. The next section, "Using Custom ASP Components in ASP Applications," demonstrates how an ASP application can interface with the custom ASP component created in this section.

10

Figure 10.8.

Use the clipboard to transfer the data structure and function definition information.

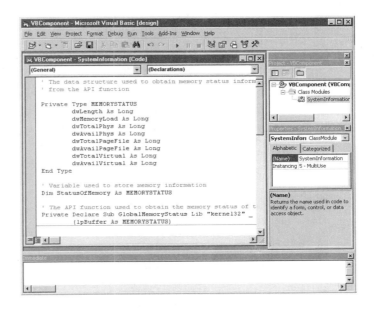

Listing 10.1. A Win32 API function is used to obtain system memory resource values.

```
 1: ' The data structure used to obtain memory status information
 2: ' from the API function
 3:
 4: Private Type MEMORYSTATUS
 5:         dwLength As Long
 6:         dwMemoryLoad As Long
 7:         dwTotalPhys As Long
 8:         dwAvailPhys As Long
 9:         dwTotalPageFile As Long
10:         dwAvailPageFile As Long
11:         dwTotalVirtual As Long
12:         dwAvailVirtual As Long
13: End Type
14:
15: ' Variable used to store memory information
16: Dim StatusOfMemory As MEMORYSTATUS
17:
18: ' The API function used to obtain the memory status of the Web server
19: Private Declare Sub GlobalMemoryStatus Lib "kernel32" _
20:         (lpBuffer As MEMORYSTATUS)
21:
22: ' Returns the amount of total physical memory on the Web server
23: Public Function GetTotalPhysicalMemory() As Long
24:   GlobalMemoryStatus StatusOfMemory
25:   GetTotalPhysicalMemory = StatusOfMemory.dwTotalPhys
26: End Function
```

continues

Listing 10.1. continued

```
27:
28: ' Returns the amount of available physical memory on the Web server
29: Public Function GetAvailablePhysicalMemory() As Long
30:    GlobalMemoryStatus StatusOfMemory
31:    GetAvailablePhysicalMemory = StatusOfMemory.dwAvailPhys
32: End Function
33:
34: ' Returns the amount of total page memory on the Web server
35: Public Function GetTotalPageMemory() As Long
36:    GlobalMemoryStatus StatusOfMemory
37:    GetTotalPageMemory = StatusOfMemory.dwTotalPageFile
38: End Function
39:
40: ' Returns the amount of available page memory on the Web server
41: Public Function GetAvailablePageMemory() As Long
42:    GlobalMemoryStatus StatusOfMemory
43:    GetAvailablePageMemory = StatusOfMemory.dwAvailPageFile
44: End Function
45:
46: ' Returns the amount of total virtual memory on the Web server
47: Public Function GetTotalVirtualMemory() As Long
48:    GlobalMemoryStatus StatusOfMemory
49:    GetTotalVirtualMemory = StatusOfMemory.dwTotalVirtual
50: End Function
51:
52: ' Returns the amount of available virtual memory on the Web server
53: Public Function GetAvailableVirtualMemory() As Long
54:    GlobalMemoryStatus StatusOfMemory
55:    GetAvailableVirtualMemory = StatusOfMemory.dwAvailVirtual
56: End Function
```

Using Custom ASP Components in ASP Applications

Custom components you create can be used from ASP applications in the same way that components included with Active Server Pages are used. The ASP application in Listing 10.2 demonstrates how to interface with the custom ASP component created in the previous section. The ASP application instantiates the custom ASP component with the statement Set InstanceOfComponent = Server.CreateObject ("VBComponent.SystemInformation"). Afterwards, public functions of the ASP component can be called as illustrated in lines 40–51 of Listing 10.2. The output of the ASP application in Listing 10.2 is shown in Figure 10.9.

Listing 10.2. Interfacing with a custom ASP component created with Visual Basic.

```
 1: <%@ LANGUAGE="VBSCRIPT" %>
 2:
 3: <HTML>
 4: <HEAD>
 5: <META NAME="GENERATOR" Content="Microsoft Visual InterDev 1.0">
 6: <META HTTP-EQUIV="Content-Type" content="text/html; charset=iso-8859-1">
 7: <TITLE>
 8:    Interfacing With Visual Basic Components
 9: </TITLE>
10: </HEAD>
11:
12: <BODY BGCOLOR=FFFFFF>
13:
14: <H3>
15: This ASP application interfaces with a Visual Basic component
16: to determine the status of memory resources on the server.
17: </H3>
18:
19: <%
20:
21: ' Variable used to instantiate the ASP component
22:    Dim InstanceOfComponent
23:
24: ' Variables used to store memory information
25:
26:    Dim TotalPhysicalMemory
27:    Dim AvailablePhysicalMemory
28:    Dim TotalPageMemory
29:    Dim AvailablePageMemory
30:    Dim TotalVirtualMemory
31:    Dim AvailableVirtualMemory
32:
33:
34: ' Create an instance of the VB ASP component
35:    Set InstanceOfComponent = _
36:       Server.CreateObject ("VBComponent.SystemInformation")
37:
38: ' Obtain memory information from the ASP component
39:
40:    TotalPhysicalMemory = _
41:       InstanceOfComponent.GetTotalPhysicalMemory()
42:    AvailablePhysicalMemory = _
43:       InstanceOfComponent.GetAvailablePhysicalMemory()
44:    TotalPageMemory = _
45:       InstanceOfComponent.GetTotalPageMemory()
46:    AvailablePageMemory = _
47:       InstanceOfComponent.GetAvailablePageMemory()
48:    TotalVirtualMemory = _
49:       InstanceOfComponent.GetTotalVirtualMemory()
50:    AvailableVirtualMemory = _
51:       InstanceOfComponent.GetAvailableVirtualMemory()
52:
```

10

continues

Listing 10.2. continued

```
53: %>
54:
55: <TABLE BORDER=3 >
56: <TR><TD>
57: Total Physical Memory</TD><TD ALIGN=RIGHT>
58: <%= TotalPhysicalMemory %>
59: </TD></TR><TR><TD>
60: Available Physical Memory</TD><TD ALIGN=RIGHT>
61: <%= AvailablePhysicalMemory %>
62: </TD></TR><TR><TD>
63: Total Page Memory</TD><TD ALIGN=RIGHT>
64: <%= TotalPageMemory %>
65: </TD></TR><TR><TD>
66: Available Page Memory</TD><TD ALIGN=RIGHT>
67: <%= AvailablePageMemory %>
68: </TD></TR><TR><TD>
69: Total Virtual Memory</TD><TD ALIGN=RIGHT>
70: <%= TotalVirtualMemory %>
71: </TD></TR><TR><TD>
72: Available Virtual Memory</TD><TD ALIGN=RIGHT>
73: <%= AvailableVirtualMemory %>
74: </TD></TR>
75: </TABLE>
76:
77: <HR>
78:
79: <%= "This Web page was generated on " & Date & " at " & Time & "." %>
80:
81: </BODY>
82: </HTML>
```

Figure 10.9.

*Output of the
ASP application in
Listing 10.2.*

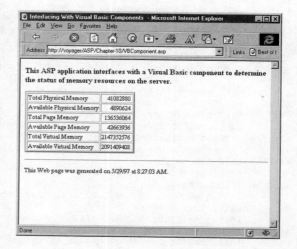

NOTE

See Day 15, "Bonus Day: Practical Applications of ASP," to learn how to develop a Web e-mail gateway using a custom ASP component.

Sending HTML Text to the Web Browser

Rather than sending data to the ASP application each time you need to display information to the user, it would be nice if custom ASP components could send HTML text directly to the Web browser. HTML text can be written directly to the Web browser by referencing the ScriptingContext object in the OnStartPage method of the ASP component and saving the reference for future use. The ScriptingContext object acts as an interface between the ASP component and the Web page generated by the ASP application. Before you can use the ScriptingContext object in your VB application, you must add a reference to the Active Server Pages DLL file (asp.dll). Do so by selecting Project | References from the Visual Basic menu bar and selecting the Microsoft Active Server Pages 1.0 Object Library checkbox, as shown in Figure 10.10. After you select the checkbox, you can send HTML text directly to the Web browser using the Write method of the Response object, as demonstrated in Listing 10.3.

Figure 10.10.
Select the Microsoft Active Server Pages 1.0 Object Library checkbox.

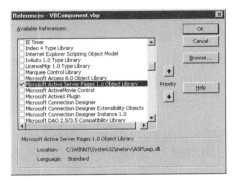

Listing 10.3. Sending HTML text to the Web browser.

```
' A global variable is used to create a reference to the
' ScriptingContext object.
Dim MyResponse As Response
Public Function OnStartPage(MyScriptingContext As ScriptingContext)
```

continues

Listing 10.3. continued

```
    ' A reference is created to the Response object
    Set MyResponse = MyScriptingContext.Response

    ' The Write method of the Response object is used to
    ' send HTML text to the Web browser.
    MyResponse.Write "<B>Hello User!</B>"

End Function
```

Distributing ASP Components

Custom ASP components need to be registered on your system before they can be used by ASP applications. When you create an ASP component with VB 5.0, Visual Basic automatically registers it on your system. In order for your ASP component to function properly, it must be registered on the target computer (unless the component was developed on that computer). To register an ASP component, open a command prompt window, change to the directory containing the ASP component file, and type the following command:

```
REGSVR32 <ASPComponentFile.dll>
```

Replace `<ASPComponentFile.dll>` with the name of the ASP component file. After the component is registered, you will see a conformation message (see Figure 10.11).

Figure 10.11.
The ASP component was successfully registered.

Do   **Don't**

DO keep all your custom ASP components in one directory to make it easier to keep track of them. `C:\WINNT\system32\inetsrv\ASP\Cmpnts` is a good location because components shipped with Active Server Pages are stored there as well.

Do	Don't

DO install at least a minimal version of Visual Basic 5.0 on the production Web server. This will ensure that all the files needed to execute VB applications are properly installed. As an added incentive, the VB installation can be used to debug your ASP component if necessary.

Summary

Custom ASP components can be developed through the use of a variety of application development environments that allow the creation of ActiveX controls. Visual Basic 5.0 can be easily used to develop custom ASP components. Your VBScript skills can be leveraged to develop custom ASP components because Visual Basic is very similar to VBScript. Custom ASP components promote data encapsulation, easy code distribution, security, and centralized code management. When developing large projects, you should create your own custom ASP components to handle those tasks that can be more efficiently and easily carried out through the use of another application development environment such as Visual Basic or Visual C++. You will then be able to mix and match the best features of each application development environment. Do not develop overly complicated ASP components. Concentrate on developing well-defined, small, and efficient ASP components that handle a certain task extremely well. You will then be able to efficiently reuse your custom ASP components when you develop future Web applications. Think of ActiveX components as bricks that you use to develop a large structure. If the bricks are too small, the project will become unnecessarily complicated; if the bricks are too large, you will not be able to design a refined structure.

What's Next?

Microsoft Visual InterDev is a rapid application development (RAD) tool for developing interactive Web applications. Tomorrow, you will learn how Microsoft Visual InterDev's integrated development environment (IDE) can be used to develop ASP applications.

10

Q&A

Q I need to display the current date and time on a Web page. Should I create an ASP component to display the time?

A For a task as simple as displaying the current time, I do not recommend that you create an ASP component. The current date and time can be displayed by simply using the ASP statement `<%= "This Web page generated on " & Date & " at " & Time & "." %>`. Consider creating an ASP component when you need to perform a task outlined in the section "Benefits of Developing Custom ASP Components."

Q I just finished creating an ASP component, and now it has to be moved to my production Web server. How do I register it on my production server?

A Register an ASP component register on another computer by opening a command prompt window, changing to the directory containing the ASP component (the DLL file), and typing the command `REGSVR32 <ASPComponentFile.dll>`. Replace `<ASPComponentFile.dll>` with the name of the ASP component file, and you will see a message confirming that the ASP component was successfully registered.

Q After I made some changes and recompiled my ASP application, Visual Basic informed me that it cannot replace the DLL file. How can I fix this?

A Most likely, the DLL file is being used by the World Wide Web publishing service. Temporarily stop the World Wide Web publishing service using the command `net stop "World Wide Web publishing service"` so Visual Basic can replace the DLL file. Do not forget to restart the World Wide Web publishing service using the command `net start "World Wide Web publishing service"`.

Q How can I write HTML text directly to the Web browser from an ASP component?

A HTML text can be directly written to the Web browser by getting a reference to the `ScriptingContext` object in the `OnStartPage` method of the ASP component and saving the reference for future use. The `Write` method of the `Response` object can then be used to write HTML directly to the Web browser.

Exercises

1. Develop a custom ASP component that can be used to change the system date/time.
2. Transfer the ASP component created in Exercise 1 to another IIS 3.0 Web server by properly registering it and calling it from an ASP application.

10

Chapter 11

Introduction to Microsoft Visual InterDev

by Kelly Held

Visual InterDev is the newest member of Microsoft Visual Studio 97. Visual Studio 97 is a suite of visual development tools designed to help programmers create applications in an integrated, GUI-driven environment. Currently, Visual Studio 97 consists of

☐ Visual Basic 5.0

☐ Visual C++ 5.0

☐ Visual FoxPro 5.0

☐ Visual J++ 1.1

☐ Visual InterDev

☐ Microsoft Developers Network (MSDN)

Visual InterDev allows you to develop Web page applications based on the HTML standard, Active Server Pages, and any of the custom components you produce.

Why use Visual InterDev? There is in fact almost nothing you can do with Visual InterDev that you could not do with Notepad, ASP, or any third-party applications such as image editors, FTP clients, HTML editors, and the like. What Visual InterDev has to offer is an integrated development environment where you can do everything you need from one familiar GUI-based tool. It allows for rapid application development (RAD) on a team or an individual basis. Microsoft specifically cites the following features and benefits in Visual InterDev:

- ☐ Rapid, visual development
- ☐ Powerful, integrated database tools
- ☐ Team-based and standalone project development
- ☐ Standards-based results viewable from standards-based client browsers

Microsoft is really targeting the professional developer with this product. It is, in my opinion, the first product on the market that is suitable for the professional development of Web applications from start to finish, all integrated into a single package. If you are in the corporate world, one of InterDev's best features is its capability to work in a team-based environment with other Web developers as well as Web authors.

It is important to make a distinction here. If you are reading this book, you are a Web developer (a programmer). Visual InterDev is a development tool. However, with WYSIWYG HTML authoring tools such as FrontPage 97, more and more nonprogrammers are contributing to Web content. For example, marketing might work on wording and page layout in FrontPage 97 while you work out the details of forms and the database interface in Visual InterDev. The two tools, FrontPage and Visual InterDev, have a lot in common, but are geared toward different audiences. The exciting thing is that they are so well integrated.

If you are used to working in teams, Visual InterDev has another strong point: It integrates with Microsoft Visual SourceSafe. This allows users to work on projects together without conflicting, losing old code, or worrying about revisions.

The database tools make working with ActiveX Data Objects (refer to Day 8, "Introduction to Web Database Programming Using ActiveX Data Objects") and SQL Server 6.5 much easier. From within Visual InterDev, you can link up many data sources and build optimized queries for your ODBC data stores. The links to your databases are live, so you do not have to guess or wait until runtime to see the results. There is even point-and-click administration for SQL Server 6.5 databases.

Finally, you will find something in Visual InterDev that cannot be found elsewhere just yet: *design time ActiveX controls*. These are used to generate scripting and scripting logic in Visual

InterDev. Design time controls are different from standard controls in that they contain no binary runtime code; their output is client-independent scripting. Design time controls are still based on the Microsoft COM and DCOM models, with the benefits of component software. You or third parties might also develop new design time ActiveX controls to augment the more than 15 controls that come standard with Visual InterDev.

After you go through the installation procedure today, you will see screenshots and an introduction to this newest member of the visual tools family. Tomorrow you will develop a sample application with Visual InterDev. You will find that it can make your life as an ASP developer much easier.

 TIP

If you need more specific marketing information on Visual InterDev, visit www.microsoft.com/vinterdev. You can also find the latest news and samples there.

What Is Included with Visual InterDev?

Visual InterDev has everything you need to get started with Web development using ASP. It includes both client and server components. You should already have a server and Active Server Pages installed; if you do not, you can install them from the Visual InterDev CD-ROM.

The following server components are included

- ☐ Personal Web Server
- ☐ Active Server Pages
- ☐ FrontPage server extensions

The following client components are included

- ☐ Visual InterDev Client
- ☐ Image Composer 1.0
- ☐ Media Manager 1.0
- ☐ Music Producer 1.0

Image Composer, Media Manager, and Music Producer are optional, but allow you to build more sophisticated Web sites.

You probably already have the server components (or at least recognize them from earlier chapters). ASP and the FrontPage extensions are available via Microsoft's Web site.

Notice that Visual InterDev is not just a development and authoring tool, but also a deployment tool. After you finish developing, you can upload and even manage your content on any server that supports FrontPage via FrontPage server extensions.

Web servers are provided so that you can test your work in a standalone environment. Personal Web Server is the Windows 95 version of IIS. It also supports ASP. This product is included so that you can develop and test your ASP applications on a Windows 95 workstation. You can also develop from Windows NT workstations by using the Peer Web Services product that is included on the Workstation CD.

Although the server components might be familiar to you, the client components will not be familiar. The Visual InterDev client contains all the integrated tools you need to develop and deploy your ASP applications. Besides the development environment, Microsoft has provided a few tools that have been until now in the domain of third parties. Microsoft's goal is to give you all the basic tools you need in a single package, so you have no need to hunt for, learn, or use any third-party tools. You will definitely want to install the Visual InterDev client, and I'll talk more about this component after installation. Before you install the other InterDev client components, you will want to have an idea of what they are and what they do.

Image Composer

Image Composer might be Microsoft's answer to Adobe Photoshop. Although Image Composer is not as advanced or developed as Photoshop, the Photoshop user will notice many similarities in the products. The most obvious is Image Composer's capability to use standard plug-ins, including Photoshop plug-ins. Using Image Composer, you can create advanced images for your Web pages or for other purposes. Figure 11.1 shows a screenshot of the Image Composer workspace.

Figure 11.1.
The Microsoft Image Composer 1.0 workspace.

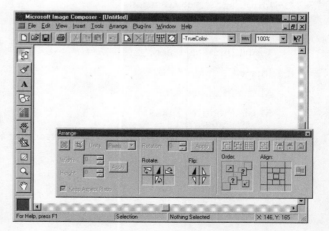

Inside Image Composer, you can create a new image, directly scan an image from a TWAIN source, or combine and modify other saved images. Image Composer currently recognizes the following formats:

- [ ] TIFF (*.TIF)
- [ ] CompuServe GIF (*.GIF)
- [ ] JPEG (*.JPG)
- [ ] Targa (*.TGA)
- [ ] Photoshop (*.PSD)
- [ ] Microsoft composition (*.MIC)

The last entry, Microsoft's new standard, is called a *composition*. A composition is object-based; the basic image object is known as a *sprite*. Sprites are defined by a shape, transparency, and bounding box. Image Composer comes standard with many sample images that can be imported into your composition as sprites. Sprites can be acted on as individual objects; in this way they are much like layers (but more advanced). Figure 11.2 shows an example of a composition. You can find this example and many more in the help files of Image Composer.

Figure 11.2.

A sample composition created with Microsoft Image Composer.

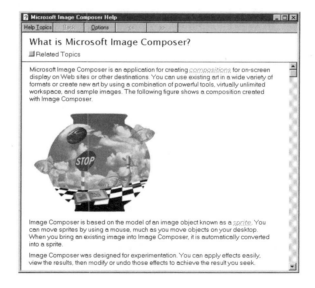

Be careful when creating images. The only universally supported image files on the Web are JPEG and GIF image formats. Others may not be supported by all browsers or even at all.

Granted, you cannot do everything you need to in Image Composer; animated GIFs are conspicuously missing. If you are not accustomed to using graphics programs, some of the more powerful features might be hard to use. Also, Image Composer will probably not make you an artist if you are not one already. However, if you want to experiment with a powerful tool that is very likely to mature, you should install Image Composer.

Music Producer

Microsoft Music Producer makes it easy for you to create original music that can be used on Web pages or other applications. Music Producer supports two standard file formats: Microsoft Music Technology (*.MMT) and MIDI (*.MID).

Music Producer creates and plays musical compositions (not to be confused with Image Composer's graphic compositions). A composition has seven characteristics that you can alter to change its sound:

- ☐ Key
- ☐ Tempo
- ☐ Style
- ☐ Personality
- ☐ Instrument
- ☐ Shape
- ☐ Length

From inside Music Producer, you can change these characteristics and vastly alter the sound of a composition. Figure 11.3 shows the controls.

Best of all, you don't have to know anything about music to create original and catchy sounds. All you have to do is play with the controls until you find the sound you like. You can modify the sample compositions or create you own. Just click Compose.

Figure 11.3.
Microsoft Music Producer.

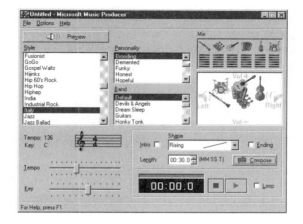

Media Manager

Media Manager helps you track and manage your multimedia and Office files. This is an important tool because you can accumulate quite a library when working with a Web project, and filenames are not always as descriptive as you would like.

Media Manager uses a different type of folder or container to help track your files. Type-specific information is extracted and is viewalbe for supported file types. You can easily add or remove files from a Media Manager folder just by dragging and dropping.

After installing Media Manager, you will see three new multimedia folders, as in Figure 11.4.

Figure 11.4.
The multimedia container for Media Manager.

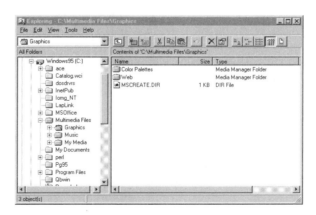

Media Manager uses two methods to track your multimedia. The first method is a searchable annotations database. Annotating where and how you use or intend to use a file will make it easier for you to track it, and is essential in a team-based environment. The second method Media Manager uses to help you track and manage your files is direct browsing from Explorer.

Direct browsing involves different concepts for different types of files, but the idea is to preview your files without a third-party application. For graphics files, this means that you can preview thumbnails directly from Explorer. From the View pull-down in Windows Explorer, choose Thumbnail. Figure 11.5 shows you some of the sample pictures that are installed in the Media Manager installation process.

Figure 11.5.

Thumbnail views of graphics that are inside multimedia containers.

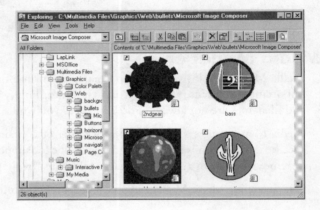

Direct browsing for audio files means playing from within Explorer. Microsoft calls this capability *play in place*. The installation installs only interactive multimedia files that work with the Music Producer product; these cannot be used with the play-in-place feature. However, if you are using Windows 95, you can see how play in place works by dragging a .wav file from the windows/media directory into a Media Manager folder (any sound file will do). To use play in place, you must be in Thumbnail view as described previously. Each audio file now has a Play button that you can use to hear the sound from within Windows Explorer, as shown in Figure 11.6.

You can add annotations to your media files by editing their properties. Right-click any Media Manager file and select Properties from the pop-up menu. Figure 11.7 shows the Properties window of an audio multimedia file.

11

Figure 11.6.

Using the play-in-place feature of Media Manager.

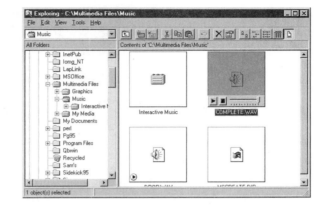

Using the Annotations tab, you can add your own text to describe different annotation properties for the media files. Several annotation properties are built in, and you can add your own using the Modify button. The file in Figure 11.7 has several annotations.

You can search for multimedia files using Media Manager Find, which is available from the Start menu or from the Tools menu of Windows Explorer. You can search based on any of the properties set in the Annotations tab or you can perform a full-text search! Figure 11.8 shows the Media Manager Find tool.

Figure 11.7.

Adding annotations to Media Manager files.

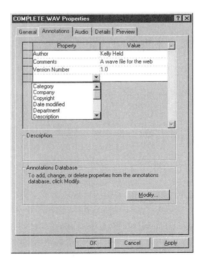

Figure 11.8.

The Media Manager
Find tool.

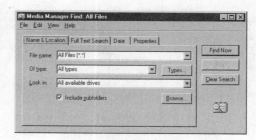

System Requirements

Before installing any product, you should always check the system requirements to make sure your computer can run the application. Requirements listed on the box are always minimum requirements. To get the performance you expect out of Visual InterDev, you will want to exceed the requirements in the places indicated. The following list tells you what you need to make full use of Visual InterDev.

Hardware requirements and recommendations include the following:

☐ InterDev runs only on Intel-based PCs. Microsoft requires a 486 CPU, but I suggest a Pentium 133 or better. This is especially true if you are testing your applications with a Web server and browser installed on the same computer and likely running at the same time.

☐ InterDev requires 16MB of RAM if you are running Windows 95 and 24MB if you are running NT. I suggest 32MB to be comfortable.

☐ InterDev installs via CD-ROM, so you will need one unless you plan on down-loading it from the Web.

 TIP
> Microsoft has added a new online purchase and download feature on its Web site, and Visual InterDev is one of the products you can download. Just be prepared for a 26-hour download at 14.4Kbps!

☐ If you install the minimum, you will need 40MB of hard-drive space. The typical installation requires 65MB of hard-drive space and the full install takes up 100MB. Remember to leave room for your swap file to grow; it probably will when you start developing. If you are developing intensive multimedia applications, consider a high-performance drive specially designed for audio and video.

TIP

Windows 95 and NT both build swap files that are extensions of your physical memory. You can see where the swap file is installed by using the System applet in the control panel. If you install Visual InterDev on a drive with a swap file, leave room for the swap file to grow. As a rule of thumb, you should never let a drive with a swap file have less than 20MB of free space.

☐ You will need a VGA card that supports 256,000 colors and a monitor capable of rendering VGA resolution and color. If you plan to work with Image Composer or other graphics, consider a higher-end card. I suggest a PCI card with at least 2MB of RAM.

☐ A sound card is optional. If you plan to use the Music Producer, you will want the sound card; otherwise, it is not needed.

☐ A mouse is required. Hotkeys are still there, but with all the visual tools, you really need that mouse.

Software requirements and recommendations include the following:

☐ Operating systems: Windows 95, Windows NT Server 4.0, or Windows NT Workstation. You can fully develop an application on any of these platforms, so you have maximum flexibility of where you work.

☐ Web hosting: Microsoft lists Web hosting software as optional, but you cannot test your applications without a Web server. Microsoft has three Web servers you could use, or you could use your ISP's server (IIS, I hope) to test your applications.

Preparing for Installation

Before you start with Visual InterDev, there are a few things to consider:

☐ Ensure that your server meets the minimum requirements listed in the previous section.

☐ Everything needs to be up to date. Visual InterDev works with and integrates all the components listed in the preceding sections. Therefore, you should have the current components installed. If you have a beta version of ASP or Visual InterDev, you should uninstall it.

NOTE

The beta version of Visual InterDev has several keys, listed next, that should be removed using `REGEDIT.EXE` (see Day 13, "Advanced Topics," for more information about `REGEDIT.EXE`):

- [ ] `HKEY_CURRENT_USER\Software\Microsoft\Devstudio\5.0\Html`
- [ ] `HKEY_CURRENT_USER\Software\Microsoft\DevStudio\5.0\IstudioProject`
- [ ] `HKEY_CURRENT_USER\Software\Microsoft\FrontPage` (Internet Studio edition)
- [ ] `HKEY_CURRENT_USER\Software\Microsoft\FrontPage` (Visual InterDev edition)
- [ ] `HKEY_CURRENT_USER\Software\Microsoft\FrontPage` (Visual Studio edition)
- [ ] `HKEY_LOCAL_MACHINE\SOFTWARE\Microsoft\DevStudio\5.0\Products\Microsoft Visual InterDev`
- [ ] `HKEY_LOCAL_MACHINE\Software\Microsoft\DevStudio\5.0\Products\Microsoft Internet Studio`

In some cases, you will have to uninstall all the products and delete the directories. *As a last resort only*, beta-testers might have to uninstall all Internet-related programs and manually delete the binary directories. Programs that could cause problems are Internet Explorer, FrontPage, and your Web server. Reinstall these components after uninstalling to get a clean working environment.

If you have not already installed a Web server and the FrontPage extensions, you should do so in the next section. Installing the FrontPage server extensions allows you to make full use of FrontPage and Visual InterDev's live site links. When using a server that has FrontPage server extensions, you can create, delete, and alter content on the Web site. Obviously this is a very powerful tool and, like all powerful tools, it can be abused. In a standalone testing environment, there should be no real security concerns; however, if you are sharing the server with others, you want to make sure your content is protected from accidental or malicious tampering or destruction. To protect your server, you should review the material in Day 13 when installing FrontPage server extensions. If you have already installed FrontPage server extensions, you might want to go back and make sure your setup has the proper security precautions.

For the latest information about Visual InterDev, click Readmes on the install screen (see Figure 11.9). The readme files are in HTML format, so you must use a browser such as Internet Explorer or Netscape Navigator to view them.

NOTE

> You should always read the readmes. They contain the latest information and problem reports that are not included in the help files or manuals of a product. Most users skip installation notes because most people are not affected by what is contained within them. However, you are developing an application and not just playing a game or typing on a word processor. It is much more likely that you will experience problems that are not your fault and that can easily be solved if you just read the readmes.

Installing Visual InterDev

Visual InterDev ships on CD-ROM (or can be downloaded from Microsoft). To get started, simply insert the CD-ROM. If you have enabled autoload, the setup program will automatically launch. If not, you must start the setup.exe program from the command line or Windows Explorer. The very first thing you are required to do is type in your CD-KEY in the Registration window. The CD-KEY is located on the back of your CD-ROM jewel case. This number is very important, and you will need it if you ever have to reinstall Visual InterDev.

Visual InterDev ships with Visual Studio 97, but it can be purchased separately. Figure 11.9 shows the install screen for Visual Studio 97 and its components.

If you are not ready to move into Visual Studio, you can purchase and install Visual InterDev separately. When you insert the Visual InterDev CD-ROM and click the Visual InterDev text shown in Figure 11.10, you reach the Visual InterDev install screen.

After you have read the readme files, you need to decide which components to install. If you are going to do testing on the machine where you are installing Visual InterDev, you will need to install the server components. If you already have the latest version of the server components installed on your machine, you do not need to reinstall them. However, you must have the latest versions and builds.

11

Figure 11.9.

*The Visual Studio 97
install screen.*

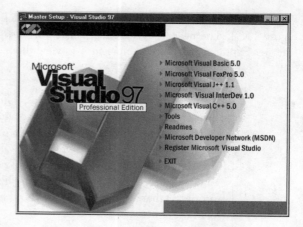

Figure 11.10.

*The Visual InterDev
install screen.*

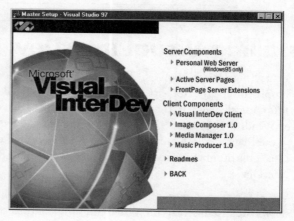

Installing Server Components

To use Visual InterDev, you must have access to a Web server that supports both ASP and FrontPage server extensions. There are only three servers that support both; all are made by Microsoft and all are free. IIS comes with Windows NT Server, Peer Web Services is shipped with NT Workstation 4.0, and the Personal Web Server for Windows 95 comes with the Visual InterDev CD-ROM. You should have installed a server and Active Server Pages on Day 1, "Introduction to Active Server Pages and IIS." If you have not, please refer to Day 1 and do so.

After you have installed a server with Active Server Pages, you need to install the FrontPage 97 server extensions. From the setup screen shown in Figure 11.10, click the FrontPage Server Extensions option to start the install. For the install to proceed, your server must be stopped. Hopefully you have picked a time when there is no traffic to the site and you can continue. Click through the Welcome screen and the license agreement.

On the next screen you can choose where to install FrontPage server extensions. If you already have a version of the server extensions installed, you cannot move the installation directory unless you uninstall the current version and rerun Setup. When you have chosen a directory, click the Next button.

Setup will now detect all the Web servers that are running on your machine. Choose the one on which you want to install the FrontPage server extensions. If Setup does not detect a Web server, you might need to reinstall by following the directions given on Day 1. Click the Next button when you have chosen which Web servers to install on.

The next screen is a confirmation screen. Click the Next button to begin copying the FrontPage server extension files to your machine. If you have a multihosted server (more than one IP address), you must choose which IPs will be FrontPage-enabled. Click the OK button when you have made your decision.

When setup is complete, you should get a dialog box telling you that everything went OK.

SECURITY

> If you installed FrontPage server extensions on a non-NTFS partition, you get a warning about a huge security hole. If you are working on a standalone machine, you have nothing to worry about. If not, consider taking the advice in the dialog box and reinstalling your server and FrontPage extensions on an NTFS partition.

Installing the Visual InterDev Client

After you install the server components, move on to the client components. This section covers the installation of only the Visual InterDev client. The installation of the other client components in not required, and all three are straightforward. For more information about the other client components, see the first section of this chapter.

Make sure that you have closed all other applications before starting. Setup will suggest you close them if you have not done so. Click Visual InterDev Client to start the installation. You will be presented with a welcome box that tells you a little about Visual InterDev. Click Continue. Next you will enter and verify your name, organization, and product ID. Place a copy of the product ID in a safe place; you will need it for registration and technical support. The next dialog box is the license agreement. After reading and agreeing to the license, you are presented with three installation options:

☐ The compact (minimum) installation requires 40MB of disk space.

☐ The typical installation requires 65MB of disk space.

☐ The full installation requires 100MB of disk space.

Just so you can see all the components, click the Custom Installation button. Figure 11.11 shows the possible components. From this screen you can specify the location of the Visual InterDev client. Click the Change Folder button to alter the default location of the files.

Figure 11.11.

Installable options for the Visual InterDev client.

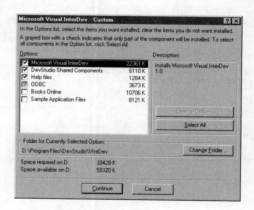

Components shown in Figure 11.11 include the following:

☐ The Microsoft Visual InterDev option installs the binaries and is required.

☐ The DevStudio Shared Components option is applicable only if you are installing Visual InterDev as part of Visual Studio 97.

☐ The Help files option installs the help files onto your hard drive. This option is highly recommended.

☐ The ODBC option installs the drivers necessary to connect you to ODBC data stores. By clicking the Change Options button, you can choose which drivers to install. By default, all drivers except the Oracle driver are installed.

☐ The Books Online option is suggested if you are new to VBScript or development. Remember that you can always remove this option later if you do not need it.

☐ The Sample Application Files option is suggested at least in the beginning.

WARNING

> You do not have to install the Books Online or help file features on your hard drive. You can read both from the CD-ROM. Although this is slower and sometimes less convenient (since you need the CD), it is a good way save space. The Books Online feature can be found on the CD in the `VI1.0\client\sharedide\help` directory.

After you have chosen your options and changed the install directory if necessary, click Continue to start transferring the files and configuring your system. You will need to reboot after the installation process is complete.

The Integrated Development Environment (IDE)

Now that you have Visual InterDev on your hard drive, let's take a look at some of its features up close. The time remaining today is not nearly adequate to cover every part of Visual InterDev in detail. Instead, I want to give you a preview of Visual InterDev's powerful tools and provide a concept model of Visual InterDev.

When you open Visual InterDev, you will see a new shell (shown in Figure 11.12) that will soon be common among all the visual products (Visual J++ and Visual C++ already share this shell).

Remember that all the tools share the same shell and workspace. That means you can have J++, C++, and Visual InterDev projects simultaneously open for integration. Remember: Visual InterDev is a component consumer in the visual tools family.

11

Figure 11.12.

The new visual tools shell.

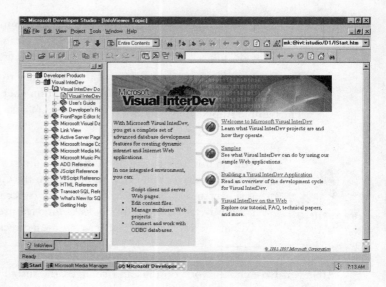

This shell is your launching point for all the features of Visual InterDev. To the left is your project workspace pane, and to the right is a window that can be used for many tasks. I will talk more about the shell and the different panes and views tomorrow.

Visual InterDev contains a multitude of wizards and templates to help you build your application. Select File | New; you will be presented with several choices (see Figure 11.13).

Figure 11.13.

Using wizards and templates in Visual InterDev.

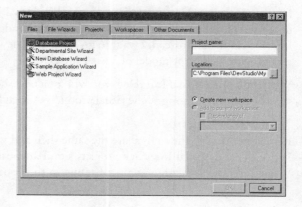

Each tab contains different templates or wizards for creating new objects. You'll learn more about wizards and templates tomorrow; for now, you should just be impressed with the amount of help Visual InterDev gives you in developing your application.

You will want to set some important options in Visual InterDev before moving on. Select Tools | Options, then choose the HTML tab. Your screen should resemble Figure 11.14. Note the box on the right labeled Default Languages. You should select VBScript as your default language for the Script wizard and for Active Server Pages because we decided to use VBScript on Day 1.

Figure 11.14.

Setting the default language.

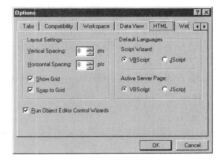

Because Visual InterDev uses HTTP to communicate with the server, you can easily pass through a proxy to retrieve and save your file. Click the Web Project Proxy tab in the Options box; your screen should resemble Figure 11.15.

Figure 11.15.

Setting up a proxy server.

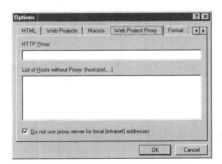

Enter the name of your proxy server in the first box. In the second box, enter a list of servers you connect to that should not go through the proxy. You can specify through the checkbox whether local intranet traffic (on the same subnet) should go through the proxy server.

There are many other options you can select from the Options box, and you might want to customize Visual InterDev after you are comfortable with it. For now, though, you have configured Visual InterDev as much as required to complete the rest of the tasks today and tomorrow. Refer to the Visual InterDev documentation for configuring the other controls. Right now, you are ready to move on and look at what else Visual InterDev has to offer.

Authoring and Site Management

The main purpose of Visual InterDev is to be a RAD tool for creating Web pages and applications that use Active Server Pages, but Visual InterDev is much more than just a scripting engine. It is a full-featured authoring and site-management tool.

The authoring tools in Visual InterDev are extensive. As you have seen, there are many wizards and templates to help you get started. Visual InterDev includes a version of the FrontPage HTML editor, so it provides a WYSIWYG environment for designing Web pages (you'll learn more about FrontPage tomorrow). You can also directly edit HTML or ASP pages from an enhanced text editor.

Next you will create a new ASP file and edit it using the enhanced editor. Select File | New; your screen should look as it did in Figure 11.13. From the Files tab, choose Active Server Pages and click OK. InterDev creates a new ASP scripting page for you with the default language and HTML tags already filled in, as shown in Figure 11.16.

Figure 11.16.

The enhanced HTML and ASP editor.

In Visual InterDev's enhanced editor, HTML tags, attributes, and attribute assignments have different colors while ASP script appears highlighted. Close this file from the File pull-down menu and choose not to save it.

Visual InterDev is standards based, so everything you build is viewable from any browser on any platform. The new HTML 3.2 standard is supported, plus a few other features. There is an HTML Layout tool (see Figure 11.17) to help you with frames and other layout problems. The Layout tool is more of an advanced tool because it is based on a nonstandardized proposal, so not all browsers support this yet. You will learn more about it tomorrow.

Figure 11.17.

The HTML Layout tool.

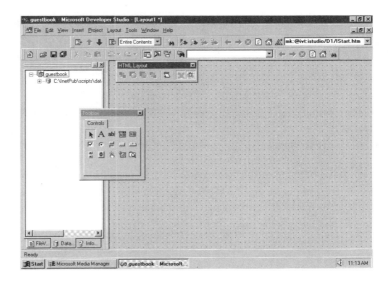

Finally, you can preview the results inside the shell with a built-in, full-featured browser called InfoViewer. The built-in browser includes support for Java, ActiveX controls, and frames. It's a real browser, and if you are connected to the Internet, you can use it. In the upper-right corner of your screen, there is a fill-in box. Try visiting the Sams.net site by typing www.mcp.com/sams in the box; you can actually pull up the page so that your screen resembles Figure 11.18.

Figure 11.18.

*Using InfoViewer, Visual
InterDev's internal
browser.*

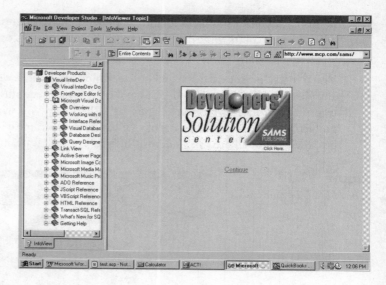

Site management is also important to the developer. You should not have to spend all your
time looking for broken links or changing link names if you change a filename. Visual
InterDev includes Automatic Link Repair, Link Listing, and a Link View to help you track
and manage your links. You will get some practical experience with Link View tomorrow,
but if you have access to a site that supports FrontPage, you can preview its uses now. From
the Tools pull-down menu, select View Links on WWW. Take a look at www.mcp.com—there
are more than just a few links, as shown in Figure 11.19!

Figure 11.19.

Link view of
www.mcp.com.

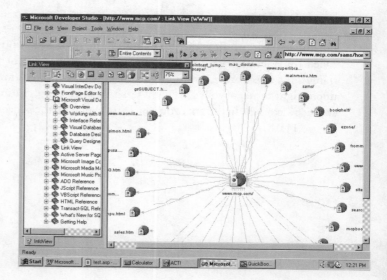

Click a page to see the links contained on that page. In your own projects, you can easily find broken links (which appear red) and you can turn on Automatic Link Repair so that InterDev automatically updates your links when you move files. Remember: Time saved here is time spent developing. But site management is not confined to links. Indeed, you are directly connected to the server if that server is using FrontPage extensions. You can drag and drop content, create new directories, or delete old ones.

Integrated Database Tools

Visual InterDev uses ActiveX Data Objects (ADO) to connect to databases and present information (refer to Day 8). The shell offers many visual tools for creating and organizing links to databases. Refer to Figure 11.13 and note that there is a wizard to get you started on a database project, including a dialog to make the ODBC connection. There are also design time ActiveX controls, which I will discuss more tomorrow.

The important thing is that you have a live link to view your data directly from your ODBC data source. You can use the information from this link to build your SQL queries and design your forms. Use the visual Query Designer in Visual InterDev if you do not feel like designing your queries manually. If you are using a SQL 6.5 data source, there is a built-in Database Designer to help you administer and build your SQL Server databases. The HTML Form Designer will design your HTML forms for you based on database fields. You will learn more about that tomorrow.

Let's jump in and use some of these tools! First you will connect to a database and then you will see your data live and even build a simple query using Visual InterDev.

1. Select File | New, then select the Projects tab.
2. Highlight the Database Project option and fill in the dialog boxes to the right so that your screen resembles the one shown in Figure 11.20. (You will learn more about the Project option tomorrow.)

Figure 11.20.

Creating a database project.

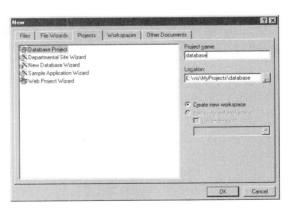

3. Click OK. Now you must choose a data source. The dialog box shown in Figure 11.21 offers two choices: File Data Source or Machine Data Source. Machine Data Source uses a registered DSN name. Every machine that uses this data source must have this DSN registered through the ODBC32 administrator applet. A File Data Source is much more portable, especially if the data file itself resides on a network drive. In this example, you will use the File Data Source, and tomorrow you will use the Machine Data Source.

Figure 11.21.

The Select Data Source dialog box.

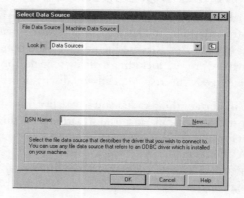

4. You will be using the sample guestbook database file `guestbook.mdb` located on the MCP Web site. If you did not install it on Day 8, do so now. In this example, the `guestbook.mdb` file is installed in the network directory `\\laptop\c\inetpub\scripts\database`.

5. Click the New button shown in Figure 11.21; the next window should be familiar to you from Day 8.

6. Choose the Microsoft Access Driver and click Next. In the next window, give the data source a name. Use `guestbook` and click Next.

7. The next window lets you verify the information you have entered. Click Finish even though there are a few more steps to complete.

8. Now you need to select the database file. In the dialog box shown in Figure 11.22, click Select, locate the `guestbook.mdb` file, and click OK.

9. Click OK one more time to return to the screen shown in Figure 11.21.

10. Choose the newly created `guestbook.dsn` and click OK to finish.

11

Figure 11.22.

Choosing the database file.

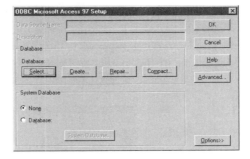

You have just created your first database project. Now you see just what Visual InterDev can do. Expand the data connection by double-clicking the folders until your screen resembles Figure 11.23. There are two folders for your database: The Tables folder contains the tables stored in your database and the Views folder holds the queries contained in your database. Notice that you automatically switch windows as you explore the database. You will learn more about the different views and windows tomorrow.

Figure 11.23.

The expanded database project.

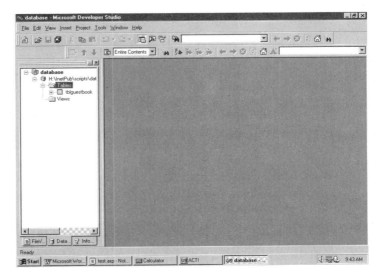

Now double-click the table tblguestbook. What you see on your screen and in Figure 11.24 is a live view of your data. From the floating Query toolbar, you can build SQL queries and save them for later use. You can write them manually and have Visual InterDev verify your work, or you can use the familiar grid plane to build them visually. You cannot perform live edits on your Microsoft Access data from Visual InterDev.

Figure 11.24.

A live view of the data in guestbook.mdb.

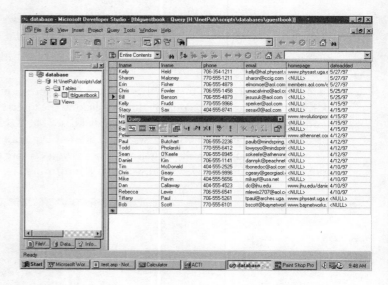

To demonstrate the power of the integrated database tools, let's now build and save a query using the grid pane. Click the Diagram Pane and the Grid Pane buttons on the toolbar (they are the first and second buttons, respectively). You should feel very comfortable with building a query if you have ever worked in Microsoft Access because the interface is almost the same. Place your mouse on the table in the diagram pane (see Figure 11.25) and clear all the checkboxes. All the rows in the grid pane should also be clear because they are connected to the checkboxes in the diagram pane.

Now select the fname box in the diagram pane. Click the Run button (the one with an exclamation point) on the toolbar to see the results live in the results pane. Then save your work from the File pull-down menu. That should do it for you and the database tools today. From the File pull-down menu, select Close Workspace.

Figure 11.25.

The diagram (top), grid (middle), and results (bottom) panes.

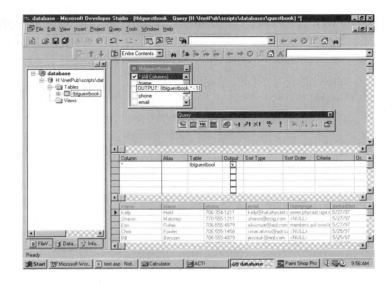

Summary

Microsoft Visual InterDev is the newest member of the Microsoft Visual Studio family. It is designed to make you more productive as a Web developer by making your life easier through use of visual tools and an integrated environment. If you are a developer in one of the other Visual Studio 97 products, you will already be familiar with InterDev's look and feel. If you plan to develop complicated ASP applications, ASP components, or if you work as a member of a team to develop applications, you should invest in Visual InterDev.

What's Next

Tomorrow you will develop an application from start to finish using Visual InterDev. You will learn much more about projects, webs, workspaces, and other concepts in Visual InterDev. You will be amazed at how quickly you can create a professional-looking application that is sophisticated enough to meet even your most demanding needs.

Q&A

Q Is Visual InterDev necessary to develop ASP applications?

A No. Visual InterDev is a tool that allows you to more quickly develop your applications, but unfortunately, it is not free. If you have more time than money, you do not need Visual InterDev. However, if you work in a large, team, deadline-oriented environment, Visual InterDev is invaluable.

Q How does Visual InterDev relate to Microsoft FrontPage 97?

A Visual InterDev is a member of the Visual Studio family, while FrontPage is a member of the Office family. Visual InterDev is geared toward programmers, while FrontPage is built for nonprogrammers.

Q Is it necessary to install Image Composer, Music Producer, and Media Manager?

A No, but they are designed to meet your basic needs so you do not have to deal with other (usually costly) third-party applications. However, Image Composer and Music Producer are not top-of-the-line programs, and they may not meet all your needs. Media Manager, on the other hand, is essential if you have a lot of files to keep up with. It makes finding your work easy, like it should be.

Exercises

1. If you have installed Media Manager, use the Thumbnail view to see some of the sample files. Add annotations to these files or drag some of your own files to a Media Manager folder and annotate those. Finally, conduct a search to find the file you annotated.

2. Click around in the Visual InterDev shell if you have it installed on your hard drive. Try creating new projects or opening the sample workspaces. Tomorrow you will begin a new project of your own.

Chapter **12**

Developing Active Server Pages with Visual InterDev

by Kelly Held

Visual InterDev allows you to develop applications in a very powerful way. It is important to understand how the process works so that you can fully exploit all the benefits that are offered. After receiving an explanation of the basics, you will spend the rest of the day redesigning the guestbook application from Day 8, "Introduction to Web Database Programming Using ActiveX Data Objects."

Visual InterDev's Development Architecture

There are two main concepts you need to understand to build an application in Visual InterDev: projects and workspaces. If you are used to using the visual tools family of products, you already know about workspaces; but the concept of a project might be a little different than what you are used to. Web projects are covered in the next section, and workspaces are covered in the section titled "Workspaces."

Web Projects

Everything you do in Visual InterDev is part of a project. You cannot create a new file without that file being part of a project. However, you can open and edit a file that is not part of a project.

A *project* is a collection of your work that is physically stored on a Web server in a structure called a *web*. A web is simply a virtual directory (and all the files and subdirectories contained in that directory) that is located on the server. The project is really only a file (.dsp) on the client machine that points to the server and web.

Projects reside in their own directories on the Visual InterDev client machine, as they do on the server. The directory name is the same as the name of the root directory on the server. The directory structure of the server's web is also copied into the project's root directory, but working copies of the files are not created until they are needed for editing.

WARNING

There are several things you need to know about folders in Visual InterDev. First, creating a new folder is not done from the File pull-down menu; instead, you must use the Project pull-down menu. Position your cursor where you want the new folder added. From the Project pull-down menu, select Add to Project, and then select New Folder.

Second, your project cannot contain virtual directories inside the virtual root. To use virtual directories, you must create them as new projects in the same workspace (see the next section).

When you edit a file, the Visual InterDev client downloads a working copy to the client machine via HTTP. When you save changes, the file is automatically updated via HTTP. Because the Visual InterDev client communicates with the server via HTTP, no direct connection is necessary, and you can even use a proxy server to connect to the Web server.

Because files are stored on the Web server, many people can work on the same project at the same time. Some people might be working with HTML content using FrontPage, while you might be developing ASP applications. If you are working in a team environment, you will want to refresh the Project pane often to keep up with additions and deletions made by others.

WARNING

> In a team environment, there is the possibility of more than one person working on the same file at the same time. This is not a good idea. Visual InterDev supports the check-in and check-out of files using Visual SourceSafe. If you have Visual SourceSafe, activate this feature by selecting Enable Web Source Control from the Project pull-down menu.

The Visual InterDev developer has some control over project security, but proper security cannot be realized without coordination with the administrator of the Web server. Security in Visual InterDev can be managed on a project-by-project basis. Security is limited to controlling user access and not access type. By default, the project inherits its security from the server root or the parent directory where the virtual directory was created. You can change this behavior from the Project pull-down menu (select Web Permissions). From the first tab, you can specify whether this project inherits permissions. From the second tab, you can specify which users have permission to browse the project's content.

Copy a Web

If you need to work on a deployed project from a standalone machine or if you need to move files from one server to another, you can use the Copy Web feature. This is a very important feature because it allows you to work on a web project from any machine and then deploy the project later. To use the Copy Web feature, select Project | Copy Web; the dialog box shown in Figure 12.1 should appear.

12

Figure 12.1.

The Copy Web dialog box.

You must select a valid destination server. You can choose to connect using Secure Socket Layers (SSL) to protect your data from being intercepted. If you are connecting to an NT machine, you may also be asked to log in to that server.

If you are creating a new web on the server, you should clear the Add to an existing Web checkbox. When creating a new web, the Web Name at Destination entry cannot already exist or the process will fail.

If you will be copying files only to an existing web, enable the Add to an existing Web checkbox. You can save time by enabling the Copy changed files only checkbox. If you are copying the root web, you can also choose to copy or not to copy all the child webs. The last option applies only to root webs.

Click OK when you are finished, and the copy process will begin. If you have a lot of content, the process might take a while. While InterDev is copying a web, you cannot use the program to perform other tasks. That way, you do not make changes to a file while it is being copied.

Workspaces

In Visual InterDev, projects and the related files are further organized into workspaces. A workspace might contain many projects and files. Within the workspace, you, the developer, can integrate all the projects to form a cohesive application.

When you create a new project, that project must be associated with a workspace. You can create a new workspace or add projects to an existing workspace. All projects in a workspace can be viewed, edited, and integrated, because they can share information within Visual InterDev. Projects from different workspaces cannot share information, because only one workspace at a time can be open. If you need related projects and files to share information, they must be in the same workspace.

Do	Don't

DO feel free to use the same project in different workspaces. Remember: Projects are just collections of related files. If you build an application in a modular way, you might be able to reuse some of your projects in different workspaces. For example, you might have a project that functions as a counter. This project could be useful in all your workspaces.

Workspace information is contained inside a DSW workspace file. This file points to different projects and files. Unlike projects, workspaces can contain projects and files located in any directory, not just subdirectories of the project root directory.

The important thing about workspaces is that they can house many heterogeneous projects. Your application might consist of a database project, a Visual Basic project, and several web projects that will all fit together to accomplish your task. Microsoft's development model is modular. Modules of different forms and functions are connected to make the whole. In Visual InterDev, your individual projects should have specific purposes and then be integrated to form the whole of your application.

The Project Workspace Pane

Within workspaces, it is important to keep up with the different projects and project files that each project contains. You can view all the active projects and the related files in a window called the Project Workspace pane. From the View pull-down menu, select Workspace. The Project Workspace pane can be seen in the left portion of Figure 12.2.

Figure 12.2.

The Project Workspace pane.

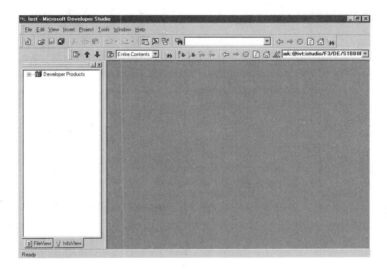

There are three ways to view your projects, but not all views are available for all types of projects. All projects support the File view. From File view, you can see the different projects, project files, and connections. If you double-click files in the Project pane, they are brought up in the default editor. By right-clicking files in the Project pane, you invoke a pop-up menu where you can choose to edit or preview files or properties (more on editing and previewing later).

Data projects and connections have another view called Data view, which allows you to view the different objects inside your data objects. These objects can be tables or stored procedures. Object details in Data view are displayed to the right in a window outside the Project pane but still within the Data view. From here, details can be viewed and in some cases edited live from within Visual InterDev.

The InfoView view allows you to read help files for Visual InterDev or your project. The InfoView browser, which is really an integrated version of Internet Explorer, can be used to preview your work from within Visual InterDev.

 NOTE

> The shell itself (not the Project pane) has other views that you might find useful but that you will not use today. Read the InfoView topic *Developer Studio Environment* from the InfoView pane for more information.

Developing a Sample Application

To illustrate how to use Visual InterDev, we will develop an application together. There are two ways to read this section. You can read along without your computer or Visual InterDev and still learn a great deal from the figures and discussion. Or you can use your own copy of Visual InterDev and the sample files to follow along interactively and learn first-hand the power of Visual InterDev.

If you intend to follow along on your own computer, there are several steps you need to take before you even open Visual InterDev:

1. If you have not already done so, install Visual InterDev, following the directions from yesterday.

2. You will need a connection to the Web server on which you will be working. If there is not one available, you can install IIS, Personal Web Services, or Personal Web Server editions that shipped with the appropriate Microsoft operating system, or on the Visual InterDev CD.

3. You must install FrontPage server extensions on the server you will use. (See Day 11, "Introduction to Microsoft Visual InterDev," for more details on installing the Web server and server extensions).

4. Copy the sample database guestbook.mdb from the MCP Web site onto your hard drive if you did not do so on Day 8.

5. If you did not do so on Day 8, you should create a System DSN entry for the file guestbook.mdb. If the server and client are on different machines, you will have to create the System DSN on each machine, using the ODBC applet.

You are now ready to get started. Open Visual InterDev and select File | New. Choose the Projects tab and select Web Project wizard. Type Sample Guestbook as a project name. Your screen should look something like Figure 12.3.

Figure 12.3.

Creating a new web project.

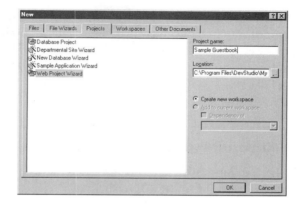

Click OK. The next step requires you to choose the name of the server to which you will be connecting. If the server is on the local machine, you can simply type your machine name. If the server is remote, you should type the fully qualified domain name (FQDN) of the server. If you are not directly connected to the server, make your connection. Note that if you have connected to a server before, it will appear in the pull-down menu, so you do not have to retype it each time.

If you are concerned about security when accessing a remote server, you can choose to connect using SSL so that your information is encrypted before it is sent to the server. After making your selections, click Next.

Visual InterDev will now try to connect to the server you specified. If there is a problem with the server name or your connection to the server, you will receive an error message and be unable to continue. If the connection was successful, your screen will resemble the one in Figure 12.4.

12

Figure 12.4.

Specifying your web when creating a project.

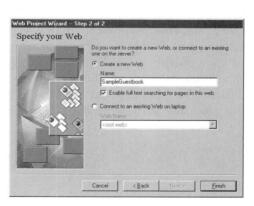

On this screen, you must choose whether to connect to an existing web or create a new one. Remember from earlier today that a web contains all your files. For our purposes, let's create a new web and a new virtual root to house our files. The default name for the new web is the same as the project name stripped of the spaces. If you have Microsoft Index Server 1.1 installed, you can enable full-text searching on your new web. Click Finish to get started on the sample project.

Microsoft Index Server 1.1

IIS 3.0 ships with a new product called Index Server 1.1, which allows users to search your site for text. You could build a search engine yourself to handle searching with ASP if you wish, but Index Server is unique.

First, it is very optimized. Searches are very fast. Second, Index Server allows users to search a wide variety of media for text. Most search engines allow users to search HTML, but Microsoft goes a step further by allowing users to search HTML, text, ASP, and Microsoft Office documents. If you have IIS 3.0, consider installing Index Server 1.1.

NOTE

You can choose to add the project to an existing web. This combines all the functionality into one web. However, for organizational purposes and for sticking with the paradigm of modular and portable code, it is usually better to create a new web that you can link to from your other webs.

You have created your first project. Notice in Figure 12.5 that two files and one folder appear in the Project pane. Use the images folder as a common place to store all your images for your web. It might even be a good idea to nest folders if you have a lot of images to organize. The global.asa file is created but not functional. Double-click it to open the file and see that there are no commands specified inside. The other file pictured, search.htm, is created only if you chose to make your web searchable.

12

Figure 12.5.
Your first project.

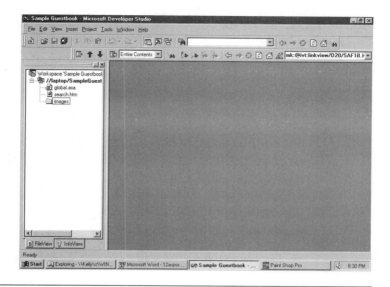

WARNING

Visual InterDev does not close a file until you tell it to do so. You can easily have 30 or more windows open at a time if you are not careful. This not only makes organization difficult, it also taxes resources. Make sure you close files you do not need, and make sure you do not open two copies of the same file. To see what files are open, use the Window pull-down menu.

Now that you have created your project, all you have to do is add files, pages, and scripting to it. The first thing you want to add to your project is a database connection:

1. Select Project | Add To Project.
2. Click Data Connection.
3. The resulting screen lets you select a data source. The first tab, File Data Source, allows you to set up a new data source. You have already set up your data source, so you want to select the second tab: Machine Data Source.
4. Choose the guestbook DSN, as shown in Figure 12.6. Although you might not have as many installed DSNs as are shown in Figure 12.6, you should have the guestbook DSN.

12

Figure 12.6.

Choosing the machine data source DSN.

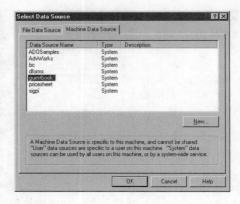

 TIP

If you are working in a team environment, you might want to select File DSN. This is a bit more difficult to set up, but when done, makes your application very portable across Visual InterDev clients. This is because developers do not have to install the System DSN on their workstation or the Web server to access the data as they do with the System Data Source choice.

You have added a database connection to your project workspace. Note that the default name `DataConn` was used for your connection. Your Project pane should resemble Figure 12.7.

Figure 12.7.

The workspace with the data connection added.

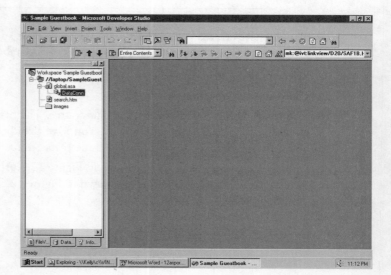

Note that the data connection is associated with the global.asa file and not with the project in general. This is because the connection to the database is made in the global.asa file by default. Open the global.asa file by double-clicking it. You will see that the following lines have been added:

```
</SCRIPT>
<SCRIPT LANGUAGE=VBScript RUNAT=Server>
Sub Session_OnStart
'==Visual InterDev Generated - DataConnection startspan==
'--Project Data Connection
    Session("DataConn_ConnectionString") ="DSN=guestbook;
➡DBQ=C:\InetPub\scripts\databases\guestbook.mdb;
➡DriverId=25;FIL=MSAccess;MaxBufferSize=512;PageTimeout 5;"
Session("DataConn_ConnectionTimeout") = 15
Session("DataConn_CommandTimeout") = 30
Session("DataConn_RuntimeUserName") = ""
Session("DataConn_RuntimePassword") = ""
'==Visual InterDev Generated - DataConnection endspan==
End Sub
</SCRIPT>
```

There is not much to notice here; you have just stored some strings in a Session object. A new Session object is created each time a new user accesses the first ASP page. The connection information is stored in the Session object until the session times out or is abandoned (see Day 4, "Web Application Development with ASP Objects," and Day 8 for more information on the global.asa file and ASP objects). Notice that you have not opened a connection, but that you have all the information needed to open one later. The information is conveniently stored in a Session object that can be easily referenced.

You now have everything you need to get started building the guestbook application. You will use most of the tools in Visual InterDev to build this project. The only toolset that is not extensively covered is the database toolset. However, most of your simple database needs can be met with the Data Form wizard.

You do not want to start the application from the default page. The default or home page gives the user directions on how to use the guestbook and explains what the guestbook is. The Connection object is not stored in the Session object until the user decides to use the guestbook. In this way, you avoid wastefully creating a Connection object for every new user if they do not want to use the database.

Now that you have a good idea of how the application is planned, let's jump right in and create one of the pages. You will start with the bottom four pages on the chart, which allow one to view, edit, add, and filter the guestbook. These pages involve complex code, but are easy to create using the Data Form wizard.

12

The Data Form Wizard

The Data Form wizard is a very powerful tool. First, it offers two different views of your data. Form view allows you to see each data field and value one record at a time. List view lets you list your data to the user in Data Sheet view one page at a time. The Data Form wizard allows you to choose which actions you want users to be able to perform on your database. The form it creates has several buttons, so you are able to perform many operations from a single page. You can filter records, add new records, edit the current record, or delete a record.

Select File | New. From the File Wizards tab, choose Data Form Wizard. Name the file guestbook, so that your screen resembles the one in Figure 12.8.

Figure 12.8.

Starting the Data Form wizard.

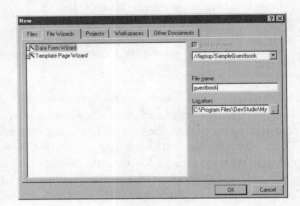

You have started a pretty intense process, and it might take the wizard a minute to display the next screen. There are seven steps in this wizard, so you will see only screenshots of the important or more confusing steps.

Step 1: Choosing the Data Connection

When the next screen appears, you must choose a data connection. Note you have the option of creating a new connection, but you have already made one, so use the DataConn choice in the pull-down menu. Next you want to give this page a title. Use The Guestbook Database. Click Next.

Step 2: Choosing a Record Source

The next screen wants you to decide which type of object you want to build your form from. You have three choices: Table, View, or SQL Statement. Choose Table, because all the information you need is in a single table. If you need to see information from several tables, you should choose a stored procedure or enter an SQL statement that selects the correct fields from each table.

Step 3: Choosing the Fields for the Form

The next screen allows you to choose which table you wish to build from. Choose the table `tblguestbook`. Next, choose which fields from that table you want included on your form. The `dateadded` field is automatically updated, so you want to choose all fields but that one.

Next, choose the order in which you want the fields presented on your form by clicking the arrows at the bottom to move fields up and down. Your screen should resemble Figure 12.9 when you are finished. Finally, click the Advanced button.

Figure 12.9.

Step 3 of the Data Form wizard.

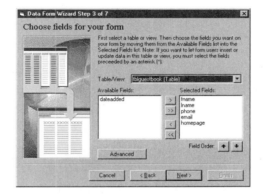

Contrary to the name of the button that led you to this screen, this screen is not really for advanced users at all, and taking this extra step will make your final product much more readable. Chances are you have field names that are descriptive to the programmer, but not to the user. For example, the field name for the first name field in the guestbook database is `fname`. This is not what you want to appear on your form as the label for this field. To change the label, first select the `fname` field in the Field Name box. Type `First Name` in the Alternative field label box. Your screen should resemble Figure 12.10.

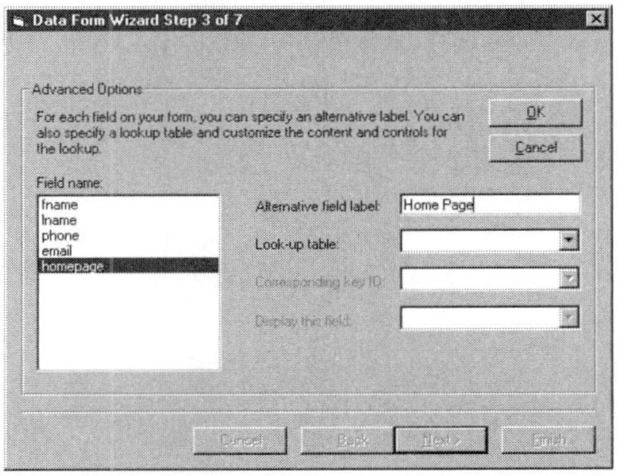

12

Figure 12.10.

The Advanced Options screen.

For this example, you should use the alternative field labels from Table 12.1.

Table 12.1. Alternative field labels.

Field name	Alternative label
fname	First Name
lname	Last Name
phone	Phone
email	E-mail
homepage	Home Page

You will also notice that you can specify a look-up for fields. A look-up gathers information from a field in another table or list. The data retrieved appears as a combo box or menu on your screen, and you can select from the different look-up values when editing or adding a new record. This example does not use look-ups, but they can be very useful tools.

Do   **Don't**

DO use look-ups if you want to limit or define the choices the user has for a field. For example, say you have a field named `state` and a table named `States` with all the states in it. You could use a look-up based on the `States` table to display a drop-down box with all the state names. The user simply chooses his state from the list created by the look-up. No more worries about spelling or abbreviations! See the Visual InterDev documentation for more information on look-ups.

Step 4: Specifying Allowed User Actions

The next screen is where you choose the types of actions you want the user to perform on this database. Essentially, you are giving Visual InterDev enough information to choose an appropriate cursor (refer to Day 8). Allow users to insert new records, browse records, and filter records. Your screen should resemble Figure 12.11.

12

Figure 12.11.
Allowed user actions.

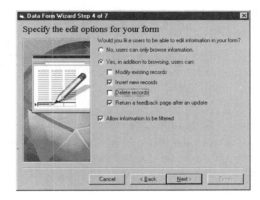

Step 5: Select Viewing Options

From this screen, you specify how data is presented to the user. There are two types of views: List view (or Data Sheet view) and Form view. For List view, you can specify pages and record count per page. Remember from Day 8 that the use of pages requires at minimum a KeySet cursor. For this application, leave all the boxes checked (default). This way you generate code for Form and List view and add a status line that tells which record you are positioned on.

Step 6: Choosing a Theme

Themes and style sheets have been mentioned, but not discussed in depth. Themes and style sheets control the way your pages look and behave. They give your pages a consistent look with the same background, border, link colors, font, and so on. Style sheets have not yet been officially incorporated into HTML 3.2, but Microsoft supports them here.

There are several built-in themes to choose from, and you can even specify your own. The theme names are to the right and a sample layout is to the left. For this application, use the Redside theme. You will notice when you are finished that a folder called Style Sheets, which contains the Redside theme, has been added to your project.

Step 7: Finishing Up

The only thing to do in step 7 is to click Finish. You can use the Back button to go back and check your options before creating the data forms.

When you have finished, there are three new files and a new folder added to your project. The files guestbookAction.asp, guestbookForm.asp, and guestbookList.asp are discussed in more detail in the following sidebar. The only one you need to link to is the guestbookAction.asp file. The others are linked internally to this one. Now let's preview the files.

12

The Data Form Files

It is important to understand the basic function of each generated file if you are going to alter them later. Chances are the generated files will not do everything you want them to do, so you will have to modify them. The name of each file gives away a lot of its function.

The file with the Action extension has all the subroutines that handle the different user actions and displays the correct view or result based on user actions. You can link directly to this file from other pages, and it will default to the Form view if no other view is specified. You can change the default value from within the Action file.

The file with the Form extension handles everything needed to present the information in Form view. This includes data entry and data editing views. The specific data views and which buttons are displayed is based on the FormMode variable passed in the URL. Another important feature is handled inside this file: defining the record set. If you need to alter the record set of the data forms, you can do it here.

The file with the List extension handles everything needed to present the information to the user in List or Data Sheet view. Based on step 5 in the wizard, you can display all records at once or pages at a time. If you need to alter the page size or whether or not to use pages, do so from within this file.

Right-click the guestbookAction.asp file and choose Preview in Browser. Your screen should resemble Figure 12.12.

Figure 12.12.

The finished guestbook in Form view.

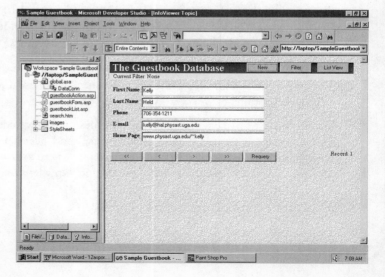

This is the Form view of the database. From here, the user can add information, view all the records, or filter the records for a certain user/users. Try each operation for yourself. Figure 12.13 shows the guestbook in List view.

Figure 12.13.

The finished guestbook in List view.

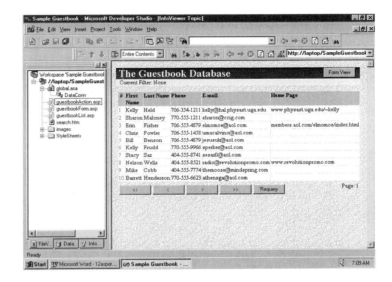

Although you have quickly developed a good-looking page, there is still some work to be done. First, you need to add script so that the dateadded field is handled correctly. Second, you need to include links from both views back to the home page.

Adding Links to the Data Form Files

You need to add a link back to the home page and a mailto: link for changes to the generated data forms. Open guestbookForm.asp with the editor. Use the Page Down key or the Ctrl+End keystroke to move to the end of the file. The section is titled FOOTER. Here you can add code that will appear at the bottom of the page. You could also add code at the top of the page from the section HEADER. You want to insert your HTML before the </BODY> tag but after any VBScript. The insertion point is shown in Listing 12.1.

Listing 12.1. The footer insertion point.

```
<!------------------------- Footer Section ------------------------->
<%
' Display a message if there are no records to show
If strFormMode = "Edit" And fEmptyRecordset Then
Response.Write "<p align=left>No Records Available</p>"
End If
' TEMP: This is here until we get a drop of the data range that has
' the CacheRecordset property
```

continues

Listing 12.1. continued

```
If fNeedRecordset Then
Set Session("rsguestbooktblguestbook_Recordset") = rsguestbooktblguestbook
End If
%>
--> INSERTION POINT IS HERE  <--
</BODY>
</HTML>
```

You now need to add code at the insertion point that gives a link back to the home page and an e-mail link. I used the code in Listing 12.2 to accomplish both goals, with the added feature of tag-lining.

Listing 12.2. Add this text at the insertion point.

```
<P align="center"> <A Href="index.html">Go Back To Home Page</A>
<BR> E-mail changes and deletions to Web Master below.
<HR>
This page is maintained by
<A HREF="http://www.book-connection.com/quantum">Quantum Consulting
Services</A>. &copy; 1997 All Rights Reserved.<BR>
Please direct questions and comments to the
<A HREF="mailto:quantum@book-connection.com">Web Master.</A>
```

NOTE

You might need to set up the preferences of Visual InterDev's internal browser (InfoViewer) to your liking. You can set up the preferences by selecting Options from the Tools pull-down menu. Look for the InfoViewer tab.

Also realize that InfoViewer does not recognize all the HTML 3.2 standards yet. The `<p align="center">` code will not display correctly. Version 3.02 of Internet Explorer does likewise. To fix this behavior, upgrade to a later version.

Preview the changes you made in the browser. Right-click the file you are editing and choose Preview in Browser. Your screen should resemble Figure 12.14.

Figure 12.14.

Preview of the revised data form.

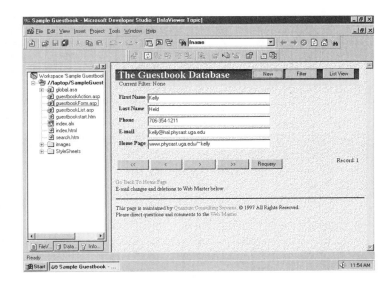

Make this same addition to the FOOTER section of the other generated file, guestbookList.asp. You do not need to edit the guestbookAction.asp file.

Adding the DateAdded Script to the Data Form Files

If you are well versed in the languages of databases and ASP code, you will understand this section. If you still feel a little shaky about dealing with lines and lines of code, you might save this section for later. But don't be daunted; all you are doing is making the guestbook *more* functional.

The dateadded field in the database is automatically updated and should not be presented to the user for fill-in. However, you want the field to update when a new user is added. You don't have time here, but you might also want to display the dateadded field only in List view in the data form.

The dateadded field should be automatically filled in via the now() function when the record is added to the database. To make sure the dateadded field is correctly updated, you need to remember some things from Day 8. Microsoft does a good job of documenting its generated code, so the insertion point for the code you need to add is not difficult to find. You will need to make two changes: one to the guestbookAction.asp file and one to the guestbookForm.asp file.

In the guestbookForm.asp file, look for the section labeled Form Section. You are interested specifically in line 457, where the SQL statement is given. Following is a code snippet from the file that contains the pertinent code.

```
If fNeedRecordset Then
    Set DataConn = Server.CreateObject("ADODB.Connection")
    DataConn.ConnectionTimeout = Session("DataConn_ConnectionTimeout")
    DataConn.CommandTimeout = Session("DataConn_CommandTimeout")
    DataConn.Open Session("DataConn_ConnectionString"),
    ➥Session("DataConn_RuntimeUserName"),
Session("DataConn_RuntimePassword")
    Set cmdTemp = Server.CreateObject("ADODB.Command")
    Set rsguestbooktblguestbook = Server.CreateObject("ADODB.Recordset")
    cmdTemp.CommandText = "SELECT `fname`, `lname`, `phone`, `email`,
    ➥`homepage` FROM `tblguestbook`"
    cmdTemp.CommandType = 1
    Set cmdTemp.ActiveConnection = DataConn
    rsguestbooktblguestbook.Open cmdTemp, , 1, 3
End If
```

Notice that the `dateadded` field is not part of the record set. It needs to be part of the record set so that you can alter it later. Change line 457 to read

```
cmdTemp.CommandText = "SELECT `dateadded`,`fname`, `lname`,
➥`phone`, `email`, `homepage` FROM `tblguestbook`"
```

Now you can change the `dateadded` field later.

The actual updating of the database occurs in the `guestbookAction.asp` file. Open the file in the editor and find the section labeled `Action Handler`. You are interested in the `Case Insert` case. This code is run after the user enters new information and clicks the Insert button, as shown in Figure 12.15.

Figure 12.15.

Inserting a new record.

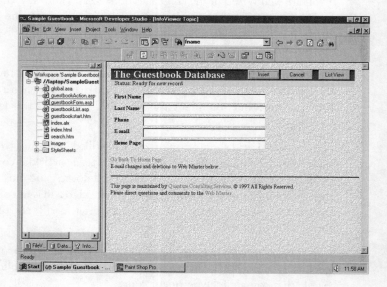

Following is a snippet of the pertinent code, starting at line 487:

```
Case "Insert"
On Error Resume Next
' Make sure we exit and re-process the form if session has timed out
If IsEmpty(Session("rsguestbooktblguestbook_Recordset")) Then
Response.Redirect "guestbookForm.asp?FormMode=Edit"
End If
Set rsguestbooktblguestbook = Session("rsguestbooktblguestbook_Recordset")
rsguestbooktblguestbook.AddNew
Do
If Not InsertField("fname") Then Exit Do
If Not InsertField("lname") Then Exit Do
If Not InsertField("phone") Then Exit Do
If Not InsertField("email") Then Exit Do
If Not InsertField("homepage") Then Exit Do
rsguestbooktblguestbook.Update
Exit Do
Loop
```

The actual record insertion takes place inside the Do loop. To change the dateadded field you need to insert the following line just before the Update method is called:

```
rsguestbooktblguestbook("dateadded")= Now()
```

Now the date and time a user was added to the database will appear as part of his record.

NOTE

It is really not important to follow all the logic of Microsoft's code. Instead, look for the important points such as where the record set is created and where insertion actually occurs. The code is well documented, and you should not have problems customizing the generated code to fit your needs, as long as they are relatively small changes.

12

Creating HTML Content

Now that you are finished with the data form files, you want to create the guestbook application's home page and, later, the Start page. These pages are HTML, so you could use the editor to create the code. However, with Visual InterDev, you do not have to manually create the code. You can use a tool called the FrontPage editor for Visual InterDev for regular HTML or the HTML Layout editor for complex layout of ActiveX controls.

WARNING

Use the FrontPage editor only to edit HTM and HTML files that contain no scripting. If you attempt to use FrontPage to edit a file with scripting, the results will be unpredictable at best.

To create a new blank HTML file, do the following:

1. From the File pull-down menu, select New.
2. From the File tab, choose HTML Page.
3. Name the page index.html.
4. Repeat the previous three steps, but this time name the page guestbookStart.html.

Visual InterDev has generated two blank HTML pages with HTML wrappers for your page. You insert your code between the HTML container tags. Not only can you insert code, you can also insert HTML layouts generated by the Layout tool, HTML generated from wizards, or ActiveX controls. To insert any of these or to edit the page properties, simply right-click the page. Figure 12.16 shows a view of the options on the right-click menu.

Figure 12.16.

The right-click menu for HTML pages.

Creating index.html with the HTML Layout Editor

The home page is really not necessary for this example, but most sites have one. Because you are trying to emulate a full site, you need a home page, even if there is not much on it. The point for today is to learn how to use the tools Visual InterDev has, not to produce a glamorous result. With that in mind, you need only one simple control.

> **NOTE**
>
> Mastering the use of the Layout editor would take most of a day. Worse still is that the Layout editor is based on a draft of a standard and not a standard. You will not find a lot of information about using the Layout editor (which used to be the ActiveX Control Pad). The best place to find information is on the Web at http://www.microsoft.com/layout or at http://www.w3.org/WWW.

Active X controls are really an advanced topic, but you can create a simple control that works without a lot of hassle.

DON'T use the HTML Layout editor unless you know that 100% of your user base is using Internet Explorer 3.0 or later. Pages created using the HTML Layout editor might look very nice in preview, but they will not be available to most browsers. At present only Microsoft's Internet Explorer supports this type of control.

Select New from the File pull-down menu. From the Files tab, select HTML Layout. Name the file `index.alx`. Note that the extensions you use when naming these files are important. You can insert layouts only into files with the extension `.htm`, `.html`, or `.asp`. All layout files should have an extension of `.alx`, and their roots should (as a convention) have a matching `.htm`, `.html`, or `.asp` file (for example, `index.html` and `index.alx`).

When working with layouts, you must realize that creating the layout and generating the HTML code are two separate steps, whereas with most WYSIWYG editors, they comprise a single step.

TIP

You can use the Form Template wizard to automatically link the layout and the code at the same time. Changes to the layout are automatically updated because the layout is linked to the code and not in the code. In this example, you will not use the Form Template wizard.

You should now have a blank HTML layout. Right-click the empty page and select Properties from the pop-up menu. Change the width and height values to `200`. You should now have a square.

From the Controls toolbar, select a command button. To place a button on the layout, place your cursor where you would like the upper-left corner of the control to be. Click and hold the right button and expand the box to the size you want. You can change the label by placing the mouse over the button's text. Place and label a button so that it is similar to the one in Figure 12.17.

12

Figure 12.17.
*Your first command
button.*

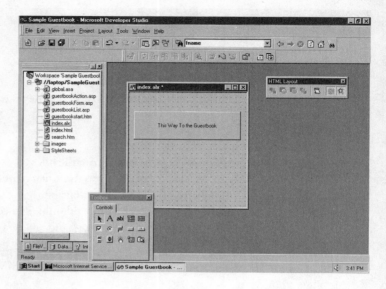

Right-click the new command button. Choose Script Wizard from the pop-up menu or click
the Script Wizard button on the toolbar. The Script wizard (see Figure 12.18) has three
panes. The first window defines an event, the second defines an action you want to associate
with that event, and the third lists event-action relationships.

Figure 12.18.
The Script wizard.

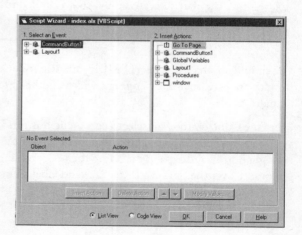

Expand the `CommandButton1` object in the first window. Find and select the `Click` event. In the second window, expand the `window` object. Expand the `location` object under that and double-click the `href` object. In the dialog box, enter the text `guestbookstart.htm`. Your screen should resemble Figure 12.19.

Figure 12.19.

Linking the guestbook Start page to the `Click` *event.*

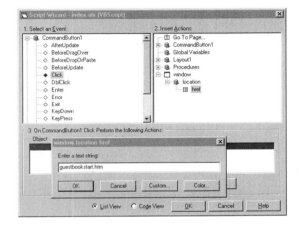

Now when users click the button, they will be linked to the guestbook Start page. Click OK to leave the Scripting wizard. From the File pull-down menu, choose Close. When prompted, select Yes to save changes. Now open `index.html` by double-clicking it or switch to the correct window if it is already open.

Position your cursor at the insertion point `<!--Insert Your HTML code here--!>`. Right-click the mouse and select Insert HTML Layout (refer to Figure 12.15). Choose `index.alx` from the file list. The following code has been inserted into your HTML file.

```
<OBJECT CLASSID="CLSID:812AE312-8B8E-11CF-93C8-00AA00C08FDF"
ID="Html_Layout1" STYLE="LEFT:0;TOP:0">
<PARAM NAME="ALXPATH" REF VALUE="index.alx">
</OBJECT>
```

This code links your HTML file to the blank `index.alx` layout. Notice that because the ALX file is embedded in the HTML file, changes to the `.alx` file appear automatically when the HTML file is displayed.

Finally, you will need to add the link to the guestbook Start page, the tag line, and the theme elements. You will start with the tag line and link. Start at the bottom of the page. Just before the `</BODY>` tag, add the following lines of code:

```
<H1 align="center"><A href="guestbookStart.htm">This Way to Guestbook
</A></H1>
<HR>
This page is maintained by
```

12

```
<A HREF="http://www.book-connection.com/quantum">Quantum Consulting
Services</A>. &copy; 1997 All Rights Reserved.<BR>
Please direct questions and comments to the
<A HREF="mailto:quantum@book-connection.com">Web Master.</A>
```

You now have a link to the guestbook Start page and a tag line. Next you will add the style sheet elements. Move to the top of the page and look for the `<TITLE>` tag. Change the document's title to `Bogus Home Page`. After the `</TITLE>` tag, add the following line:

```
<LINK rel="STYLESHEET" href="./Stylesheets/Redside/Style2.css">
```

Now replace the `<BODY>` tag with the following line:

```
<BODY background="images/redside/background/Back2.jpg" bgcolor="#FFFFFF">
```

Now the home page has a title and will have the same look as the other pages. Right-click the page again and choose Preview in Browser. Your screen should resemble Figure 12.20.

Figure 12.20.
Preview of the
`index.html` *file.*

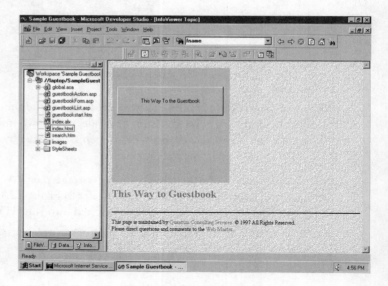

You now have only one more page to create, and this one will be easy.

Creating `GuestbookStart.htm` with FrontPage

Microsoft has made the FrontPage editor for Visual InterDev easy to use, but hard to find. I even reinstalled to make sure I had installed this component. You cannot activate FrontPage editor from any of the pull-down menus. Instead, you must select the file you want to work with in the Project pane and then right-click to get the pop-up menu. Choose Open With. Your screen should resemble Figure 12.21, except that `netscape.exe` will not appear on your screen unless you have installed it yourself.

Figure 12.21.

The Open With screen.

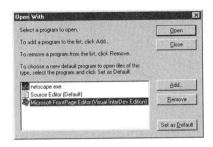

From this screen, you can choose to add your own custom editors. When you save the file in the editor, Visual InterDev knows and deploys the changes to the server. You can use any third-party tool, and can set any tool as your default. Note that the Source editor is the out-of-the-box default.

WARNING

When you create a new file using FrontPage editor for Visual InterDev or another third-party application, that file is not automatically added to your project even if it is in the project directory. You can manually add a file created with FrontPage or another editor from the Project pull-down menu. Select Add To Project | Files.... Add each file manually. Alternatively, you can drag files into your Project pane from Explorer to add them to the project.

Open the guestbookstart.htm file with the FrontPage editor using the previous instructions. The FrontPage editor is a WYSIWYG HTML editor that works a lot like Microsoft Word. Entire books can be written on the use of FrontPage, so in this section you will get only a quick introduction. For more information about FrontPage, see *Laura Lemay's Web Workshop: Microsoft FrontPage 97* or *Teach Yourself Microsoft FrontPage 97 in a Week*, both published by Sams.net.

The first thing you should do is edit the properties of the page so that you can set the background and the title. From the File pull-down menu, select Page Properties. On the General tab, change the title to Guestbook Start Page. Next, choose the Background tab. Check Background Image and type image/redside/background/back2.jpg. Your screen should resemble Figure 12.22.

12

Figure 12.22.

Editing page properties in FrontPage.

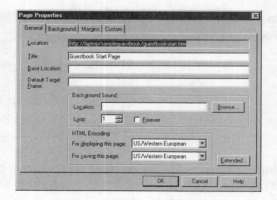

On the first line, type `Guestbook Sample Application`. Highlight the text and change its style to Heading 1. Change the text alignment to center. Your screen should resemble Figure 12.23.

Figure 12.23.

Editing the file `guestbookStart.htm` *with FrontPage.*

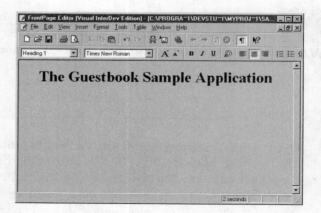

Use the Enter key to get to a new line. Change the style back to normal and alignment back to left. Type the following text exactly as it appears. Do not use the Enter key except at the end of the paragraphs.

```
The Guestbook is a database that contains current information on visitors to
your Web site. You can enter your information, or you can browse or even search
through information of others. However, you cannot make changes even to your own
data.
If changes need to be made, or you would like your name removed then please
e-mail the Web Master below.
```

Now that you have written the instructions, you need to add links to the actual database for those who wish to proceed and links to the home page for those who want to go back. Type the following text with center alignment:

```
Proceed to Guestbook
Nevermind, I Want To Go Back
```

Highlight the first line. From the Insert pull-down menu, select Hyperlink. Under the World Wide Web tab, type `guestbookAction.asp` as the URL. Your screen should resemble Figure 12.24.

Figure 12.24.

Creating a hyperlink with FrontPage.

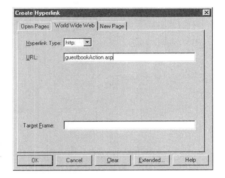

Click OK. Highlight the second line and repeat the procedure, but this time type `index.html` as the URL. You can visually add images and tables to your layouts in the same way, but you have done enough to get the idea. Feel free to experiment with FrontPage at the end of the day.

Save your page and exit FrontPage. Now open `guestbookstart.htm` with the Source editor to see all the generated HTML. You still need to add the tag line to this page, and you might as well do it manually. Add the following HTML to the end of the file just before the `</BODY>` tag.

```
<HR>
This page is maintained by
<A HREF="http://www.book-connection.com/quantum">Quantum Consulting
Services</A>. &copy; 1997 All Rights Reserved.<BR>
Please direct questions and comments to the
<A HREF="mailto:quantum@book-connection.com">Web Master.</A>
```

Save your work and close the file.

12

Using FrontPage editor, it is just as easy to work with tables, images, and all other elements of HTML. Now you can take a look at the finished product. Select the `guestbookstart.htm` file in the Project pane. Right-click it for the pop-up menu. Choose Preview in Browser. Your screen should resemble Figure 12.25.

Figure 12.25.

Preview of `guestbookstart.htm`.

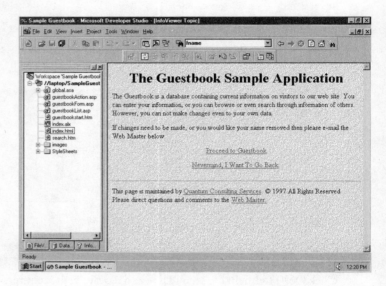

You have finished creating an application that looks great, works well, and did not take a lot of time to develop. What more could you ask for from Visual InterDev? Well, Microsoft thought you might want a little more, so it included even more tools to make your life easier and to help validate your final product.

The Link View Tool and Automatic Link Repair

Visual InterDev includes a Link View tool that is similar to the one found in FrontPage. With the Link View tool, you can see the relationship between different pages and how they are linked together. Link view can also find broken links so they can be repaired before production.

From the Tools pull-down menu, select View Links on WWW. Enter the name of the page from which you wish to start viewing links. You can choose to show incoming as well as outgoing links to that page. The default is outgoing only. Type the `guestbookStart.html` URL. Your screen should resemble Figure 12.26.

Figure 12.26.

The Link View tool.

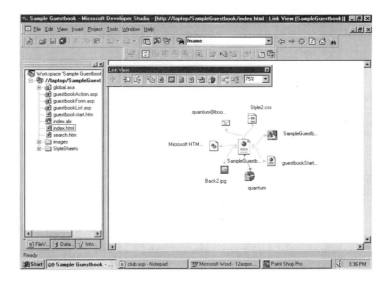

Alternately, you can right-click the file in the Project pane and select View Links.

The image in Figure 12.26 is taken from a standalone machine that is not connected to the Internet, so those links to the Internet appear broken. Notice in Figure 12.26 that you see all objects. You can pick and choose which types of objects you see from the toolbar. Try viewing the link structure of different pages, expanding the links, viewing secondary links, and viewing different object sets in the project. All these tasks can be accomplished from the toolbar. Simply position your mouse over a button to see the pop-up help text on the button's function. Give them all a try.

There are a few time-saving shortcuts in Link view that will make your life easier. By double-clicking any of the objects, you open them with their default editor. By positioning your mouse over a link, you can see the link's full URL. If the link is broken, you also see any server-generated HTTP error codes.

Besides Link view, there is another tool that will make your life as a developer a lot easier. Many times you find that you have to rename files or reorganize the structure of a web. When you do this, you often have to change the hyperlinks that connect those files. Visual InterDev has a feature called Automatic Link Repair. To activate it, select the project in the Project pane. From the View pull-down menu, select Properties. You can also right-click an object to see its properties.

12

> **TIP** There is more overhead involved when Automatic Link Repair is active. If you will not be using this feature, you should deactivate it to increase performance.

Under the General tab is a box called Link Repair. Turn it on to activate link repair. Anytime you change the name of a file, all hyperlinks will be automatically updated to reflect your changes. You can turn this feature on and off as need arises.

Summary

Visual InterDev is a powerful RAD tool for developing Web pages that utilize Active Server Pages. An application is made of one or many projects. All projects are contained in the workspace. Only one workspace can be loaded at one time. You can view the results of your development immediately because your files are automatically updated on the server. You can view the results using the internal browser or a third-party application.

Visual InterDev quickly develops professional-looking pages and complex script. Remember that Visual InterDev does not really understand your application and you might have to make changes to get better performance and functionality. In fact, this might be the hardest part of using Visual InterDev.

What's Next

Tomorrow you will learn about advanced security topics. The Web is a nasty place; if you are going to put information out there that you do not want others to see, you need to take extra steps to ensure that your information remains private. Day 13, "Advanced Topics," covers some of the strategies for keeping data safe and points out some of the places that hackers attack most often.

Q&A

Q How many projects can I work with at one time?

A As many as you need, but organizationally, they should all be related.

Q How many workspaces can I have open at once?

A Only one workspace at a time can be open.

Exercises

1. Use FrontPage to insert an image and a table into the `gueststart.htm` file.

2. Examine Figures 12.12 and 12.13. Notice the record and page numbers, respectively, but that the total number of records or pages is not indicated. Use the `Page.Count` and `Record.Count` properties to display the total records and pages for each view.

3. Edit the `guestbookList.asp` file so that the `dateadded` field is displayed in List view, but not in Form view where it could be edited. Can you display it in Form view so that it cannot be edited or changed when you add a new record?

12

Chapter 13

Advanced Topics

Although you now know how to create various types of ASP applications, topics such as Web server security, server variables, and the use of other scripting languages such as Perl have not yet been covered. Topics covered today will help you realize the potential of Active Server Pages and make your ASP applications more secure. Today, you will learn about the following:

☐ Server variables—These are used to obtain information about the current HTTP session.

☐ Using Perl to script ASP applications—Perl is a powerful scripting language and can be used to develop ASP applications. If you already know Perl, you will be able to immediately leverage your Perl skills to develop ASP applications by the end of the day. If you are new to Perl, I will refer you to Perl resources on the Internet.

☐ Active Server Pages Registry settings—Learn how to customize Active Server Pages using the Registry.

☐ Web server/Active Server Pages security—Security is a most important aspect of any Web application. Use information presented today to enhance the security of your Web server.

Accessing Server Variables

Each time an ASP application is executed, the Web server creates a number of environment variables that contain information about the server, the browser, and how the ASP application is being invoked. This section discusses useful server variables that can be accessed by ASP scripts. By accessing these variables, ASP scripts can obtain useful information about the current HTTP transaction. After you read the following discussion about environment variables, you will be shown how to find their values from an ASP application.

NOTE   Depending on how the ASP script is invoked, some environment variables cannot be available in some cases.

NOTE   Environment variables supplied to ASP scripts are always uppercase. When accessing environmental variables, use all uppercase letters.

AUTH_TYPE

If the Web server has authenticated a user, the authentication type used to validate the user is stored in the AUTH_TYPE variable. The authentication type is determined by an examination of the authorization header that the Web server receives with an HTTP request.

CONTENT_LENGTH

Sometimes ASP applications are invoked with additional information. This information is typically input for the ASP application. The amount of this information is specified by the number of bytes. If an ASP script is called with additional information, CONTENT_LENGTH contains the amount of the input in bytes.

CONTENT_TYPE

MIME content types are used to label types of objects (HTML files, Microsoft Word files, GIF files, and so on). The MIME content type for data being submitted to the ASP script is stored in CONTENT_TYPE. For example, if data is submitted to an ASP script through the use of the GET method, CONTENT_TYPE contains the value application/x-www-form-urlencoded. This is because responses to the form are encoded according to URL specifications.

GATEWAY_INTERFACE

The CGI specification revision number is stored in the GATEWAY_INTERFACE environment variable. The format of this variable is CGI/*revision*. By examining this variable, an ASP application can determine what version of CGI the Web server is using. This variable is particularly useful if your ASP application uses newer CGI specifications and you need to verify that the Web server supports the new CGI specification.

HTTP_ACCEPT

Web clients can handle different MIME types. These MIME types are described in the HTTP_ACCEPT variable. MIME types accepted by the Web client calling the ASP application appear as a list separated by commas. This list takes the format *type/subtype, type/subtype*. For example, if the Web client supports GIF and JPEG image types, the HTTP_ACCEPT list contains the items image/gif, image/jpeg.

HTTP_USER_AGENT

By examining this value, the Web browser being used by the client can be determined. For example, if Netscape 2.0 beta 4 is being used by the client, the HTTP_USER_AGENT variable contains the value Mozilla/2.0b4 (WinNT; I). The general format of this variable is *software/ version library/version*.

PATH_INFO

The PATH_INFO variable is generally used to pass options/input to an ASP program. These options follow the script's URL. Clients can invoke ASP scripts with additional information after the URL of the ASP script. PATH_INFO always contains the string that was used to call the ASP script after the name of the ASP script. For example, PATH_INFO has the value /These/ Are/The/Arguments if the ASP script FunWithNT.ASP is called with the URL http:// your_server.your_domain/cgi-bin/FunWithNT.ASP/These/Are/The/Arguments.

PATH_TRANSLATED

If the ASP script needs to know its absolute pathname, it can obtain this information from PATH_TRANSLATED. For example, if the ASP script being invoked is HelloNTWorld.ASP, the ASP script is physically located at H:\www\http\ns-home\root\cgi-bin, and the ASP script is accessed with the URL http://your_server.your_domain/root/cgi-bin/HelloNTWorld.ASP. PATH_TRANSLATED contains the value H:\www\http\ns-home\root\cgi-bin\HelloNTWorld.ASP. If the ASP program needs to save or access any temporary files in its home directory, it can examine the PATH_TRANSLATED variable to determine its absolute location.

13

QUERY_STRING

You might have noticed that when you submit certain forms, a string of characters appears after a question mark, followed by the URL name of the script being called. This string of characters is referred to as the *query string*, and contains everything after the question mark. When an ASP script is called with the GET method, QUERY_STRING typically contains variables and their values as entered by the person who filled in the form. QUERY_STRING is sometimes used by search engines to examine the input when a form is submitted for a keyword search. For example, if an ASP application is executed using the URL http://www.server.com/cgi-bin/application.asp?WindowsNT=Fun, QUERY_STRING contains the string WindowsNT=Fun.

REMOTE_ADDR

The IP address of the client that called the ASP program is stored in the REMOTE_ADDR environment variable. For security reasons, the value of this variable should never be used for user-authentication purposes. It's not hard to trick your Web server into believing a client is connecting from a false IP address.

REMOTE_HOST

If the Web server performs a DNS lookup of the client's IP address and finds the alias of the IP address, the REMOTE_HOST variable contains that alias. Some Web servers allow DNS lookups to be turned on or off. If you plan to use this variable to find the IP address alias of clients, be sure the DNS lookup option is turned on. The Web server can find the IP address alias of most, but not all, clients. If the Web server cannot find the IP address alias of a client, the REMOTE_HOST variable is not assigned the client's DNS alias value; it contains just the client's IP address. This value should never be used for user-authentication purposes.

REQUEST_METHOD

A client can call an ASP script in a number of ways. The method used by the client to call the ASP script is in the REQUEST_METHOD variable. This variable can have a value such as HEAD, POST, GET, or PUT.

SCRIPT_NAME

Files on a Web server are usually referenced relative to their document root directory. SCRIPT_NAME contains the virtual pathname of the script called relative to the document root directory. For example, if the document root directory is c:\www\http\ns-home\root, all ASP scripts are stored in c:\www\http\ns-home\root\cgi-bin\, and the ASP script HelloNTWorld.asp is called, the SCRIPT_NAME variable contains the value \cgi-bin\HelloWorld.asp. The advantage of this variable is that it allows the ASP script to refer to itself. This is handy if, somewhere in the output, the script's URL needs to be made into a hypertext link.

SERVER_NAME

The domain name of the Web server that invoked the ASP script is stored in SERVER_NAME. This domain name can be an IP address or DNS alias. The SERVER_NAME variable can be used by ASP applications to construct self-referencing URLs with the Web server name.

SERVER_PORT

Typically, Web servers listen to HTTP requests on port 80. However, a Web server can listen to any port that's not in use by another application. An ASP program can determine at what port the Web server is handling HTTP requests by looking at the value of the SERVER_PORT environment variable. When you display self-referencing hypertext links at runtime by examining the contents of SERVER_NAME, be sure to append the port number of the Web server (typically port 80) by concatenating it with the value of SERVER_PORT.

SERVER_PROTOCOL

Web servers speak the Hypertext Transport Protocol (HTTP) language. The version of HTTP that the Web server is using can be determined by examining the SERVER_PROTOCOL environment variable. This variable contains the name and revision data of the protocol being used. This information is in the format *protocol/revision*. For example, if the server speaks HTTP 1.0, this variable has the value HTTP/1.0.

SERVER_SOFTWARE

The name of the Web server that invoked the ASP script is stored in the SERVER_SOFTWARE environment variable. This variable is in the format *name/version*. If an ASP script is designed to use special capabilities of a Web server (such as IIS), the ASP script can determine what Web server is being used by examining this variable before those special capabilities are used.

Accessing Server Variables from ASP Applications

Server variables can be easily accessed by ASP applications through the use of the ServerVariables method of the Request object. The syntax of the ServerVariables method is

```
Request.ServerVariables ("NameOfServerVariableName")
```

NameOfServerVariableName can be replaced with any of the CGI variables discussed in the previous section. For example, the following command can be used to determine the value of the SERVER_SOFTWARE variable:

```
Request.ServerVariables ("SERVER_SOFTWARE")
```

13

Listing 13.1 demonstrates how an ASP application can display all the available server variable values. The application in Listing 13.1 simply uses the `Request.ServerVariables()` method to display the values of server variables. See Figure 13.1 for the output of the ASP script in Listing 13.1.

Listing 13.1. Accessing CGI environment variables from ASP applications.

```
 1: <%@ LANGUAGE="VBSCRIPT" %>
 2: <!DOCTYPE HTML PUBLIC "-//IETF//DTD HTML//EN">
 3: <html>
 4:
 5: <head>
 6: <meta http-equiv="Content-Type"
 7: content="text/html; charset=iso-8859-1">
 8: <title>Accessing Values of Server Variables</title>
 9: </head>
10:
11: <body bgcolor="#FFFFFF">
12:
13: <p><font color="#FF0000" face="Comic Sans MS"><Strong>
14: Server Variables can be used to obtain information about the
15: current HTTP session.
16: </Strong></font></p>
17:
18: <div align="left">
19:
20: <table border="4" width="400">
21:     <tr>
22:         <td width="100" bgcolor="#000000"><font color="#FFFFFF">
23:         <strong>Server Variable</strong></font></td>
24:         <td bgcolor="#000000"><font color="#FFFFFF">
25:         <strong>Value of Server Variable</strong></font></td>
26:     </tr>
27: <%
28:         Dim LoopCount
29:         LoopCount = 0
30:
31:         For Each ServerVariable In Request.ServerVariables
32:         LoopCount = LoopCount + 1
33:         If LoopCount Mod 2 = 0 Then
34: %>
35:         <TR><td bgcolor="#FFDDBB">
36:           <%= ServerVariable %>
37:         </td>
38:         <td bgcolor="#FFDDBB">
39:           <%= Request.ServerVariables(ServerVariable) %>
40:         </td></TR>
41: <%     Else %>
42:         <TR><td bgcolor="#E3FFB0">
43:           <%= ServerVariable %>
44:         </td>
45:         <td bgcolor="#E3FFB0">
```

13

```
46:              <%= Request.ServerVariables(ServerVariable) %>
47:          </td></TR>
48: <%      End If
49:          Next %>
50: </table>
51: </div>
52:
53: <hr>
54:
55: <p>
56: This Web page was generated on <%= Date %> at <%= Time %>.
57: </p>
58: </body>
59: </html>
```

Figure 13.1.
*Output of the ASP
application in
Listing 13.1.*

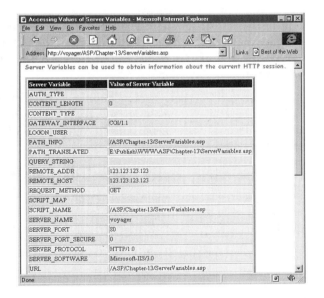

Developing ASP Applications with Perl

13

Practical Extraction and Report Language (Perl) is one of the most widely used CGI scripting languages. In this section, you will learn how to use PerlScript (a version of Perl for Active Server Pages) to develop ASP applications.

Numerous Perl scripts can be found in various Internet Perl script archives. By customizing these scripts to suit your needs, you can easily improve your Web site. A comprehensive tutorial of Perl is beyond the scope of this book. The purpose of this section is to demonstrate how you can use Perl to develop ASP applications.

NOTE

> Perl for Windows NT is available for the Intel and Alpha platforms.

Benefits of Using Perl to Develop ASP Applications

Many of the best features of C, SED, AWK, and sh (these are scripting languages that are most widely used in the UNIX environment) are incorporated into Perl; therefore, you can develop Perl scripts quickly because you don't have to reinvent the wheel for fundamental tasks such as string manipulation. Perl's expression syntax corresponds quite closely to the expression syntax of C programs, which makes Perl very easy to learn if you are already familiar with C.

One of the best things about Perl is its portability. Perl is an interpreted language that is available for several hardware platforms, including PCs, Macs, and different types of UNIX systems. Because of its portability, you will be able to port Perl scripts to Active Server Pages with very few modifications.

Unlike most scripting languages and utilities, Perl does not impose limits on data size. As long as you have enough system resources, Perl will happily read the contents of a multi-megabyte file into a string. Thanks to the optimizing algorithms built into Perl, scripts written in Perl are robust and fast.

Downloading and Installing PerlScript

Before you develop ASP applications using Perl, you must download PerlScript and install it on your system. PerlScript can be freely downloaded from the Internet from http:// www.activeware.com/welcome.htm. Perl for Windows NT is distributed as three files:

- ☐ The Perl for Win32 binary file (available for Intel and Alpha platforms).
- ☐ The PerlScript binary file (available for Intel and Alpha platforms). PerlScript requires the Perl for Win32 binary file.
- ☐ The Perl ISAPI file (available for Intel and Alpha platforms) can be used to develop ISAPI applications in Perl. Perl for ISAPI requires the Perl for Win32 binary file.

You must download at least the Perl for Win32 and PerlScript binary files to develop ASP applications in Perl. Download the files to a temporary directory, and then execute the Perl for Win32 distribution file. Acknowledge the dialog box you see in Figure 13.2 to proceed with the installation.

Figure 13.2.

Execute the Perl for Win32 distribution file to install Perl.

Use the dialog box shown in Figure 13.3 to specify the target directory of Perl for Win32. Either accept the default path or specify a new path, and make sure the checkbox to run `PerlW32-install.bat` is checked. This is to ensure that Perl is installed in your system as soon as the distribution file is decompressed.

Figure 13.3.

Select the target directory of Perl for Win32.

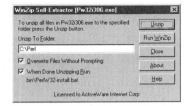

After the Perl distribution file is decompressed, a Windows NT command window runs the Perl installation script, as shown in Figure 13.4. I recommend that you answer yes to all the questions. Perl for Win32 is now installed and ready for use.

Figure 13.4.

Perl for Win32 is installed and ready for use.

Do not copy any Perl for Win32 executable files (such as PERL.EXE) to a CGI directory of your Web server. This enables a user with malicious intentions to execute Windows NT commands by hacking Perl!

13

Before you begin developing ASP applications using Perl, you must install PerlScript in the same directory as Perl for Win32. Execute the PerlScript distribution file to begin installing PerlScript (see Figure 13.5).

Figure 13.5.

Execute the PerlScript distribution file.

The dialog box shown in Figure 13.6 is used to specify the target directory of PerlScript. This directory should be the same as the directory specified in Figure 13.3 (the target directory of Perl for Win32). Make sure the checkbox to run `PerlScript-install.bat` is checked.

Figure 13.6.

Select the target directory of PerlScript.

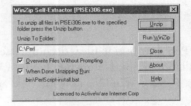

After the PerlScript distribution file is decompressed, a Windows NT command window will run the PerlScript installation script, as shown in Figure 13.7. After the installation script terminates, PerlScript is installed and ready for use.

Figure 13.7.

PerlScript is installed and ready for use.

After you install Perl, log off and log back on for the Perl directory paths to become effective.

Your First Perl Active Server Pages Application

On Day 2, "The Fundamentals of ASP Application Development," you learned how to develop as ASP application using VBScript and JScript at the same time. Now that you have Perl installed on your system, you also can use PerlScript. The ASP application in Listing 13.2 demonstrates how to use VBScript, JScript, and PerlScript in the same application. See Figure 13.8 for the output of the ASP application in Listing 13.2. To use Perl in your ASP applications, simply replace `LANGUAGE=VBSCRIPT` of the `SCRIPT` parameter with `LANGUAGE=PerlScript`, as shown in line 29 of Listing 13.2.

Listing 13.2. Using Perl to develop ASP applications.

```
 1: <%@ LANGUAGE="VBSCRIPT" %>
 2:
 3: <SCRIPT RUNAT=SERVER LANGUAGE=VBSCRIPT>
 4:
 5: Sub UserDefinedVBScriptFunction ()
 6:
 7:   Response.Write("<H3>UserDefinedVBScriptFunction has been called.<BR>")
 8:   Response.Write("Today's date is " & Date & " </H3>")
 9:
10: End Sub
11:
12: </SCRIPT>
13:
14: <SCRIPT RUNAT=SERVER LANGUAGE=JSCRIPT>
15:
16: function  UserDefinedJScriptFunction ()
17: {
18:
19:   var DateObject = new Date()
20:   Response.Write("<H3>UserDefinedJScriptFunction has been called.<BR>")
21:   Response.Write("Today's time is " + DateObject.getHours() + " : " +
22:                  DateObject.getMinutes() + " : " +
23:                  DateObject.getSeconds() + " </H3>")
24:
25: }
26:
27: </SCRIPT>
28:
29: <SCRIPT RUNAT=SERVER LANGUAGE=PerlScript>
30: sub UserDefinedPerlScriptFunction
31: {
32:
33:   $BrowserCapabilities = $Server->CreateObject("MSWC.BrowserType");
34:
35:   $Response->write
36:     ("<H3>UserDefinedJScriptFunction has been called.<BR>");
37:   $Response->write
38:     ("The Web browsre you are using is ");
39:   $Response->write ($BrowserCapabilities->browser);
40:   $Response->write ($BrowserCapabilities->version);
41:   $Response->write ("</H3>");
42:
43: }
44: </SCRIPT>
45:
46: <HTML>
47: <HEAD>
48: <META HTTP-EQUIV="Content-Type"
49:       content="text/html; charset=iso-8859-1">
50: <TITLE>
51:   Using PerlScript With VBScript And JScript
52: </TITLE>
53: </HEAD>
54:
```

13

continues

Listing 13.2. continued

```
55: <BODY bgcolor="#DBFFBF" link="#0000FF" vlink="#800080">
56:
57: <TABLE BORDER=3><TR><TD>
58: <H1>VBScript, JScript, and PerlScript can be used in
59: the same ASP application!</H1>
60: </TD></TR></TABLE>
61:
62: <H2>About to call VBScript subroutine</H2>
63: <% Call UserDefinedVBScriptFunction %>
64:
65: <HR>
66:
67: <H2>About to call JScript subroutine</H2>
68: <% Call UserDefinedJScriptFunction %>
69:
70: <HR>
71:
72: <H2>About to call PerlScript subroutine</H2>
73: <% Call UserDefinedPerlScriptFunction %>
74:
75: </BODY>
76: </HTML>
```

Figure 13.8.

VBScript, JScript, and PerlScript can be used at the same time.

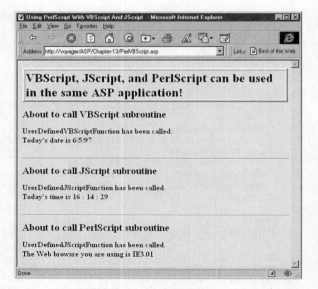

NOTE

To learn more about developing ASP applications with Perl, experiment with PerlScript sample applications found in `C:\Perl\aspSamples` (assuming you installed Perl in the `C:\Perl` directory).

Perl Resources on the Internet

You might want to visit the following sites for sample Perl scripts and general information about Perl.

Yahoo!

Visit Yahoo!'s page about Web programming with Perl scripts at the following URL:

```
http://www.yahoo.com/Computers_and_Internet/Internet/World_Wide_Web/Programming/
PERL_Scripts/
```

Check out Yahoo!'s Web page about Internet applications of Perl at the following URL:

```
http://www.yahoo.com/Computers_and_Internet/Languages/PERL/
```

Mailing Lists

To keep abreast of the latest news on Perl for Windows NT, join the following mailing lists:

- ☐ PERL-Win32—To subscribe, send an e-mail message to majordomo@mail.hip.com and include subscribe PERL-Win32 in the message body.

> **NOTE**   The Perl discussion list is a relatively high-volume list. However, this list is read by many Windows NT Perl programmers, and answers virtually any question you might have about Perl for Win32.

- ☐ PERL-Win32_announce—Perl announcements. To subscribe, send an e-mail message to majordomo@mail.hip.com and include subscribe PERL-Win32_announce in the message body.

Active Server Pages Registry Settings

Various options and features of Active Server Pages can be customized through the use of the Windows NT Registry. Be very careful when editing the Windows NT Registry; never change or delete a Windows NT Registry setting unless you completely understand the ramifications of your actions. An improper Registry modification can result in the required reinstallation of Windows NT. The following Registry values can be modified by executing the Windows NT Registry editor located at C:\WINNT\system32\regedt32.exe.

Allowing Session States

By default, Active Server Pages keeps track of user sessions using a cookie. You can disable this feature by setting this Registry value to 0. After this Registry setting is changed and IIS is restarted, session ID cookies will not be sent to Web browsers. I do not recommend that you modify this Registry value unless you have a very good reason for doing so (for example, if none of your Web browsers allows cookies).

Default Value:

1

Data Type:

REG_DWORD

Registry Key:

```
HKEY_LOCAL_MACHINE\SYSTEM
\CurrentControlSet
 \Services
  \W3SVC
   \ASP
    \Parameters
     \ AllowSessionState
```

NOTE   You must stop and restart IIS if you change this Registry key.

Buffering ASP Output

Active Server Pages can be configured to buffer output to the browser. By default, buffering is turned off (this is why you had to specify HTTP headers before outputting any HTML text). If you set this value to 1, you can specify HTTP headers anywhere in your ASP application.

NOTE   You can use the Buffer method of the Response object to override this Registry value.

Default Value:

0

Data Type:

REG_DWORD

Registry Key:

```
HKEY_LOCAL_MACHINE\SYSTEM
\CurrentControlSet
 \Services
  \W3SVC
   \ASP
    \Parameters
     \ BufferingOn
```

13

NOTE You do not need to stop and restart IIS if you change this Registry key.

Specifying the Default Scripting Language

Use this Registry setting to specify the default scripting language used by ASP applications.

Default Value:

VBScript

Data Type:

REG_SZRange

Registry Key:

```
HKEY_LOCAL_MACHINE\SYSTEM
\CurrentControlSet
 \Services
  \W3SVC
   \ASP
    \Parameters
     \DefaultScriptLanguage
```

NOTE You must stop and restart IIS if you change this Registry key.

Allowing Paths Relative to the Current Directory

This Registry setting specifies whether Active Server Pages should allow paths relative to the current directory. If this value is set to 0 (false), Active Server Pages cannot access files using "..". I recommend that you not change this value unless it poses a specific security risk.

Default Value:

1

Data Type:

REG_DWORD

Registry Key:

```
HKEY_LOCAL_MACHINE\SYSTEM
\CurrentControlSet
 \Services
  \W3SVC
   \ASP
    \Parameters
     \EnableParentPaths
```

13

NOTE

> You must stop and restart IIS if you change this Registry key.

Logging Unsuccessful HTTP Requests

Set this Registry setting to 1 to log unsuccessful HTTP requests to the Windows NT Event Log, and 0 to turn this feature off. Use this Registry setting to detect and log unsuccessful HTTP requests.

Default Value:

1

Data Type:

REG_DWORD

Registry Key:

```
HKEY_LOCAL_MACHINE\SYSTEM
\CurrentControlSet
 \Services
  \W3SVC
   \ASP
    \Parameters
     \LogErrorRequests
```

NOTE

> You do not need to stop and restart IIS if you change this Registry key.

Specifying the Amount of Memory Available to Active Server Pages

Use this Registry setting to specify the amount of memory available to Active Server Pages (as a percentage of the used memory list). If you need to use this Registry setting to severely limit the memory available to ASP applications, it's a good indication that your Web server needs more memory.

Default Value:

50

Data Type:

REG_DWORD

13

Registry Key:

```
HKEY_LOCAL_MACHINE\SYSTEM
\CurrentControlSet
 \Services
  \W3SVC
   \ASP
    \Parameters
     \MemFreeFactor
```

NOTE   You must stop and restart IIS if you change this Registry key.

Specifying the Minimum Length of the Used Memory List

Use this Registry setting to specify the minimum length of the used memory list.

Default Value:

```
10
```

Data Type:

```
REG_DWORD
```

Registry Key:

```
HKEY_LOCAL_MACHINE\SYSTEM
\CurrentControlSet
 \Services
  \W3SVC
   \ASP
    \Parameters
     \MinUsedBlocks
```

NOTE   You must stop and restart IIS if you change this Registry key.

13

Specifying the Number of Initial ASP Threads

Specify the number of initial ASP threads using this Registry value. This value should be less than `ProcessorThreadMax`; otherwise, `ProcessorThreadMax` threads will be created. Use this Registry setting if your Web server hosts a high-volume ASP Web site and you always need more than two threads. I do not recommend that you change this Registry setting to a value greater than 10.

Default Value:

2

Data Type:

REG_DWORD

Registry Key:

```
HKEY_LOCAL_MACHINE\SYSTEM
\CurrentControlSet
 \Services
  \W3SVC
   \ASP
    \Parameters
     \NumInitialThreads
```

NOTE

You must stop and restart IIS if you change this Registry key.

Specifying the Maximum Number of ASP Threads

This Registry setting specifies the maximum number of threads to create for each processor.
I recommend that you not change this value.

Default Value:

10

Data Type:

REG_DWORD

Registry Key:

```
HKEY_LOCAL_MACHINE\SYSTEM
\CurrentControlSet
 \Services
  \W3SVC
   \ASP
    \Parameters
     \ProcessorThreadMax
```

NOTE

You must stop and restart IIS if you change this Registry key.

Specifying the Maximum Number of ASP Requests to Be Handled

This Registry setting specifies the maximum number of ASP requests to be handled at any given time.

Default Value:

500

Data Type:

REG_DWORD

Registry Key:

```
HKEY_LOCAL_MACHINE\SYSTEM
\CurrentControlSet
 \Services
  \W3SVC
   \ASP
    \Parameters
     \RequestQueueMax
```

NOTE

You must stop and restart IIS if you change this Registry key.

Specifying the Maximum Number of Scripting Language Engines to Cache

Use this Registry setting to specify the maximum number of scripting language engines to cache. Even after you install PerlScript, you will not have more than 30 scripting languages. Because you are unlikely to exceed this value, I recommend you do not change it unless you need to.

Default Value:

30

Data Type:

REG_DWORD

Registry Key:

```
HKEY_LOCAL_MACHINE\SYSTEM
\CurrentControlSet
 \Services
  \W3SVC
   \ASP
    \Parameters
     \ScriptEngineCacheMax
```

13

NOTE

> You must stop and restart IIS if you change this Registry key.

Specifying the Script Error Message

Use this Registry key to specify the error message displayed in the event of an error condition. You might want to include a URL here that can be used to send e-mail about the error condition.

Default Value:

```
"An error occurred on the server when processing the URL. Please contact
the system administrator."
```

Data Type:

```
REG_SZ
```

Registry Key:

```
HKEY_LOCAL_MACHINE\SYSTEM
\CurrentControlSet
 \Services
  \W3SVC
   \ASP
    \Parameters
     \ScriptErrorMessage
```

NOTE

> You do not need to stop and restart IIS if you change this Registry key.

Writing Debug Information to the Web Browser

Set this Registry value to 1 if you would like ASP debugging information to be sent to the Web browser. Although I recommend that you set this Registry setting to 1 on a development machine, I recommend that you set this value to 0 on a production server so your users do not see any part of your ASP code (or debugging messages).

Default Value:

1

Data Type:

```
REG_DWORD
```

13

Registry Key:

```
HKEY_LOCAL_MACHINE\SYSTEM
\CurrentControlSet
 \Services
  \W3SVC
   \ASP
    \Parameters
     \ScriptErrorsSentToBrowser
```

NOTE

You do not need to stop and restart IIS if you change this Registry key.

Specifying the Size of the ASP Script Cache

Use this Registry setting to specify the size (in bytes) of the ASP script cache. A value of -1 causes all ASP scripts to be cached; a value of 0 causes no ASP scripts to be cached. I strongly discourage you from setting this value to 0 because it will adversely affect the performance of Active Server Pages.

Default Value:

-1

Data Type:

```
REG_DWORD
```

Registry Key:

```
HKEY_LOCAL_MACHINE\SYSTEM
\CurrentControlSet
 \Services
  \W3SVC
   \ASP
    \Parameters
     \ScriptFileCacheSize
```

NOTE

You do not need to stop and restart IIS if you change this Registry key.

13

Specifying How Long ASP Scripts Are Kept in Memory Cache

This Registry setting specifies how long an ASP script should remain in memory (Active Server Pages cache). Use a value of 0 to indefinitely cache ASP scripts.

Default Value:

300

Data Type:

REG_DWORD

Registry Key:

```
HKEY_LOCAL_MACHINE\SYSTEM
\CurrentControlSet
 \Services
  \W3SVC
   \ASP
    \Parameters
     \ScriptFileCacheTTL
```

NOTE

You must stop and restart IIS if you change this Registry key.

Specifying the ASP Script Timeout Value

This setting specifies how long Active Server Pages will allow a script to run. If the script does not terminate before the timeout value specified in this Registry value, the script is terminated and an event is written to the Event Log. You can use the ScriptTimeout method of the Server object to override this value. The default value (-1) allows ASP scripts to run forever. I recommend that you change this Registry setting to a value such as 90 (seconds).

Default Value:

90

Data Type:

REG_DWORD

Registry Key:

```
HKEY_LOCAL_MACHINE\SYSTEM
\CurrentControlSet
 \Services
  \W3SVC
   \ASP
    \Parameters
     \ScriptTimeout
```

NOTE

You do not need to stop and restart IIS if you change this Registry key.

Specifying How Long an ASP Session Object Lasts

This Registry value specifies, in minutes, how long an ASP session object lasts. You might want to increase this value if your users tend to have time intervals greater than 20 minutes between HTTP sessions. For most purposes, the default value should suit you just fine.

Default Value:

```
20
```

Data Type:

```
REG_DWORD
```

Registry Key:

```
HKEY_LOCAL_MACHINE\SYSTEM
\CurrentControlSet
 \Services
  \W3SVC
   \ASP
    \Parameters
     \SessionTimeout
```

NOTE

You can override this Registry value using the `Timeout` method of the `Session` object.

Specifying ODBC Connection Pooling

This Registry setting controls whether ODBC connection pooling is on or off. I do not recommend that you change this value because ODBC connection pooling generally enhances the performance of database-intensive ASP applications.

Default Value:

```
1
```

Data Type:

```
REG_DWORD
```

Registry Key:

```
HKEY_LOCAL_MACHINE\SYSTEM
\CurrentControlSet
 \Services
  \W3SVC
   \ASP
    \Parameters
     \StartConnectionPool
```

13

NOTE

> You must stop and restart IIS if you change this Registry key.

Specifying the Number of ASP Requests Handled by an ASP Thread

Use this Registry setting to specify the number of ASP requests that can be handled by an ASP thread. If the number of ASP requests handled by the thread pool exceeds the number specified in this Registry setting, a new ASP thread is created (provided the size of the thread pool is less than `ProcessorThreadMax`).

Default Value:

5

Data Type:

REG_DWORD

Registry Key:

```
HKEY_LOCAL_MACHINE\SYSTEM
\CurrentControlSet
 \Services
  \W3SVC
   \ASP
    \Parameters
     \ThreadCreationThreshold
```

NOTE

> You must stop and restart IIS if you change this Registry key.

Web Server/Active Server Pages Security

Security is an important aspect of any Internet server. When you publish information on the Internet, you should be aware of various security threats and take precautions to guard against them. In this section, you'll examine various ways of making your Internet server more secure. The purpose of this section is to provide an overview of ways you can make an NT server on the Internet more secure. Security risks are nearly always associated with connecting a server to the Internet. However, this threat to security does not mean that you should not set up a server on the Internet. You should simply take whatever precautions necessary to make it harder and more expensive for someone to break into your system.

13

This section consists of two parts. The first part is devoted to various security countermeasures that you can implement to secure an NT server on the Internet. The second part is devoted to various security resources on the Internet. You should visit Web sites listed here to obtain the most up-to-date information about Windows NT/Internet security.

Disabling the Windows NT Guest Account

If you have not done so already, disable the Windows NT guest account. Anyone can use this account to gain access to your system. If you have an FTP server set up at your site, this account can be especially dangerous because a user with malicious intent can destroy information on your system using this account.

Using NTFS Security and Disk Partitions

Devoting an entire disk partition to Internet publishing is recommended if you can afford to do so. This partition should contain not only the FTP and Web server document root directories, but also binary files of various Internet services. This setup makes it easier for you to control access to various directory structures and to manage security. If you follow this advice, you can use NTFS security to restrict access to all other disk partitions. Using NTFS partitions exclusively is highly recommended. As shown in Figure 13.9, access to files and directories in an NTFS partition can be restricted to only certain users and user groups. Figure 13.9 demonstrates how you can revoke access to a certain directory from the Internet guest account (the account used by Internet Information Server) and assign it to the Administrators group, a certain user, or the system user.

Figure 13.9.

You can restrict access to files and directories in NTFS partitions by using the File Manager.

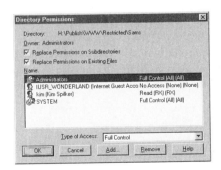

Controlling Directory Browsing

Directory browsing is a feature available in most Web servers. A URL typically contains a directory and a filename. If a user types a URL without a filename at the end of it, a listing of files in the directory is sent to the user if the default document (usually, `index.html`) is not present in that directory. See Figure 13.10 for an example of how a user can use the directory browsing feature to obtain a list of files and directories.

Figure 13.10.

Listing of files and directories when directory browsing is turned on.

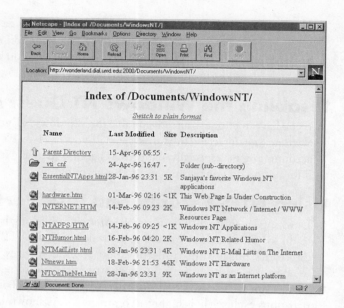

Depending on the structure and nature of information at your Web site, this capability has advantages as well as disadvantages. If your Web site is an open Web site and you want to share as much information as possible, enable directory browsing. If your Web site contains information that should be accessed in a particular order, however, disable directory browsing. You can, for example, distribute software using a Web server. All the applications distributed via the Web server can be in a certain directory. For record-keeping and statistical-analysis purposes, you might have users fill out a form and submit it before they are given permission to download various applications. If directory browsing is enabled, a technically inclined user might figure out how to skip registering by typing the name of the directory in which the applications are located and downloading all the applications in that directory.

Note that a middle ground also exists. You can disable directory browsing only on certain directories. For these directories, simply create a default document (usually index.html) Web page and copy it to directories in which you want to disable directory browsing. Your Web server might allow you to disable directory browsing on certain directories using a special menu or configuration file. Refer to your Web server documentation for more information.

Controlling Access to CGI/ISAPI/ASP Directories

Controlling access to CGI, ISAPI, and ASP directories of your Web server is very important. Only trusted users should have access to these directories. Any user who has access to a CGI directory of the Web server can easily execute programs on the server using a Web browser. For this reason, never allow any user to have access to the CGI directory via FTP. FTP uses clear-text usernames and passwords. Someone who has access to part of your local network

13

or to the part of the Internet over which the authentication data is transmitted can monitor FTP transactions with a simple protocol analyzer. A protocol analyzer can be used to obtain usernames and passwords of users authorized to access your system. An unauthorized user, possibly with malicious intent, then can access your system via FTP by pretending to be an authorized user, and execute any application on your system by copying it to the CGI directory.

Enabling Auditing

Use resource-auditing capabilities of Windows NT to monitor critical resources of your Internet server. From the User Manager's main menu, select Policies | Audit. The Audit Policy dialog box that appears can be used to turn on auditing (see Figure 13.11).

Figure 13.11.

You can audit various system resources by using User Manager.

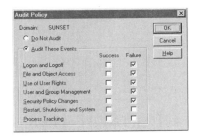

After you enable auditing with User Manager, select a directory and then choose Security | Auditing from the File Manager main menu. The Directory Auditing dialog box, shown in Figure 13.12, appears. Use the options in this dialog box to audit critical areas of your Internet server.

Figure 13.12.

The Directory Auditing dialog box.

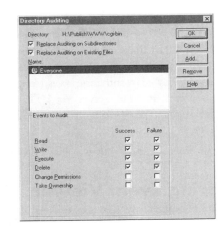

You can use the Event Detail dialog box shown in Figure 13.13 to monitor possible breaches of security. Invoke the Event Detail dialog box by selecting an event from the Windows NT Event Viewer. The event in this figure was logged as a result of an unsuccessful login attempt.

Figure 13.13.

Unsuccessful login attempt recorded.

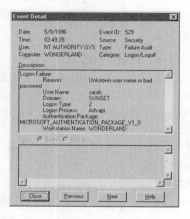

WARNING

Do not get carried away and audit too many activities; otherwise, you'll clutter your Event Log. When the Event Log becomes cluttered with too many events, it makes it virtually impossible for you to locate critical information. Auditing too many events can also slow down your system. Nonetheless, at the very least, I recommend that you audit access failures.

Allowing FTP Access to Your Web Site

You can use FTP to allow users to upload contents to your Web site. When you allow users to FTP to your server, make sure they are aware that anything they upload to the Web server via FTP can be viewed by someone eavesdropping on the network connection. If users upload sensitive material to your server via FTP, make them use a powerful data encryption mechanism such as Pretty Good Privacy (PGP). Visit the following Web site for information about PGP:

```
http://www.yahoo.com/Computers_and_Internet/Security_and_Encryption/
PGP___Pretty_Good_Privacy/
```

Monitoring Event Viewer

You should periodically (once every few days) monitor Event Viewer entries to detect suspicious activities. The Event Log contains valuable information that should be monitored. (The Event Viewer allows you to view items in the Event Log.) See Figure 13.14 for a typical Event Viewer listing.

Figure 13.14.
An Event Viewer listing.

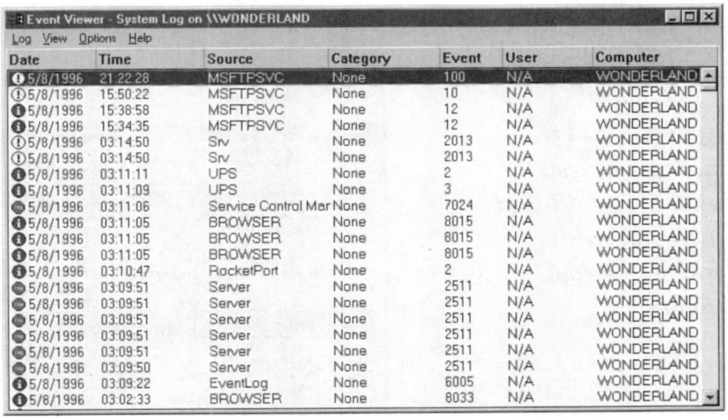

You can obtain additional information about various events displayed in the Event Viewer by selecting an event and double-clicking it. For example, invoke the dialog box shown in Figure 13.15 by double-clicking the event selected in Figure 13.14.

Figure 13.15.
Detailed information about an event displayed in the Event Viewer.

Monitoring Access Log Files

If you detect suspicious activity, monitoring access log files is a good idea. Log files can be several megabytes in size, so manually examining access log files is not a very good idea. If you detect repeated suspicious activity, however, you can use access log files to obtain additional information. If several messages similar to the one shown in Figure 13.15 appear in the Event Log, you can use the access log file to obtain additional information such as the IP address of the user who tried to access the system. Figure 13.16 demonstrates how the access log file can be used to obtain detailed information about the event in Figure 13.15. In this example, the time and date of the event in Figure 13.15 are used as indexes to locate the corresponding access log file entry. Refer to your Web or FTP documentation and configuration settings for the location of the access log file.

Figure 13.16.

You can use access log files to obtain detailed information about various suspicious activities.

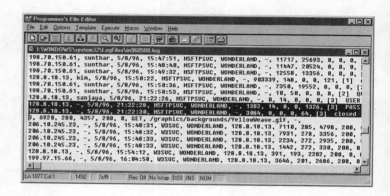

Hide PERL.EXE

Perl is a powerful language that you can use for a variety of purposes. It is especially suitable for creating CGI, ISAPI, and, of course, ASP applications to process user input. However, do not place PERL.EXE in a CGI directory. A user with malicious intent can potentially use PERL.EXE to execute commands on your NT Server. Rather than place PERL.EXE in your CGI directory, you should create a CGI extension mapping and place PERL.EXE in a directory that's not accessible via your Web server (an extension mapping is automatically created when you install Perl 5.0 or better). Refer to IIS documentation for more information about creating CGI extension mappings.

Publishing Sensitive Information

Sensitive information should never be distributed via a Web server unless the data is encrypted before it is transmitted. Although you can restrict access to parts of a Web site by IP address, users can spoof IP addresses. Therefore, you should never use IP addresses to restrict access to sensitive information. The same goes for basic user authentication. Unless Windows NT challenge/response user authentication is used, someone monitoring connections to your Web server can easily intercept usernames and passwords of authorized users and use them to gain unauthorized access to your system.

Enabling Encryption on the Web Server

If you use your Web server to conduct sensitive transactions over the Internet, you should enable encryption on your Web server to make it virtually impossible for someone to monitor your Web server traffic. Although a user who has a great deal of processing power can still monitor HTTP transactions to and from your server, doing so is prohibitively expensive. The purpose of enabling encryption is to make monitoring encrypted Web server traffic by using a mechanism such as SSL too expensive.

Using Windows NT Challenge/Response User Authentication

If you are hosting your Web site with IIS, you can use Windows NT challenge/response user authentication to ensure that usernames and passwords are encrypted before they are transmitted over the Internet. Although doing so improves security, there is a tradeoff. At the time of this writing, only Internet Explorer supports Windows NT challenge/response user authentication. Use this method of authentication to improve security if you are certain all your users use Internet Explorer. Note that Windows NT challenge/response user authentication does not encrypt information transmitted via the Internet; it encrypts only usernames and passwords.

Simulating Unauthorized Break-ins

You would be wise to test the security of your NT system by trying to gain unauthorized access to it. You can do so with the aid of various administrative tools. ScanNT is one utility that can be used to find weak passwords on NT systems. You can use such a utility to ensure that poor passwords chosen by your users do not compromise the security of your system by detecting them before a potential breach of security occurs. Find ScanNT at the following URL:

```
http://www.omna.com/yes/AndyBaron/pk.htm
```

Internet Security Resources on the Internet

Many Internet security resources are available on the Internet. You should visit the Web sites listed in the following sections to learn more about Internet security and various ways of protecting an Internet server against unauthorized access. Monitor these Web sites for the most up-to-date information related to Internet security.

The World Wide Web Security FAQ

The World Wide Web Security FAQ contains many Internet security resources. Visit it to find information about various security holes and how to protect your system from unauthorized accesses.

```
http://www-genome.wi.mit.edu/WWW/faqs/www-security-faq.html
```

Information Security Web Site

Visit the Information Security Web site for news articles related to information data security and Internet Web security.

```
http://www.newspage.com/NEWSPAGE/cgi-bin/walk.cgi/NEWSPAGE/info/d2/d10/
```

Almost Everything You Ever Wanted to Know

Visit the Almost Everything Web site to learn about various Internet security topics. Although some topics discussed apply only to UNIX systems, reading about them will give you a thorough understanding of some of the broader issues related to Internet security.

```
http://www.cis.ohio-state.edu/hypertext/faq/usenet/security-faq/faq.html
```

13

Yahoo!'s Internet Security and Encryption Web Page

Yahoo!'s Internet Security and Encryption Web page lists numerous Internet security Web pages. Visit it often to find the most up-to-date information related to Internet security and encryption.

```
http://www.yahoo.com/Computers_and_Internet/Security_and_Encryption/
```

NT Web Server Security Issues

The following Web site lists many useful suggestions for securing an NT Web server on the Internet. Visit it to learn about various security precautions that you can take to prevent unauthorized access to an NT Web server.

```
http://www.telemark.net/~randallg/ntsecure.htm
```

NT FTP Server Security Issues

If you need help setting up the Windows NT FTP server and securing it to prevent unauthorized access to your system, visit the following Web page. It contains information about Windows NT FTP server security issues.

```
http://mushin.wes.army.mil/ntpermit.htm
```

Maximum Security: A Hacker's Guide to Protecting Your Internet Site and Network

For an alternative view of Internet security, check out *Maximum Security: A Hacker's Guide to Protecting Your Internet Site and Network* (published by Sams.net). This book offers comprehensive coverage of security issues on several platforms, and provides plenty of resources for additional knowledge.

Summary

Server variables can be used to obtain useful information about the current HTTP session. Server variables are accessed using the ServerVariables() method of the Request object.

You can take various steps to protect an NT server on the Internet from unauthorized access. Although setting up an Internet server that is immune to unauthorized access is virtually impossible, there are ways to make it harder and, in some cases, prohibitively expensive for someone to gain unauthorized access. The following is a summary of steps that can be taken to make your NT Web server more secure:

- ☐ Use NTFS partitions (you cannot enforce Windows NT security on FAT partitions)
- ☐ Limit members of the Administrators group
- ☐ Monitor security logs
- ☐ Enable auditing
- ☐ Enable Web server access logging
- ☐ Consult Web server access logs to track down suspicious activities
- ☐ Encrypt sensitive information
- ☐ Limit access to CGI/ASP directories
- ☐ Limit the number of CGI directories
- ☐ Physically secure the server

What's Next

Active Server Pages is ideal for developing Web database applications. Tomorrow, you'll learn how to create a CD cataloging system with ASP.

Q&A

Q Is Perl supported by Active Server Pages in ASP's out-of-the-box form?

A No. You must download and install PerlScript from `http://www.activeware.com/welcome.htm`.

Q Do I need to install the Perl for Win32 binary file before installing PerlScript?

A Yes. PerlScript uses the Perl for Win32 binary file to execute Perl ASP applications.

Q Is PerlScript compatible with the Alpha platform?

A Yes.

Q Should I copy `PERL.EXE` to a Web server CGI directory?

A No. Doing so will dangerously compromise the security of your system because users with malicious intent can hack `PERL.EXE` to execute Windows NT commands.

Q How do I access the server variable `SERVER_SOFTWARE` (provide the ASP statement)?

A `Request.ServerVariables ("SERVER_SOFTWARE")`

13

Exercises

1. Use PerlScript to develop an ASP application that randomly greets the user with one of five greetings.

2. Use the HTTP_USER_AGENT server variable to display a special Web page for users using a Web browser other than Internet Explorer or Netscape Navigator.

Chapter 14

Developing a CD Cataloging System with ASP

You've made it to Day 14! Today you will learn how to develop a CD cataloging database ASP application using tips and techniques you learned during the last two weeks. This database can be used to catalog and easily locate audio CDs. Figure 14.1 shows the data fields of the CD cataloging database.

Figure 14.1.
Data fields of the CD cataloging database.

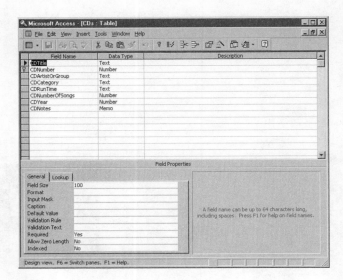

NOTE

Although today is technically the last day of this book, a bonus day, "Practical Applications of ASP," is included to give you an overview of various tasks that can be accomplished with ASP. I encourage you to modify applications presented in Day 15 to activate your Web site.

Overview of the CD Cataloging Application

By developing the CD cataloging database application, you will learn how to create a Web interface to a Microsoft Access database. On Days 8, "Introduction to Web Database Programming Using ActiveX Data Objects," and 9, "Advanced Web Database Programming," you learned how to develop ASP database applications. Today you will learn how to apply skills learned on previous days to develop a complete database application that allows entries to be added, deleted, viewed, and searched. When the ASP application is invoked, the user sees the Web page shown in Figure 14.2. (See Listing 14.1 for the ASP source code of the main menu).

NOTE

Rigorous error checking is not performed in the application presented today because you already know how to use VBScript to examine the values of variables and perform error checking. The purpose of the application presented today is to demonstrate how you can develop a complete database application using skills learned on previous days.

Figure 14.2.

The main menu of the ASP application.

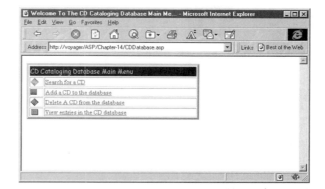

Listing 14.1. The ASP code that generates the main menu of the ASP application.

```
 1: <table border="4" width="350">
 2:     <tr>
 3:         <td bgcolor="#000000" colspan=2>
 4:         <font color="#FFFFFF" face="Comic Sans MS">
 5:         CD Cataloging Database Main Menu</font>
 6:         </td>
 7:     </tr>
 8:     <tr>
 9:         <td width=25>
10:         <img src="Blue_Diamond41.gif" width="17" height="17">
11:         </td><td>
12:         <A href="CDDatabase.asp?Action=SearchForm">
13:         Search for a CD</A></td>
14:     </tr>
15:     <tr>
16:         <td width=25>
17:         <img src="Square_Key49.gif" width="13" height="12">
18:         </td><td>
19:         <A href="CDDatabase.asp?Action=AddForm">
20:         Add a CD to the database</A></td>
21:     </tr>
22:     <tr>
23:         <td width=25>
24:         <img src="Red_Diamond45.gif" width="17" height="17">
25:         </td><td>
26:         <A href="CDDatabase.asp?Action=DeleteForm">
```

continues

14

Listing 14.1. continued

```
27:          Delete A CD from the database</A></td>
28:      </tr>
29:      <tr>
30:          <td width=25>
31:          <img src="Square_Maze47.gif" width="25" height="13">
32:          </td><td>
33:          <A href="CDDatabase.asp?Action=View">
34:          View entries in the CD database</td></A>
35:      </tr>
36: </table>
```

ANALYSIS Notice how the URLs in Listing 14.1 (lines 12, 19, 26, and 33) communicate the selected link by using the ACTION parameter. The ASP application can use the Request.QueryString("Action") statement to extract the values specified in lines 12, 19, 26, and 33 of Listing 14.1. This technique can be employed to avoid creating a separate ASP file to handle each task that has to be performed.

Adding Records to the Database

You can add CDs to the database by selecting the Add a CD to the database link (refer to Figure 14.2). When this link is selected, the Web page shown in Figure 14.3 is displayed to gather information about the CD being added. Add CDs to the database by entering information about the CD and clicking the submit button. See Listing 14.2 for the ASP source code of the data entry form shown in Figure 14.3.

Figure 14.3.

Adding a new entry to the CD database.

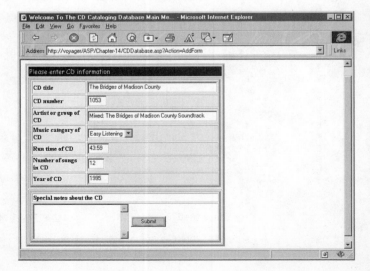

14

Listing 14.2. The source code of the data entry form shown in Figure 14.3.

```
 1: <Form name=CDInformationForm method=Get action="CDDatabase.asp">
 2:
 3: <input type="hidden" name="Action" value="Add">
 4:
 5: <table border="4" width="400">
 6:     <tr>
 7:         <td bgcolor="#000000"><font color="#FFFFFF"
 8:             face="Comic Sans MS">
 9:         Please enter CD information</font></td>
10:     </tr>
11:     <tr>
12:         <td><div align="center"><center><table border="4"
13:         width="400">
14:             <tr>
15:                 <td width="150" bgcolor="#FFFFC1"><strong>
16:                 CD title</strong></td>
17:                 <td width="250" bgcolor="#DDFDB9">
18:                 <input type="text" size="50" name="CDTitle"></td>
19:             </tr>
20:             <tr>
21:                 <td width="155" bgcolor="#FFFFC1"><strong>
22:                 CD number</strong></td>
23:                 <td width="250" bgcolor="#DDFDB9">
24:                 <input type="text" size="4" name="CDNumber"></td>
25:             </tr>
26:             <tr>
27:                 <td width="155" bgcolor="#FFFFC1"><strong>
28:                 Artist or group of CD</strong></td>
29:                 <td width="250" bgcolor="#DDFDB9">
30:                 <input type="text" size="50"
31:                     name="CDArtistOrGroup"></td>
32:             </tr>
33:             <tr>
34:                 <td width="155" bgcolor="#FFFFC1"><strong>
35:                 Music category of CD</strong></td>
36:                 <td width="250" bgcolor="#DDFDB9">
37:                     <select name="CDCategory" size="1">
38:                     <option selected value="EasyListening">
39:                         Easy Listening</option>
40:                     <option value="Oldies">
41:                         Oldies</option>
42:                     <option value="NewAge">
43:                         New Age</option>
44:                     <option value="Mixed">
45:                         Mixed</option>
46:                     <option value="Instrumental">
47:                         Instrumental</option>
48:                     <option value="Rock">
49:                         Rock</option>
50:                     <option value="Up-Beat">
51:                         Up-Beat</option>
```

continues

14

Listing 14.2. continued

```
52:                         <option value="Techno">
53:                             Techno</option>
54:                         </select>
55:                     </td>
56:                 </tr>
57:                 <tr>
58:                     <td width="155" bgcolor="#FFFFC1"><strong>
59:                     Run time of CD</strong></td>
60:                     <td width="250" bgcolor="#DDFDB9">
61:                     <input type="text" size="5" name="CDRunTime"></td>
62:                 </tr>
63:                 <tr>
64:                     <td width="155" bgcolor="#FFFFC1"><strong>
65:                     Number of songs in CD</strong></td>
66:                     <td width="250" bgcolor="#DDFDB9">
67:                     <input type="text" size="3"
68:                         name="CDNumberOfSongs"></td>
69:                 </tr>
70:                 <tr>
71:                     <td width="155" bgcolor="#FFFFC1"><strong>
72:                     Year of CD</strong></td>
73:                     <td width="250" bgcolor="#DDFDB9">
74:                     <input type="text" size="5" name="CDYear"></td>
75:                 </tr>
76:             </table>
77:             </center></div></td>
78:         </tr>
79:         <tr>
80:             <td><div align="center"><center><table border="4"
81:             width="400">
82:                 <tr>
83:                     <td><strong>
84:                         Special notes about the CD
85:                     </strong></td>
86:                 </tr>
87:                 <tr>
88:                     <td>
89:                     <textarea name="CDNotes" rows="4" cols="40">
90:                     </textarea>
91:                     <input type="submit" name="SubmitForm"
92:                             value="Submit">
93:                     </td>
94:                 </tr>
95:             </table>
96:             </center></div></td>
97:         </tr>
98: </table>
99:
100: </Form>
```

The Web page shown in Figure 14.4 is displayed to confirm that a new CD was successfully added to the database. The ASP source code that inserts the data into the database is given in Listing 14.3.

Figure 14.4.

The new entry is successfully added to the CD database.

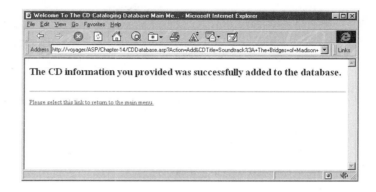

Listing 14.3. The ASP source code that inserts a new CD record into the database.

```
 1: ' Create a connection to the CD database
 2:
 3: Set DatabaseConnection = Server.CreateObject ("ADODB.Connection")
 4: DatabaseConnection.Open "CDDatabase"
 5:
 6: ' Retrieve information entered by the user
 7: UserCDTitle         = _
 8:    CStr (Request.QueryString("CDTitle"))
 9: UserCDNumber        = _
10:    CStr (Request.QueryString("CDNumber"))
11: UserCDArtistOrGroup = _
12:    CStr (Request.QueryString("CDArtistOrGroup"))
13: UserCDCategory      = _
14:    Cstr (Request.QueryString("CDCategory"))
15: UserCDRunTime       = _
16:    CStr (Request.QueryString("CDRunTime"))
17: UserCDNumberOfSongs = _
18:    CStr (Request.QueryString("CDNumberOfSongs"))
19: UserCDYear          = _
20:    CStr (Request.QueryString("CDYear"))
21: UserCDNotes         = _
22:    CStr (Request.QueryString("CDNotes"))
23:
24: ' Build the SQL statement that actually inserts the data
25:
26:    SQLStatement = "INSERT INTO CDs" _
27:                  & "(CDTitle,CDNumber,CDArtistOrGroup,CDCategory," _
28:                  & "CDRunTime,CDNumberOfSongs,CDYear,CDNotes) " _
29:                  & "SELECT '" & UserCDTitle & "' As CDTitle, '" _
30:                  & UserCDNumber & "' As CDNumber, '" _
31:                  & UserCDArtistOrGroup & "' As CDArtistOrGroup, '" _
32:                  & UserCDCategory & "' As CDCategory, '" _
33:                  & UserCDRunTime & "' As CDRunTime, '" _
34:                  & UserCDNumberOfSongs & "' As CDNumberOfSongs, '" _
35:                  & UserCDYear & "' As CDYear, '" _
```

continues

14

Listing 14.3. continued

```
36:                 & UserCDNotes & "' As CDNotes;"
37:
38:   DatabaseConnection.Execute (SQLStatement) %>
39:
40: <H2>
41: The CD information you provided was successfully
42: added to the database.
43: </H2>
44:
45: <HR>
46:
47: <A href=CDDatabase.asp>
48: Please select this link to return to the main menu.</A>
```

ANALYSIS Lines 7–22 of Listing 14.3 retrieve information entered by the user through the use of `(Request.QueryString("<FormVariable>")` statements. Afterwards, a SQL statement is created to insert the data into the CD cataloging database. Line 38 of Listing 14.3 executes the SQL statement created by lines 26–36 through the use of the `DatabaseConnection.Execute()` method.

Look at Figure 14.5 and notice how the information provided in Figure 14.3 is added to the CDs table of the CD cataloging database.

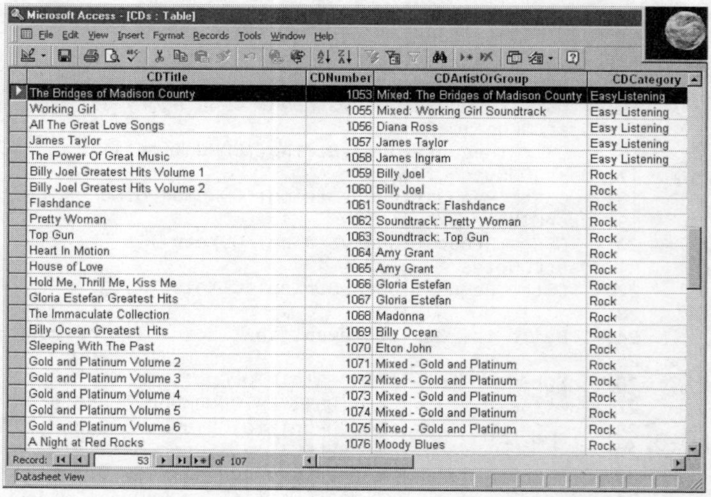

CDTitle	CDNumber	CDArtistOrGroup	CDCategory
The Bridges of Madison County	1053	Mixed: The Bridges of Madison County	EasyListening
Working Girl	1055	Mixed: Working Girl Soundtrack	Easy Listening
All The Great Love Songs	1056	Diana Ross	Easy Listening
James Taylor	1057	James Taylor	Easy Listening
The Power Of Great Music	1058	James Ingram	Easy Listening
Billy Joel Greatest Hits Volume 1	1059	Billy Joel	Rock
Billy Joel Greatest Hits Volume 2	1060	Billy Joel	Rock
Flashdance	1061	Soundtrack: Flashdance	Rock
Pretty Woman	1062	Soundtrack: Pretty Woman	Rock
Top Gun	1063	Soundtrack: Top Gun	Rock
Heart In Motion	1064	Amy Grant	Rock
House of Love	1065	Amy Grant	Rock
Hold Me, Thrill Me, Kiss Me	1066	Gloria Estefan	Rock
Gloria Estefan Greatest Hits	1067	Gloria Estefan	Rock
The Immaculate Collection	1068	Madonna	Rock
Billy Ocean Greatest Hits	1069	Billy Ocean	Rock
Sleeping With The Past	1070	Elton John	Rock
Gold and Platinum Volume 2	1071	Mixed - Gold and Platinum	Rock
Gold and Platinum Volume 3	1072	Mixed - Gold and Platinum	Rock
Gold and Platinum Volume 4	1073	Mixed - Gold and Platinum	Rock
Gold and Platinum Volume 5	1074	Mixed - Gold and Platinum	Rock
Gold and Platinum Volume 6	1075	Mixed - Gold and Platinum	Rock
A Night at Red Rocks	1076	Moody Blues	Rock

Figure 14.5.
The entry in Figure 14.3 is added to the CDs table of the CD cataloging database.

Deleting Records from the Database

You can delete CDs from the database by selecting the Delete A CD from the database link from the main menu (refer to Figure 14.2). The Web page shown in Figure 14.6 obtains the ID number of the CD to be deleted. See Listing 14.4 for the ASP source code of the Web page shown in Figure 14.6.

Figure 14.6.

You can delete a CD by specifying its ID number.

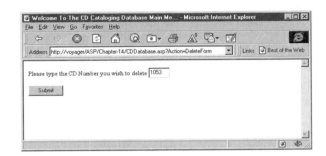

Listing 14.4. An HTML form is used to obtain the ID number of the CD to be deleted.

```
1: <Form name=CDInformationForm method=Get action="CDDatabase.asp">
2:
3: <input type="hidden" name="Action" value="Delete">
4:
5: Please type the CD Number you wish to delete
6: <input type="text" size="5" name="CDNumber"><P>
7: <input type="submit" name="SubmitForm"
8: value="Submit">
9: </Form>
```

After the form in Figure 14.6 is submitted, the ASP statements in Listing 14.5 delete the CD whose ID number was entered by the user (see the SQL statement in lines 15 and 16).

Listing 14.5. An SQL statement is used to delete a CD from the database.

```
1: <%
2: ' Delete a CD from the database
3: ElseIf (Request.QueryString("Action")="Delete") Then
4:
5: ' Create a connection to the CD database
6:   Set DatabaseConnection = _
```

continues

14

Listing 14.5. continued

```
 7:     Server.CreateObject ("ADODB.Connection")
 8:   DatabaseConnection.Open "CDDatabase"
 9:
10: ' Obtain the CD number entered by the user
11:   UserCDNumber       = _
12:     CStr (Request.QueryString("CDNumber"))
13:
14: ' Delete the CD number entered by the user
15:   DatabaseConnection.Execute _
16:     "DELETE * FROM CDs WHERE CDNumber = " & UserCDNumber
17:
18: %>
19:
20: <H2>
21: The CD was successfully deleted from the database.
22: </H2>
23:
24: <HR>
25:
26: <A href=CDDatabase.asp>
27: Please select this link to return to the main menu.</A>
```

Viewing Records in the Database

You can view all the records in the CD database by selecting the View entries in the CD database link in the main menu (refer to Figure 14.2). The Web page shown in Figure 14.7 uses a table to display all the records in the CD database, and is generated by the ASP code in Listing 14.6.

Figure 14.7.

All the records of the CD database.

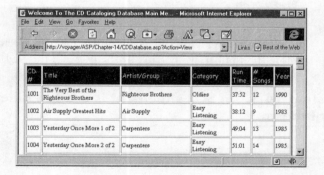

14

Listing 14.6. A loop is used to display all the records of the CD database.

```
 1: <%
 2: ' Display all the records of the CD database
 3:   ElseIf (Request.QueryString("Action")="View") Then
 4:
 5: ' Create a connection to the CD database
 6:   Set DatabaseConnection = _
 7:     Server.CreateObject ("ADODB.Connection")
 8:   DatabaseConnection.Open "CDDatabase"
 9:
10:   Set CurrentRecordSet = _
11:     DatabaseConnection.Execute ("SELECT * FROM CDs ")
12:
13: ' To make sure we are at the first record
14:   CurrentRecordSet.MoveFirst %>
15:
16: <table border="4">
17:     <tr>
18:         <td bgcolor="#000000"><font color="#FFFFFF"
19:         face="Comic Sans MS">CD #</font></td>
20:         <td bgcolor="#000000"><font color="#FFFFFF"
21:         face="Comic Sans MS">Title</font></td>
22:         <td bgcolor="#000000"><font color="#FFFFFF"
23:         face="Comic Sans MS">Artist/Group</font></td>
24:         <td bgcolor="#000000"><font color="#FFFFFF"
25:         face="Comic Sans MS">Category</font></td>
26:         <td bgcolor="#000000"><font color="#FFFFFF"
27:         face="Comic Sans MS">Run Time</font></td>
28:         <td bgcolor="#000000"><font color="#FFFFFF"
29:         face="Comic Sans MS"># Songs</font></td>
30:         <td bgcolor="#000000"><font color="#FFFFFF"
31:         face="Comic Sans MS">Year</font></td>
32:     </tr>
33:
34: <%
35:
36:     Do While Not CurrentRecordSet.EOF
37:
38:       Response.Write ("<tr><td>")
39:       Response.Write (CurrentRecordSet.Fields("CDNumber"))
40:       Response.Write ("</td><td>")
41:       Response.Write (CurrentRecordSet.Fields("CDTitle"))
42:       Response.Write ("</td><td>")
43:       Response.Write (CurrentRecordSet.Fields("CDArtistOrGroup"))
44:       Response.Write ("</td><td>")
45:       Response.Write (CurrentRecordSet.Fields("CDCategory"))
46:       Response.Write ("</td><td>")
47:       Response.Write (CurrentRecordSet.Fields("CDRunTime"))
48:       Response.Write ("</td><td>")
49:       Response.Write (CurrentRecordSet.Fields("CDNumberOfSongs"))
50:       Response.Write ("</td><td>")
51:       Response.Write (CurrentRecordSet.Fields("CDYear"))
```

continues

14

Listing 14.6. continued

```
52:     Response.Write ("</td></tr>")
53:     CurrentRecordSet.MoveNext
54:
55:   Loop
56:
57: %>
58:
59:   </table>
60:
61:   <HR>
62:
63:   <A href=CDDatabase.asp>
64:   Please select this link to return to the main menu.</A>
```

ANALYSIS The records are displayed by establishing a connection to the database (see line 8 of Listing 14.6), selecting the records to be viewed (see lines lines 10–11 of Listing 14.6), and using a `Do While…Loop` (see lines 36–55 of Listing 14.6) to loop through all the records.

Searching for Records in the Database

Select the `Search for a CD link` from the main menu (refer to Figure 14.2) to search for records in the CD database. The Web page shown in Figure 14.8 obtains search criteria from the user. This form can be used to search for CDs by title, ID number, artist, and category. See Listing 14.7 for the ASP source code of the page shown in Figure 14.8.

Figure 14.8.
Searching for all CD titles with the string Greatest Hits.

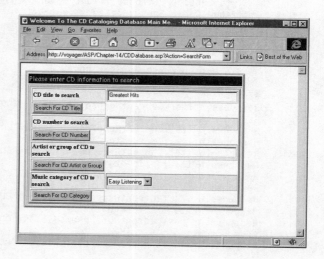

Listing 14.7. The form used to obtain search criteria from the user.

```
 1: <table border="4" width="400">
 2:     <tr>
 3:         <td bgcolor="#000000"><font color="#FFFFFF"
 4:             face="Comic Sans MS">
 5:         Please enter CD information to search</font></td>
 6:     </tr>
 7:     <tr>
 8:         <td><div align="center"><center><table border="4"
 9:         width="400">
10:             <tr>
11:                 <Form name=CDInformationForm method=Get
12:                     action="CDDatabase.asp">
13:                 <input type="hidden" name="Action"
14:                     value="Search">
15:                 <input type="hidden" name="SearchWhat"
16:                     value="CDTitle">
17:                 <td width="150" bgcolor="#FFFFC1"><strong>
18:                 CD title to search</strong></td>
19:                 <td width="250" bgcolor="#DDFDB9">
20:                     <input type="text" size="50" name="CDTitle"></td>
21:             </tr>
22:             <tr><td>
23:                     <input type="submit" name="SubmitForm"
24:                         value="Search For CD Title">
25:                     </Form>
26:             </td></tr>
27:
28:             <tr>
29:                 <Form name=CDInformationForm method=Get
30:                     action="CDDatabase.asp">
31:                 <input type="hidden" name="Action"
32:                     value="Search">
33:                 <input type="hidden" name="SearchWhat"
34:                     value="CDNumber">
35:                 <td width="155" bgcolor="#FFFFC1"><strong>
36:                 CD number to search</strong></td>
37:                 <td width="250" bgcolor="#DDFDB9">
38:                     <input type="text" size="4" name="CDNumber"></td>
39:             </tr>
40:             <tr><td>
41:                     <input type="submit" name="SubmitForm"
42:                         value="Search For CD Number">
43:                     </Form>
44:             </td></tr>
45:
46:             <tr>
47:                 <Form name=CDInformationForm method=Get
48:                     action="CDDatabase.asp">
49:                 <input type="hidden" name="Action"
50:                     value="Search">
51:                 <input type="hidden" name="SearchWhat"
52:                     value="CDArtistOrGroup">
```

continues

14

Listing 14.7. continued

```
 53:                         <td width="155" bgcolor="#FFFFC1"><strong>
 54:                         Artist or group of CD to search</strong></td>
 55:                         <td width="250" bgcolor="#DDFDB9">
 56:                         <input type="text" size="50"
 57:                           name="CDArtistOrGroup"></td>
 58:                 </tr>
 59:                 <tr><td>
 60:                         <input type="submit" name="SubmitForm"
 61:                                 value="Search For CD Artist or Group">
 62:                         </Form>
 63:                 </td></tr>
 64:
 65:                 <tr>
 66:                         <Form name=CDInformationForm method=Get
 67:                                 action="CDDatabase.asp">
 68:                         <input type="hidden" name="Action"
 69:                                 value="Search">
 70:                         <input type="hidden" name="SearchWhat"
 71:                                 value="CDCategory">
 72:                         <td width="155" bgcolor="#FFFFC1"><strong>
 73:                         Music category of CD to search</strong></td>
 74:                         <td width="250" bgcolor="#DDFDB9">
 75:                         <select name="CDCategory" size="1">
 76:                         <option selected value="Easy Listening">
 77:                            Easy Listening</option>
 78:                         <option value="Oldies">
 79:                            Oldies</option>
 80:                         <option value="NewAge">
 81:                            New Age</option>
 82:                         <option value="Mixed">
 83:                            Mixed</option>
 84:                         <option value="Instrumental">
 85:                            Instrumental</option>
 86:                         <option value="Rock">
 87:                            Rock</option>
 88:                         <option value="Up-Beat">
 89:                            Up-Beat</option>
 90:                         <option value="Techno">
 91:                            Techno</option>
 92:                         </select>
 93:                            </td>
 94:                 </tr>
 95:                 <tr><td>
 96:                         <input type="submit" name="SubmitForm"
 97:                                 value="Search For CD Category">
 98:                         </Form>
 99:                 </td></tr>
100:            </table>
101:            </center></div></td>
102:       </tr>
103: </table>
```

ANALYSIS   Notice how all four forms in Listing 14.7 submit the search criteria to the same ASP script—you do not use four ASP scripts to handle the forms. The hidden form variable `SearchWhat` is examined by the ASP application to determine what to search for. This technique can be used to avoid having multiple ASP files to accomplish a task that can be completed with a single ASP file.

Figure 14.9.

A list of CDs in the database that contain the string Greatest Hits *in their titles.*

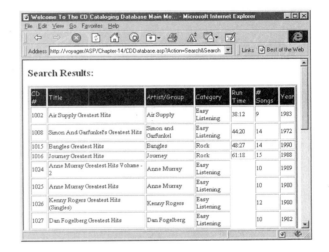

When search criteria are submitted to the server-side script by the user, the ASP application in Listing 14.8 searches the database and displays the matching records.

Listing 14.8. An SQL statement is used to obtain records that match the user's search criteria.

```
 1: <H2>
 2: Search Results:
 3: </H2>
 4:
 5: <%
 6:
 7: ' Create a connection to the CD database
 8:
 9:    Set DatabaseConnection = _
10:      Server.CreateObject ("ADODB.Connection")
11:    DatabaseConnection.Open "CDDatabase"
12:
13: ' Determine what to search
14:    UserSearchChoice  = CStr (Request.QueryString("SearchWhat"))
15:
```

14

continues

Listing 14.8. continued

```
16: ' Obtain records matching user's search criteria
17:    Select Case UserSearchChoice
18:      Case "CDTitle"
19:        UserCDTitle            = _
20:        CStr (Request.QueryString("CDTitle"))
21:        Set CurrentRecordSet = _
22:          DatabaseConnection.Execute _
23:          ("SELECT * FROM CDs WHERE CDTitle LIKE'%" & _
24:          UserCDTitle & "%'")
25:      Case "CDNumber"
26:        UserCDNumber           = _
27:        CStr (Request.QueryString("CDNumber"))
28:        Set CurrentRecordSet = _
29:          DatabaseConnection.Execute _
30:          ("SELECT * FROM CDs WHERE CDNumber = " & _
31:          UserCDNumber )
32:      Case "CDArtistOrGroup"
33:        UserCDArtistOrGroup = _
34:        CStr (Request.QueryString("CDArtistOrGroup"))
35:        Set CurrentRecordSet = _
36:          DatabaseConnection.Execute _
37:          ("SELECT * FROM CDs WHERE CDArtistOrGroup LIKE '%" & _
38:          UserCDArtistOrGroup & "%'")
39:      Case Else
40:        UserCDCategory         = _
41:        Cstr (Request.QueryString("CDCategory"))
42:        Set CurrentRecordSet = _
43:          DatabaseConnection.Execute _
44:          ("SELECT * FROM CDs WHERE CDCategory = '" & _
45:          UserCDCategory & "'")
46:    End Select
47:
48: ' Check to see if there were not matches
49:    If CurrentRecordSet.EOF Then %>
50:
51:    <H3>No Matching records found.</H3>
52:
53: <% Else
54:
55: ' To make sure we are at the first record
56:    CurrentRecordSet.MoveFirst %>
57:
58: <table border="4">
59:    <tr>
60:        <td bgcolor="#000000"><font color="#FFFFFF"
61:        face="Comic Sans MS">CD #</font></td>
62:        <td bgcolor="#000000"><font color="#FFFFFF"
63:        face="Comic Sans MS">Title</font></td>
64:        <td bgcolor="#000000"><font color="#FFFFFF"
65:        face="Comic Sans MS">Artist/Group</font></td>
66:        <td bgcolor="#000000"><font color="#FFFFFF"
67:        face="Comic Sans MS">Category</font></td>
68:        <td bgcolor="#000000"><font color="#FFFFFF"
69:        face="Comic Sans MS">Run Time</font></td>
```

14

```
70:          <td bgcolor="#000000"><font color="#FFFFFF"
71:          face="Comic Sans MS"># Songs</font></td>
72:          <td bgcolor="#000000"><font color="#FFFFFF"
73:          face="Comic Sans MS">Year</font></td>
74:      </tr>
75:
76: <%
77:
78: ' Use a loop to display all the records
79:   Do While Not CurrentRecordSet.EOF
80:
81:     Response.Write ("<tr><td>")
82:     Response.Write (CurrentRecordSet.Fields("CDNumber"))
83:     Response.Write ("</td><td>")
84:     Response.Write (CurrentRecordSet.Fields("CDTitle"))
85:     Response.Write ("</td><td>")
86:     Response.Write (CurrentRecordSet.Fields("CDArtistOrGroup"))
87:     Response.Write ("</td><td>")
88:     Response.Write (CurrentRecordSet.Fields("CDCategory"))
89:     Response.Write ("</td><td>")
90:     Response.Write (CurrentRecordSet.Fields("CDRunTime"))
91:     Response.Write ("</td><td>")
92:     Response.Write (CurrentRecordSet.Fields("CDNumberOfSongs"))
93:     Response.Write ("</td><td>")
94:     Response.Write (CurrentRecordSet.Fields("CDYear"))
95:     Response.Write ("</td></tr>")
96:     CurrentRecordSet.MoveNext
97:   Loop
98:
99: %>
100:
101:   </table>
102:
103: <% End If %>
104:
105:   <HR>
106:
107:   <A href=CDDatabase.asp>
108:   Please select this link to return to the main menu.</A>
```

ANALYSIS   The ASP application in Listing 14.8 first determines what to search for by examining the SearchWhat hidden form variable in line 14. The ASP application uses an appropriate SQL statement in lines 17–46 to obtain the records that match the user's search criteria. Afterwards, a Do While...Loop is used in lines 79–97 to display the records matching the user's search criteria.

Figure 14.10 demonstrates how the pull-down list defined in lines 75–92 of Listing 14.7 is used to display all the oldies CDs in the database. The results of the search can be found in Figure 14.11.

14

TIP

Whenever the user should select a value from a set of predefined values, use a pull-down list to simplify data entry and error checking.

Figure 14.10.

Searching for oldies CDs in the database.

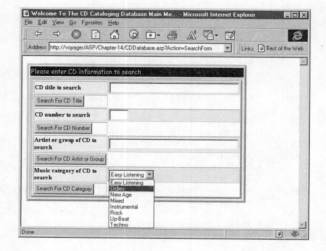

Figure 14.11.

Oldies CDs in the database.

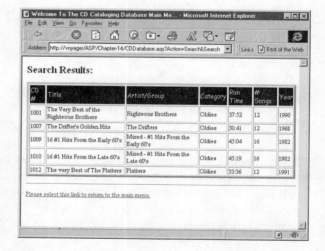

14

The CD Cataloging Application

For your reference, the complete source code of the CD cataloging application is provided in Listing 14.9.

Listing 14.9. The complete source code of the CD database ASP application.

```
 1: <%@ LANGUAGE="VBSCRIPT" %>
 2: <!DOCTYPE HTML PUBLIC "-//IETF//DTD HTML//EN">
 3:
 4: <html>
 5:
 6: <head>
 7: <meta http-equiv="Content-Type"
 8: content="text/html; charset=iso-8859-1">
 9: <title>
10: Welcome To The CD Cataloging Database Main Menu!
11: </title>
12: </head>
13:
14: <body bgcolor="#FFFFFF">
15:
16: <div align="left">
17:
18: <%
19: ' If the user has not selected an action, we display the
20: ' main menu.
21:
22:    If (IsEmpty(Request.QueryString("Action"))) Then
23: %>
24:
25: <table border="4" width="350">
26:     <tr>
27:         <td bgcolor="#000000" colspan=2>
28:         <font color="#FFFFFF" face="Comic Sans MS">
29:         CD Cataloging Database Main Menu</font>
30:         </td>
31:     </tr>
32:     <tr>
33:         <td width=25>
34:         <img src="Blue_Diamond41.gif" width="17" height="17">
35:         </td><td>
36:         <A href="CDDatabase.asp?Action=SearchForm">
37:         Search for a CD</A></td>
38:     </tr>
39:     <tr>
40:         <td width=25>
41:         <img src="Square_Key49.gif" width="13" height="12">
42:         </td><td>
43:         <A href="CDDatabase.asp?Action=AddForm">
```

14

continues

Listing 14.9. continued

```
44:             Add a CD to the database</A></td>
45:         </tr>
46:         <tr>
47:             <td width=25>
48:             <img src="Red_Diamond45.gif" width="17" height="17">
49:             </td><td>
50:             <A href="CDDatabase.asp?Action=DeleteForm">
51:             Delete A CD from the database</A></td>
52:         </tr>
53:         <tr>
54:             <td width=25>
55:             <img src="Square_Maze47.gif" width="25" height="13">
56:             </td><td>
57:             <A href="CDDatabase.asp?Action=View">
58:             View entries in the CD database</td></A>
59:         </tr>
60: </table>
61:
62: <%
63: ' Display the form used to add CDs
64:     ElseIf (Request.QueryString("Action")="AddForm") Then
65: %>
66:
67: <Form name=CDInformationForm method=Get action="CDDatabase.asp">
68:
69: <input type="hidden" name="Action" value="Add">
70:
71: <table border="4" width="400">
72:         <tr>
73:             <td bgcolor="#000000"><font color="#FFFFFF"
74:                 face="Comic Sans MS">
75:             Please enter CD information</font></td>
76:         </tr>
77:         <tr>
78:             <td><div align="center"><center><table border="4"
79:             width="400">
80:                 <tr>
81:                     <td width="150" bgcolor="#FFFFC1"><strong>
82:                     CD title</strong></td>
83:                     <td width="250" bgcolor="#DDFDB9">
84:                     <input type="text" size="50" name="CDTitle"></td>
85:                 </tr>
86:                 <tr>
87:                     <td width="155" bgcolor="#FFFFC1"><strong>
88:                     CD number</strong></td>
89:                     <td width="250" bgcolor="#DDFDB9">
90:                     <input type="text" size="4" name="CDNumber"></td>
91:                 </tr>
92:                 <tr>
93:                     <td width="155" bgcolor="#FFFFC1"><strong>
94:                     Artist or group of CD</strong></td>
95:                     <td width="250" bgcolor="#DDFDB9">
96:                     <input type="text" size="50"
```

14

```
 97:                         name="CDArtistOrGroup"></td>
 98:                 </tr>
 99:                 <tr>
100:                     <td width="155" bgcolor="#FFFFC1"><strong>
101:                     Music category of CD</strong></td>
102:                     <td width="250" bgcolor="#DDFDB9">
103:                         <select name="CDCategory" size="1">
104:                         <option selected value="EasyListening">
105:                             Easy Listening</option>
106:                         <option value="Oldies">
107:                             Oldies</option>
108:                         <option value="NewAge">
109:                             New Age</option>
110:                         <option value="Mixed">
111:                             Mixed</option>
112:                         <option value="Instrumental">
113:                             Instrumental</option>
114:                         <option value="Rock">
115:                             Rock</option>
116:                         <option value="Up-Beat">
117:                             Up-Beat</option>
118:                         <option value="Techno">
119:                             Techno</option>
120:                         </select>
121:                     </td>
122:                 </tr>
123:                 <tr>
124:                     <td width="155" bgcolor="#FFFFC1"><strong>
125:                     Run time of CD</strong></td>
126:                     <td width="250" bgcolor="#DDFDB9">
127:                     <input type="text" size="5" name="CDRunTime"></td>
128:                 </tr>
129:                 <tr>
130:                     <td width="155" bgcolor="#FFFFC1"><strong>
131:                     Number of songs in CD</strong></td>
132:                     <td width="250" bgcolor="#DDFDB9">
133:                     <input type="text" size="3"
134:                         name="CDNumberOfSongs"></td>
135:                 </tr>
136:                 <tr>
137:                     <td width="155" bgcolor="#FFFFC1"><strong>
138:                     Year of CD</strong></td>
139:                     <td width="250" bgcolor="#DDFDB9">
140:                     <input type="text" size="5" name="CDYear"></td>
141:                 </tr>
142:             </table>
143:             </center></div></td>
144:         </tr>
145:         <tr>
146:             <td><div align="center"><center><table border="4"
147:             width="400">
148:                 <tr>
149:                     <td><strong>
150:                         Special notes about the CD
151:                     </strong></td>
152:                 </tr>
```

continues

Listing 14.9. continued

```
153:                <tr>
154:                    <td>
155:                    <textarea name="CDNotes" rows="4" cols="40">
156:                    </textarea>
157:                    <input type="submit" name="SubmitForm"
158:                            value="Submit">
159:                    </td>
160:                </tr>
161:        </table>
162:        </center></div></td>
163:    </tr>
164: </table>
165:
166: </Form>
167:
168: <%
169: ' Display the form used to search for CDs
170:    ElseIf (Request.QueryString("Action")="SearchForm") Then
171: %>
172:
173: <table border="4" width="400">
174:    <tr>
175:        <td bgcolor="#000000"><font color="#FFFFFF"
176:            face="Comic Sans MS">
177:        Please enter CD information to search</font></td>
178:    </tr>
179:    <tr>
180:        <td><div align="center"><center><table border="4"
181:        width="400">
182:            <tr>
183:                <Form name=CDInformationForm method=Get
184:                        action="CDDatabase.asp">
185:                <input type="hidden" name="Action"
186:                        value="Search">
187:                <input type="hidden" name="SearchWhat"
188:                        value="CDTitle">
189:                <td width="150" bgcolor="#FFFFC1"><strong>
190:                CD title to search</strong></td>
191:                <td width="250" bgcolor="#DDFDB9">
192:                <input type="text" size="50" name="CDTitle"></td>
193:            </tr>
194:            <tr><td>
195:                <input type="submit" name="SubmitForm"
196:                        value="Search For CD Title">
197:                </Form>
198:            </td></tr>
199:
200:            <tr>
201:                <Form name=CDInformationForm method=Get
202:                        action="CDDatabase.asp">
203:                <input type="hidden" name="Action"
204:                        value="Search">
205:                <input type="hidden" name="SearchWhat"
206:                        value="CDNumber">
```

```
207:                    <td width="155" bgcolor="#FFFFC1"><strong>
208:                    CD number to search</strong></td>
209:                    <td width="250" bgcolor="#DDFDB9">
210:                    <input type="text" size="4" name="CDNumber"></td>
211:              </tr>
212:              <tr><td>
213:                    <input type="submit" name="SubmitForm"
214:                           value="Search For CD Number">
215:                    </Form>
216:              </td></tr>
217:
218:              <tr>
219:                    <Form name=CDInformationForm method=Get
220:                          action="CDDatabase.asp">
221:                    <input type="hidden" name="Action"
222:                           value="Search">
223:                    <input type="hidden" name="SearchWhat"
224:                           value="CDArtistOrGroup">
225:                    <td width="155" bgcolor="#FFFFC1"><strong>
226:                    Artist or group of CD to search</strong></td>
227:                    <td width="250" bgcolor="#DDFDB9">
228:                    <input type="text" size="50"
229:                       name="CDArtistOrGroup"></td>
230:              </tr>
231:              <tr><td>
232:                    <input type="submit" name="SubmitForm"
233:                           value="Search For CD Artist or Group">
234:                    </Form>
235:              </td></tr>
236:
237:              <tr>
238:                    <Form name=CDInformationForm method=Get
239:                          action="CDDatabase.asp">
240:                    <input type="hidden" name="Action"
241:                           value="Search">
242:                    <input type="hidden" name="SearchWhat"
243:                           value="CDCategory">
244:                    <td width="155" bgcolor="#FFFFC1"><strong>
245:                    Music category of CD to search</strong></td>
246:                    <td width="250" bgcolor="#DDFDB9">
247:                      <select name="CDCategory" size="1">
248:                      <option selected value="Easy Listening">
249:                        Easy Listening</option>
250:                      <option value="Oldies">
251:                        Oldies</option>
252:                      <option value="NewAge">
253:                        New Age</option>
254:                      <option value="Mixed">
255:                        Mixed</option>
256:                      <option value="Instrumental">
257:                        Instrumental</option>
258:                      <option value="Rock">
259:                        Rock</option>
260:                      <option value="Up-Beat">
261:                        Up-Beat</option>
262:                      <option value="Techno">
```

14

continues

Listing 14.9. continued

```
263:                          Techno</option>
264:                      </select>
265:                    </td>
266:                </tr>
267:                <tr><td>
268:                    <input type="submit" name="SubmitForm"
269:                         value="Search For CD Category">
270:                    </Form>
271:                </td></tr>
272:            </table>
273:            </center></div></td>
274:        </tr>
275: </table>
276:
277: <%
278: ' Search for user's search criteria
279:    ElseIf (Request.QueryString("Action")="Search") Then
280: %>
281:
282: <H2>
283: Search Results:
284: </H2>
285:
286: <%
287:
288: ' Create a connection to the CD database
289:
290:    Set DatabaseConnection = _
291:      Server.CreateObject ("ADODB.Connection")
292:    DatabaseConnection.Open "CDDatabase"
293:
294: ' Determine what to search
295:    UserSearchChoice  = CStr (Request.QueryString("SearchWhat"))
296:
297: ' Obtain records matching user's search criteria
298:    Select Case UserSearchChoice
299:      Case "CDTitle"
300:        UserCDTitle         = _
301:        CStr (Request.QueryString("CDTitle"))
302:        Set CurrentRecordSet = _
303:          DatabaseConnection.Execute _
304:          ("SELECT * FROM CDs WHERE CDTitle LIKE'%" & _
305:          UserCDTitle & "%'")
306:      Case "CDNumber"
307:        UserCDNumber        = _
308:        CStr (Request.QueryString("CDNumber"))
309:        Set CurrentRecordSet = _
310:          DatabaseConnection.Execute _
311:          ("SELECT * FROM CDs WHERE CDNumber = " & _
312:          UserCDNumber )
313:      Case "CDArtistOrGroup"
314:        UserCDArtistOrGroup = _
315:        CStr (Request.QueryString("CDArtistOrGroup"))
316:        Set CurrentRecordSet = _
```

```
317:          DatabaseConnection.Execute _
318:          ("SELECT * FROM CDs WHERE CDArtistOrGroup LIKE '%" & _
319:          UserCDArtistOrGroup & "%'")
320:     Case Else
321:       UserCDCategory       = _
322:       Cstr (Request.QueryString("CDCategory"))
323:       Set CurrentRecordSet = _
324:          DatabaseConnection.Execute _
325:          ("SELECT * FROM CDs WHERE CDCategory = '" & _
326:          UserCDCategory & "'")
327:    End Select
328:
329: ' Check to see if there were not matches
330:    If CurrentRecordSet.EOF Then %>
331:
332:    <H3>No Matching records found.</H3>
333:
334: <% Else
335:
336: ' To make sure we are at the first record
337:    CurrentRecordSet.MoveFirst %>
338:
339: <table border="4">
340:     <tr>
341:         <td bgcolor="#000000"><font color="#FFFFFF"
342:         face="Comic Sans MS">CD #</font></td>
343:         <td bgcolor="#000000"><font color="#FFFFFF"
344:         face="Comic Sans MS">Title</font></td>
345:         <td bgcolor="#000000"><font color="#FFFFFF"
346:         face="Comic Sans MS">Artist/Group</font></td>
347:         <td bgcolor="#000000"><font color="#FFFFFF"
348:         face="Comic Sans MS">Category</font></td>
349:         <td bgcolor="#000000"><font color="#FFFFFF"
350:         face="Comic Sans MS">Run Time</font></td>
351:         <td bgcolor="#000000"><font color="#FFFFFF"
352:         face="Comic Sans MS"># Songs</font></td>
353:         <td bgcolor="#000000"><font color="#FFFFFF"
354:         face="Comic Sans MS">Year</font></td>
355:     </tr>
356:
357: <%
358:
359: ' Use a loop to display all the records
360:    Do While Not CurrentRecordSet.EOF
361:
362:      Response.Write ("<tr><td>")
363:      Response.Write (CurrentRecordSet.Fields("CDNumber"))
364:      Response.Write ("</td><td>")
365:      Response.Write (CurrentRecordSet.Fields("CDTitle"))
366:      Response.Write ("</td><td>")
367:      Response.Write (CurrentRecordSet.Fields("CDArtistOrGroup"))
368:      Response.Write ("</td><td>")
369:      Response.Write (CurrentRecordSet.Fields("CDCategory"))
370:      Response.Write ("</td><td>")
371:      Response.Write (CurrentRecordSet.Fields("CDRunTime"))
372:      Response.Write ("</td><td>")
```

14

continues

Listing 14.9. continued

```
373:        Response.Write (CurrentRecordSet.Fields("CDNumberOfSongs"))
374:        Response.Write ("</td><td>")
375:        Response.Write (CurrentRecordSet.Fields("CDYear"))
376:        Response.Write ("</td></tr>")
377:        CurrentRecordSet.MoveNext
378:    Loop
379:
380: %>
381:
382:    </table>
383:
384: <% End If %>
385:
386:    <HR>
387:
388:    <A href=CDDatabase.asp>
389:    Please select this link to return to the main menu.</A>
390:
391: <%
392: ' Add a new CD
393: ElseIf (Request.QueryString("Action")="Add") Then
394:
395: ' Create a connection to the CD database
396:
397: Set DatabaseConnection = Server.CreateObject ("ADODB.Connection")
398: DatabaseConnection.Open "CDDatabase"
399:
400: ' Retrieve information entered by the user
401: UserCDTitle        = _
402:    CStr (Request.QueryString("CDTitle"))
403: UserCDNumber       = _
404:    CStr (Request.QueryString("CDNumber"))
405: UserCDArtistOrGroup = _
406:    CStr (Request.QueryString("CDArtistOrGroup"))
407: UserCDCategory     = _
408:    Cstr (Request.QueryString("CDCategory"))
409: UserCDRunTime      = _
410:    CStr (Request.QueryString("CDRunTime"))
411: UserCDNumberOfSongs = _
412:    CStr (Request.QueryString("CDNumberOfSongs"))
413: UserCDYear         = _
414:    CStr (Request.QueryString("CDYear"))
415: UserCDNotes        = _
416:    CStr (Request.QueryString("CDNotes"))
417:
418: ' Build the SQL statement that actually inserts the data
419:
420:    SQLStatement = "INSERT INTO CDs" _
421:                    & "(CDTitle,CDNumber,CDArtistOrGroup,CDCategory," _
422:                    & "CDRunTime,CDNumberOfSongs,CDYear,CDNotes) " _
423:                    & "SELECT '" & UserCDTitle & "' As CDTitle, '" _
424:                    & UserCDNumber & "' As CDNumber, '" _
425:                    & UserCDArtistOrGroup & "' As CDArtistOrGroup, '" _
426:                    & UserCDCategory & "' As CDCategory, '" _
```

14

```
427:                    & UserCDRunTime & "' As CDRunTime, '" _
428:                    & UserCDNumberOfSongs & "' As CDNumberOfSongs, '" _
429:                    & UserCDYear & "' As CDYear, '" _
430:                    & UserCDNotes & "' As CDNotes;"
431:
432:    DatabaseConnection.Execute (SQLStatement) %>
433:
434: <H2>
435: The CD information you provided was successfully
436: added to the database.
437: </H2>
438:
439: <HR>
440:
441: <A href=CDDatabase.asp>
442: Please select this link to return to the main menu.</A>
443:
444: <%
445: ' Obtain information about the CD to delete
446:   ElseIf (Request.QueryString("Action")="DeleteForm") Then
447: %>
448:
449: <Form name=CDInformationForm method=Get action="CDDatabase.asp">
450:
451: <input type="hidden" name="Action" value="Delete">
452:
453: Please type the CD Number you wish to delete
454: <input type="text" size="5" name="CDNumber"><P>
455: <input type="submit" name="SubmitForm"
456: value="Submit">
457: </Form>
458:
459: <%
460: ' Delete a CD from the database
461: ElseIf (Request.QueryString("Action")="Delete") Then
462:
463: ' Create a connection to the CD database
464:   Set DatabaseConnection = _
465:     Server.CreateObject ("ADODB.Connection")
466:   DatabaseConnection.Open "CDDatabase"
467:
468: ' Obtain the CD number entered by the user
469:   UserCDNumber        = _
470:     CStr (Request.QueryString("CDNumber"))
471:
472: ' Delete the CD number entered by the user
473:   DatabaseConnection.Execute _
474:     "DELETE * FROM CDs WHERE CDNumber = " & UserCDNumber
475:
476: %>
477:
478: <H2>
479: The CD was successfully deleted from the database.
480: </H2>
481:
482: <HR>
```

14

continues

Listing 14.9. continued

```
483:
484: <A href=CDDatabase.asp>
485: Please select this link to return to the main menu.</A>
486:
487: <%
488: ' Display all the records of the CD database
489:   ElseIf (Request.QueryString("Action")="View") Then
490:
491: ' Create a connection to the CD database
492:   Set DatabaseConnection = _
493:     Server.CreateObject ("ADODB.Connection")
494:   DatabaseConnection.Open "CDDatabase"
495:
496:   Set CurrentRecordSet = _
497:     DatabaseConnection.Execute ("SELECT * FROM CDs ")
498:
499: ' To make sure we are at the first record
500:   CurrentRecordSet.MoveFirst %>
501:
502: <table border="4">
503:     <tr>
504:         <td bgcolor="#000000"><font color="#FFFFFF"
505:         face="Comic Sans MS">CD #</font></td>
506:         <td bgcolor="#000000"><font color="#FFFFFF"
507:         face="Comic Sans MS">Title</font></td>
508:         <td bgcolor="#000000"><font color="#FFFFFF"
509:         face="Comic Sans MS">Artist/Group</font></td>
510:         <td bgcolor="#000000"><font color="#FFFFFF"
511:         face="Comic Sans MS">Category</font></td>
512:         <td bgcolor="#000000"><font color="#FFFFFF"
513:         face="Comic Sans MS">Run Time</font></td>
514:         <td bgcolor="#000000"><font color="#FFFFFF"
515:         face="Comic Sans MS"># Songs</font></td>
516:         <td bgcolor="#000000"><font color="#FFFFFF"
517:         face="Comic Sans MS">Year</font></td>
518:     </tr>
519:
520: <%
521:
522:   Do While Not CurrentRecordSet.EOF
523:
524:     Response.Write ("<tr><td>")
525:     Response.Write (CurrentRecordSet.Fields("CDNumber"))
526:     Response.Write ("</td><td>")
527:     Response.Write (CurrentRecordSet.Fields("CDTitle"))
528:     Response.Write ("</td><td>")
529:     Response.Write (CurrentRecordSet.Fields("CDArtistOrGroup"))
530:     Response.Write ("</td><td>")
531:     Response.Write (CurrentRecordSet.Fields("CDCategory"))
532:     Response.Write ("</td><td>")
533:     Response.Write (CurrentRecordSet.Fields("CDRunTime"))
534:     Response.Write ("</td><td>")
535:     Response.Write (CurrentRecordSet.Fields("CDNumberOfSongs"))
536:     Response.Write ("</td><td>")
```

14

```
537:        Response.Write (CurrentRecordSet.Fields("CDYear"))
538:        Response.Write ("</td></tr>")
539:        CurrentRecordSet.MoveNext
540:
541:    Loop
542:
543: %>
544:
545:    </table>
546:
547:    <HR>
548:
549:    <A href=CDDatabase.asp>
550:    Please select this link to return to the main menu.</A>
551:
552: <% Else %>
553:
554:    <H1>The selection you made is not a valid selection!</H1>
555:
556:    <HR>
557:
558:    <A href=CDDatabase.asp>
559:    Please select this link to return to the main menu.</A>
560:
561: <%
562:    End If
563: %>
564:
565: </div>
566:
567: </body>
568: </html>
```

Summary

Active Server Pages is ideal for developing Web database applications. The Active Database component that is included with ASP can be used to easily create Web interfaces to ODBC databases. Today, you learned how to use information presented on previous days to create a complete database application. As you discovered today, Active Server Pages can be used to easily develop a database application complete with the capability to search, insert, and delete records.

What's Next

The bonus day that follows has been included to provide an overview of some of the tasks that can be accomplished using Active Server Pages. By developing the following ASP

14

applications, you will discover how to put to use tips and techniques presented in previous days in order to create

☐ A Web e-mail gateway

☐ An application that allows the user to select a URL using a pull-down list

☐ An application that inserts a time stamp in a Web page and greets the user with a special message the first time he invokes the Web page

Q&A

Q How do I determine whether I have reached the end of the `CurrentRecordSet` record set?

A Use the following control structure:

```
<% If CurrentRecordSet.EOF Then %>
```

Q How do I create a connection to the System DSN named `GuestList`?

A Use the following ASP statements:

```
<%
  Set DatabaseConnection = _
    Server.CreateObject ("ADODB.Connection")
  DatabaseConnection.Open "GuestList"
%>
```

Q How do I select all the records of the `CurrentInventory` table of the `DatabaseConnection` database connection?

A Use the following ASP statement:

```
<%
  Set CurrentRecordSet = _
  DatabaseConnection.Execute ("SELECT * FROM CurrentInventory ")
%>
```

Q How do I move to the first record?

A Use the following ASP statement:

```
<% CurrentRecordSet.MoveFirst %>
```

Q How do I delete a record in the CD table whose `CDNumber` field is 5?

A Use the following ASP statement:

```
<%
  DatabaseConnection.Execute _
    "DELETE * FROM CDs WHERE CDNumber = 5"
%>
```

Q How do I create a record set with CDs containing the string `Greatest Hits` in the `CDTitle` field of the `CDs` table?

A Use the following ASP statement:

```
<%
  UserCDTitle           = _
  Set CurrentRecordSet = _
    DatabaseConnection.Execute _
    ("SELECT * FROM CDs WHERE CDTitle LIKE'%Greatest Hits%'")
%>
```

Exercises

1. Modify the CD cataloging application so that it can be used to catalog songs of CDs.

2. Create an option that randomly selects five CDs when a music category is given.

14

WEEK 2

In Review

The Data Access component and ActiveX data objects (ADOs) can be used to easily interface with databases. ADO's advantages include speed, small disk footprint, low memory usage, and the capability to function in a connectionless and stateless environment like the Internet. ADO (and OLE DB) exposes data from a data provider in a tabular form. The most important exposed object in ADO is the Recordset object. The other exposed objects and methods enable the creation or manipulation of Recordset objects. Performance should always be a consideration when developing Web database applications. Because there is usually more than one way to accomplish a task, your challenge is to understand ADO and find the best method.

Although IIS 3.0 supports the Internet Database Connector, Active Server Pages is far more suitable for developing dynamic Web database applications. Various components and utilities that can be freely downloaded from Microsoft's Web site can be used to aid in the development of ASP applications (or even to port IDC applications to ASP). Both Microsoft Visual InterDev and Microsoft Access support Active Server Pages and can be used to easily develop Web interfaces to databases using Active Server Pages.

You can extend the capabilities of Active Server Pages by developing your own custom ASP components. Custom ASP components can be developed through a variety of application development environments that allow the creation of ActiveX controls. Visual Basic 5.0 can be used to easily develop custom ASP components. Your VBScript skills can be leveraged to develop custom ASP components because the syntax of Visual Basic is very similar to VBScript. Custom ASP components promote data encapsulation, ease of code distribution, security, and centralized code management. When developing large projects, you should develop your own custom ASP components to handle tasks that can be more efficiently and easily carried out through the use of another application development environment such as Visual Basic or Visual C++. You will then be able to mix and match the best features of each application development environment. Do not develop ASP components that are overly complicated. Concentrate on developing well-defined, small, and efficient ASP components that handle a certain task extremely well. You will then be able to efficiently reuse your custom ASP components when developing future Web applications. Think of ActiveX components as bricks you are using to develop a large structure. If the bricks you use are too small, you are going to make the project unnecessarily complicated. On the other hand, if you make your bricks too large, you will not be able to design a refined structure.

Microsoft Visual InterDev is the newest member of Microsoft's Visual Studio family. Visual InterDev is designed to make you more productive as a Web developer by making your life easier through the use of visual tools and an integrated development environment.

Visual InterDev quickly develops professional-looking pages and complex ASP statements. If you plan to develop complicated ASP applications or components, or if you work with others to develop applications, you should seriously consider investing in Visual InterDev.

Server variables can be used to obtain useful information about the current HTTP session. Server variables are accessed through the `ServerVariables()` method of the `Request` object.

You can take various steps to protect an NT server on the Internet against unauthorized access. Although setting up an Internet server that is immune to unauthorized access is virtually impossible, you can take steps to make it harder, and in some cases, prohibitively expensive for someone to gain unauthorized access. The following is a summary of steps that can be taken to make your NT Web server more secure:

☐ Use NTFS partitions (you cannot enforce Windows NT security on FAT partitions)

☐ Limit membership to the Administrators group

☐ Monitor security logs

☐ Enable auditing

☐ Enable Web server access logging

☐ Consult Web server access logs to track down suspicious activities

☐ Encrypt sensitive information

☐ Limit access to CGI/ASP directories

☐ Limit the number of CGI directories

☐ Physically secure your server

The Active Database component included with Active Server Pages can be used to easily create Web interfaces to ODBC databases. On Day 14, "Developing a CD Cataloging System with ASP," you learn how to use tips and techniques presented on previous days to develop a CD-cataloging database.

Bonus Day 15

Chapter 15

Bonus Day: Practical Applications of ASP

Congratulations! You made it to the last day of *Teach Yourself Active Server Pages in 14 Days*! This bonus day has been included to provide an overview of some of the tasks you can accomplish using Active Server Pages and to reinforce tips and techniques presented on previous days. No new information will be presented to you today; all the information required to develop the Web applications presented today has been covered in previous days. Today you will be shown how to do the following using Active Server Pages:

☐ Insert a time stamp into a Web page and greet the user with a special message the first time he invokes the Web page.

☐ Create a Web application that allows the user to select a URL to navigate using a pull-down list.

☐ Create a Web e-mail gateway that uses a custom Visual Basic component to e-mail a file to a given e-mail address.

Time-Stamping Web Pages

When displaying time-sensitive information in a Web page, it is useful to display when the Web page was generated. The ASP application in Listing 15.1 can be used to insert a time stamp into a Web page. As an added incentive, the ASP application displays a special welcome message to the user the first time he invokes the Web page, as shown in Figure 15.1.

Listing 15.1. Time-stamping Web pages.

```
 1: <%@ LANGUAGE="VBSCRIPT" %>
 2:
 3: <%
 4:
 5:   Dim FirstVisit
 6:
 7:   LastAccessTime = Request.Cookies ("LastTime")
 8:   LastAccessDate = Request.Cookies ("LastDate")
 9:
10:   If (Request.Cookies ("FirstVisit")="") Then
11:     Response.Cookies ("FirstVisit") = FALSE
12:     FirstVisit = TRUE
13:     Response.Cookies ("FirstVisit").Expires = Date + 365
14:   Else
15:     FirstVisit = FALSE
16:   End If
17:
18:   Response.Cookies ("LastDate") = Date
19:   Response.Cookies ("LastDate").Expires = Date + 365
20:
21:   Response.Cookies ("LastTime") = Time
22:   Response.Cookies ("LastTime").Expires = Date + 365
23:
24: %>
25:
26: <HTML>
27: <HEAD>
28: <META NAME="GENERATOR" Content="Microsoft Visual InterDev 1.0">
29: <META HTTP-EQUIV="Content-Type" content="text/html; charset=iso-8859-1">
30: <TITLE>Time Stamping Web Pages</TITLE>
31: </HEAD>
32: <BODY BGCOLOR=FFFFFF>
33:
34: <H2>
35: Contents of the Web page go here
36: </H2>
37:
38: <HR>
39:
40: <!-- Display when the current system date/time
41:      of the Web server -->
42: This Web page was generated on <%= FormatDateTime(date,vbLongDate)%>
43: at <%= FormatDateTime(time,vbLongTime)%>.<BR>
```

15

```
44:
45: <!-- If the Web browser supports cookies, we
46:      display when the user last visited this
47:      Web page -->
48: <%
49:
50:   Set BrowserCapabilities = Server.CreateObject("MSWC.BrowserType")
51:   If (BrowserCapabilities.cookies = TRUE) Then %>
52:
53:     <% If FirstVisit Then %>
54:       Thanks for visiting this Web page for the
55:       first time!
56:     <% Else %>
57:     You last visited this Web page
58:     on <%= FormatDateTime(LastAccessDate,vbLongDate)%>
59:     at <%= FormatDateTime(LastAccessTime,vbLongTime)%>.<BR>
60:     <% End If %>
61:
62: <% End If %>
63:
64: </BODY>
65: </HTML>
```

Figure 15.1.

A special greeting is displayed the first time the ASP application is invoked via Internet Explorer.

Each subsequent time the user invokes the Web page, he is shown the date and time the Web page was generated along with the last date and time he visited the Web page (see Figure 15.2). The ASP application uses cookies to keep track of information between HTTP sessions.

Figure 15.2.

The user is shown the date and time he last visited the Web page.

The ASP application in Listing 15.1 first determines whether the user has previously visited the Web page. If so, the local variable FirstVisit is set to TRUE (lines 10–16). If the user has not visited the Web page before, the local variable FirstVisit is set to FALSE and a cookie is created to note that the user has visited the Web page before (lines 11–13).

 NOTE
When creating a cookie you intend to use in a future HTTP session, it is important that you define an expiration date as shown in line 13 of Listing 15.1. Otherwise, the cookie will be discarded when the Web browser session is terminated.

The ASP application in Listing 15.1 uses cookies to retain information between HTTP sessions. Because cookies are an Internet standard, the ASP application in Listing 15.1 works with any Web browser that supports cookies. Notice how this ASP application produces identical output when viewed with Internet Explorer (refer to Figures 15.1 and 15.2) or Netscape Navigator (see Figures 15.3 and 15.4).

Figure 15.3.

A special greeting is displayed the first time the ASP application is invoked via Netscape Navigator.

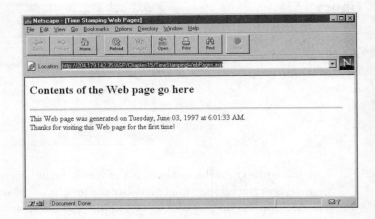

If the Web browser does not support cookies, the ASP application in Listing 15.1 displays the Web page shown in Figure 15.5. The Browser Capabilities component defined in line 50 of Listing 15.1 is used to determine whether the Web browser supports cookies. Lines 50–62 demonstrate how the Browser Capabilities component can be used to provide an information-rich Web-browsing experience while ensuring that technologically challenged Web browsers are not forgotten.

Figure 15.4.

The ASP application is reloaded via Netscape Navigator.

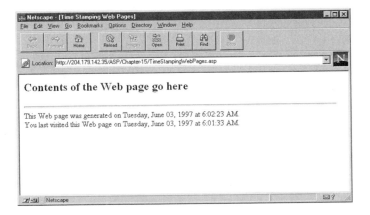

Figure 15.5.

The ASP application browsed using a Web browser that does not support cookies.

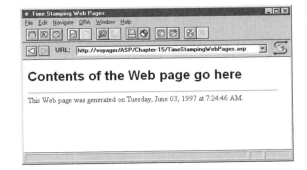

Creating a Pull-Down List of URLs

The Redirect method of the Response object is very useful because it can be used to redirect the Web browser to another Web page. The ASP application in Listing 15.2 takes advantage of the Redirect method to implement a pull-down list of URLs. When a user invokes the ASP application in Listing 15.2, he sees a pull-down menu. The user can use this menu to select a Web page, as shown in Figure 15.6.

Listing 15.2. Creating a pull-down list of URLs.

```
1: <%@ LANGUAGE="VBSCRIPT" %>
2: <%
3:
4: ' If the user has selected a URL to visit,
5: ' we transfer him/her there.
```

continues

Listing 15.2. continued

```
 6:
 7:
 8: RedirectURL = Request.QueryString("URLToNavigate")
 9:
10: IF NOT ( RedirectURL = "") THEN
11:
12: Select Case RedirectURL
13:   Case "WebPage01"
14:     Response.Redirect "WebPage01.html"
15:   Case "WebPage02"
16:     Response.Redirect "WebPage02.html"
17:   Case "WebPage03"
18:     Response.Redirect "WebPage03.html"
19: End Select
20:
21: End If
22: %>
23: <!DOCTYPE HTML PUBLIC "-//IETF//DTD HTML//EN">
24: <html>
25:
26: <head>
27: <meta http-equiv="Content-Type"
28: content="text/html; charset=iso-8859-1">
29: <title>Select A URL To Navigate</title>
30: </head>
31:
32: <body bgcolor="#FFFFFF">
33:
34: <div align="center"><center>
35:
36: <table border="4" width="400">
37:     <tr>
38:         <td bgcolor="#000000"><p align="center"><font
39:         color="#FFFF80" size="4" face="Verdana"><strong>Please
40:         Select A URL To Navigate</strong></font></p>
41:         </td>
42:     </tr>
43:     <tr>
44:         <td bgcolor="#FFFFB9"><form method="Get"
45:         name="PullDownListOfURLs.asp">
46:             <select name="URLToNavigate" size="1">
47:                 <option selected value="WebPage01">Web Page 01</option>
48:                 <option value="WebPage02">Web Page 02</option>
49:                 <option value="WebPage03">Web Page 03</option>
50:             </select>
51:             <input type="submit" name="SubmitURL"
52:             value="Submit">
53:         </form>
54:         </td>
55:     </tr>
56: </table>
57: </center></div>
58: </body>
59: </html>
```

15

Users select a Web page to navigate using the pull-down list declared in lines 46–50 of Listing 15.2. After the user selects a Web page to navigate, the If statement declared in lines 10–21 transfers the user to the selected Web page.

Figure 15.6.

The user selects Web Page 03.

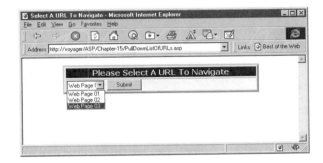

Lines 8–19 of the ASP application in Listing 15.2 redirect the user to the Web page selected in Figure 15.6, as shown in Figure 15.7.

Figure 15.7.

The ASP application redirects the Web browser to WebPage03.html.

The source code of the HTML file WebPage03.html can be found in Listing 15.3.

Listing 15.3. The source code of WebPage03.html.

```
1: <!DOCTYPE HTML PUBLIC "-//IETF//DTD HTML//EN">
2: <html>
3:
4: <head>
5: <meta http-equiv="Content-Type"
6: content="text/html; charset=iso-8859-1">
7: <title>You have selected Web Page 03!</title>
8: </head>
9:
```

continues

Listing 15.3. continued

```
10: <body bgcolor="#FFFFFF" text="#000000">
11:
12: <p align="center">
13: <img src="Target170.gif" width="48" height="51">
14: </p>
15:
16: <p align="center">
17: <font color="#FF0000" size="5" face="Comic Sans MS">
18: <strong>You have selected Web Page 03!</strong>
19: </font></p>
20:
21: <hr>
22:
23: <p><a href="PullDownListOfURLs.asp">
24: Please select this URL to return to the ASP application
25: </a></p>
26:
27: </body>
28: </html>
```

Developing a Web E-Mail Gateway

It is sometimes convenient to e-mail certain files to users browsing your Web site. For example, a user might be browsing your Web site at home using a slow, analog modem connection. Rather than download a multi-megabyte file, the user can select to have the file sent to her e-mail address. The user can then retrieve the file via her e-mail account when she can afford to spare the bandwidth (possibly when she's at work and connected to the Internet with a higher-bandwidth Internet connection).

The ASP application discussed in this section demonstrates how to develop a Web e-mail gateway using an ASP application. The ASP application uses Blat (a very useful Windows NT utility application that can be used to e-mail files from the NT command prompt) to actually send the e-mail message.

Installing and Configuring Blat for E-Mail

Before you begin developing the ASP application presented in this section, ensure that Blat is installed on your system. If you are familiar with C/C++, you will be happy to know that Blat's source code is included with the distribution file. After you download the latest version of Blat from http://gepasi.dbs.aber.ac.uk/softw/blat.html, follow these directions to install and configure Blat on your computer:

15

1. Before you install Blat, make sure you are connected to the Internet. This is because Blat needs access to an SMTP server to send e-mail messages. You will also need the address of your SMTP server. Consult your network administrator or ISP if you do not know the address of your SMTP server.

2. Download Blat, then decompress the distribution file. Locate the file `gwinsock.dll` and copy it to your `\WINNT\SYSTEM32` directory.

NOTE

Replace an existing `gwinsock.dll` file only if the version you downloaded is more recent than the version in the `\WINNT\SYSTEM32` directory.

3. Copy the file `Blat.exe` to your Windows System32 directory (`\WINNT\SYSTEM32`). You can copy `Blat.exe` to a different directory if you wish, provided that the directory you use is in the Windows `PATH`.

4. Install Blat on your computer by opening a Windows NT command prompt and typing `Blat -install` `smtp.address.of.mail.server YourEmailAddress@YourDomain.com`. Simply replace `smtp.address.of.mail.server` with the address of your SMTP server and `YourEmailAddress@YourDomain.com` with your e-mail address. Your e-mail address is used as the default From address when e-mail is sent out.

5. Blat is now configured and ready for use. In the next section, you will learn how to invoke Blat from an ASP custom component developed using Visual Basic.

After Blat is installed, you can e-mail a file to a user via the command `Blat C:\Filename.txt -t email@address.com`, as shown in Figure 15.8. Replace `C:\Filename.txt` with the name of the file you wish to e-mail and replace `email@address.com` with the recipient's e-mail address.

Figure 15.8.

Blat can be used to send e-mail messages from the Windows NT command prompt.

For a list of Blat command-line switches and arguments, use the command `Blat -h`, as shown in Figure 15.9.

Figure 15.9.

Command-line switches and arguments of Blat.

Developing a Custom ASP Component to Interact with Blat

Create a custom ASP component using Visual Basic as shown in the "Developing a Custom ASP Component" section of Day 10, "Developing Custom ActiveX Components." Name the custom ASP component EMail and create a class inside the component named EMailFile, as shown in Figure 15.10. Create a Public function (using the text in Listing 15.4) inside the class EMailFile, as shown in Figure 15.10, and compile it into a DLL file.

NOTE

If you have to recompile the DLL file, make sure all services (World Wide Web, FTP, Gopher, and so on) of IIS are stopped before compiling the DLL file. You can restart the IIS services after the DLL file is compiled.

Figure 15.10.

The custom ASP component uses the Visual Basic Shell() command to invoke Blat.

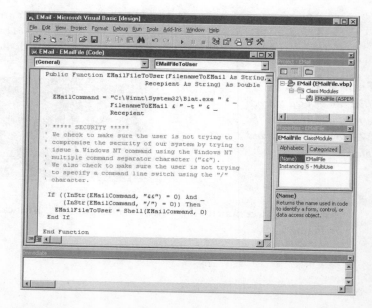

The Visual Basic function in Listing 15.4 uses the `Shell()` command to invoke Blat. Because the VB function is declared as a `Public` function, it is exposed to the ASP application in Listing 15.5 after an instance of the VB component is instantiated.

SECURITY

Pay particular attention to the security check in lines 17–20 of Listing 15.4. These lines examine the two arguments passed into the function to ensure that they do not compromise the security of your system. Windows NT uses the character sequences `"&&"` and `"/"` to specify additional commands and command-line switches. A user might try to exploit this feature by appending character sequences to the e-mail message (for example, the character sequence `&& del C:\*.*`, which would delete all the files in the root directory of your C drive). Always examine input provided by users (especially if the input will be used as a command-line argument) to avoid a breach in security.

Listing 15.4. Source code of the Active Server Pages VB component.

```
 1: Public Function EMailFileToUser(FilenameToEMail As String, _
 2:                         Recipient As String) As Double
 3:
 4:    EMailCommand = "C:\Winnt\System32\Blat.exe " & _
 5:                   FilenameToEMail & " -t " & _
 6:                   Recipient
 7:
 8: ' ***** SECURITY *****
 9: ' We check to make sure the user is not trying to
10: ' compromise the security of our system by trying to
11: ' issue a Windows NT command using the Windows NT
12: ' multiple command separator character ("&&").
13: ' We also check to make sure the user is not trying
14: ' to specify a command line switch using the "/"
15: ' character.
16:
17:    If ((InStr(EMailCommand, "&&") = 0) And _
18:        (InStr(EMailCommand, "/") = 0)) Then
19:      EMailFileToUser = Shell(EMailCommand, 0)
20:    End If
21:
22: End Function
```

Developing the Web E-Mail Gateway ASP Application

The ASP application in Listing 15.5 uses the ASP component developed in the previous section to implement a Web e-mail gateway. When the ASP application in Listing 15.5 is invoked, the HTML form in Figure 15.11 is displayed. This HTML form is used to select a file and specify an e-mail address.

SECURITY

> When addressing security issues, redundancy never hurts. Notice how both the ASP component and the ASP application examine the user's input to ensure that security of the system is not compromised.

Listing 15.5. Developing a Web e-mail gateway.

```
 1: <%@ LANGUAGE="VBSCRIPT" %>
 2:
 3: <HTML>
 4: <HEAD>
 5: <META NAME="GENERATOR" Content="Microsoft Visual InterDev 1.0">
 6: <META HTTP-EQUIV="Content-Type" content="text/html; charset=iso-8859-1">
 7: <TITLE>Implementing A Web E-mail Gateway</TITLE>
 8: </HEAD>
 9: <BODY BGCOLOR=FFFFFF>
10:
11: <BR><BR>
12:
13: <%
14:
15: ' User's EMailAddress
16:    Dim EMailAddress
17:
18: ' Filename selected by the user
19:    Dim UserSelectedFile
20:
21: ' Filename to e-mail
22:    Dim FileToEMail
23:
24:    EMailAddress     = Request.QueryString("EMailAddress")
25:    UserSelectedFile = Request.QueryString("FileToEMail")
26:
27: ' First we check to see if the user has filled in the form.
28: ' If not, we display a form.
29:
30:    IF ( EMailAddress = "") THEN
31:
32: %>
33:
34: <div align="left">
35:
36: <form method="GET" name="WebEMailGateway.asp">
37: <table border="4" width="400">
38:     <tr>
39:         <td bgcolor="#FEEBAF">
40:           <Strong>
41:             Please select the file you wish to receive via e-mail
42:           </Strong>
```

15

```
43:            </td>
44:        </tr>
45:        <tr>
46:            <td>
47:                <p><select name="FileToEMail" size="1">
48:                    <option selected value="WebPage01">Web Page 01</option>
49:                    <option value="WebPage02">Web Page 02</option>
50:                    <option value="WebPage03">Web Page 03</option>
51:                </select></p>
52:            </td>
53:        </tr>
54:        <tr>
55:            <td bgcolor="#FEEBAF">
56:                <Strong>
57:                    Please type your e-mail address below
58:                </Strong>
59:            </td>
60:        </tr>
61:        <tr>
62:            <td>
63:                <input type="text" size="40" name="EMailAddress">
64:            </td>
65:        </tr>
66:        <tr>
67:            <td>
68:                <input type="submit" name="SubmitForm"
69:                value="Press here to submit your form">
70:            </td>
71:        </tr>
72: </table>
73: </form>
74: </div>
75:
76: <%
77: ' If the user has filled in the form, we process it.
78:
79:    Else
80:
81: ' Variables used to instantiate the ASP component
82:    Dim EMailComponent
83:    Dim Result
84:
85:    Select Case UserSelectedFile
86:       Case "WebPage01"
87:          FileToEMail = "E:\Publish\WWW\ASP\Chapter-15\WebPage01.html"
88:       Case "WebPage02"
89:          FileToEMail = "E:\Publish\WWW\ASP\Chapter-15\WebPage02.html"
90:       Case Else
91:          FileToEMail = "E:\Publish\WWW\ASP\Chapter-15\WebPage03.html"
92:    End Select
93:
94: ' ***** !!!!! SECURITY !!!!! *****
95: ' We check to make sure the user is not trying to
96: ' compromise the security of our system by trying to
97: ' issue a Windows NT command using the Windows NT
98: ' multiple command separator character ("&&").
99: ' We also check to make sure the user is not trying
```

continues

Listing 15.5. continued

```
100: ' to specify a command line switch using the "/"
101: ' character.
102:
103:    If ((InStr(EMailAddress, "&&") = 0) And _
104:        (InStr(EMailAddress, "/") = 0)) Then
105:
106: ' Create an instance of the VB ASP component
107:        Set EmailComponent = _
108:          Server.CreateObject ("EMail.EMailFile")
109:        Result = EmailComponent.EMailFileToUser (CStr(FileToEMail),
➥CStr(EMailAddress))
110: %>
111:
112:        <table border=0>
113:        <tr>
114:          <td bgcolor="#000000"><font color="#FFFFFF"
115:          size="4" Face="Comic Sans MS">
116:            The file you selected has been
117:            e-mailed to you!</font> </td>
118:        </tr>
119:        </table>
120:
121:        <hr>
122:
123:        <p>
124:        Please select<a href="WebEMailGateway.asp"> this link</a>
125:        to return to the ASP application.
126:        </p>
127:
128: <%
129:    Else
130:
131: ' ***** !!!!! SECURITY !!!!! *****
132: ' If the user attempted to compromise the security of the
133: ' system, an error message is displayed.
134:
135:        Response.Write "<TABLE BORDER=3><TR><TD>"
136:        Response.Write "<H1>Error code: SEC-001</H1>"
137:        Response.Write "Your request cannot be processed.<P>"
138:        Response.Write "Please report the error code to the "
139:        Response.Write "system administrator."
140:        Response.Write "</TD></TR></TABLE>"
141:
142:    End If
143: %>
144:
145: <%
146:    End If
147: %>
148:
149: </BODY>
150: </HTML>
```

15

ANALYSIS After the specified e-mail address is examined for any attempts to breach system security (see lines 103–104 of Listing 15.5), the selected file is sent to the e-mail address specified via the Visual Basic custom ASP component developed in the previous section. Line 109 of Listing 15.5 calls the Visual Basic function in Listing 15.4.

Figure 15.11.

A file and an e-mail address are specified.

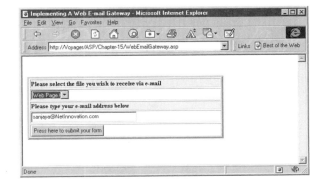

The ASP application displays a confirmation message (see Figure 15.12) after the file has been e-mailed to the user. See Figure 15.13 for the actual file e-mailed by the ASP application.

Figure 15.12.

The confirmation message displayed by the ASP application.

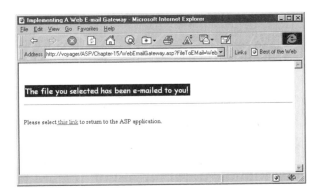

Figure 15.13.

*The selected file is
e-mailed to the e-mail
address specified in
Figure 15.11.*

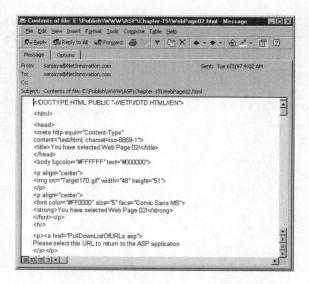

Exercises

1. Modify the CD cataloging database application so that the user can specify custom text and background colors.

2. Use cookies to keep track of previous search values. For example, if a user searched for the string Greatest Hits, the next time the user invokes the search form, it automatically fills in the data-entry field with the string Greatest Hits.

3. Expand the CD cataloging database application to also keep track of songs. (Hint: create a Songs table to keep track of songs.)

Where to Go from Here

Congratulations! You've just completed the final day of learning about Active Server Pages. During the last two weeks, you learned how you can develop your own dynamic and interactive Web applications using ASP. You also learned how to extend the default functionality of ASP by developing your own custom components and using a different scripting language such as Perl.

Active Server Pages is a very powerful technology that can be used to develop highly sophisticated Web applications. It accomplishes this by providing a simple development environment that still manages to expose very powerful Web application development interfaces to the Web application developer. For example, an ASP application can use components created using Visual Basic, Visual C++, Visual J++, and Delphi all at the same

15

15

time! What's more, an ASP application can use VBScript, JavaScript, and even Perl to script Web applications and interface with ASP components. As you see, the ASP framework provides you with the freedom and flexibility to tackle virtually any Web project. All you really need to write ASP applications is IIS 3.0 and a text editor (yes, even Notepad will do!).

If you are not using Visual InterDev already, I highly recommend that you invest in a copy. Visual InterDev makes it easier to develop ASP applications—especially database-intensive applications. If you are already using one of Microsoft's other Visual tools, such as Visual J++, Visual C++, or Visual Basic, you will be happy to know that Visual InterDev is well integrated with these tools.

Skills you learned during the last 15 days can be employed to make the best use of Microsoft's most powerful Web application development technology: Active Server Pages. So what are you waiting for? Activate the Internet—one Active Server Page at a time!

APPENDIX A

VBScript Primer

Nearly all ASP applications in this book are written using VBScript. The purpose of this appendix is to introduce you to VBScript, to demonstrate how to use various features of VBScript, and to illustrate the development of simple, client-side VBScript applications. By taking advantage of scripting capabilities on the server using Active Server Pages and scripting capabilities on the client using VBScript, you can present information to your users in a compelling manner.

A long time ago (which translates to about 18 months with respect to the Internet), people were discovering the virtues of providing dynamic information to users browsing a Web site. CGI applications were typically used to create Web pages that displayed dynamic information. Although this worked well in some cases, it did not work well for some people. The development of a CGI application typically obligated the developer to learn a programming language such as C or C++, compile the CGI application, transfer it to the CGI directory of a Web server, and test the CGI application for bugs. Even the slightest change to the application meant that the application had to be recompiled and the process of copying the application to a CGI directory and testing the application for bugs had to be repeated. To solve this problem, Web scripting languages such as JavaScript and VBScript were developed to aid in the development of client-side and server-side CGI applications. Although Web scripting languages are widely used in the development of client-side Web applications that run on the Web browser, Web scripting languages are also used to develop server-side applications in the form of Active Server Pages. Therefore, skills you learn in this section can be used to not only develop interactive client-side Web applications, but also to develop server-side Web applications.

Why Use VBScript?

Developed by Microsoft, VBScript is designed to leverage the skills and investments of millions of VB programmers to the Internet. VBScript boasts the following advantages:

☐ VBScript is powerful—Various capabilities of VBScript can be used to develop richly interactive Web pages that respond to user input in an intelligent manner. For example, when a user submits a form, a VBScript subroutine can be triggered to verify that the form has been properly filled in with valid values. In the case of a server-side CGI application, VBScript can be used to process data submitted by users with the aid of ActiveX controls designed especially for Microsoft Active Server Pages.

☐ VBScript is lightweight—Because VBScript code is lightweight, fast, and has been optimized to be transmitted via the Internet, it can be quickly transmitted to users browsing a Web site—even via relatively slow Plain Old Telephone Service (POTS) links to the Internet.

☐ VBScript is easy to use—Compared to scripting languages such as JavaScript, VBScript is easier to use because it is based on the easy-to-learn BASIC (Beginner's All Purpose Symbolic Instruction Code) language.

☐ VBScript is freely available—Microsoft has made VBScript freely available to software vendors so they can add scripting capabilities to their applications with the aid of VBScript.

☐ VBScript is cross-platform—By the time you read this, VBScript will be functioning on UNIX as well as Macintosh computers in addition to Windows 95 and Windows NT computers.

☐ VBScript is cross-language—VBScript supports any language, such as C++ and Java, that allows objects to be compiled as ActiveX controls.

Because VBScript is supported by Microsoft, expect to see a great deal of integration between VBScript and Internet Explorer, Windows NT/95, Microsoft Office, and Microsoft BackOffice in the near future.

VBScript is a subset of Microsoft Visual Basic and is upwardly compatible with Visual Basic for Applications (VBA). VBA is shipped with Microsoft Office applications to make it easier for developers to build custom solutions using Microsoft Office applications. The capability to provide scripting, automation, and customization for Web browsers and Web servers is a major feature of VBScript. If you are already familiar with Visual Basic, very shortly you will be able to leverage your skills to the Internet using VBScript. Even if you are not familiar with another programming language, after reading this appendix you will be able to create interactive Web pages using VBScript. However, familiarity with a programming language will make it easier for you to grasp various concepts such as type casting, control structures, and Boolean arithmetic presented in later sections of this appendix.

URL

Visit the Microsoft VBScript information Web site for the latest information about VBScript:

`http://www.microsoft.com/VBScript`

But What About JavaScript?

You've probably heard about JavaScript by now; you might have already developed JavaScript applications to accomplish various tasks. You may be wondering why you should bother to learn JavaScript if you know VBScript or vice versa.

If you know neither scripting language, you should start out with VBScript and learn how VBScript is used to develop interactive Web applications. As mentioned earlier, VBScript is easy to learn, and you can use it to start developing interactive Web applications in no time—even if you are new to programming.

If you are familiar with Visual Basic or VBA, you already know VBScript and you will be able to easily leverage your skills to the Internet using VBScript. Except for a few differences in the language and the availability of additional objects for obtaining information about Web transactions, VBScript is very similar to Visual Basic and VBA.

If you know JavaScript, learning VBScript will make it easier for you to learn Visual Basic and VBA. Visual Basic 5.0 can be used to easily develop ActiveX controls. Information presented in this appendix will help you learn VBScript and leverage your VBScript skills when developing ActiveX controls with Visual Basic.

After you learn VBScript and JavaScript, you can select the language with which you are most comfortable developing Web applications.

How VBScript Works

VBScript programs are defined within the `<SCRIPT LANGUAGE=VBS>` and `</SCRIPT>` HTML tags. Browsers that support VBScript read the VBScript application contained within these tags and execute it after checking the code for syntax errors. VBScript works as shown in Figure A.1.

Figure A.1.
How VBScript works.

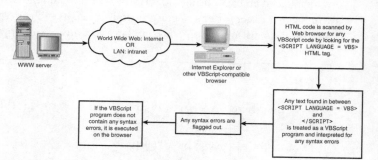

When a Web browser that supports VBScript encounters the `<SCRIPT LANGUAGE=VBS>` HTML tag, all text between that tag and `</SCRIPT>` is treated as a VBScript application and is checked for syntax errors. If the application contains no syntax errors, it is executed on the Web browser. If syntax errors are detected, they are flagged by the VBScript interpreter, as shown in Figure A.2.

Figure A.2.
Syntax errors in VBScript programs are flagged by the VBScript interpreter.

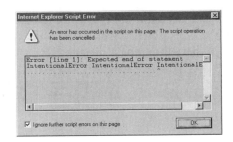

Dealing with Technologically Challenged Web Browsers

To hide VBScript code from technologically challenged Web browsers, you can enclose it in two HTML comment tags as shown in Listing A.1. This prevents technologically challenged Web browsers from attempting to display the VBScript application as though it is part of the HTML code of the Web page.

Listing A.1. Hiding VBScript code from technologically challenged Web browsers.

```
<SCRIPT LANGUAGE=VBS>
<!-- To hide VBScript code from technologically challenged
     Web browsers
…VBScript code…
!-->
</SCRIPT>
```

Hello World! VBScript

Writing the classic Hello World! application with VBScript is very easy. For the purpose of this example, you will be shown how to create a Web page similar to the one in Figure A.3. This Web page will have three buttons: The first will display a message box with a greeting, the second will display the current time, and the third will display the current date.

The Hello World! Dialog Box

The Hello World! dialog box, shown in Figure A.4, is displayed each time a user clicks the Please click here for message box button shown in Figure A.3. If you look at the HTML page of the VBScript application (see lines 22 and 23 of Listing A.5), you will see that the command button associated with the Hello World! dialog box is named. As shown in line 1 of Listing A.2, the OnClick event of the BtnHello command button is associated with the

`BtnHello_OnClick` subroutine. Each time a user clicks the Please click here for message box button, the Web browser invokes the `BtnHello_OnClick` subroutine and any VBScript code defined in that subroutine is executed.

Figure A.3.

The classic Hello World! application written with VBScript.

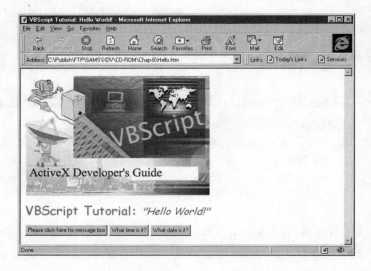

The `BtnHello_OnClick` subroutine is very simple. The first three lines create strings displayed in the dialog box shown in Figure A.4. Note how the string concatenation operator (&) is used in line 4 to merge two strings and assign the result to a variable. The result is then displayed in the message box shown in Figure A.4.

Figure A.4.

The Hello World! dialog box.

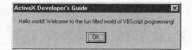

NOTE

Lines numbers are not part of the VBScript code. Line numbers have been inserted to make it easier to refer to various lines of code. This applies to all subsequent code listings with line numbers.

Listing A.2. The `BtnHello_OnClick` subroutine.

```
1: Sub BtnHello_OnClick
2:   titleString = "ActiveX Developer's Guide"
3:   helloString = "Hello world! Welcome to the fun filled "
```

```
4:  helloString = helloString & "world of VBScript programming!"
5:  MsgBox helloString, 0, titleString
6: End Sub
```

The Time Dialog Box

The `BtnTime_OnClick` subroutine is very similar to the `BtnHello_OnClick` subroutine. The only difference is that rather than concatenating two strings, it concatenates a string with the result of a function. The `time` function returns the current time. Line 3 of Listing A.3 displays the current time in a dialog box (see Figure A.5). The `BtnTime_OnClick` subroutine is associated with the `OnClick` event of the `BtnTime` command button.

Listing A.3. The `BtnTime_OnClick` subroutine.

```
1: Sub BtnTime_OnClick
2:  timeString = "So, you want to know the time? The time is " & time
3:  MsgBox  timeString , 0, "Time Dialog Box"
4: End Sub
```

Figure A.5.
The Time dialog box.

The Date Dialog Box

The Date dialog box displays the current date, as shown in Figure A.6. As you can see in line 2 of Listing A.4, the result of one function (`date`) can be used as an argument (input) of another function (`DateValue`).

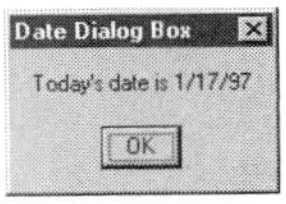

Figure A.6.
The Date dialog box.

Listing A.4. The `BtnDate_OnClick` Subroutine.

```
1: Sub BtnDate_OnClick
2:  dateString = "Today's date is " & DateValue(date)
3:  MsgBox  dateString , 0, "Date Dialog Box"
4: End Sub
```

For your reference, the full source code of the Hello World! application is provided in Listing A.5.

Listing A.5. The Hello World! Web page.

```
 1: <!--
 2: © 1996 Sanjaya Hettihewa
 3: http://www.NetInnovation.com/sanjaya
 4: !-->
 5:
 6: <HTML>
 7: <HEAD>
 8: <TITLE>VBScript Tutorial: Hello World!</TITLE>
 9: </HEAD>
10:
11: <BODY BGCOLOR="#FFFFFF" TEXT="#0000FF"
12:       LINK="#B864FF" VLINK="#670000" ALINK="#FF0000">
13:
14: <IMG SRC="vbscript.jpg"><P>
15:
16: <B><FONT FACE="Comic Sans MS" SIZE=6 COLOR=RED>
17: VBScript Tutorial: <FONT></B>
18: <I><FONT FACE="Comic Sans MS" SIZE=5 COLOR=BLUE>
19:  "Hello World!" </I><P><FONT>
20:
21: <form>
22: <INPUT TYPE=BUTTON VALUE="Please click here for message box"
23:       NAME="BtnHello">
24: <INPUT TYPE=BUTTON VALUE="What time is it?"
25:       NAME="BtnTime">
26: <INPUT TYPE=BUTTON VALUE="What date is it?"
27:       NAME="BtnDate">
28: </form>
29:
30: <SCRIPT LANGUAGE="VBScript">
31: <!-- To hide VBScript code from technologically challenged browsers
32:
33: Sub BtnHello_OnClick
34:  titleString = "ActiveX Developer's Guide"
35:  helloString = "Hello world! Welcome to the fun filled "
36:  helloString = helloString & "world of VBScript programming!"
37:  MsgBox helloString, 0, titleString
38: End Sub
39:
40: Sub BtnTime_OnClick
41:  timeString = "So, you want to know the time? The time is " & time
42:  MsgBox  timeString , 0, "Time Dialog Box"
43: End Sub
44:
45: Sub BtnDate_OnClick
46:  dateString = "Today's date is " & DateValue(date)
47:  MsgBox  dateString , 0, "Date Dialog Box"
48: End Sub
49: !-->
50: </SCRIPT>
51:
52: </BODY>
53:
54: </HTML>
```

Fundamentals of VBScript

VBScript is used by Web page developers to add scripting, automation, and customization capabilities to Web pages and to develop richly interactive Web applications. This section covers the fundamentals of VBScript Web application development. If you're already familiar with the basics of VBScript, you might want to skim this section and proceed to the section titled "Using VBScript Data Structures."

The client-side VBScript engine is part of Internet Explorer and is installed on your system when you install Internet Explorer. If Internet Explorer 3.0 or better is not installed on your system, please install it before you proceed. Even if you have Internet Explorer 3.0 installed on your system, visit Microsoft's Internet Explorer Web page to find out the availability of a more recent version of Internet Explorer (Internet Explorer 4.0 or better should be available for download by the time you read this).

> **URL**
>
> Visit Microsoft's Internet Explorer Web site at `http://www.microsoft.com/ie/default.asp` for the most up-to-date information about Internet Explorer.

Figure A.7 shows a graphical representation of how client-side VBScript applications are executed by Web browsers. When a VBScript-compatible Web browser downloads a Web page containing VBScript code, it executes that code whenever an object of the Web page triggers a VBScript subroutine contained in the VBScript code.

The Structure of a VBScript Application

Before you develop VBScript applications, it is important that you understand their structure. A typical VBScript application is composed of the following:

- ☐ HTML code—The HTML code can contain any number of valid HTML statements. For example, Listing A.6 contains valid HTML statements in every line of code except lines 23–42.

- ☐ VBScript code delimiters—These separate VBScript code from the HTML code of a Web page. Lines 23–24 and 41–42 of Listing A.6 are examples of VBScript code delimiters. Notice how the HTML comment tags (`<!--` and `-->`) are used to enclose the VBScript source code. These tags prevent VBScript-challenged Web browsers from interpreting the VBScript code as part of the text of the Web page and displaying it on the browser window.

Figure A.7.

How VBScript applications are executed by Web browsers.

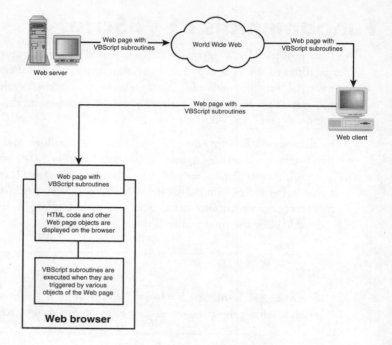

☐ VBScript subroutines—A VBScript application is composed of one or more VBScript subroutines. VBScript subroutines are defined using the following syntax:

```
Sub name of subroutine
…VBScript statements…
End Sub
```

VBScript subroutines are contained within the `<SCRIPT LANGUAGE="VBScript">` and `</SCRIPT>` tags. Certain events associated with various objects of a Web page trigger VBScript subroutines to perform certain tasks. For example, when a user submits a form, a VBScript subroutine can examine and validate the data entered by the user before it is sent to the Web server for processing.

See lines 25–30, 32–35, and 37–40 in Listing A.6 for examples of VBScript subroutines.

Listing A.6. A typical VBScript application.

```
1: <HTML>
2: <HEAD>
3: <TITLE>VBScript Tutorial: Hello World!</TITLE>
4: </HEAD>
5:
6: <BODY BGCOLOR="#FFFFFF" TEXT="#0000FF"
7:      LINK="#B864FF" VLINK="#670000" ALINK="#FF0000">
8:
```

```
 9: <B><FONT FACE="Comic Sans MS" SIZE=6 COLOR=RED>
10: VBScript Tutorial: <FONT></B>
11: <I><FONT FACE="Comic Sans MS" SIZE=5 COLOR=BLUE>
12:  "Hello World!" </I><P><FONT>
13:
14: <FORM>
15: <INPUT TYPE=BUTTON VALUE="Please click here for message box"
16:        NAME="BtnHello">
17: <INPUT TYPE=BUTTON VALUE="What time is it?"
18:        NAME="BtnTime">
19: <INPUT TYPE=BUTTON VALUE="What date is it?"
20:        NAME="BtnDate">
21: </FORM>
22:
23: <SCRIPT LANGUAGE=VBS>
24: <!-- To hide VBScript code from technologically challenged browsers
25: Sub BtnHello_OnClick
26:  titleString = "Windows NT Internet & Intranet Development"
27:  helloString = "Hello world! Welcome to the fun filled "
28:  helloString = helloString & "world of VBScript programming!"
29:  MsgBox helloString, 0, titleString
30: End Sub
31:
32: Sub BtnTime_OnClick
33:  timeString = "So, you want to know the time? The time is " & time
34:  MsgBox  timeString , 0, "Time Dialog Box"
35: End Sub
36:
37: Sub BtnDate_OnClick
38:  dateString = "Today's date is " & DateValue(date)
39:  MsgBox  dateString , 0, "Date Dialog Box"
40: End Sub
41: -->
42: </SCRIPT>
43:
44: </BODY>
45: </HTML>
```

The Role of VBScript in Web Page Development

Prior to client-side scripting languages such as VBScript, Web pages were largely static entities. Interactivity in a Web page required the execution of a CGI application on the server and the display of the results of that application on the Web browser. Although this worked well for some applications, it tied up valuable network and system resources. VBScript allows Web page developers to create multimedia-rich, interactive Web pages with great ease while conserving network bandwidth and system resources.

Automation of ActiveX Controls

ActiveX controls are powerful components that can be used to build sophisticated Web applications. By themselves, ActiveX controls are capable of performing limited tasks. For example, the Microsoft Forms 2.0 ComboBox ActiveX control is capable of displaying a list of items, and the Microsoft Forms 2.0 Image ActiveX control is capable of displaying a graphical image. Although these two components perform very limited tasks by themselves, VBScript can be used to glue together the two ActiveX controls and develop a VBScript application that automates ActiveX controls. For example, a VBScript subroutine can allow a user to change the image displayed in the Microsoft Forms 2.0 Image ActiveX control when an image is selected using the Microsoft Forms 2.0 ComboBox ActiveX control.

Dynamic Web Applications

VBScript is ideal for developing dynamic Web applications that immediately respond to user interactions. The Mr. Potato Head application discussed next is an example of a Web application that is better implemented with a client-side scripting language such as VBScript as opposed to a server-side CGI application.

The application in Figure A.8 is the CGI version of Mr. Potato Head. After a user selects various physical attributes of Mr. Potato Head, that information is transmitted to the Web server. A CGI application creates a graphic of Mr. Potato Head according to the physical attributes selected by the user and transmits the image to the Web browser as shown in Figure A.9. The CGI implementation of Mr. Potato Head is network intensive because data must be transferred between the Web browser and the Web server each time a user makes a selection. The CGI implementation is also processor intensive for the Web server because the server must process a CGI request and create a Mr. Potato Head each time the user changes the appearance of Mr. Potato Head.

URL

Browse `http://winnie.acsu.buffalo.edu/cgi-bin/potatoe-cgi` to experiment with the CGI version of Mr. Potato Head.

The ActiveX version of Mr. Potato Head (see Figure A.10) addresses limitations of the CGI version of Mr. Potato Head. As you can see, the ActiveX version is more interactive and is easier to use because it allows the user to change physical attributes of Mr. Potato Head on the fly, without interacting with the Web server. Users can select physical attributes and drag-and-drop them onto Mr. Potato Head. The ActiveX version of Mr. Potato Head is less processor intensive because it does not communicate with the Web server each time the user makes a change; it is less network intensive because all the processing is done locally.

Figure A.8.

Selecting physical properties of Mr. Potato Head.

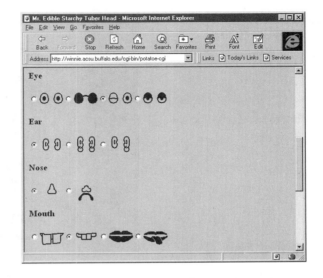

Figure A.9.

An image of Mr. Potato Head created by a CGI application.

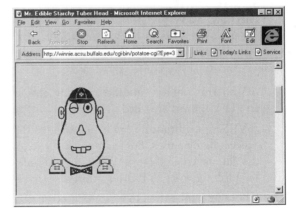

URL

Browse the Web page at `http://www.microsoft.com/ie/most/howto/layout/eggplant/begin.htm` to experiment with the ActiveX version of Mr. Potato Head.

Figure A.10.

The ActiveX version of
Mr. Potato Head.

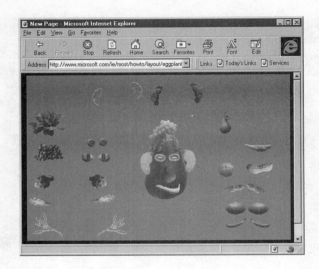

Error Checking

Error checking is a very important aspect of Web application development. Lack of error checking usually results in flaky applications that are frustrating to use. Listed next are examples of how VBScript is used to perform error checking and to validate data entered by users.

☐ A VBScript application can be used to ensure that all required data-entry fields of an HTML form are filled in.

☐ A VBScript subroutine can be used to ensure that invalid data is not submitted for processing by a user. For example, a VBScript application can inform the user that the date he entered (45/67/1996, for example) is invalid—without the expense of establishing an HTTP connection to a server-side CGI application.

☐ VBScript can be used to verify that certain data is accurate before processing the data. For example, an online grocery-shopping application developed using VBScript can verify that the user really wants to order four eggs (since most people buy eggs by the dozen).

Manipulating Web Browser Objects

VBScript applications can modify Web browser objects such as the background color of the current Web page. This feature is particularly useful when you create sophisticated Web applications. For example, a VBScript subroutine of a multiframe Web application can change the contents of several frames when a user selects a URL or clicks a button.

VBScript Programming Tips

When developing applications using VBScript (or any other programming language), you should create source code that is easy to maintain and read. Messy source code often leads to buggy applications that are hard to maintain and debug. The following tips will help you develop VBScript applications that are easy to maintain.

Indent Source Code

While indentation does not affect the way a VBScript application is executed, the lack of indentation can make an application extremely difficult to debug and maintain. You should indent control structures of applications as shown in Listing A.7—particularly if it is a complex or large VBScript application. Also, don't be afraid to add blank lines between VBScript code segments to enhance readability and clarity.

Listing A.7. Indentation makes it easier to read VBScript source code.

```
Sub BtnEvaluate_OnClick
  If (OperatorBox.Value = "?") Then
     MsgBoxString = "A valid operator is required to carry out "
     MsgBoxString = MsgBoxString & "an evaluation."
     MsgBoxString = MsgBoxString & chr(10)
     MsgBoxString = MsgBoxString & "Valid operators are: +, -, *"
     MsgBox MsgBoxString , 48 , "Invalid operator!"
  Else
     If (OperatorBox.Value = "+")  Then
        answer = CDbl(Operand1Box.Value) + CDbl(Operand2Box.Value)
     ElseIf (OperatorBox.Value = "-")  Then
        answer = CDbl(Operand1Box.Value) - CDbl(Operand2Box.Value)
     ElseIf (OperatorBox.Value = "*")  Then
        answer = CDbl(Operand1Box.Value) * CDbl(Operand2Box.Value)
     End If
     MsgBox answer , 64 , "Results of calculation"
     Operand1Box.Value = answer
     Operand2Box.Value = 0
  END If
End Sub

Sub AddDigit ( digit )
 REM Just in case there are any preceeding zeros or spaces
 Operand1Box.Value = CDbl (Operand1Box.Value)
 If (OperatorBox.Value = "?") Then
    If (Len (Operand1Box.Value) < 14) Then
       Operand1Box.Value = Operand1Box.Value & digit
       Operand1Box.Value = CDbl (Operand1Box.Value)
    Else
       TooManyDigits
    END If
```

continues

A

Listing A.7. continued

```
Else
    If (Len (Operand2Box.Value) < 14) Then
        Operand2Box.Value = Operand2Box.Value & digit
        Operand2Box.Value = CDbl (Operand2Box.Value)
    Else
        TooManyDigits
    END If
 END If
End Sub
```

Use the Code-Continuation Character

The code-continuation character is used to split relatively long VBScript statements. Generally, if a VBScript statement is more than 80 characters long, you should use the code-continuation character to break the statement into two or more lines. This makes it easier to indent the application for easy reading, as shown in Listing A.8. The code-continuation character is an underscore (_) placed at the point where the long line is to be broken, as demonstrated in lines 3–5 of Listing A.8. Notice how the code-continuation character makes the VBScript source code easier to read by preserving the indentation of the VBScript code.

Listing A.8. VBScript code with the code-continuation character.

```
1: Sub OperatorBox_OnChange
2:
3:     If (NOT((OperatorBox.Value = "+" ) OR _
4:            (OperatorBox.Value = "-" ) OR _
5:            (OperatorBox.Value = "*" ) OR _
6:            (OperatorBox.Value = "?" ))) Then
7:        MsgString = "Do not type invalid characters "
8:        MsgString = MsgString & "into the operator text box! "
9:        MsgString = MsgString & chr(10)
10:        MsgString = MsgString & "The operator text box will now be reset."
11:        MsgString = MsgString & chr(10) & chr(10)
12:        MsgString = MsgString & "Valid input: +, -, *"
13:        MsgBox MsgString , 48 , "Invalid input detected!"
14:        OperatorBox.Value = "?"
15:     END If
16:
17:  End Sub
```

Comment Your Source Code

Commenting your source code can save hours or even days of application development time. In the software development industry, more time is often spent maintaining existing applications than developing new ones. Commenting your source code makes it easier for you (or someone else) to understand your application and modify it without creating undue side effects. To insert a comment in VBScript applications, precede the comment with an apostrophe (') or the keyword Rem like so:

```
' This is a comment
```

or

```
Rem This is a comment
```

TIP

> When you are working on a complex application, use VBScript comments to document your code. Although you might understand how your application works when you are coding it, you might have a hard time remembering three months later.

Using VBScript Data Structures

Virtually all VBScript applications use data structures. Data structures are the building blocks of VBScript applications because they hold all the information a VBScript application needs. Unlike some other programming languages, VBScript stores all data in a data type called Variant. A variable of Variant data type can store many different kinds of information, such as strings of characters (Hello!), numbers (123), Boolean values (TRUE), and so on. This makes things easier for you, the programmer, because you no longer need to worry about certain variable type mismatches. For example, if you are using a strongly typed language and try to assign a 2-byte value to a 1-byte variable, unpredictable things happen. On the other hand, VBScript intelligently uses variables by analyzing the value to be stored in the variable and allocating enough storage space for the variable.

TIP

> When you develop complex applications with dozens of variables, it can be confusing to determine the purpose of a variable by looking at the variable's name. Always give your variables descriptive names. Giving descriptive names to variables goes a long way in reducing confusion when you (or others) debug and maintain the program.

To accommodate the need to store different kinds of data, the Variant data type consists of several data subtypes. This section covers how VBScript applications store and manipulate data that belongs to subtypes of Variant. A brief description of each subtype, as well as its range (when applicable), is provided in Table A.1.

Table A.1. Subtypes of `Variant`.

Subtype	Description	Range
Boolean	A Boolean value	TRUE or FALSE
Byte	A byte value	An integer between 0 and 255
Date	A date	A date between January 1, 100 and December 31, 9999
Double	A double-precision floating-point number	A number between -1.79769313486232E308 and -4.94065645841247E-324 for negative numbers, and a number between 4.94065645841247E-324 and 1.79769313486232E308 for positive numbers
Empty	An uninitialized value	0 for numeric variables, " " (empty string) for string variables
Error	An error code	N/A
Integer	An integer value	An integer between -32,768 and 32,767
Long	Relatively large integer values	An integer between -2,147,483,648 and 2,147,483,647
Null	Empty variable—does not contain any value	N/A
Object	An OLE automation object	N/A
Single	A single-precision floating-point number	A number between -3.402823E38 and -1.401298E-45 for negative values, and a number between 1.401298E-45 and 3.402823E38 for positive values
String	A string of characters	Up to about 2 billion characters in length
Time	A time	A time between January 1, 100 and December 31, 9999

See the section "Converting and Validating Data with VBScript" later in this appendix to learn how to convert data of one subtype to another subtype.

VBScript Data Structures

VBScript data structures can be broken into two categories:

☐ Scalar data structures (also called *scalar variables*)—These generally hold a single data value, such as a number, a string of characters, or the date and time. See Figure A.11 for an illustration of a scalar variable. As you can see in Figure A.11, a scalar variable consists of only *one* data value.

Figure A.11.

A scalar data structure.

VariableName
VariableValue

☐ Multidimensional data structures (also called *array variables*)—Unlike scalar variables, array variables contain many data values. Arrays are useful when data is stored and accessed sequentially. Arrays are especially ideal for performing the same set of operations on a series of data locations.

The simplest nonscalar data type is a single-dimensional array, which has only one index to data storage locations. Multidimensional data structures, on the other hand, have two or more indexes to data storage locations. Think of a multidimensional data structure as being like a spreadsheet, which has two dimensions: rows and columns (see Figure A.12 for a two-dimensional data structure). The variable name alone is not sufficient for determining the value of a two-dimensional variable. The row and column of the data field are also needed.

Figure A.12.

A two-dimensional structure.

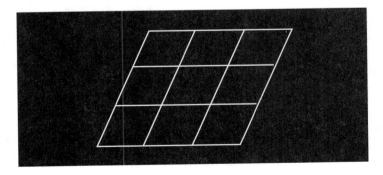

A multidimensional VBScript data structure can contain many additional dimensions for storing data. Figure A.13 illustrates a three-dimensional data structure. Notice how the row, column, and height of the data storage location are required to store or retrieve data from a three-dimensional data structure.

Figure A.13.
A three-dimensional structure.

Generally, you should avoid using more than three dimensions in a data structure. Higher dimensions require large amounts of memory, and make the task of programming significantly harder. This is simply because it is difficult for the programmer to visualize data structures that contain more than three dimensions.

Data Structure Manipulation Functions

VBScript includes several functions for manipulating data structures. Before discussing how data structures are created and manipulated in a VBScript application, let's explore the functions provided by the VBScript language for manipulating data structures. Use the following functions to define and manage data structures in your VBScript applications. In

the sections "Scalar Data Structures" and "Multidimensional Data Structures" later in this appendix, you will learn how to use the Dim, Redim, Private, Public, IsArray, LBound and UBound functions to create and manage VBScript data structures.

The Dim Statement

The Dim statement is used to declare variables, such as arrays, and assign them storage space. When numeric variables are declared with Dim, they are initialized with the value 0. Otherwise, they are assigned an empty string. The Dim statement can be used to declare several types of variables.

The ReDim Statement

For those occasions when you are unsure about the size of an array when it is declared, VBScript allows the creation of dynamic arrays. Dynamic arrays can be expanded or reduced as needed. Dynamic arrays can be created using the following syntax:

```
Dim NameOfArray()
```

Storage space for additional elements can be allocated for a dynamic array through the use of the ReDim statement, as shown in the following syntax (simply indicate, in parentheses, the number of elements the array should have):

```
ReDim NameOfArray(10)
```

As an added advantage, VBScript dynamic arrays can be expanded while preserving existing array values. Do this by adding a Preserve keyword between the ReDim statement and the array name like so:

```
ReDim Preserve NameOfArray(20)
```

WARNING

If a data type was defined for a dynamic array through the use of the As statement, the array's data type cannot be changed using the ReDim statement. Also, if a dynamic array is reduced in size through the use of the ReDim statement, any data stored in the portion of the array that was deleted is permanently lost.

The Private Statement

By preceding a variable declaration with the Private keyword, you can limit the variable's scope to the script in which it was declared.

The `Public` **Statement**

By preceding a variable declaration with the `Public` keyword, the scope of a variable can be extended to other scripts.

The `IsArray` **Statement**

The `IsArray` statement returns `TRUE` if a data structure is an array and `FALSE` otherwise.

The `Erase` **Statement**

The `Erase` statement is used to free memory used by dynamic arrays and to reinitialize elements of static arrays. If the array is dynamic, all space taken up by the array is freed. Dynamic arrays then need to be reallocated through the use of the `ReDim` statement before they can be used again. If the array is static, all array elements are initialized with `0` if its elements are numeric. However, the array's elements are initialized with empty strings if the elements are nonnumeric. The syntax of the `Erase` statement is as follows:

```
Erase NameOfArray
```

The `LBound` **Statement**

`LBound` can be used to determine the minimum index of an array dimension. For example, if `ArrayVariable` is a three-dimensional array defined with the statement `Dim ArrayVariable(5 To 100, 10 To 200, 20 To 300)`, `UBound(ArrayVariable,1)` returns 5, `LBound(ArrayVariable,2)` returns 10, and, of course, `LBound(ArrayVariable,3)` returns 20.

The `UBound` **Statement**

Use `UBound` to determine the maximum size of an array dimension. For example, if `ArrayVariable` is a three-dimensional array defined with the statement `Dim ArrayVariable (100,200,300)`, `UBound(ArrayVariable,1)` returns 100, `UBound(ArrayVariable,2)` returns 200, and, of course, `UBound(ArrayVariable,3)` returns 300.

Scalar Data Structures

Virtually all subtypes of `Variant` are scalar data structures. Declare a scalar data structure by using the keyword `Dim` and following it with the name of the variable. A variable name can contain letters, numbers, and underscore characters (_). However, there are a few restrictions:

☐ The variable name cannot be a reserved VBScript keyword. `Dim` is not a valid variable name.

☐ The variable must begin with an alphabetic character. `10TimesTheFunWithNT` is not a valid variable name.

☐ The variable name should not exceed 255 characters. In general, you should avoid very long variable names because they make it hard to develop and debug applications.

☐ The variable name must be unique in the scope in which it is declared. You cannot define two variables with the same name within a VBScript subroutine.

TIP

Give variables descriptive names. The variable name RowCount is far less ambiguous than X2.

See Listing A.9 for an example of how a scalar data structure is declared and used in a VBScript application. Line 3 of Listing A.9 declares a scalar data structure named ThisIsAScalarVariable. Line 5 assigns it the value 5, line 6 adds 5 to it, and line 7 displays the value of ThisIsAScalarVariable in a message box (see Figure A.14).

Listing A.9. Declaring and using a scalar VBScript data structure.

```
 1: <SCRIPT LANGUAGE="VBScript">
 2:
 3: Dim ThisIsAScalarVariable
 4:
 5: ThisIsAScalarVariable = 5
 6: ThisIsAScalarVariable = ThisIsAScalarVariable + 5
 7: Msgbox "The value of ThisIsAScalarVariable is " & _
 8:         ThisIsAScalarVariable
 9:
10: </SCRIPT>
```

Figure A.14.
Value of the variable
ThisIsAScalarVariable.

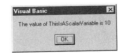

Multidimensional Data Structures

Multidimensional data structures are used to store several data values in a single variable. A value known as an *index* is used to refer to individual data fields of a multidimensional data structure.

NOTE A multidimensional data structure in VBScript can contain as many as 60 dimensions. Nonetheless, you should avoid using more than 3 or 4 dimensions; otherwise, the complexity of your source code (not to mention the amount of RAM required to create the data structure) will skyrocket.

Types of Multidimensional Data Structures

There are two main types of arrays: static arrays and dynamic arrays. Both are similar when it comes to storing and accessing data. However, unlike data arrays, which can be changed dynamically during program execution, the size of static arrays does not change while the program is being executed. Use static arrays whenever you are certain about the size of the array, and use dynamic arrays when you have no way of knowing the size of an array until execution time. For example, a spreadsheet application is of little use to anyone if it is implemented with a static array and therefore has a fixed spreadsheet size. A dynamic array is used in a spreadsheet application to dynamically change the size of the spreadsheet as data is inserted and deleted.

NOTE In VBScript, the index of multidimensional data structures begins at 0. This means that the data structure declared using the VBScript statement `Dim Array(20)` actually contains 21 data fields.

Static Arrays

Static arrays are declared via the `Dim` keyword. Listing A.10 demonstrates how a one-dimensional array containing six elements is declared.

NOTE The following examples apply to one-dimensional as well as multidimensional arrays. The only difference is that multidimensional arrays contain multiple indexes, each separated from the others with a comma. In the case of a two-dimensional array, the first value is the row index and the second value is the column index. For example, `ArrayVariable(2,3)` refers to the data stored in the second row and third column of the `ArrayVariable` data structure.

Listing A.10. Declaring an array.

```
<SCRIPT LANGUAGE="VBScript">
<!--
  Dim VariableName(5)
-->
</SCRIPT>
```

Values are assigned to VariableName through the use of the index of the data field. Listing A.11 demonstrates how to assign twice the value of each array index to data fields of the variable declared in Listing A.10. For example, the first data field will be assigned the value 2, the second data field will be assigned the value 4, and so on.

Listing A.11. Assigning values to an array.

```
<SCRIPT LANGUAGE="VBScript">
<!--
  VariableName(0) = 0
  VariableName(1) = 2
  VariableName(2) = 4
  VariableName(3) = 6
  VariableName(4) = 8
-->
</SCRIPT>
```

You can access values of array elements by including the array index in parentheses after the name of the array. For example, Listing A.12 demonstrates how to display the value of the array declared in Listing A.10 whose index is 4.

Listing A.12. Retrieving values from an array.

```
<SCRIPT LANGUAGE="VBScript">
<!--
Msgbox "Value of element = " & VariableName(4)
-->
</SCRIPT>
```

Dynamic Arrays

Dynamic arrays are declared in much the same way as static arrays. The only difference is that no array size is specified at the time of the array declaration. The VBScript keywords Dim and ReDim are used to declare dynamic arrays, as demonstrated in Listing A.13.

Listing A.13. Declaring a dynamic array.

```
<SCRIPT LANGUAGE="VBScript">
<!--
  ReDim ArrayName()
  Dim    SecondArrayName()
-->
</SCRIPT>
```

The ReDim keyword is used to modify the size of a dynamic array. Listing A.14 demonstrates how to set the size (15 storage locations) of the variable ArrayName, which was declared in Listing A.13.

Listing A.14. Resizing a dynamic array.

```
<SCRIPT LANGUAGE="VBScript">
<!--
  ReDim ArrayName(15)
-->
</SCRIPT>
```

The ReDim keyword can be used as many times as necessary to modify the size of an array. Listing A.15 demonstrates how the ReDim statement is used to modify the size (increase to 25 storage locations) of the variable ArrayName, which was declared in Listing A.14 with 15 storage locations. The keyword Preserve is preceded by the variable name to ensure that the data of the array ArrayName is not lost when the array is resized.

WARNING

Data will be lost when you reduce the size of an array—even if the Preserve keyword is used.

Listing A.15. Resizing a dynamic array while preserving its data.

```
<SCRIPT LANGUAGE="VBScript">
<!--
  ReDim Preserve ArrayName(25)
-->
</SCRIPT>
```

When the size of a dynamic array is reduced, the data contained in the reduced portion of the array is permanently lost.

Understanding Variable Scopes

It is important that you fully understand the concept of variable scope before you develop VBScript applications. Failure to do so can result in applications with bugs that are hard to detect and fix.

Variable scopes define which subroutines of an application have access to the data stored in a variable. When developing VBScript applications, do not depend on global variables. All subroutines of an application have access to global variables that are defined at the application level of an ASP application. On the other hand, a local variable is accessible only to the subroutine in which the variable is declared. The use of local variables also increases the portability of subroutines. When a subroutine depends on a globally declared variable, it is not very portable.

Although it might seem complicated at first, the concept of variable scope is very simple. If a variable is declared in a subroutine, that variable is only accessible within that subroutine. On the other hand, if a variable is declared at the same level as subroutines of an application, that variable is accessible throughout the application. Such a variable is called a *global variable* because it is accessible throughout the application. The only time global variables are not accessible throughout the application is in a special case known as *local-variable precedence*. This occurs when a local variable is declared with the same name as a global variable.

The variable scope layout of the application in Listing A.16 is shown in Figure A.15. Refer to Figure A.15 while manually stepping through the application in Listing A.17, taking into account how variable scopes function (as explained in the preceding paragraph). While stepping through the application in Listing A.17, fill in the values at the end of each line of Listing A.16. If you understand variable-scope rules correctly, the values you enter in Listing A.16 will resemble those of Listing A.18. (Try to fill in the values in Listing A.16 without looking at Listing A.18.) See Figure A.16 for the output of the application in Listing A.17.

Figure A.15.

*Scope layout of the
variables declared in
Listing A.17.*

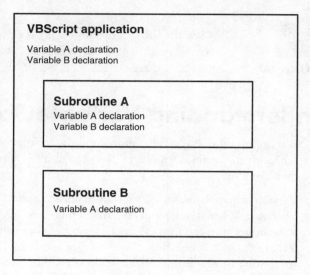

Listing A.16. Fill in values of the variables at each point of execution.

```
Value of variable A in subroutine A = ____
Value of variable B in subroutine A = ____
Value of variable A in subroutine B = ____
Value of variable B in subroutine B = ____
Value of variable A outside subroutine A and B = ____
Value of variable B outside subroutine A and B = ____
```

Listing A.17. Working with the scope of data structures.

```
 1: <HTML>
 2: <HEAD>
 3:
 4: <TITLE>Working With The Scope Of Data Structures</TITLE>
 5: </HEAD>
 6: <BODY BGCOLOR=FFFFFF>
 7:
 8:     <SCRIPT LANGUAGE="VBScript">
 9:     <!--
10:
11:         Dim A
12:         Dim B
13:
14:         Sub SubroutineA ()
15:
16:         Dim A
17:         Dim B
18:
```

```
19:         A = 20
20:         B = 30
21:
22:         document.write "Value of variable A in subroutine A =  " _
23:                        & A & "<BR>"
24:         document.write "Value of variable B in subroutine A =  " _
25:                        & B & "<BR>"
26:
27:         End Sub
28:
29:         Sub SubroutineB ()
30:
31:         Dim A
32:
33:         A = 35
34:
35:         document.write "Value of variable A in subroutine B =  " _
36:                        & A & "<BR>"
37:         document.write "Value of variable B in subroutine B =  " _
38:                        & B & "<BR>"
39:
40:         End Sub
41:
42:         A = 5
43:         B = 10
44:
45:         Call SubroutineA
46:         Call SubroutineB
47:
48:         document.write "Value of variable A outside subroutine _
49:                        & A and B =  " & A & "<BR>"
50:         document.write "Value of variable B outside subroutine _
51:                        & A and B = " & B & "<BR>"
52:
53:         -->
54:         </SCRIPT>
55:
56:  </BODY>
57:  </HTML>
```

Figure A.16.

Results of the application in Listing A.17.

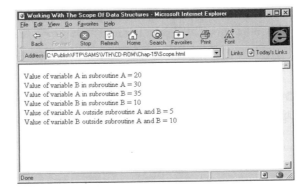

How the Variable Scope Application Works

A and B are global variables of the VBScript application. The values 5 and 10 are assigned to them respectively at the beginning of application execution. Afterwards, program flow is transferred to SubroutineA, which declares variables A and B as local variables. Due to local variable precedence, whenever A or B is referenced inside SubroutineA, the reference is made to the local variables A and B declared inside SubroutineA. Therefore, lines 22 and 24 of Listing A.17 print the values 20 and 30 because these values are assigned to the local variables A and B at lines 19 and 20. The situation is almost the same in the case of SubroutineB, which declares its own variable A. Therefore, when a reference is made to variable A within SubroutineB, that reference is made to the local variable declared in SubroutineB. However, because B is not declared as a local variable, all references made to B refer to the global variable B. Finally, lines 48 and 50 print the values of the global variables A and B.

Listing A.18. Output of the VBScript application in Listing A.17.

```
Value of variable A in subroutine A = 20
Value of variable B in subroutine A = 30
Value of variable A in subroutine B = 35
Value of variable B in subroutine B = 10
Value of variable A outside subroutine A and B = 5
Value of variable B outside subroutine A and B = 10
```

Operators, Control Structures, and Iterative Structures

Operators, control structures, and iterative structures allow VBScript developers to create intelligent and interactive Web applications. The following topics are covered in this section:

☐ Performing calculations using VBScript operators

☐ Transferring program flow of a VBScript application to a VBScript function or subroutine based on a Boolean expression

☐ How control structures are used to iterate a series of VBScript statements until a certain Boolean condition is met

Operators

Operators either assign the result of a certain calculation to a variable or use the result to perform more calculations. VBScript supports several operators for various string, Boolean, and number-manipulation operations.

The Addition Operator

Syntax: *operand1 + operand2*

The addition operator can be used to add two operands together. If both operands are numeric, the result of the addition operator is also numeric. If the operands are strings, VBScript performs a string concatenation instead of a numeric addition.

 NOTE

> To avoid ambiguity, use the string concatenation operator (&) when joining strings, and the addition operator (+) when adding numeric expressions.

The Subtraction Operator

Syntax: *operand1 - operand2*

Syntax: *-OperandToNegate*

The subtraction operator is used as the unary minus as well as the binary subtraction operator. When used as the binary subtraction operator, it subtracts *operand2* from *operand1* and returns the resulting value. When used as the unary minus, it negates the numeric operand with which it is used.

The Multiplication Operator

Syntax: *operand1 * operand2*

The multiplication operator multiplies two numeric operands and returns the resulting value.

The Exponential Operator

Syntax: *operand1 ^ operand2*

The exponential operator returns the resulting value of *operand1* raised to the *operand2* power.

The Floating-Point Division Operator

Syntax: *operand1 / operand2*

The floating-point division operator is used to divide *operand1* with *operand2*. Both *operand1* and *operand2* must be numeric expressions, and the resulting value is a floating-point number. Do not confuse the floating-point division operator with the integer-division operator. The result of 23/4 (floating-point division operator is used) is 5.75 and the result of 23\4 (integer division operator is used) is 5.

Watch out for division by zero when using either the floating-point division operator or integer-division operator by ensuring that the denominator (<*operand2*>) is not zero.

The Integer-Division Operator

Syntax: *operand1* \ *operand2*

The integer-division operator is somewhat similar to the floating-point division operator: It returns an integer number after dividing *operand1* with *operand2*. Examples of the integer-division operator are given next for your reference.

```
(23 \ 4) = 5
(4 \ 23) = 0
(4 \ 2) = 2
(5 \ 2) = 2
```

The String-Concatenation Operator

Syntax: *operand1* & *operand2*

The string-concatenation operator can be used to join *operand1* and *operand2*. For example, the result of "Windows NT" & " is fun!" is "Windows NT is fun!"

The MOD Operator

Syntax: *operand1* MOD *operand2*

The MOD operator is similar to the integer-division operator, except that it returns the remainder of *operand1* divided by *operand2*. Examples of the MOD operator are given next for your reference.

```
(23 MOD 4) = 3
(4 MOD 23) = 4
(4 MOD 2) = 0
(5 MOD 2) = 1
```

Boolean Operators

VBScript supports a number of Boolean operators. The best way to illustrate how Boolean operators work is with a truth table. Figure A.17 provides truth tables of a number of useful VBScript Boolean operators.

Figure A.17.

Truth tables of VBScript Boolean operators.

AND				
TRUE	AND	TRUE	=	TRUE
TRUE	AND	FALSE	=	FALSE
FALSE	AND	TRUE	=	FALSE
FALSE	AND	FALSE	=	FALSE
OR				
TRUE	OR	TRUE	=	TRUE
TRUE	OR	FALSE	=	TRUE
FALSE	OR	TRUE	=	TRUE
FALSE	OR	FALSE	=	FALSE
XOR				
TRUE	XOR	TRUE	=	FASLE
TRUE	XOR	FALSE	=	TRUE
FALSE	XOR	TRUE	=	TRUE
FALSE	OR	FALSE	=	FALSE
NOT				
	NOT	TRUE	=	FALSE
	NOT	FALSE	=	TRUE

The AND Operator

Syntax: *<operand1>* AND *<operand2>*

The AND operator returns TRUE if both *<operand1>* and *<operand2>* are true. If not, it returns FALSE. The AND operator can be used with expressions and functions that return a Boolean value.

The OR Operator

Syntax: *<operand1>* OR *<operand2>*

The OR operator returns TRUE if either *<operand1>* or *<operand2>* is true. The OR operator can be used with expressions and functions that return a Boolean value.

The NOT Operator

Syntax: NOT *<operand>*

A Boolean value can be negated using the NOT operator. The NOT operator can be used with expressions and functions that return a Boolean value.

The XOR Operator

Syntax: *<operand1>* XOR *<operand2>*

The XOR operator is very similar to the OR operator, except that in order for the XOR operator to return TRUE, *<operand1>* or *<operand2>* must be true. However, they both can't be true at the same time. The XOR operator can be used with expressions and functions that return a Boolean value.

The Equivalence Operator

Syntax: `<operand1> Eqv <operand2>`

The equivalence operator can be used to determine whether `<operand1>` is equal to `<operand2>`. If either `<operand1>` or `<operand2>` is NULL, the resulting value is also NULL. The truth table of the equivalence operator is listed next:

```
TRUE Eqv TRUE = TRUE
FALSE Eqv TRUE = FALSE
TRUE Eqv FALSE = FALSE
FALSE Eqv FALSE = TRUE
```

(TRUE may be replaced with binary 1 and FALSE may be replaced with the binary 0.)

The Object-Reference Operator

Syntax: `<operand1> IS <operand2>`

The object-reference operator is used to compare two object reference variables. If `<operand1>` refers to the same object as `<operand2>`, the object-reference operator returns TRUE; otherwise, it returns FALSE.

Comparison Operators

VBScript supports several comparison operators, which can be used to compare strings as well as numbers. Comparison operators that can be used in VBScript programs are listed next.

The Equal Operator (=)

Syntax: `<operand1> = <operand2>`

The equal operator returns TRUE if `<operand1>` and `<operand2>` are equal to each other. If either `<operand1>` or `<operand2>` is NULL, the equal operator returns NULL.

The Unequal Operator (<>)

Syntax: `<operand1> <> <operand2>`

The unequal operator returns TRUE if `<operand1>` and `<operand2>` are unequal to each other. If either `<operand1>` or `<operand2>` is NULL, the unequal operator returns NULL.

The Less-Than Operator (<)

Syntax: `<operand1> < <operand2>`

The less-than operator returns TRUE if `<operand1>` is less than `<operand2>`. If either `<operand1>` or `<operand2>` is NULL, the less-than operator returns NULL.

The Less-Than-Or-Equal-To Operator (<=)

Syntax: `<operand1> <= <operand2>`

The less-than-or-equal-to operator returns TRUE if `<operand1>` is less than or equal to `<operand2>`. If either `<operand1>` or `<operand2>` is NULL, the less-than-or-equal-to operator returns NULL.

The Greater-Than Operator (>)

Syntax: *<operand1>* > *<operand2>*

The greater-than operator returns TRUE if *<operand1>* is greater than *<operand2>*. If either *<operand1>* or *<operand2>* is NULL, the greater-than operator returns NULL.

Greater-Than-Or-Equal-To Operator (>=)

Syntax: *<operand1>* >= *<operand2>*

The greater-than-or-equal-to operator returns TRUE if *<operand1>* is greater than or equal to *<operand2>*. If either *<operand1>* or *<operand2>* is NULL, the greater-than-or-equal-to operator returns NULL.

Control Structures

Control structures are an important part of any programming language. They give a programming language life by allowing programmers to add intelligence to programs with the aid of conditional and iterative statements. A control structure transfers program flow to a series of VBScript statements or a VBScript subroutine based on a certain Boolean expression. The next few sections discuss how VBScript control structures are used in VBScript programs to transfer program flow.

Call

Call is used to transfer program control to another VBScript subroutine. When Call is used to transfer control to subroutines having parameters, the parameters should be enclosed in parentheses. If Call is omitted, subroutine arguments do not need to be enclosed in parentheses. Return values of functions are ignored when they are invoked with the Call statement.

NOTE

> The Call keyword is mentioned here because it is part of the VBScript language specification. The Call keyword is generally superfluous because it can be omitted when calling subroutines.

See Listing A.19 for an example of how program control is transferred to other VBScript subroutines through the use of the Call statement. Notice how the subroutine ThisSubroutineWillBeCalledWithCall, declared in lines 7–9, is called with the Call statement in line 20. See Figure A.18 for the message box displayed when the VBScript application in Listing A.19 is executed.

Listing A.19. Transferring program control via the `Call` statement.

```
 1: <HTML>
 2:
 3: <HEAD>
 4:
 5:     <SCRIPT LANGUAGE="VBScript">
 6: <!--
 7: Sub ThisSubroutineWillBeCalledWithCall
 8: MsgBox "Inside subroutine ThisSubroutineWillBeCalledWithCall"
 9: end sub
10: -->
11:     </SCRIPT>
12:
13: <TITLE>Transferring Program Control Using Call</TITLE>
14: </HEAD>
15:
16: <BODY BGCOLOR="FFFFFF">
17:
18:     <SCRIPT LANGUAGE="VBScript">
19: <!--
20: Call ThisSubroutineWillBeCalledWithCall
21: -->
22:     </SCRIPT>
23:
24: </BODY>
25: </HTML>
```

Figure A.18.

*This message box is
displayed when the
application in Listing
A.19 is executed.*

Select...Case

The `Select...Case` control structure is used to execute a series of VBScript statements based on an expression. The syntax of the `Select...Case` structure is as follows:

```
Select Case <ExpressionToTest>
  Case <ResultOfExpression>
   ...VBScript statement(s)...
  Case Else
   ...VBScript statement(s)...
End Select
```

Listing A.20 demonstrates how the `Select...Case` control structure is used to transfer program control to certain VBScript statements based on the value of an expression. When a user selects a color via the drop-down list shown in Figure A.19, the `Select...Case` control structure in lines 27–41 of Listing A.20 changes the background color of the Web page (as shown in Figure A.20).

Figure A.19.

Selecting a background color via the pull-down menu.

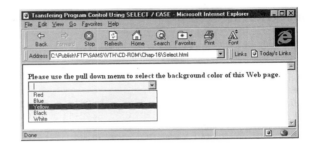

Listing A.20. Using the `Select…Case` **control structure.**

```
 1: <HTML>
 2: <HEAD>
 3:
 4:     <SCRIPT LANGUAGE="VBScript">
 5: <!--
 6: Sub window_onLoad()
 7:   BackgroundColorSelector.AddItem ("Red")
 8:   BackgroundColorSelector.AddItem ("Blue")
 9:   BackgroundColorSelector.AddItem ("Yellow")
10:   BackgroundColorSelector.AddItem ("Black")
11:   BackgroundColorSelector.AddItem ("White")
12: end sub
13: -->
14:     </SCRIPT>
15:
16: <TITLE>Transferring Program Control Using SELECT / CASE</TITLE>
17: </HEAD>
18: <BODY BGCOLOR="FFFFFF">
19: <B>
20: Please use the pull down menu to select the background
21: color of this Web page.
22: </B>
23:
24:     <SCRIPT LANGUAGE="VBScript">
25: <!--
26: Sub BackgroundColorSelector_Change()
27: Select Case BackgroundColorSelector.Value
28:   Case "Red"
29:     Document.bgColor      = "Red"
30:   Case "Blue"
31:     Document.bgColor      = "Blue"
32:   Case "Yellow"
33:     Document.bgColor      = "Yellow"
34:   Case "Black"
35:     Document.bgColor      = "Black"
36:   Case "White"
37:     Document.bgColor      = "White"
38:   Case Else
39:     MsgBox "Please select a a valid color!"  &
40:           document.ColorSelectorForm.BackgroundColorSelector.text
```

continues

A

Listing A.20. continued

```
41: End Select
42: end sub
43: -->
44:     </SCRIPT>
45:
46:     <OBJECT ID="BackgroundColorSelector" WIDTH=269 HEIGHT=21
47:      CLASSID="CLSID:8BD21D30-EC42-11CE-9E0D-00AA006002F3">
48:         <PARAM NAME="VariousPropertyBits" VALUE="746604571">
49:         <PARAM NAME="BackColor" VALUE="14417394">
50:         <PARAM NAME="DisplayStyle" VALUE="3">
51:         <PARAM NAME="Size" VALUE="7112;556">
52:         <PARAM NAME="MatchEntry" VALUE="1">
53:         <PARAM NAME="ShowDropButtonWhen" VALUE="2">
54:         <PARAM NAME="FontCharSet" VALUE="0">
55:         <PARAM NAME="FontPitchAndFamily" VALUE="2">
56:     </OBJECT>
57:
58: </BODY>
59: </HTML>
```

Figure A.20.

*The VBScript application
changes the background
color of the Web page.*

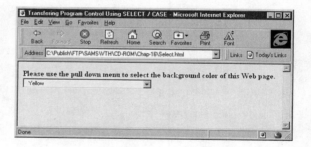

TIP

It is a good programming practice to include a `Case Else` statement in
every `Select...Case` statement. Failure to do so can result in applications
that behave erratically as a result of unanticipated circumstances. Try to
think of all possible cases and structure your `Select...Case` statements to
handle each case properly.

NOTE

A `Select...Case` structure can be nested inside another `Select...Case`
structure provided that each `Select...Case` structure has a matching `End
Select` statement.

If...Then

The If...Then statement is used to execute certain VBScript statements based on a Boolean expression. The syntax of the If...Then control structure is as follows:

```
If <BooleanExpression> Then
…VBScript statement…
END If
```

As shown in the previous example, an If...Then control structure can execute certain VBScript statements based on the value of a Boolean expression.

If...Then...Else

The If...Then...Else statement can be used to execute certain VBScript statements based on Boolean expressions. The syntax of the If...Then...Else control structure is as follows:

```
If <BooleanExpression> Then
…VBScript statement…
Else If <BooleanExpression> Then
…VBScript statement…
Else
…VBScript statement…
END If
```

As shown in the previous example, an If...Then...Else statement can execute certain VBScript statements based on the values of various Boolean expressions.

You might be wondering when you should use an If...Then...Else control structure and when you should use a Select...Case control structure. Use Select...Case if certain VBScript statements must be executed based on the value of a single expression. Use If...Then...Else if certain VBScript statements must be executed based on the values of different Boolean expressions.

For example, if subroutine ALessThanB() must be executed if the variable A is less than B, the subroutine AGreaterThanB() must be executed if the variable A is greater than B, and the subroutine AEqualsB() must be executed if A equals B, use an If...Then...Else control structure. On the other hand, if certain VBScript statements must be executed based on the value of a single expression (the value of a string variable for example), use a Select...Case control structure. For example, a Select...Case control structure is ideal for executing the subroutine Red() if the variable VariableColor equals "Red", executing the subroutine Blue() if the variable VariableColor equals "Blue", and executing the subroutine Green() if the variable VariableColor equals "Green".

Iterative Structures

When developing applications, it is sometimes necessary to perform a series of tasks more than once. VBScript provides several iterative structures that can be used to repeatedly perform a series of actions. There are two kinds of iterative structures—those that repeat until a certain condition is met, and those that repeat for a certain number of iterations.

WARNING

> Be careful when using iterative structures that repeat until a certain condition is met. If you are not careful, you can inadvertently create an infinite loop. Always choose well-defined starting and ending conditions when using this type of iterative structure.

For...Next

The For...Next control structure can be used to iterate a series of VBScript statements a certain number of times. The syntax of the For...Next control structure is as follows:

```
For <LoopCount> = <BeginLoop> To <EndLoop> Step <StepCount>
…VBScript statements…
Next
```

The previous definition can be used to iterate a series of VBScript statements a certain number of times by replacing certain placeholders (enclosed in pointed braces) of the definition as follows:

- ☐ `<LoopCount>`—This variable is used to keep track of the number of iterations. It's best if your VBScript statements do not alter the value of this variable because doing so can easily complicate your code and make it harder to debug.

- ☐ `<BeginLoop>`—This is the first value of the iteration sequence.

- ☐ `<EndLoop>`—This is the last value of the iteration sequence.

- ☐ `Step <StepCount>`—`<StepCount>` can be replaced with the value that the variable `<LoopCount>` is incremented after each iteration of the loop. The `Step <StepCount>` statement is optional; by default, `<LoopCount>` is incremented by one.

NOTE

> The Exit For statement can be used to exit a For loop.

The application in Listing A.21 demonstrates how the For...Next control structure is used to iterate a series of VBScript statements. In this case, For...Next does this by printing all even numbers between 0 and 20, and printing an asterisk for each number. The output of the application in Listing A.21 is shown in Figure A.21. Notice how the For...Next loop found in lines 14–20 of Listing A.21 is nested inside the For...Next loop found in lines 16–18.

Listing A.21. A For...Next **control structure is used to iterate a series of** VBScript statements.

```
 1: <HTML>
 2: <HEAD>
 3: <TITLE>Using the FOR / NEXT control structure</TITLE>
 4: </HEAD>
 5: <BODY BGCOLOR="FFFFFF">
 6: <H3>
 7: Printing even numbers from 0 to 20 using the FOR / NEXT
 8: control structure and printing a histograph of the numbers
 9: using asterisks.
10: </H3>
11:     <SCRIPT LANGUAGE="VBScript">
12: <!--
13:
14: For LoopCountVariable = 0 To 20 Step 2
15:   document.write (LoopCountVariable-1)
16:   For AsterisksCountVariable = 0 To LoopCountVariable
17:     document.write "*"
18:   Next
19:   document.write "<BR>"
20: Next
21: -->
22:     </SCRIPT>
23:
24: </BODY>
25: </HTML>
```

Figure A.21.

The For...Next *control structure is used to iterate a series of VBScript statements.*

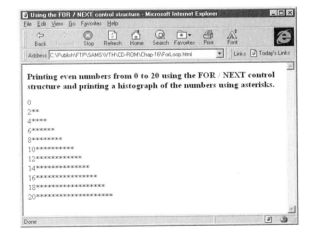

For Each...Next

The For Each...Next control structure is useful for iterating VBScript statements for each object in a collection or each element in an array. The syntax of the For Each...Next loop is as follows:

```
For Each <LoopIndex> In <ArrayOrCollection>
…VBScript statements…
Next <LoopIndex>
```

You can add a For Each...Next loop to a VBScript program by substituting certain placeholders of the preceding example as follows:

☐ <LoopIndex>—This is the variable used to traverse the elements of an array or objects in a collection.

☐ <ArrayOrCollection>—This is the name of an array or collection of objects.

The Exit For statement can be used to exit a For Each...Next loop. Also, <LoopIndex> can be omitted in the Next <LoopIndex> statement. However, this is not recommended; it can complicate things and cause errors if a For Each...Next loop is nested inside another For Each...Next loop.

While...Wend

The While...Wend control structure can be used to iterate a series of VBScript statements while a certain Boolean expression is true. The syntax of the While...Wend control structure is as follows:

```
While <BooleanExpression>
…VBScript statements…
Wend
```

Listing A.22 demonstrates how the While...Wend control structure is used to iterate a series of VBScript statements. See Figure A.22 for the output of the VBScript application in Listing A.22.

Listing A.22. A While...Wend **control structure is used to iterate a series of VBScript statements.**

```
 1: <HTML>
 2: <HEAD>
 3: <TITLE>Using the While/Wend control structure</TITLE>
 4: </HEAD>
 5: <BODY BGCOLOR="FFFFFF">
 6: <H3>
 7: Printing even numbers from 0 to 20 using the While/Wend control structure
 8: and printing a histograph of the numbers using asterisks.</H3>
 9:     <SCRIPT LANGUAGE="VBScript">
10: <!--
11:
```

```
12: Dim LoopCountVariable, AsterisksCountVariable
13:
14: LoopCountVariable = 0
15: While LoopCountVariable <= 20
16:   If ( LoopCountVariable MOD 2 = 0 ) Then
17:     document.write LoopCountVariable
18:     AsterisksCountVariable = 0
19:     While AsterisksCountVariable < LoopCountVariable
20:       document.write "*"
21:       AsterisksCountVariable = AsterisksCountVariable + 1
22:     Wend
23:     document.write "<BR>"
24:   End If
25:   LoopCountVariable = LoopCountVariable + 1
26: Wend
27:
28: -->
29:     </SCRIPT>
30:
31: </BODY>
32: </HTML>
```

Figure A.22.

The While...Wend *control structure is used to iterate a series of VBScript statements.*

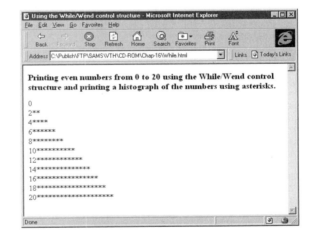

Do/While...Until/Loop

The Do...Loop control structure can be used to iterate a series of VBScript statements until a certain Boolean expression becomes true. The syntax of the Do...Loop control structure is listed next. As shown in the following examples, the Boolean test condition of a Do...Loop structure can be placed either at the beginning or the end of the control structure (in the first example, the Boolean expression appears at the beginning of the control structure).

```
Do <condition> <BooleanExpression>
…VBScript statements…
Loop
```

In this example, the Boolean expression is placed at the end of the control structure.

```
Do
…VBScript statements…
Loop <condition> <BooleanExpression>
```

The preceding examples repeatedly execute VBScript statements enclosed in the loop structure until `<BooleanExpression>` becomes true. In the examples, `<condition>` can be replaced with either `While` or `Until`. As the name implies, if `While` is used, the loop iterates while `<BooleanExpression>` is true. Likewise, if `Until` is used, the loop iterates until `<BooleanExpression>` is true.

Listing A.23 demonstrates how the `Do/While…Until/Loop` control structure is used to iterate a series of VBScript statements. See Figure A.23 for the output of Listing A.23.

Listing A.23. A `Do/While…Until/Loop` control structure is used to iterate a series of VBScript statements.

```
 1: <HTML>
 2: <HEAD>
 3: <TITLE>Using the Do/While/Until/Loop control structure</TITLE>
 4: </HEAD>
 5: <BODY BGCOLOR="FFFFFF">
 6: <H3>
 7: Printing even numbers from 0 to 20 using the Do/While/Until/Loop
 8: control structure and printing a histograph of the numbers
 9: using asterisks.
10: </H3>
11:     <SCRIPT LANGUAGE="VBScript">
12: <!--
13:
14: Dim LoopCountVariable, AsterisksCountVariable
15:
16: LoopCountVariable = 0
17:
18: Do
19:   If ( LoopCountVariable MOD 2 = 0 ) Then
20:     document.write LoopCountVariable
21:     AsterisksCountVariable = 0
22:     Do While AsterisksCountVariable < LoopCountVariable
23:       document.write "*"
24:       AsterisksCountVariable = AsterisksCountVariable + 1
25:     Loop
26:     document.write "<BR>"
27:   End If
28:   LoopCountVariable = LoopCountVariable + 1
29: Loop While LoopCountVariable <= 20
30: .
31: -->
32:     </SCRIPT>
33:
34: </BODY>
35: </HTML>
```

Figure A.23.
The Do/While...Until/
Loop *control structure is
used to iterate a series of
VBScript statements.*

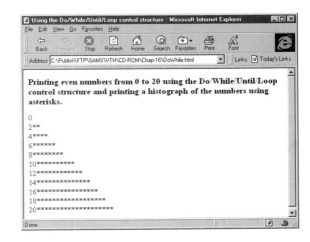

The Exit Statement

The Exit statement causes program control to be transferred out of the control structure in which it is used. The control structure can be a loop or a subroutine. Forms of the Exit command are listed next:

☐ Exit Do—Exits a Do loop

☐ Exit For—Exits a For loop

☐ Exit Function—Exits a function

☐ Exit Sub—Exits a procedure

Converting and Validating Data with VBScript

Data conversion and validation are important aspects of application development. Poor data-validation and -conversion strategies often result in applications that behave erratically when they are presented with unanticipated input. Data-conversion and -validation functions of the VBScript language can be used to develop robust applications that do not fall apart when presented with invalid input. VBScript data conversion and validation functions are used to develop robust Web applications that gracefully handle invalid input. For example, say a user enters a string in place of a number. In such an event, VBScript data-conversion and -validation functions can be used to examine the data entered by the user, display an error message, and ask the user to enter a number.

NOTE Time, string, and mathematical expression conversion functions are not covered in this section. See the section "Time- and String-Manipulation Functions" to learn how to convert time, string, and mathematical expressions.

Data-Conversion Functions

VBScript includes a number of functions that can be used to convert data from one subtype of Variant to another. Data-conversion functions are especially valuable when interfacing with other applications and ActiveX components. For example, an ActiveX control might require input in the form of a hexadecimal (base 16) number. In such an event, the Hex() function can be used to convert a base 10 numeric expression to base 16.

Int(), Fix()

Both Int() and Fix() convert numeric expressions into integers. The only difference is that Int() converts a negative number with a fraction into a smaller integer, and Fix() converts a negative number with a fraction into a larger integer. The following examples illustrate how Int() and Fix() handle numbers with fractions. The Int() and Fix() functions can be used to perform various mathematical calculations such as approximate the area under a curve.

```
Int(11.75) = 11

Fix(11.75) = 11

Int(12.45) = 12

Fix(12.45) = 12

Int(-17.75) = -18

Fix(-17.75) = -17

Int(-7.25) = -8

Fix(-7.25) = -7
```

Hex()

Hex() returns the hexadecimal (base 16) value of a numeric expression. For example, Hex(10) returns A.

Oct()

Oct() returns the octal value (base 8) of a numeric expression. For example, Oct(10) returns 12.

CBool()

CBool() returns the Boolean value of an expression passed into the function. For example, CBool(A=B) returns TRUE if both A and B contain the same value.

CByte()

Cbyte() converts a number passed to the function into a number of type byte and returns it. For example, if Cbyte() is called with the number 123.678, it returns 123.

CDbl()

CDbl() converts an expression passed into the function into a variant of subtype double.

Chr()

Chr() returns the ASCII character of an ASCII code. For example, Chr(65) returns the character A. The Chr() function is particularly handy for including special ASCII characters that are hard to include in VBScript string expressions.

CInt()

CInt() converts an expression into a variant of subtype Integer. For example, CInt(1234.567) returns 1235.

CLng()

CLng() returns a variant of subtype long after the expression passed into the function is converted into long. For example, CLng(12345.67) returns 12346.

CSng()

CSng() converts a numeric expression passed to the function into a variant of subtype Single. For example, CSng(12.123456) returns 12.12346.

CStr()

CStr() converts an expression passed to CStr() into a string and returns it. For example, CStr(123.456) returns the value "123.456".

Val()

Val() can be used to obtain a number contained in a string. The function scans the string until it encounters a character that is not part of a number. For example, Val("1234 567 in a string") returns the number 1234567.

Data-Validation Functions

Data-validation functions are used to determine what type of data is stored in an object/expression. For example, IsDate() can be used to validate a date entered by the user. IsDate() returns TRUE if an expression can be converted to a valid date and FALSE otherwise. The following data-validation functions are available to VBScript application developers.

IsArray()

IsArray() returns TRUE if a variable is an array and FALSE otherwise.

IsDate()

IsDate() returns TRUE if an expression can be converted to a valid date and FALSE otherwise.

IsEmpty()

IsEmpty() returns TRUE if a variable has been initialized and FALSE otherwise.

IsError()

IsError() returns TRUE if an expression is an error code and FALSE otherwise.

IsNull()

IsNull() returns TRUE if an expression is NULL and FALSE otherwise.

IsNumeric()

IsNumeric() returns TRUE if an expression is numeric and FALSE otherwise.

IsObject()

IsObject() returns TRUE if an expression references an OLE automation object and FALSE otherwise.

VarType()

The type of variable can be determined via the VarType() function. For example, if IntVariable is an integer variable, VarType(IntVariable) returns 2. The type of variable can be determined by examining the return value of VarType(). Return values are interpreted in Table A.2.

Table A.2. Variable type codes.

Value returned	Type of variable
0	Empty
1	Null
2	Integer
3	Long integer
4	Single-precision, floating-point number
5	Double-precision, floating-point number
6	Currency
7	Date
8	String
9	OLE automation object
10	Error
11	Boolean
12	Variant
13	Non-OLE automation object
8192	Array

Validating Data

You should always perform data validation when you accept input from users. Failure to do so can result in runtime errors that crash your application. Data validation is very easy to perform. A typical data-validation algorithm consists of a data-entry control, a data-validation condition, and a loop, and functions as illustrated in Figure A.24.

A Simple Data-Validation Application

The application in Listing A.24 demonstrates the implementation of a simple data-validation application using VBScript. The application continues to function until the user types 5 and selects another area of the Web page using the mouse (or presses the Tab key to shift focus from the input box).

Figure A.24.

*The data-entry control
obtains data from the
user until the control is
satisfied.*

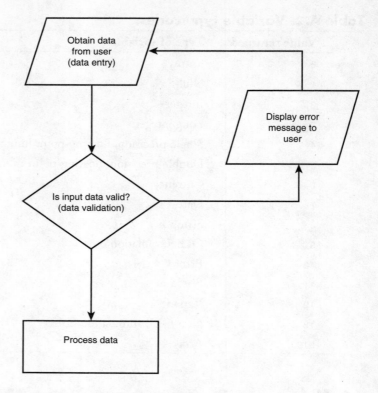

Listing A.24. A simple data-validation application.

```
1: <!--
2:  © 1996 Sanjaya Hettihewa (http://www.NetInnovation.com/)
3:   All Rights Reserved.
4:  !-->
5: <HTML>
6: <HEAD>
7: <SCRIPT LANGUAGE="VBScript">
8: <!--
9: Sub ValidateData()
10:  If ( IsNumeric (DataEntryForm.Input.Value) ) Then
11:   If ( DataEntryForm.Input.Value=5 ) Then
12:    Call ThankUser
13:   Else
14:    MsgBox "Please enter the number five!" & chr(10) & _
15:       "The number you entered (" & DataEntryForm.Input.Value _
16:       & ") is not the number 5."
17:   End If
18:  Else
19:   MsgBox "Please enter the number five!" & chr(10) & _
20:      "Your input (" & DataEntryForm.Input.Value _
21:      & ") is not a valid numeric expression."
```

```
22:    End If
23: End sub
24:
25: Sub ThankUser
26:    document.open
27:    document.write "<BODY BGCOLOR=FFFFFF>"
28:    document.write "<H1>"
29:    document.write "Thank you for entering the number 5!"
30:    document.write "</H1>"
31:    document.write "<H2>"
32:    document.write "<Have a nice day!>"
33:    document.write "</H2>"
34:    document.close
35: End Sub
36: -->
37:    </SCRIPT>
38: <TITLE>Simple Data Validation</TITLE>
39: </HEAD>
40: <BODY BGCOLOR="#F7FFF4">
41:    <FORM NAME="DataEntryForm">
42: <p>Please enter the number 5
43:    <INPUT LANGUAGE="VBScript"
44:    TYPE=text ONCHANGE="call ValidateData()"
45:    SIZE=20 NAME="Input"></p>
46:    </FORM>
47: </BODY>
48: </HTML>
```

The user interface of the data-validation application in Listing A.24 is shown in Figure A.25. When a user types an expression and selects another area of the Web page using the mouse, the call ValidateData() statement defined in line 44 of Listing A.24 is executed. The ValidateData() subroutine validates user input by first checking whether the user's input is a numeric expression.

Figure A.25.

The simple data-validation application.

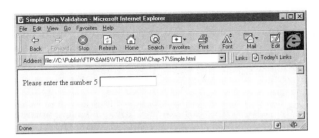

If the user enters a nonnumeric expression, the dialog box shown in Figure A.26 is displayed. Notice how this dialog box displays the user's input.

Figure A.26.

Error message displayed when a nonnumeric expression is entered.

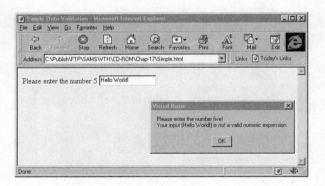

If the user enters a numeric expression that does not equal the number 5, the dialog box shown in Figure A.27 is displayed. Again, notice how the user's input is returned to the user to point out the mistake.

Figure A.27.

Error message displayed when a numeric expression other than the number 5 is entered.

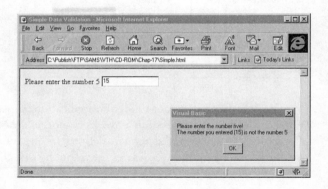

TIP

When validating data, it is always a good idea to echo what the user enters (as shown in Figures A.26 and A.27) if the user's input is not valid.

When a user types the number 5, the ThankUser subroutine defined in lines 25–35 is executed. The output of the ThankUser subroutine is shown in Figure A.28.

Figure A.28.
Output of the
`ThankUser` *subroutine.*

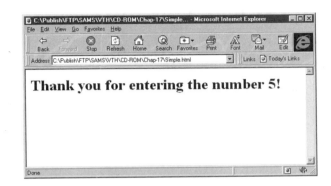

Validating Data in an HTML Form

HTML forms are generally used to obtain input from users browsing a Web site. When the HTML form is submitted to the Web server for processing, the HTML form data is processed by a CGI application. This transaction can be unnecessarily resource intensive if a form's data-entry field contains invalid input. The guestbook application in Listing A.25 (see Figure A.29) demonstrates how VBScript is used to validate data in an HTML form before the form is submitted to a CGI application for processing.

Most HTML forms contain the following line of HTML code:

```
<input type="submit" value="Submit Comments">
```

This instructs the Web browser to establish an HTTP connection and submit the data of the HTML form. Although this works well for submitting data to the server for processing, it does not allow a client-side VBScript application to validate the data before it is transmitted. This problem is solved through the use of the following line of code:

```
<input type="button" name="SubmitData" value="Submit Comments">
```

Compare this line of code to the line of code before it, and you will notice that the only difference between the two statements is how the data is submitted, and the additional HTML field `name="SubmitData"`. This field assigns the name `SubmitData` to the button used to submit the HTML form. When a Submit button (defined through the use of the HTML statement `<input type="submit"…>`) is used to submit the data as soon as the button is clicked, the Web browser transmits the HTML form data to the CGI application defined in the `action=` tag of the form declaration. But when a regular HTML form button (defined through the use of the HTML statement `<input type="button"…>`) is used to submit the data, the HTML form data is not automatically submitted to the Web server by the Web browser. Instead, if the HTML form data is valid, a VBScript subroutine validates the data and submits it to a CGI application via the `Submit` method of the `Form` object (see lines 54 and 57 of Listing A.25).

Listing A.25. Validating data in an HTML form.

```
 1: <!--
 2:  © 1996 Sanjaya Hettihewa (http://www.NetInnovation.com/)
 3:  All Rights Reserved.
 4: !-->
 5: <HTML>
 6: <HEAD>
 7:
 8:    <SCRIPT LANGUAGE="VBScript">
 9: <!--
10:
11:  Sub SubmitData_OnClick()
12:
13:  ' The following VBScript statements verify HTML form data.
14:
15:    If (GuestBookForm.FirstName.Value = "") Then
16:     MsgBox "Invalid Input Detected." & Chr(10) & _
17:        "Required data entry field not filled in." & Chr(10) & _
18:        "Please fill in the First Name data entry field and " & _
19:        "try again.", 4112, "Invalid Input Detected"
20:    Else If (GuestBookForm.LastName.Value = "") Then
21:     MsgBox "Invalid Input Detected." & Chr(10) & _
22:        "Required data entry field not filled in." & Chr(10) & _
23:        "Please fill in the Last Name data entry field and " & _
24:        "try again.", 4112, "Invalid Input Detected"
25:    Else If (GuestBookForm.EMailAddress.Value = "") Then
26:     MsgBox "Invalid Input Detected." & Chr(10) & _
27:        "Required data entry field not filled in." & Chr(10) & _
28:        "Please fill in the E-Mail Address data entry field and " & _
29:        "try again.", 4112, "Invalid Input Detected"
30:    Else If (GuestBookForm.Country.Value = "") Then
31:     MsgBox "Invalid Input Detected." & Chr(10) & _
32:        "Required data entry field not filled in." & Chr(10) & _
33:        "Please fill in the Country data entry field and " & _
34:        "try again.", 4112, "Invalid Input Detected"
35:    Else If (GuestBookForm.City.Value = "") Then
36:     MsgBox "Invalid Input Detected." & Chr(10) & _
37:        "Required data entry field not filled in." & Chr(10) & _
38:        "Please fill in the City data entry field and " & _
39:        "try again.", 4112, "Invalid Input Detected"
40:    Else If (GuestBookForm.Comments.Value = "") Then
41:     MsgBox "Invalid Input Detected." & Chr(10) & _
42:        "Required data entry field not filled in." & Chr(10) & _
43:        "Please fill in the Comments data entry field and " & _
44:        "try again.", 4112, "Invalid Input Detected"
45:    Else If (GuestBookForm.Birthdate.Value <> "") Then
46:    If (IsDate (GuestBookForm.Birthdate.Value) = FALSE) Then
47:     MsgBox "Invalid Input Detected." & Chr(10) & _
48:        "I'm sorry but the birthday you entered is " & Chr(10) & _
49:        "not a valid earth day. Please enter a valid " & Chr(10) & _
50:        "birthday and try again." & Chr(10) & Chr(10) & _
51:        "Ps: Please e-mail Webmaster if you are not from earth." _
52:        , 4112, "Invalid Input Detected"
53:    Else
54:     GuestBookForm.Submit ' Submit HTML form data to the server.
55:    End If
56:    Else
```

```
57:    GuestBookForm.Submit ' Submit HTML form data to the server.
58:    End If
59:    End If
60:    End If
61:    End If
62:    End If
63:    End If
64:    End If
65:    End sub
66: -->
67:    </SCRIPT>
68: <TITLE>Submit Guest Book Entry</TITLE>
69: </HEAD>
70:
71: <BODY BGCOLOR="#F7FFF4">
72: <CENTER><TABLE BORDER=3 BGCOLOR=FFFFCC>
73: <TR><TD>
74: <FONT SIZE=+2>Thank you for signing the guest book!</FONT>
75: </TD></TR></TABLE></CENTER>
76: <p>Thanks for taking the time to sign the NetInnovation guest
77: book. As soon as you fill in the following form and press the
78: submit button, your guest book entry will be added to the
79: NetInnovation.Com guest book.</p>
80: <P><B>Please note that data entry fields with a white backgound
81: are optional.</B></P>
82:
83: <form name="GuestBookForm"
84:      action="http://www.NetInnovation.com/cgi-bin/GuestBookSubmit.IDC"
85:      method="POST">
86:
87: <TABLE BGCOLOR=FFFFCC>
88: <TR>
89: <TD>First Name Please: </TD><TD><INPUT NAME="FirstName"
90: TYPE="TEXT" COLS=50 SIZE="43" ALIGN=left></TD>
91: </TR>
92: <TR>
93: <TD>Last Name Please: </TD><TD><INPUT NAME="LastName"
94: TYPE="TEXT" COLS=50 SIZE="43" ALIGN=left></TD>
95: </TR>
96: <TR>
97: <TD>E-mail Address Please: </TD><TD><INPUT NAME="EMailAddress"
98: TYPE="TEXT" COLS=50 SIZE="43" ALIGN=left></TD>
99: </TR>
100: <TR BGCOLOR=FFFFFF>
101: <TD>Your Birthdate Please: </TD><TD>
102: <INPUT NAME="Birthdate" TYPE="TEXT" COLS=10 SIZE="10"
103:    ALIGN=left> (Example: 02/29/1976)</TD></TR>
104: <TR>
105: <TD>Country </TD><TD><INPUT NAME="Country" TYPE="TEXT"
106: COLS=50 SIZE="43" ALIGN=left></TD>
107: </TR>
108: <TR>
109: <TD>City / State / Province </TD><TD>
110: <INPUT NAME="City" TYPE="TEXT" COLS=50 SIZE="43" ALIGN=left></TD>
111: </TR>
112: </TABLE>
113:
```

continues

Listing A.25. continued

```
114: <TABLE BGCOLOR=FFFFCC>
115: Please type your comments below. (Feel free to use HTML!)<BR>
116: <TEXTAREA NAME="Comments" WRAP=VIRTUAL ROWS=5 COLS=82
117: SIZE="82" ALIGN=left></TEXTAREA><BR>
118: </TABLE>
119:
120: <TABLE BGCOLOR=000000>
121: <input type="button" name="SubmitData" value="Submit Comments">
122: <input type="reset" value="Clear Form">
123: </TABLE>
124:
125: </form>
126: <HR>
127:
128: <strong>In case you are curious, after you press the submit button,
129: your guest book entry is inserted to a Microsoft Access
130: database.</strong>
131:
132: <HR>
133: <h5>Copyright &#169; 1995 Sanjaya Hettihewa.
134: All rights reserved.<br>
135: Revised: February 10, 1997.</h5>
136:
137: </body>
138: </html>
```

Figure A.29.

Data-entry fields of the guestbook application.

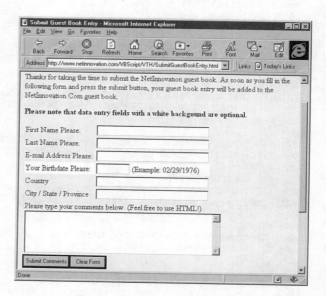

The application in Listing A.25 is composed of a series of If...Then...Else statements that check user input for invalid data. See Figure A.30 for the error message displayed when a user attempts to submit an empty form.

Figure A.30.

Error message received when the user attempts to submit an empty form.

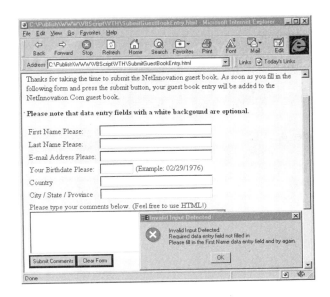

The If...Then...Else statements in lines 15–64 of Listing A.25 check all required data-entry fields to ensure that they are filled in. Notice how the VBScript application informs the user when a required data-entry field is not filled in (see Figure A.31).

Figure A.31.

The required data-entry field (Comments) is not filled in.

Lines 45–55 of Listing A.25 validate the user's birthday. If an invalid birthday is entered, the VBScript application displays a message to the user, as shown in Figure A.32. (2/29/1975 is not a valid birthday because 1975 was not a leap year.) When the guestbook form is properly filled in (as shown in Figure A.33), the VBScript application submits the form to the Web server by using the Submit method of the HTML form. See Figure A.34 for the results of the guestbook entry submission.

Figure A.32.

Error message received when the user attempts to submit an entry with an invalid date.

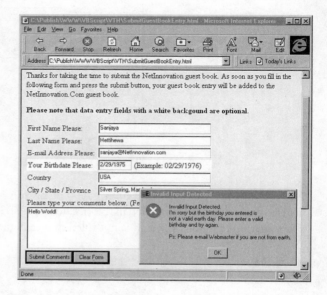

Figure A.33.

A valid guestbook entry.

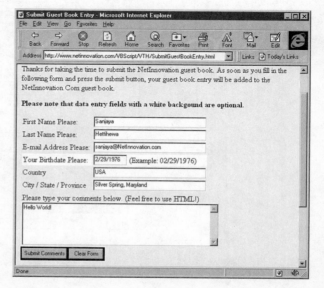

Figure A.34.

The VBScript application submits the valid guestbook entry to the Web server.

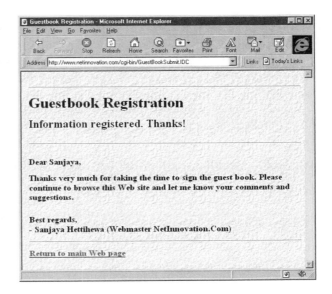

NOTE

The guestbook application presented in this section works with the Internet Database Connector.

Time- and String-Manipulation Functions

VBScript time- and string-manipulation functions are useful when developing Web applications. This section comprehensively covers these functions and demonstrates how they are used in VBScript applications.

Time-Manipulation Functions

Web applications can be refined through the use of time-manipulation functions of the VBScript language. For example, depending on the time of day, a VBScript application can greet the user (good morning, good evening, and so on) and provide time-sensitive information (stock prices, current weather, and so on). Listed next are some of the tasks that you can perform by using VBScript time-manipulation functions.

☐ Validate user input

☐ Perform calculations that involve time and date expressions

☐ Display time-sensitive messages based on the time of day

☐ Convert time/date information to a uniform time/date format

Validate User Input

VBScript can be used to validate dates entered by users. For example, the VBScript code in Listing A.26 displays a dialog box similar to the one shown in Figure A.35 if an invalid date is stored in the variable UserInput. You can replace the variable UserInput with the name of an HTML form element such as NameOfForm.NameOfFormDataEntryField.Value and use the code in Listing A.26 to validate dates in your HTML forms. The VBScript subroutine in Listing A.26 uses the IsDate() function to validate dates.

Listing A.26. Invalid date-detection subroutine.

```
1: If (IsDate (UserInput) = FALSE) Then
2:    MsgBox "Invalid Input Detected." & Chr(10) & _
3:          "I'm sorry but the date you entered is " & Chr(10) & _
4:          "not a valid day. Please enter a valid " & Chr(10) _
5:          & "date and try again." _
6:          , 4112, "Invalid Input Detected"
7: End If
```

Figure A.35.
Error message generated by lines 2–6 of Listing A.26.

Perform Calculations That Involve Time and Date Expressions

VBScript time- and date-manipulation functions can be used to perform calculations that involve dates. For example, the DateSerial() function called with the arguments DateSerial(1996,4-2,1+28) returns the exact date two months prior and 28 days later than the date 4/1/1996 (which is 2/29/1996).

Display Time-Sensitive Messages Based on the Time of Day

Time-sensitive messages can be displayed on the Web browser window based on what time a Web page is browsed, as illustrated by Listing A.27. Notice how the Hour() and Time() functions are used in line 24 of Listing A.27 to obtain the hour of day. The output of the VBScript application in Listing A.27 can be found in Figure A.36.

Listing A.27. The time-sensitive version of the Hello World! application.

```
 1: <!--
 2:    © 1996 Sanjaya Hettihewa (http://www.NetInnovation.com/)
 3:    All Rights Reserved.
 4:    Permission is hereby given to modify and distribute this code as you wish
 5:    provided that this block of text remains unchanged.
 6:    !-->
 7:
 8: <HTML>
 9:
10: <HEAD>
11: <TITLE>Hello World! (time sensitive version)</TITLE>
12: </HEAD>
13:
14: <BODY BGCOLOR=FFFFCC>
15:
16: <H1>Hello World! (time sensitive version)</H1>
17:
18: <TABLE BORDER=4 BGCOLOR="000000">
19: <TR><TD>
20: <FONT COLOR="FFFFFF">
21:    <SCRIPT LANGUAGE="VBScript">
22: <!--
23:
24:    CurrentHour = Hour(Time)
25:
26:    document.Write "<H3>Current time: " & Time & "<BR>"
27:    document.Write "Current date: " & Date & "</H3>"
28:
29:    If (CurrentHour < 6 ) Then
30:      document.Write _
31:      "<H2>Hi! What are you doing up in the wee hours of the morning?</H2>"
32:    Else If (CurrentHour < 12 ) Then
33:      document.Write _
34:      "<H2>Hi! Good morning!</H2>"
35:    Else If (CurrentHour < 14) Then
36:      document.Write _
37:      "<H2>Hi! Good afternoon!</H2>"
38:    Else
39:      document.Write _
40:      "<H2>Hi! Good evening!</H2>"
41:    End If
42:    End If
43:    End If
44:
45: -->
46:    </SCRIPT>
47: </FONT>
48: </TD></TR>
49: </TABLE>
```

continues

Listing A.27. continued

```
50:
51: </BODY>
52: </HTML>
```

Figure A.36.
Output of the VBScript application in Listing A.27.

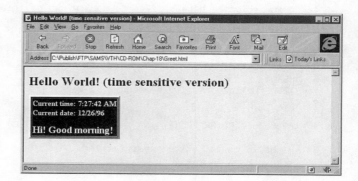

Convert Time/Date Information to a Uniform Time/Date Format

In the case of a database application, you might want to store all date values in the format 01/01/1996 as opposed to formats such as January 1, 1996 or Jan. 1, 1996. VBScript time-manipulation functions can be used to convert all date values to a uniform date format before they are submitted to the Web server for processing.

The Syntax of Time-Manipulation Functions

The syntax and usage of VBScript time-manipulation functions are given next for your reference.

CDate()

If a valid date expression is passed into the function, it is converted into Date type and returned. Before passing an expression to the CDate() function, it is possible to determine whether it can be converted by CDate() into Date type by using the IsDate() function. Always use the IsDate() function to validate dates entered by users. Do not assume dates typed by users are valid.

Date()

Date() returns the date from the system clock.

DateSerial()

DateSerial is a handy function that can be used to calculate various days. By using numeric expressions, it is possible to use the DateSerial function to count backward and forward from a date simply by adding and subtracting numbers. The syntax of the DateSerial function is as follows:

```
DateSerial(<Year>, <Month>, <Day>)
```

For example, if the current date is 4/1/1996, DateSerial(1996,4-2,1+28) returns the value 2/29/1996. Of course, if the year was 1997 (not a leap year), the result would have been 3/1/1996.

DateValue()

DateValue() converts an expression passed to the function into a variant of subtype Date and returns it. For example, DateValue("February 29, 1976") returns 2/29/1976. If the year is left out, it is obtained from the system clock.

Day()

The Day() function returns a value between 1 and 31 and can be used to find the day of a date. For example, Day("4/1/1996") returns 1.

Hour()

Hour() returns the number of hours of a time expression. For example, Hour("12:25:34") returns 12.

IsDate()

IsDate() returns TRUE if an expression can be converted to a valid date and FALSE otherwise.

NOTE

> When accepting a date from a user, always use the IsDate() function to ensure that the date entered by the user is valid.

Minute()

Minute() returns the number of minutes when called with the time. For example, Minute("23:50:45") returns 50.

Month()

Month() returns the month when called with a date. For example, Month("4/1/1996") returns 4.

Now()

Now() returns the current date and time from the system clock. The return value is followed by the date and then the time. For example, the Now command returned the string 4/1/1996 23:08:31 at the time of this writing.

Second()

Second() returns the number of seconds of a date expression. For example, Second("18:23:57") returns 57.

Time()

`Time()` returns the current time from the system clock. For example, the value `01:23:48` was returned by the `Time()` function at the time of this writing.

TimeSerial()

`TimeSerial()` is a very handy function that can be used to perform time calculations. For example, if the current time is 12:30, `TimeSerial()` can be used to calculate the time 25 minutes ago. In this case, `TimeSerial(12,30-25, 0)` returns `12:05:00`.

TimeValue()

`TimeValue()` returns an expression passed to the function after converting it into a variant of subtype `Date()`. For example, `TimeValue("2:35:17pm")` returns `14:35:17`.

Weekday()

The `Weekday()` function returns a number between 1 and 7. The numbers returned by the `Weekday()` function correspond to days of the week, as shown in Table A.3.

Table A.3. Day codes.

Day code	Day of week
1	Sunday
2	Monday
3	Tuesday
4	Wednesday
5	Thursday
6	Friday
7	Saturday

For example, `Weekday("April 2, 1996")` returns 3—which is, indeed, a Tuesday.

Year()

`Year()` returns the year of the expression. For example, `Year("February 29, 1976")` returns `1976`.

String-Manipulation Functions

String-manipulation functions are generally used to process data entered by users. The following VBScript functions can be used to manipulate string expressions.

LSet

LSet is used to copy a variable of one user-defined type to a variable of another user-defined type. When a variable is copied with the LSet command, it is *left-aligned*. The syntax of the LSet statement is as follows:

```
LSet Variable = ValueOfVariable
```

If the length of *Variable* is longer than that of *ValueOfVariable* after you copy *ValueOfVariable* to *Variable*, the remaining space is filled in with whitespaces. Likewise, if the length of *Variable* is less than that of *ValueOfVariable*, *ValueOfVariable* is truncated to fit in the space allocated for *Variable*. For example, if *Variable* can hold only four characters and *ValueOfVariable* contains the string "ABCDEFG", *Variable* will have the value "ABCD" after *ValueOfVariable* is copied to *Variable* using the LSet command.

Mid()

Mid() is a handy statement for replacing one or more characters of a string with characters from another string. The syntax of the Mid() statement is as follows:

```
Mid(<Variable>, <Begin>, <NumCharactersToReplace>) = <Replacement>
```

The Mid() function is used by replacing italicized placeholders as follows:

- [ ] *<Variable>*—The name of variable containing the string that will be modified.
- [ ] *<Begin>*—The position to begin replacing text. For example, if *<Variable>* contains the string "1234" and you want "34" to be replaced with "67", *<Begin>* is replaced with "3" because the substring "34" begins at the third position.
- [ ] *<NumCharactersToReplace>*—Lists the number of characters that should be replaced by *<Replacement>*. This value can be left out if you wish, in which case the entire *<Replacement>* string is copied over.
- [ ] *<Replacement>*—Contains string that will be copied over to *<Variable>*.

RSet

The RSet command is similar in functionality to the LSet command. The only difference is that when a variable is assigned a string using the RSet command, the value of it is assigned to the variable *right-aligned*. The syntax of the RSet command is as follows:

```
RSet <Variable> = <StringToCopy>
```

CStr()

CStr converts an expression passed to it into a string and returns it. For example, CStr(123.456) returns the value "123.456".

InStr()

InStr() returns the location of one string in another string. The syntax of InStr() is as follows:

```
InStr(<BeginPosition>, <String1>, <String2>, <ComparisonType>)
```

The InStr() function is used by replacing italicized placeholders as follows:

- ☐ *<BeginPosition>*—This argument is optional and specifies the starting position of a search.

- ☐ *<String1>*—Refers to the string being searched.

- ☐ *<String2>*—Refers to the string to be located.

- ☐ *<ComparisonType>*—This argument is optional. A value of 0 indicates a binary search, and a value of 1 indicates a case-insensitive search. The default value is 0.

The InStr() function can be used to validate an e-mail address entered by a user. By itself, VBScript cannot contact a remote mail server and verify an e-mail address provided by a user; however, the e-mail address can be examined with the aid of VBScript string-manipulation functions. The application in Listing A.28 demonstrates how the InStr() function is used to validate an e-mail address by verifying that it conforms to the format *text@text.text*. If an invalid e-mail address is entered, the e-mail address validation application displays a dialog box (shown in Figure A.37). The dialog box shown in Figure A.38 is displayed if the e-mail address conforms to the format *text@text.text*.

Listing A.28. The e-mail address validation application.

```
 1: <!--
 2:    © 1996 Sanjaya Hettihewa (http://www.NetInnovation.com/)
 3:    All Rights Reserved.
 4:    Permission is hereby given to modify and distribute this code as
 5:    you wish provided that this block of text remains unchanged.
 6:    !-->
 7: <HTML>
 8: <HEAD>
 9: <TITLE>Validating An E-Mail Address</TITLE>
10: </HEAD>
11: <BODY BGCOLOR=FFFFCC>
12: <H1>Validating An E-Mail Address</H1>
13: <TABLE BORDER=4 BGCOLOR="000000">
14: <TR><TD>
15: <FONT COLOR="FFFFFF">
16: <form name="EMailAddressEntryForm">
17: <p><H3>Please enter an e-mail address to validate</H3>
18: <input type="text" size="40" name="EMailAddress">
19: <input type="button" name="Validate" value="Validate E-Mail Address"></p>
20: </form>
21: </FONT>
```

```
22: </TD></TR>
23: </TABLE>
24:    <SCRIPT LANGUAGE="VBScript">
25: <!--
26: Sub Validate_OnClick
27:    EMailAdress = EMailAddressEntryForm.EMailAddress.Value
28:    AtSignPosition =  InStr (EMailAdress,"@")
29:    If (AtSignPosition > 0) Then
30:      PeriodPosition =  InStr (AtSignPosition,EMailAdress,".")
31:    Else
32:      PeriodPosition =  0
33:    End If
34:    AddressLength = Len(EMailAdress)
35:    If (AtSignPosition = 0) Then
36:      MsgBox "Invalid e-mail address entered!"
37:    Else If (PeriodPosition = 0) Then
38:      MsgBox "Invalid e-mail address entered!"
39:    Else If (AddressLength=PeriodPosition) Then
40:      MsgBox "Invalid e-mail address entered!"
41:    Else
42:      MsgBox "Valid e-mail address entered!"
43:    End If
44:    End If
45:    End If
46: End Sub
47: -->
48:    </SCRIPT>
49: </BODY>
50: </HTML>
```

Figure A.37.

Output of the e-mail address validation application when an invalid e-mail address is entered.

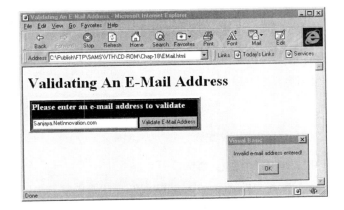

Figure A.38.

Output of the e-mail address validation application when a valid e-mail address is entered.

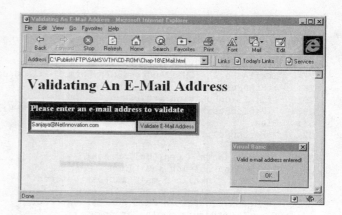

NOTE

The application in Listing A.28 is presented to give you an overview of how the Instr() function is used to validate data entered by the user—not to demonstrate how to extensively validate an e-mail address. Additional data validation may be required to validate an e-mail address.

LCase

LCase converts a string expression to lowercase and returns it.

Left()

Left() returns a certain number of characters from the left side of a string. For example, Left("Windows NT", 7) returns "Windows".

Len

Len returns the number of characters of a string expression.

LTrim, RTrim, **and** Trim

LTrim, RTrim, and Trim eliminate spaces from a string and return it. LTrim eliminates preceding spaces, RTrim eliminates trailing spaces, and Trim eliminates both trailing and preceding spaces.

Mid()

Mid() returns a certain number of characters from a string. For example, Mid("Windows NT", 0, 7) returns "Windows".

Right()

Right() returns a certain number of characters from the right side of a string. For example, Right("Windows NT", 2) returns "NT".

Str()

Str() converts a numeric expression into a string and returns it. The Str() function returns a string representation of a number while the CStr() function converts an expression to a string.

StrComp()

The StrComp() function is used to compare strings. The syntax of the StrComp() function is as follows:

StrComp(String1, String2, ComparisonMethod)

After StrComp() compares both strings, it returns 0 if both strings are identical, -1 if <String1> is less than <String2>, and 1 otherwise. The <ComparisonMethod> argument is optional. If it is 0, a binary comparison is performed, and if it is 1, a case-insensitive comparison is performed. If <ComparisonMethod> is left out, a binary comparison is performed.

String()

The String() function is handy for repeating a character a certain number of times. For example, String(5,"*") can be used to create a string containing five asterisks.

UCase()

UCase() converts strings passed to the function into uppercase and returns them. For example, UCase("Windows NT") returns "WINDOWS NT".

Val()

The Val() function can be used to obtain a number contained in a string. The function scans the string until it encounters a character that is not part of a number. For example, Val("1234 567 in a string") returns the number 1234567.

Mathematical Functions

Mathematical functions are used to perform complex calculations that cannot be easily performed through the use of simple mathematical operators. This section covers mathematical functions of the VBScript language by discussing their syntax and how they can be used to perform complex calculations. Most VBScript mathematical functions are used to perform trigonometric calculations. At the end of this section, you will be shown how to develop a VBScript application that uses all the VBScript mathematical functions discussed here.

NOTE

> Degrees can be converted to radians by multiplying the degrees by
> π/180. Multiply radians by 180/π to convert radians to degrees.

Atn()

Atn() returns the arctangent of a number.

Cos()

Cos() returns the cosine of an angle passed to the function.

Sin()

Sin() returns the sine of an angle. For example, Sin(Pi) returns 0.

Tan()

The Tan() function can be used to calculate the tangent of an angle. For example, Tan(0)
returns 0.

Exp()

Exp() returns the value of e raised to a power. For example, Exp(1) returns 2.71828182845905.

Log()

Log() returns the natural logarithm of a nonnegative, numeric expression.

Sqr()

Sqr() returns the square root of a nonnegative, numeric expression.

Randomize()

Randomize() can be used to initialize the random-number generator, and can be used either
with or without a numeric argument. If it is used with a numeric argument, that argument
is used to seed the random-number generator. If it is used without an argument, a number
from the system clock is used to seed the random-number generator. You must seed the
random-number generator before attempting to generate any random numbers. Random
numbers can be used in Web pages. For example, a random number can be used to greet the
user with a random greeting or tip of the day.

Rnd()

Rnd() returns a random number between 0 and 1. Be sure to seed the random-number
generator by calling Randomize() before using the Rnd() function.

Using VBScript Mathematical Functions

Mathematical functions discussed in previous sections can be used in VBScript applications as demonstrated in Listing A.29. You might want to experiment with the application shown in Figure A.39 to become familiar with VBScript mathematical functions. Enter a value in a text box and click the Evaluate button to see the result shown in Figure A.40.

Listing A.29. Using VBScript mathematical functions.

```
 1: <HTML>
 2: <HEAD>
 3: <TITLE>Using VBScript Mathematical Functions</TITLE>
 4: </HEAD>
 5: <BODY BGCOLOR="FFFFFF">
 6: <form name="SimpleCalculator">
 7: <H3>
 8: Atn(<input type="text" size="5" name="AtnInput" value="1">)
 9: <input type="button" name="AtnEvaluate" value="Evaluate!"><P>
10: Cos(<input type="text" size="5" name="CosInput" value="1">)
11: <input type="button" name="CosEvaluate" value="Evaluate!"><P>
12: Sin(<input type="text" size="5" name="SinInput" value="1">)
13: <input type="button" name="SinEvaluate" value="Evaluate!"><P>
14: Tan(<input type="text" size="5" name="TanInput" value="1">)
15: <input type="button" name="TanEvaluate" value="Evaluate!"><P>
16: Exp(<input type="text" size="5" name="ExpInput" value="1">)
17: <input type="button" name="ExpEvaluate" value="Evaluate!"><P>
18: Log(<input type="text" size="5" name="LogInput" value="1">)
19: <input type="button" name="LogEvaluate" value="Evaluate!"><P>
20: Sqr(<input type="text" size="5" name="SqrInput" value="1">)
21: <input type="button" name="SqrEvaluate" value="Evaluate!"><P>
22: </H3>
23: </form>
24:     <SCRIPT LANGUAGE="VBScript">
25: <!--
26: Sub AtnEvaluate_OnClick
27:     MsgBoxString = "Atn(" & SimpleCalculator.AtnInput.Value & _
28:     ") = " & Atn(SimpleCalculator.AtnInput.Value)
29:     MsgBox MsgBoxString , 64 , "Result of Calculation"
30: End Sub
31: Sub CosEvaluate_OnClick
32:     MsgBoxString = "Cos(" & SimpleCalculator.CosInput.Value & _
33:     ") = " & Cos(SimpleCalculator.CosInput.Value)
34:     MsgBox MsgBoxString , 64 , "Result of Calculation"
35: End Sub
36: Sub SinEvaluate_OnClick
37:     MsgBoxString = "Sin(" & SimpleCalculator.SinInput.Value & _
38:     ") = " & Sin(SimpleCalculator.SinInput.Value)
39:     MsgBox MsgBoxString , 64 , "Result of Calculation"
40: End Sub
41: Sub TanEvaluate_OnClick
42:     MsgBoxString = "Tan(" & SimpleCalculator.TanInput.Value & _
43:     ") = " & Tan(SimpleCalculator.TanInput.Value)
```

continues

Listing A.29. continued

```
44:     MsgBox MsgBoxString , 64 , "Result of Calculation"
45: End Sub
46: Sub ExpEvaluate_OnClick
47:     MsgBoxString = "Exp(" & SimpleCalculator.ExpInput.Value & _
48:     ") = " & Exp(SimpleCalculator.ExpInput.Value)
49:     MsgBox MsgBoxString , 64 , "Result of Calculation"
50: End Sub
51: Sub LogEvaluate_OnClick
52:     MsgBoxString = "Log(" & SimpleCalculator.LogInput.Value & _
53:     ") = " & Log(SimpleCalculator.LogInput.Value)
54:     MsgBox MsgBoxString , 64 , "Result of Calculation"
55: End Sub
56: Sub SqrEvaluate_OnClick
57:     MsgBoxString = "Sqr(" & SimpleCalculator.SqrInput.Value & _
58:     ") = " & Sqr(SimpleCalculator.SqrInput.Value)
59:     MsgBox MsgBoxString , 64 , "Result of Calculation"
60: End Sub
61: -->
62:     </SCRIPT>
63: </BODY>
64: </HTML>
```

Figure A.39.

The VBScript application in Listing A.29.

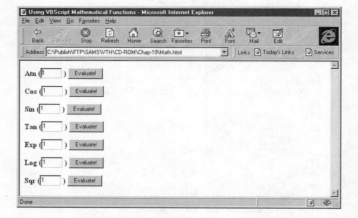

Figure A.40.

Calculating the value of
Sin(0).

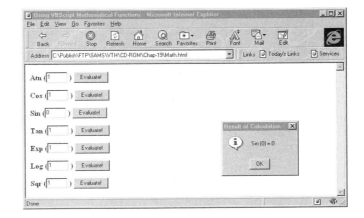

APPENDIX

B

ASP Resources on the Internet

There are many Active Server Pages resources on the Internet. Some of the more useful ASP resources on the Internet are listed in this appendix for your reference. Browse the following sites to learn more about Active Server Pages.

Microsoft's Internet News Server

If you have any ASP questions, use Internet Explorer or another Internet newsgroup reading program to connect to Microsoft's Internet news server, `msnews.microsoft.com`. You will then be able to use the `microsoft.public.inetserver.iis.activeserverpages` newsgroup to participate in online discussions related to Active Server Pages.

Active Server Pages Overview

This site provides an overview of Active Server Pages by discussing what Active Server Pages is and how it is used with Internet Information Server 3.0, and by answering frequently asked questions about Active Server Pages. This page is a jumping-off point for more detailed ASP information with links to "What is Active Server Pages?," "Using Active Server Pages with IIS 3.0," and "Frequently Asked Questions." Visit the Active Server Pages Overview Web page at

☐ `http://www.microsoft.com/iis/learnaboutiis/activeserver/default.asp`

Carl and Gary's Active Server Pages

This site contains links to many ASP-related resources on the Internet. Visit this site to learn how to develop ASP applications. Find it online at

☐ `http://www.apexsc.com/vb/asp.html`

Active Server Pages Frequently Asked Questions

Learn the answers to frequently asked questions about Active Server Pages by visiting the Active Server Pages Frequently Asked Questions Web pages at:

☐ `http://www.microsoft.com/support/activeserver/content/faq/general/default.htm`

☐ `http://www.microsoft.com/iis/LearnAboutIIS/ActiveServer/faq.htm`

The Adventure Works Demo

The Adventure Works Demo is a fine example of a sophisticated Web application that you can develop using Active Server Pages. Visit the following Web page to learn more about the Adventure Works Demo:

☐ http://www.microsoft.com/iis/usingiis/solutions/samples/default.htm

Designing Real-World Apps with Active Server Pages

For useful tips and techniques that can be used to develop real-world applications with Active Server Pages, visit the following Web page:

☐ http://www.microsoft.com/mind/0397/actservpages.htm

Developing Web Applications for IIS

The development of Active Server Pages, ISAPI applications, CGI applications, and ActiveX components for IIS is discussed in the following Web page:

☐ http://www.microsoft.com/iis/usingiis/developing/default.htm

Ken's Active Server Pages and VBScript Demos

Learn how to develop ASP applications using VBScript by visiting the following Web page:

☐ http://kencox.corinet.com/kencscripts/index.asp

Microsoft Active Server Pages Internet Database Roadmap

Browse the following Web page to learn database features of Active Server Pages:

☐ http://www.microsoft.com/sql/inet/inetdevstrat3.htm

B

The Scripting FAQ

Visit this Web page to find answers to common Web-scripting questions and problems:

☐ `http://www.frontpagechat.com/FAQ/Scripts/`

The ASP Developer's Site

This is a resource-rich Web page for ASP application developers. Source code, tools, components, tutorials, FAQs, and documentation can be found here:

☐ `http://www.genusa.com/asp/`

About Active Server Pages

This Web page provides an overview of Active Server Pages. Various attributes that make Active Server Pages ideal for developing Web applications are also discussed.

☐ `http://www.microsoft.com/iis/learnaboutiis/activeserver/about.htm`

INDEX

J-K

W

A VIACOM SERVICE

The Information SuperLibrary™

Bookstore

Search

What's New

Reference

Software

Newsletter

Company Overviews

Yellow Pages

Internet Starter Kit

HTML Workshop

Win a Free T-Shirt!

Macmillan Computer Publishing

Site Map

Talk to Us

CHECK OUT THE BOOKS IN THIS LIBRARY.

You'll find thousands of shareware files and over 1,600 computer books designed for both technowizards and technophobes. You can browse through 700 sample chapters, get the latest news on the Net, and find just about anything using our massive search directories.

All Macmillan Computer Publishing books are available at your local bookstore.

We're open 24 hours a day, 365 days a year.

You don't need a card.

We don't charge fines.

And you can be as **LOUD** as you want.

The Information SuperLibrary
http://www.mcp.com/mcp/ftp.mcp.com

MACMILLAN COMPUTER PUBLISHING USA
A VIACOM COMPANY

Technical Support:

If you need assistance with the information in this book, please access the Knowledge Base on our Web site at **http://www.superlibrary.com/ general/support**. Our most Frequently Asked Questions are answered there. If you do not find the answer to your questions on our Web site, you may contact Macmillan Technical Support **(317) 581-3833** or e-mail us at **support@mcp.com**.

Teach Yourself to Create a Home Page in 24 Hours

Rogers Cadenhead

This book is a carefully organized tutorial that is divided into 24 one-hour chapters that teach the beginning Web page author what he needs to know to make a Web page operational in the shortest time possible. No HTML is required—the book steps you through the process using Claris Home Page—a leading Web page editor for novices. The Windows and Macintosh CD-ROM includes a full working copy of Claris Home Page Lite and a collection of examples from the author.

Price: $24.99 USA/$35.95 CDN　　*User Level: New–Casual*
ISBN: 1-57521-325-7　　　　　*336 pages*

Laura Lemay's Web Workshop: Advanced Graphics and Web Page Design

Jon Duff and James Mohler

With the number of Web pages increasing daily, only the well-designed will grab the attention of those browsing the Web. This book illustrates, in classic Laura Lemay style, how to design attractive Web pages that will be visited over and over again. It covers beginning- and advanced-level design principles, and discusses advanced and emerging topics such as Shockwave, Java, VRML, and vector graphics on the Web. The CD-ROM follows the book's examples to create graphical Web pages, and contains HTML editors, graphics software, and royalty-free graphics and sound files.

Price: $49.99 USA/$70.95 CDN　　*User Level: Accomplished*
ISBN: 1-57521-317-6　　　　　*408 pages*

Teach Yourself Microsoft Internet Explorer 4 in 24 Hours

John San Fillipo

This beginner-level book shows readers how to browse the Web with Microsoft Internet Explorer, send e-mail, and find news groups. Everything from configuration to creating a Web page is covered. Each of its 24 lessons can be completed in one hour or less, making this book the best way to learn everything about Internet Explorer! Readers learn how to install, configure, and use Microsoft Internet Explorer, and they learn how to create an easy and reliable method of navigating the Web. This book also details all the new features of the latest version of Microsoft Internet Explorer.

Price: $24.99 USA/$35.95 CDN　　*User Level: New–Casual*
ISBN: 1-57521-233-1　　　　　*300 pages*

Microsoft Visual InterDev Unleashed

Jay Kottler, Glenn Fincher, et al.

Now there's an all-in-one, advanced-level guide to designing, creating, and publishing for the Web using the most sophisticated visual development environment on the market—Visual InterDev. In no time, you will learn how to use ActiveX Server scripting with databases, build ActiveX controls, and program with objects. This book provides real-world examples to highlight a variety of tasks, including database and query design, content creation, server-side scripting, and front-end scripting. The CD-ROM contains Internet Explorer 3.0, Microsoft ActiveX and HTML development tools, Java applets, tools, and all the examples from the book (plus electronic version of two Sams.net Web development books).

Price: $49.99 USA/$70.95 CDN　　*User Level: Accomplished–Expert*
ISBN: 1-57521-285-4　　　　　*1,152 pages*

Add to Your Sams.net Library Today
with the Best Books for Internet Technologies

ISBN	Quantity	Description of Item	Unit Cost	Total Cost
1-57521-325-7		Teach Yourself to Create a Home Page in 24 Hours (Book/CD-ROM)	$24.99	
1-57521-317-6		Laura Lemay Web Workshop: Advanced Graphics and Web Page Design (Book/CD-ROM)	$49.99	
1-57521-233-1		Teach Yourself Microsoft Internet Explorer 4 in 24 Hours	$24.99	
1-57521-285-4		Microsoft Visual InterDev Unleashed (Book/CD-ROM)	$49.99	
		Shipping and Handling: See information below.		
		TOTAL		

Shipping and Handling: $4.00 for the first book, and $1.75 for each additional book. If you need to have it immediately, we can ship product to you in 24 hours for an additional charge of approximately $18.00, and you will receive your item overnight or in two days. Overseas shipping and handling adds $2.00. Prices are subject to change. Call between 9:00 a.m. and 5:00 p.m. EST for availability and pricing information on latest editions.

201 W. 103rd Street, Indianapolis, Indiana 46290

1-800-428-5331 — Orders   1-800-835-3202 — Fax   1-800-858-7674 — Customer Service

Book ISBN 1-57521-330-3